DEVOUT AND DEFIANT

STUDIES IN EARLY MODERN GERMAN HISTORY
Joel F. Harrington, H. C. Erik Midelfort, and Tara Nummedal, Editors

Devout and Defiant

How Pilgrims Shaped the Franco-German Borderlands in the Age of Revolutions

Kilian Harrer

UNIVERSITY OF VIRGINIA PRESS
Charlottesville and London

The University of Virginia Press is situated on the traditional lands of the Monacan Nation, and the Commonwealth of Virginia was and is home to many other Indigenous people. We pay our respect to all of them, past and present. We also honor the enslaved African and African American people who built the University of Virginia, and we recognize their descendants. We commit to fostering voices from these communities through our publications and to deepening our collective understanding of their histories and contributions.

University of Virginia Press
© 2025 by the Rector and Visitors of the University of Virginia
All rights reserved
Printed in the United States of America on acid-free paper

First published 2025

9 8 7 6 5 4 3 2 1

LIBRARY OF CONGRESS CATALOGING-IN-PUBLICATION DATA
Names: Harrer, Kilian, author.
Title: Devout and defiant : how pilgrims shaped the Franco-German borderlands in the age of revolutions / Kilian Harrer.
Description: Charlottesville : University of Virginia Press, 2025. | Series: Studies in early modern German history | Includes bibliographical references and index.
Identifiers: LCCN 2024060718 (print) | LCCN 2024060719 (ebook) | ISBN 9780813953571 hardback | ISBN 9780813953588 trade paperback | ISBN 9780813953595 ebook
Subjects: LCSH: Christian pilgrims and pilgrimages—France—History—18th century | Christian pilgrims and pilgrimages—Germany—History—18th century | Revolutions—History—18th century | Christian pilgrims and pilgrimages—France—History—19th century | Christian pilgrims and pilgrimages—Germany—History—19th century | Revolutions—History—19th century
Classification: LCC BX2320.5.F8 H37 2025 (print) | LCC BX2320.5.F8 (ebook) | DDC 263/.04243—dc23/eng/20250514
LC record available at https://lccn.loc.gov/2024060718
LC ebook record available at https://lccn.loc.gov/2024060719

Cover art: *Description du jubilé, célébré à l'honneur de Marie, consolatrice des affligés, choisie depuis plus de cent ans pour patronne & protectrice de la ville & du duché de Luxembourg: avec le récit des décorations qui y ont paru,* héritiers d'André Chevalier, Luxembourg 1781, engraving by J. N. Sagittarius. (© Diocesan Archives Luxembourg)
Cover design: Cecilia Sorochin

To Chance

CONTENTS

List of Illustrations — ix
Acknowledgments — xi

Introduction — 1
1. Holy Place and Sacred Territory in the Age of Revolutions — 19
2. Shifting the Confessional Frontier — 49
3. Inventing Transnational Pilgrimage — 81
4. Mary's Overflowing Presence — 109
5. The Making of an Imperial Mass Pilgrimage — 139
Conclusion — 165

Notes — 173
Bibliography — 231
Index — 283

ILLUSTRATIONS

Maps

1. The Saar-Moselle-Rhine region, ca. 1802 (Saar Department and neighboring areas)   14
2. Territories of the region around Sankt Wendel and Tholey in 1770   58
3. Alsace in 1790 and the shrines across the border   84
4. Hoste and connected pilgrimage sites in the summer of 1799   117

Tables

1. Numbers of Haut-Rhin pilgrims arrested in the 1790s   101
2. Haut-Rhin pilgrims jailed and declared émigrés, 1792–1797   101

ACKNOWLEDGMENTS

A pilgrim relies on many people's hospitality as well as on various places in which to find material and spiritual sustenance. I vividly remember sitting in a youth hostel room in Kraków, Poland, in January 2019 and realizing that I had, in some sense, become a pilgrim myself while doing dissertation research on pilgrimage in revolutionary-era Europe. Now, after many scholarly and personal peregrinations, I am finally completing the journey toward my first book. One of the greatest joys of this moment is that it gives me the opportunity to express my deep gratitude to all those who have provided hospitality and help along the way.

This project took shape at the University of Wisconsin–Madison. Going there for graduate school was one of the best decisions I have ever made. My dissertation advisor and mentor, Suzanne Desan, has poured an incredible amount of enthusiasm, patience, critical insight, and sheer human sensitivity into helping me become a better writer, teacher, and thinker. Her teaching and scholarship kindled my interest in the time of the French Revolution. Suzanne recognized the full potential of my project before I did. Crucially, she has always found ways to cheer me up and get me back on track when I get discouraged and confused over where my research and writing are headed. I am enormously grateful to the other members of my dissertation committee as well. Laird Boswell introduced me to the field of modern French and European history, read and offered constructive criticism on innumerable drafts of papers and grant applications, and graciously accompanied my outbursts of Francophilia. With a unique and perfect mix of energy, rigor, and kindness, Giuliana Chamedes helped me understand modern Catholicism. Kathryn Ciancia guided me through the thickets of transnational history and remained interested in my work even after I had abandoned my plan to write a chapter on Polish pilgrimage places. Thomas DuBois immediately agreed to serve as my outside reader and offered a great deal of support even though he had never met me in person, as I first reached out to him in the midst of the COVID-19 pandemic.

I also had the great fortune of getting to know and working with many other excellent scholars and teachers at UW–Madison, including Pernille Ipsen, Lee Palmer Wandel, Karl Shoemaker, Daniel Ussishkin, Elizabeth Hennessy, William Cronon, Thomas Broman, and Lynn Nyhart. They have immeasurably enriched my thinking on topics ranging from early modern Christianity to the Enlightenment to theories of space and place.

It is hard to overstate the felicitous influence that my friendships and intellectual exchanges with former and current UW graduate students have had on me. Special thanks go to Robert Christl, John Ryan, Charlotte Whatley, and all the other members of my history program cohort. I feel not just grateful but genuinely honored to have belonged to this outstanding group. Across cohorts, I was lucky to join a thriving and extraordinarily supportive community of peers, especially my fellow adepts in French revolutionary history, Alice Main and Patrick Travens. Two former graduate students— Skye Doney and Katie Jarvis—have provided great mentorship and exciting examples of how to write about the history of pilgrimage and the French Revolution, respectively. I would like to say thank you to the amazing staff of the History Department as well, above all, to Leslie Abadie.

Writing this book has been a transatlantic endeavor from start to finish. For providing the funding that enabled me to conduct extensive research in Europe in 2018 and 2019, I thank the Social Science Research Council, the Fondation Napoléon, the Western Society for French History, and the Center for European Studies at UW–Madison. At the various waystations of my archival pilgrimage, I enjoyed truly heartwarming hospitality often combined with intellectual companionship, above all while being roommates with Adem Cobur and Christoph Gossing in Trier. The unfailingly helpful staff of more than twenty archives and libraries made it possible for me to gather the sources on which this book is built. I especially thank Roland Geiger for letting me tap into the riches of not only the Sankt Wendel parish archives but also his own treasure trove of regional history knowledge.

Countless conversations with scholars on both sides of the ocean stimulated my thinking while I was researching, writing, and revising the book manuscript. Conference and workshop participants listened closely and asked thoughtful questions, whether on Zoom or in person in Munich, Saarbrücken, Trier, Bern, Solothurn, Paris, Rome, Kraków, Madison, Tallahassee, and Atlanta. I was also lucky to get many opportunities to talk about my research to experts in informal settings. I was impressed with the generosity of Vincent Denis, Christophe Duhamelle, Laurent Jalabert, Dominique Julia, and Sébastien Schick in Paris, Philippe Martin in Lyon, Claude Muller in Colmar, Boris Fuge, Georges Hellinghausen, Sonja Kmec, Jean-Claude Muller, Bernhard Schmitt, Guy Thewes, and Martin Uhrmacher in Luxembourg, Maren Annette Baumann, Jort Blazejewski, and Bernhard Schneider in Trier, Wolfgang Hans Stein in Koblenz, Karl Solchenbach in Malberg, Christian Windler in Bern, Father Thomas at Einsiedeln, and Izabela Sołjan, Elżbieta Bilska-Wodecka, Paweł Grabowski, and Stanisław Witecki in Kraków. Moreover, I was fortunate to find four scholars—Ruth Harris, Marc Lerner, Michael Rowe, and Thomas Wallnig—who gave astute and charitable comments on chapter drafts even though I was a perfect stranger to them.

Born and raised in Germany, I came to appreciate history in German and French academic settings, long before I even considered writing my dissertation at a US university. At the University of Munich, from my undergraduate days to the postdoctoral stage, I benefited immensely from conversations with coworkers and mentors including Jonathan Alderman, Moritz Baumstark, Arndt Brendecke, Susanne Friedrich, Patrick Geiger, Mark Hengerer, Julia Herzberg, Leonard Horsch, Vitus Huber, Iryna Klymenko, Birgit Näther, Jorun Poettering, Brendan Röder, Benjamin Steiner, Maria Weber, and Hannes Ziegler. In France, during my student exchange year at the University of Tours in 2012–13, Ulrike Krampl and Robert Beck not only encouraged me for the first time to delve into the archives but also taught me how to think and write coherently about what I discovered there. Moreover, my stay in Tours marks the origin point of two especially longstanding and important friendships with Renée Pera Ros and Jared Smith.

Since 2023, the Leibniz Institute of European History in Mainz has been an ideal place for me to bring this project to completion. Nicole Reinhardt gave me the advice and freedom that I needed to write a convincing book proposal and revise my manuscript extensively. Bernhard Gißibl's mentorship was key. I learned a great deal from him, the other members of the research group on (de)sacralization, and most recently the working group on religious history, especially as I grappled with the themes of chapter 1.

I also offer my thanks to Ufuk Erol, Fani Gargova, Jaap Geraerts, Henning Jürgens, Florian Kühnel, Zornitsa Radeva, Jared Warren, Malin Wilckens, and all the other fantastic coworkers and fellows at the Institute who have made my time there extraordinarily pleasant and fruitful.

At the University of Virginia Press, my editor, Nadine Zimmerli, has gone above and beyond in encouraging and guiding this project all the way from proposal to publication. I sincerely thank her. My gratitude also goes to Susan Murray for her fantastic copyediting, as well as to the series editors of the Studies in Early Modern German History, the two reviewers who engaged deeply and constructively with my manuscript, and the other staff members at the Press who have been involved in the making of this book.

I could never have embarked on this pilgrimage if it was not for the love and support that I have received from my family members. They have all embodied the values of perseverance and care that have enabled me, quite simply and quite crucially, to get things done. *Danke.* Laura Peterson always makes me feel at home in Minneapolis, and I thank her for being the best mother-in-law I could have possibly imagined. Finally, my most profound thanks go to my spouse, Chance McMahon, whose brilliance, kindness, calmness, moral sense, and depth of feeling have sustained me every day for the last four years, all the way from Madison to Mainz via Munich. I consider myself incredibly lucky to continue on this journey with Chance by my side, and I dedicate this book to them with all my love.

DEVOUT AND DEFIANT

Introduction

A pilgrimage craze engulfed the German-speaking borderlands of revolutionary France in the summer of 1799. Such, at least, was the alarming impression that the municipal administrators of Hochfelden, a small Alsatian town thirty kilometers from Strasbourg, conveyed to the French ministry of police. "Each day," they wrote, "fanatics show up at our office to obtain passports" for trips to the "counterrevolutionary" holy well and apparition site of Hoste in the neighboring Moselle Department.[1] A slew of other police reports confirms that hundreds of thousands of Catholics had been hitting the road as pilgrims during those spring and summer months. They were all eager to visit Hoste and numerous related places of Marian apparitions, in the Moselle as well as in surrounding departments.

The passport requests indicate that Catholics' thirst for an encounter with the miraculous did not obliterate their awareness of the profane territorial boundaries they would need to cross. Then again, just how profane were these boundaries? The municipality of Hochfelden raised that question with great flourish: as part of a plan to reestablish "the Altar and the Throne on the blood-spattered debris of Liberty," the proliferating "evil" of pilgrimage and miracles "seems to be wreaking havoc across the sacred territory of the Republic."[2] With these words, local revolutionaries captured the dramatic stakes of the relationship between holy place and sacralized territory, or between pilgrimage and borders.

This book contends that pilgrims contributed significantly to reshaping Catholicism and the politics of religion in the revolutionary era, especially by engaging with a transformation of border culture. In the regions on which I focus—northeastern France, Luxembourg, and neighboring parts of present-day western Germany—pilgrimage endured and intermittently even flourished throughout the turbulent period of Enlightenment reforms, the French Revolution, and Napoleonic imperialism. While various authorities made radical efforts to curb "superstition" and securitize shifting territorial boundaries, pilgrims kept exposing the border as the state's Achilles' heel. They evaded mobility controls, crossed provocatively into Protestant territories, and went abroad to visit shrines beyond the reach of anticlerical revolutionaries. Some pilgrims engaged in anti-Protestant and anti-Jewish violence. Others became victims of state violence themselves; a few were even guillotined in 1794, during the most radical phase of the French Revolution. On the whole, pilgrims faced mounting difficulties in navigating sacred space and state territory at the same time, but they also found effective ways to respond to the challenge.

For that reason, pilgrimage catalyzed political and religious change in different moments of the revolutionary era. In the last decades of the Old Regime, pilgrims in the Holy Roman Empire championed a new form of Catholic pride, responding to a notion of Catholic backwardness that was developing on the frontier with Protestantism. Soon after 1789, they began confronting and appropriating the national ideologies bubbling up in the cauldron of revolution. During the later 1790s, pilgrims multiplied their encounters with Mary across territorial boundaries, outmaneuvering French police forces. Finally, the Napoleonic age produced a kind of imperial pilgrimage, which ostensibly complied with spatial order but actually prompted Catholics to cross borders unauthorized on a massive scale. The history of pilgrimage in the age of revolutions thus offers important clues to the riddle posed by recent, revisionist theories of the secular: if religious communities did not simply flounder and shrink in the struggles that made modern Europe, then how did these communities manage instead to adapt and actively shape the outcomes of revolutionary change?[3]

In providing elements of a fresh answer to this question, I make two major arguments, buttressed and linked by the theoretical impulse to bring together pilgrimage studies and border studies. First, pilgrimage proved resilient and transformative in the decades around 1800. By renewing the spatial and political repertoires of their faith, pilgrims helped shape the framework within which subsequent generations of Catholics would go on to confront nationalism, Protestantism, secularism, and state power. Second, this book highlights the cultural creativity that characterizes the revolutionary-era borderlands, despite their distance from well-studied centers of power. In developing my two arguments in tandem, I show how pilgrims made a difference by crossing and using borders, after realizing that they were confronting not just campaigns against "superstition" but also a novel territorial regime. Hence, instead of merely emphasizing the appeal of sacred space in its own right, this book suggests that pilgrimage fostered important frictions between sacred and territorial space.

Pilgrimage and the Many Faces of Catholicism, circa 1800

By insisting that pilgrims contributed actively to religious and political change between 1770 and 1815, I go against the grain of the existing scholarship. To be sure, historians of German- and French-speaking Europe have frequently noted that many Catholics kept making pilgrimages throughout that period.[4] By and large, however, studies of pilgrimage have periodized their subject matter as if it had been in eclipse during the late eighteenth and early nineteenth centuries.[5] The underlying assumption is that pilgrimage epitomized Catholic devotion before and after—but not during—the age of revolutions. In the culture of the Baroque, which dominated most of Catholic Europe from the late sixteenth through the mid-eighteenth century, nothing proved as effective as pilgrimage in fusing anti-Protestant triumphalism, liturgical splendor, communal cohesion via shared leisure, and popular devotion to Mary and the saints.[6] Similarly, the militant Catholicism of the mid- to late nineteenth century relied heavily on the devotional power and public spectacle of pilgrimage to outrival both Protestantism and liberalism.[7] Therefore, historians of the nineteenth century habitually use the topic of pilgrimage to support the idea that, after the troubles of the revolutionary era, a thoroughly "new," Rome-oriented (ultramontane), and politically resurgent Catholicism emerged only between the 1830s and 1860s in German- and French-speaking Europe.[8]

If this claim has remained immune to scholarly insights into Catholic renewals occurring earlier, around 1800, it is because these insights do not yield a unified picture.[9] No prevailing paradigm of Catholicism comparable to "the Baroque" or "ultramontanism" exists for the time in between, the late eighteenth and early nineteenth centuries. Some historians of that period argue that the enlightened movement for church reform laid the groundwork for the reorganizing and mobilization that became both necessary and possible after 1800.[10] Others, by contrast, emphasize the actions of clergymen who worked *against* the forces of reform and revolution: by amplifying people's fears of seeing their religious traditions destroyed by those forces, these clerics paved the way for later Catholic mass movements.[11] Yet another group of scholars has eschewed such top-down perspectives and focused instead on lay Catholics' agency, often by way of gender analysis. When the self-proclaimed shepherds—bishops and priests—faced persecution or struggled to regroup after massive expropriations and reforms of the Church, Catholic flocks tended to find themselves left to their own devices. In such situations, laymen and especially laywomen took the initiative in defense of their faith.[12] We cannot ignore the tensions between these different, equally valuable strands of scholarship.

Nor can we resolve those tensions by flattening them into chronological order. For example, we cannot claim that a short age of enlightened Catholicism was superseded, at some point in time, by the Counter-Enlightenment, in turn followed by a few years of mostly prerevolutionary sentiment among Catholics, and so on. For one thing, Catholic embrace and rejection of the Enlightenment coexisted throughout the last decades before 1789; likewise, Revolution and Counter-Revolution competed throughout the 1790s and beyond.[13] What is more, the Catholic Enlightenment persisted and even made new advances in the decades after 1800—especially in the borderlands of present-day southwestern Germany, where religious *Spätaufklärer* vied for influence with romantics and reactionaries.[14]

In sum, between the relatively coherent Baroque and ultramontane periods, Catholicism went through a unique phase of much greater cultural and political heterogeneity.[15] The Church—including laypeople as well as clergy—presented many different faces throughout this in-between moment, which has made it difficult ever since to relate the revolutionary era coherently to the bigger picture of the history of Catholicism. Yet, four decades' worth of research has demonstrated that Catholics both experienced and actively shaped momentous transformations right before, during, and right after the French Revolution. In numerous, mutually contradictory ways, they kept drawing on the Baroque legacy while already participating in the breakthrough of new forms of devotion, mass politics, and ideology.

Against this backdrop, it is astonishing that the study of pilgrimage around 1800 has mostly revolved around a single question: how far-reaching and successful were enlightened and revolutionary ambitions to control or inhibit pilgrim activity? Scholars have provided overwhelming evidence that such ambitions circulated among church and state authorities as well as reformist writers. These groups routinely denounced pilgrims' practices as almost inherently superstitious, unduly raucous if not politically suspect, and a collective waste of time that resembled vagabondage and slowed down the economy. We also know that enlightened elites tried seriously to implement their programs, although with varying degrees of severity depending on whether they subscribed to a moderate Catholic Enlightenment, more radical Josephist ideals, an uncompromising revolutionary antifanaticism, or a postrevolutionary ideology of order and "liberal authoritarianism."[16] As a result, condemnations of—and conflicts around—pilgrimage quickly became much more numerous and intense than they had been in Catholic parts of Europe before roughly 1770.[17]

Keenly aware of this fact, historians have concentrated on determining how effectively it eroded lay Catholics' participation in pilgrimage. Some argue that the word "revival" applies quite literally to mid-nineteenth-century developments in pilgrimage. Jonathan Sperber expressed this conclusion most provocatively in his work on the northern Rhineland: "By 1850, the traditional pilgrimage was dead; its triumphant resurrection in the following twenty years would see it in a new and different form."[18] Other scholars insist that lay Catholics mounted an effective resistance and stuck with their traditional pilgrim practices throughout the age of revolutions, especially in German-speaking Europe.[19] My own findings underscore the vitality of pilgrimage in the years from 1770 to 1810. I have focused on these four decades because they witnessed the successive heydays of enlightened Reform Catholicism, revolutionary activism, and Napoleonic imperial order.

Yet pilgrims and pilgrimage promoters did much more than preserve religious traditions, and their actions had more powerful political ripple effects than scholarship has recognized. To be sure, folklorists and historians have already enriched the study of religious practice in the revolutionary era with the broader insight that attachment to traditions and resistance to reforms need not imply changelessness. Thus, with regard to pilgrimage, some scholars show how laypeople also adapted. For instance, they increasingly took initiative in organizing and leading pilgrimages previously guided by clergy but now shunned by enlightened state and church authorities.[20] While my case studies corroborate this argument, I consider it insufficient in that it still responds to the question of how new political developments impacted old religious practices. In other words, most of the existing narratives begin by asking what the age of revolutions did to pilgrimage and finish by emphasizing devotional decline, persistence, or adaptation.[21] It is time to turn the question upside down and explore what pilgrimage did to the age of revolutions.

The answer is that pilgrims both challenged and shaped new spatial regimes in creative and consequential ways. While the upheavals of the revolutionary era rattled people's sense of place and belonging in general, the notion of holy place that underpinned pilgrimage came under particular attack. Many Catholics responded by engaging in spatial bricolage: they constantly adjusted the meanings and interconnections of holy sites as well as their relationship to the shifting territories in which these sites were embedded. In this way, pilgrims refreshed and reoriented their confessional pride, deepening new fault lines of strife that concerned spatial order and an alleged Catholic backwardness. Once the French Revolution had erupted, pious journeys across borders prompted pilgrims to sharpen their awareness of the nation. A little later, they inaugurated a pattern in which Marian apparitions would occur more frequently and spectacularly whenever Catholic–secular conflict would reach its highest pitch. Finally, under Napoleon's authoritarian rule, mass pilgrimage taught Catholics how to rely on state power while also exploiting its loopholes. These developments made a real difference in the larger scheme of things, not least because they touched and often changed the lives of extraordinary numbers of people. The problems of pilgrimage mattered to zealous churchmen, touchy bureaucrats, and scornful critics of popular piety, but above all to the many hundreds of thousands of lay Catholics in the borderlands who took part in pilgrimages on a regular basis.

I have chosen to describe these pilgrims' devotion as "transgressive" in order to capture an important meshing of space and politics. My point is that, in the process of moving toward and across territorial borders, pilgrims frequently crossed more metaphorical lines as well—namely, the boundaries of what reformers and revolutionaries considered appropriate or acceptable. That said, did pilgrims overstep those boundaries without meaning to cause a stir, or did they act in deliberate defiance? In other words, did pilgrims' *mobility* in quest of the sacred actually entail their *mobilization* in the sense of exercising political "resistance," struggling "intentionally" to make their own history, and thereby demonstrating "agency"?[22] This is a legitimate question even though we sometimes lack the sources that we would need in order to address it, and this book will return to the issue of resistance repeatedly, on a case-by-case basis. Yet, as geographer Tim Cresswell has argued, intentionality and resistance are in some ways secondary when we study transgressive acts: "The crossing of the line may or may not have been intended." Either way, it constitutes a transgression, at least when it is noticed and perceived as such by those who have set the line or wish to enforce it.[23] Unintended as well as intended transgressions can thus spark disputes and lead to repercussions, which in turn gives people a clearer sense of how their practices conflict with the ideals of those in power. Because of such dynamics, the transgressive devotion of revolutionary-era pilgrims could and did become politically salient.

The Transformation of Border Culture

By suggesting that pilgrimage created a great deal of border trouble, this book also intervenes in the vibrant field of historical border studies. In a famous article first published in 1928, the cofounder of the French *Annales* school Lucien Febvre claimed that "we should study and analyze the border by taking as our starting point the state rather than the border itself."[24] This state-centric view persisted for a long time, but it has gradually ceased to dominate the field since the 1980s, as historians and theorists have grown more interested in understanding what a border means to the people who live with it.[25] Many important issues have come to the fore as a result, ranging from seasonal migration, smuggling, and other forms of short- or mid-distance mobility to cross-border patterns of regional solidarity and conflict. We also know much more now about how people on territorial peripheries dealt with the geopolitical strife that usually affected them first, whether in the form of military invasions, occupation, or annexation. This scholarship has shown how, throughout the age of revolutions, a wide gamut of local social actors continued powerfully to refashion and manipulate the spatial "filters" that borders represented rather than lose all control over them to state apparatuses.[26] My aims are to shed more light on how religious themes played out in this context, as well as to provide a fresh impulse to the field as a whole by suggesting that a vast transformation of border culture took place around 1800.[27]

The concept of border culture brings together geopolitics and quotidian local constructions of belonging and difference. As characterized by Victor

Konrad and Anne-Laure Amilhat Szary, this concept is a heuristic tool, a way of attending to the relationships among "imaginaries of the border, narratives of barriers and crossings, multiple identities and states of being," as well as "the despair of conflict and violence at borders."[28] Hence, border culture refers to something different than the regional cultures of particular borderlands.[29] People everywhere—not just those living on the territorial margins—participate in elaborating those border-related imaginaries, narratives, identities, and conflicts. Still, for any study of border culture, the borderlands are an especially promising setting: it is there that geopolitical and local developments interact most directly and forcefully, constantly producing new dynamics and frictions. Crucially, the inhabitants of borderlands retain their own interests and their own ideas about how the border should function, how much connection and separation it should allow for, and how to delineate their "own" space from that of "others." Geopolitics and local borderland politics thus coevolve sometimes in relative harmony and sometimes in highly dissonant ways. Almost always, the effects of this coevolution resonate far and wide on both sides of the border.

The transformation of border culture in the age of revolutions was multifaceted rather than monolithic, and it is worth distinguishing four major interlocking aspects of this process. First, a sense of extraordinary territorial volatility spread due to the many dramatic border changes that occurred in the decades preceding the Congress of Vienna. To be sure, territorial stability in central Europe had always remained elusive in the 140 years between the Peace of Westphalia and the French Revolution. Louis XIV's quasi-incessant wars of conquest sent shock waves across and beyond the Holy Roman Empire in the late seventeenth century, as did the First Partition of Poland-Lithuania in 1772.[30] In the heyday of French revolutionary expansion and Napoleonic imperialism, however, politicians and diplomats remapped Europe much more sweepingly and in shorter intervals than previous generations had done. Above all, the territorial complexity of the Holy Roman Empire unraveled between April 1792 (when France declared war on Austria) and the end of the Alte Reich in August 1806. This unraveling began west of the Rhine where the French conquered, occupied, and annexed a multitude of territories in the 1790s. It proceeded eastward in the Napoleonic period—via additional annexations by France but also via the dissolution and subsumption of all ecclesiastical principalities (*Säkularisation*) and many other imperial estates (*Mediatisierung*) into larger territorial entities.

Especially in revolutionary France and later in areas of Napoleonic hegemony, the decades around 1800 also saw far-flung efforts to simplify and homogenize the internal subdivisions of state territory. These efforts reflect a second main aspect of the transformation of border culture. In France, its sister republics of the 1790s, and its vassal states of the Napoleonic era, territorial reforms led to the creation of "departments" (*départements*), conceived of as standardized units of administrative space—as opposed to the Old Regime's assemblages of motley regions and provinces boasting unique histories and diverse privileges.[31] Other measures targeted diocesan borders. In many parts of the Habsburg lands, for instance, Joseph II reorganized dioceses so they no longer straddled state borders. The French revolutionaries aligned diocesan boundaries exactly with departmental ones in the Civil Constitution of the Clergy (1790).[32]

Taken together, the redrawn state borders and the newly implemented system of administrative division amounted to a massive change in the forms and implications of territorial space. While the "Europe of composite monarchies" did not vanish completely in the revolutionary era, an innovative and potent type of unitary state was rapidly emerging, and the "fractal" Holy Roman Empire disappeared along with loosely constituted early modern republics such as the Old Swiss Confederacy.[33] All these changes are well known and seemingly easy to represent through lines on maps of eighteenth- and nineteenth-century Europe. What maps mostly fail to convey, however, and what cultural historians need to pay more attention to is the extent to which the very meaning of borders also shifted in the revolutionary era. As Marie-Vic Ozouf-Marignier puts it, a new generation of political elites "affirmed the primacy of spatial dependency over social dependency, the cutting of space into discrete units, the importance of the limit."[34] In other words, the transformation of border culture involved an attempt to fundamentally reimagine and reengineer the interplay between space and political power. Chapter 1 of this book further discusses the revolutionary era's burgeoning ideology of territory and borders, as well as its early modern roots.

A third aspect concerns the intensification of border security and begins to reveal how geopolitics and seemingly abstract rethinking of territory became relevant to the everyday lives of political subjects and citizens. While passport requirements for travel abroad, customs brigades, and military surveillance at border fortress towns existed long before the age of revolutions, state authorities ramped up the control of border-crossing mobility significantly in the decades after 1750—and especially after 1789. As borders acquired greater ideological cachet and demarcated "decision space" ever more sharply, they became the Achilles' heel of the body politic—a vulnerable and ever more sensitive territorial edge in need of securitization.[35] Thus, for various German principalities, Luca Scholz has recently shown an intriguing shift that took place in the mid- to late eighteenth century: officials now carried out more and more controls right at the border, whereas previously travelers had encountered checkpoints mostly along roads and rivers in the territorial interior.[36] The efforts to securitize borders did not increase in a linear fashion, either in the Holy Roman Empire or in France, where the early Revolution engaged in (ephemeral) experiments with liberal passport law. Yet the overall trend is unmistakable.[37] It manifested itself sharply in the French revolutionary border panics around émigrés, a newly invented category of people whose mobility in the 1790s was seen by revolutionaries not just as territorial transgression but as national betrayal. Chapter 3 revolves largely around this issue, which illustrates the link between new ideologies and practical border policies.

Fourth, and finally, I want to emphasize the creativity of multifarious local practices in the borderlands, which inflected or hampered the implementation of grand strategies instead of being consigned to irrelevance by geopolitics and top-down security regimes.[38] German Jacobins, for instance, used Strasbourg as a safe haven where they could publish prorevolutionary newspapers throughout the 1790s. These papers reached audiences not just in Alsace but also in the southern Holy Roman Empire, endangering German princes' geopolitical objective of preventing revolutionary ideas from spreading.[39] A little later, in the left-bank Rhineland under Napoleon, businesspeople made large fortunes by benefiting from the integration of markets and territories that French rule provided—but also by smuggling goods across the Rhine and thus circumventing the less convenient aspects of Napoleonic protectionism.[40] Overall, when territorial order came to represent a guarantee of security and social cohesion, crossing or using borders turned into more significant social strategies and means of political expression for those living in the borderlands. These people, too, fueled the transformation of border culture because they recognized rapidly shifting forms of belonging—provincial, national, transnational, and imperial—and weighed them against each other on an everyday basis.

As a hotly contested form of mobility, pilgrimage interacted at every step with the transformation of border culture in the revolutionary era. This book shows that territorialized top-down control of pilgrimage proved elusive: pilgrims and their allies exercised a great deal of power in defining and navigating the relationships between borders and holy places. The resulting conflicts unfolded in part because pilgrims crossed borders, but also because Catholics interested in pilgrimage often contested or manipulated the meanings and logics of territorial division. Things might always be different on the other side of any border.[41] Indeed, they often were—especially when a holy place was located on that other side. As I will show, pilgrims and pilgrimage organizers interpreted and utilized the border as a form of spatialized difference. In doing so, they reinforced and reshaped the specific power of pilgrimage, which consisted in seizing public spaces and displaying Catholic visibility as effectively as few other religious practices did.

Hence, far from constituting a marginal or isolated phenomenon, pilgrimage was central to border culture, at least in regions mostly inhabited by Catholics. To be sure, the story of pilgrimage cannot possibly represent the *whole* story when it comes to such large topics as the politics of religion in the age of revolutions or the history of borders and borderlands. The study of transgressive devotion can, however, shed fresh light on many of the key processes that scholars working on those topics have been debating, from nation- and empire-building to border policing. Moreover, in several chapters of this book, I point out that authorities often conflated pilgrims with other "suspect" groups of people who crossed borders, including vagabonds, deserters, emigrants, and smugglers. I hope that my findings can inspire further research on how these other groups, too, experienced and shaped the transformation of border culture.

By entering into dialogue with border studies, I also seek to break new ground in the interdisciplinary scholarship on pilgrimage. As historian Dee Dyas notes, pilgrimage studies "is emerging as an important area of study in its own right."[42] It has appropriated and refined a rich toolkit of spatial analysis in the half century since Victor and Edith Turner and Alphonse Dupront published their classic anthropological works. Evolving concepts of place, sacred space, ritual space, and landscape have successively risen to prominence and undergirded much brilliant work.[43] Moreover, the idea that pilgrimage always involves crossing anthropological boundaries of some sort has enjoyed widespread acceptance ever since the Turners characterized this religious practice as "liminal" or "liminoid."[44] The presence of these notions has not, however, sparked much interest in the ways pilgrims and pilgrimage organizers interact with territorial borders.[45] By contrast, I aim to bridge the conceptual gulf between sacred space and territory. In pivotal historical moments such as the age of revolutions, pilgrimage as a form of border trouble generated new patterns of social conflict and catalyzed important transformations in the politics of religion. These findings justify a new approach to the power of sacred sites, where people feel that Heaven and Earth are joined. I revise the history of these meetings between the *celestial* and *terrestrial* spheres by exploring when and how the *territorial* factor entered the equation.

Setting, Structure, Sources

Foregrounding territory in this way depends in part on my choice of regional setting. This book focuses on a contiguous set of borderlands including Alsace, Lorraine, the present-day Saarland, Luxembourg, and adjacent areas. Far from connoting lack of importance, the very marginality of those regions turned them into a highly neuralgic "shatterzone" of early modern and modern geopolitics.[46] From the conquest of the bishoprics of Metz, Toul, and Verdun by King Henry II of France in 1552 to the reabsorption of the Saarland into Germany in 1957, countless territorial shifts as well as political and cultural upheavals marked these borderlands as western Europe's crucial arena of "enmity and entanglement."[47] To mention this longer historical arc is not to suggest that the entangled entities remained stable; for instance, "France," "Germany," and "Luxembourg" each meant something very different in, say, 1850 compared to 1550 or even 1750. Moreover, by highlighting a transformation of border culture, this book insists that the meaning of such categories as "territory" changed profoundly, too. Yet, acknowledging the long persistence of the shatterzone status still makes sense, because it helps us appreciate the sheer geopolitical weight that the lands along the Rhine, Saar, and Moselle Rivers possessed during the revolutionary era and beyond.

In the early modern period, these lands also became a religious shatterzone, as French scholars of early modern Catholicism have long emphasized. Leaders of the Catholic Reformation poured enormous resources into this part of Europe from the sixteenth century onward. As a major "frontier of Catholicity" facing numerous beacons of Protestantism to the north (in the Dutch Republic) and to the east (Heidelberg, Basel, Geneva), the borderlands developed into an influential arena of Baroque identity formation.[48] In the revolutionary era and throughout the nineteenth century, they remained a powerhouse of European Catholicism north of the Alps.[49] Thus, the regions covered in this book deserve sustained attention—even though they were far removed from major power centers, lacked economic dynamism in some cases, and cannot be shoehorned into any one national historiographical frame.[50]

Beyond these regions, too, territorial borders and frontiers of Catholicity had been proliferating across western and central Europe for centuries, and pilgrimage was a common practice among Catholics just about everywhere. To be sure, in the absence of systematic comparative research, this book cannot and does not cover all of Europe, let alone the entire Catholic world. It does, however, include numerous glimpses into pilgrimage in other parts of German-speaking Europe and beyond. In this way, I widen the lens repeatedly to show that, at the very least, the borderlands on which this book focuses did not present an utterly exceptional situation. In particular, it is safe to say that the transformation of border culture affected most of Europe, from Brittany to the Balkans, from the Kingdom of Naples to the Netherlands. Why, then, should we expect this development to interact with a spatially salient religious practice such as pilgrimage only in the lands between Alsace and Luxembourg?

Pilgrims could encounter and cause not just one kind of border trouble but many, a diversity that this book captures thanks to its transregional scope. For example, the Saar region with its confessional diversity yields a different scenario from homogenously Catholic Luxembourg. Similarly, borders were not equally unstable in every single region during the revolutionary era. Most notably, even Napoleon preferred not to amputate the territory of the prerevolutionary ensemble of Swiss cantons, prompting one historian to speak of an "untouchable border."[51] This kind of continuity mattered: it enabled pilgrims from eastern France to begin approaching the Swiss shrines of Mariastein and Einsiedeln as mirrors in which to contemplate from the outside what it meant to be French. By contrast, most of the chapters present case studies from farther north, where French expansion entailed more dramatic and more variegated territorial changes (for the results of which see map 1).

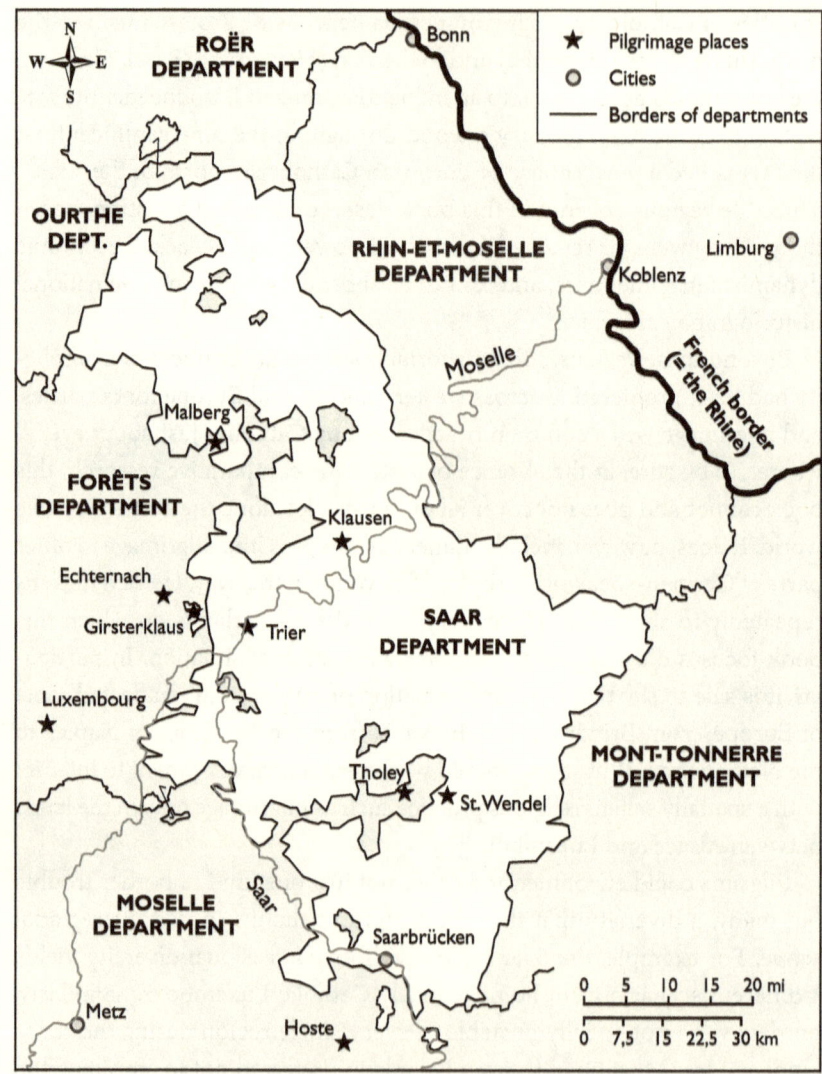

MAP 1. The Saar-Moselle-Rhine region, ca. 1802: Saar Department and neighboring areas. (Adapted from Eismann, *Umschreibung der Diözese*)

While the narrative presented in this book proceeds largely in chronological order, chapter 1 sets the scene by covering the entire period from 1770 to the heyday of Napoleonic imperialism. This chapter deals primarily with the detractors and defenders of pilgrimage rather than with the pilgrims themselves, who will take center stage in the other chapters. In the revolutionary era, pilgrimage had numerous outspoken enemies as well as committed friends. Their writings and actions can serve to give us an initial, overarching grasp of the interplay between holy places and nearby borders—between sacred and territorial space—that impacted political culture, whether on the scale of a parish or an empire. Chapter 1 addresses this issue at the level of intellectual history but also through a first case study that retraces the vicissitudes of Luxembourg City as a major pilgrimage destination in the borderlands.

The next two chapters touch on persistent confessional enmity and the roots of modern nationalism between the early 1770s and the mid-1790s. Chapter 2 moves the geographical focus from Luxembourg to the neighboring present-day Saarland, and specifically to the regionally important shrines of Sankt Wendel, Tholey, and Blasiusberg. This cluster of holy places straddled the border between the Holy Roman Empire and France while also belonging to a confessional frontier, an area where Catholic and Protestant communities lived in close, uneasy proximity. Here, borderlands pilgrimage renewed the matrix of confessional strife once enlightened reform programs made themselves felt at the local level. Chapter 3 explores the transformative trouble into which Alsatian Catholics got themselves in the revolutionary 1790s by going on pilgrimage across the Franco-Swiss border, to Einsiedeln and Mariastein. The historiography has revolved overwhelmingly around prorevolutionary constructions of the French nation and its territory. By contrast, I demonstrate that pilgrims with limited or no sympathy for the Revolution also shaped and appropriated the national frame—precisely by transgressing it through pious journeys abroad.

Dealing with the years around and after 1800, the last two chapters probe the intertwined processes of displacing and re-placing apparitions and relics as well as territorial boundaries. Chapter 4 is concerned with the intensified spatial instability of devotion in the later 1790s, when revolutionary France kept stumbling from one crisis to the next while also invading, occupying, and annexing many regions. Pilgrims' miraculous encounters with Mary proliferated during those years, inaugurating a type of apparition wave distinguished by its ephemeral, fluid, and expansive qualities. Specifically, this chapter examines the period's most spectacular series of Marian apparitions, which began just outside the tiny village of Hoste in German-speaking Lorraine. Finally, chapter 5 addresses the years of Napoleonic hegemony. I analyze the public showing of a prestigious relic known as the Holy Coat of Jesus, an event which drew more than two hundred thousand pilgrims to the small provincial city of Trier within three weeks in September 1810. This towering mass spectacle of the Napoleonic era reveals the interplay between an imperial border regime and unruly religious mobility: almost half of all pilgrims came unauthorized, from outside the territory whose inhabitants had been invited to Trier by the local bishop.

Overall, the structure of this book reflects the ambition to capture and contextualize one aspect of religious and political transformation in each chapter, rather than to say something about as many different shrines as possible.[52] That said, I did not cherry-pick my case studies so as to fill out the contours of some preconceived narrative. Rather, for each of the five borderlands covered in this book (Luxembourg, the region around Trier, the Saar region, Lorraine, and Alsace), my research concentrated on a particularly massive and well-documented phenomenon of devotional mobility. As a result, the chapters that follow consider Luxembourg's signature provincial—today national—Marian pilgrimage; the most important cluster of shrines situated in present-day Saarland; the most popular pilgrimages abroad for Catholics from Alsace; the most spectacular sequence of Marian apparitions that Europe witnessed in the revolutionary era; and the largest mass pilgrimage event of the entire Napoleonic period.

In writing these chapters, I have wrestled with the methodological issue that almost none of the available sources were produced by pilgrims themselves. To get at pilgrimage as a transformative site of border trouble, I had to contend overwhelmingly with texts written by and for state officials or clergy—police reports, administrative correspondence, pastoral visits and inquiries, and so forth. I often read these sources against the grain of the dominant clerical and anticlerical perspectives that tend, for all their mutual hostility, to agree remarkably on denying ordinary laypeople's capacity to mobilize themselves rather than be mobilized by priests. I also offer especially detailed analyses of the few bits of source material in which pilgrims' voices do appear, albeit in more or less heavily mediated ways. For instance, of the many hundreds of pilgrims arrested by French gendarmerie, almost none ended up in front of tribunals whose records have been preserved. Yet there are some felicitous exceptions to this rule, such as the interrogations of eleven pilgrims in 1799 by the Correctional Court of Habay-la-Neuve, in the present-day Belgian province of Luxembourg (see chapter 4). In other cases, communities sent petitions to defend their local pilgrimage traditions in the face of restrictive reform measures. Sources of this kind are especially helpful for understanding how pilgrims represented their own journeys and the borders they encountered.

Ultimately, this book zooms in on pilgrimage to help us understand Catholic renewal and politics during the age of revolutions and beyond. As historians have begun to show in the wake of revisionist approaches to secularization theory, the considerable success of this renewal owed much to Catholics' active, if tense engagement with wider currents of culture and politics in modern Europe. In the transition from a pre- to a postrevolutionary world, pilgrimage served as a major means of that engagement, a means through which broad swathes of the lay population navigated Enlightenment, Revolution, and Napoleonic imperialism. Their actions mattered because, on the one hand, the champions of the new regime worked hard to reshape politics, society, and people's relationships to the divine by spatial means, staking great hopes on territorial borders. On the other hand, these hopes were constantly challenged and redirected by pilgrims' mobility and by the very existence of shrines at or near borders. The ensuing struggles proved perilous, for lay Catholics, who often put themselves at risk by transgressing boundaries, but also for authorities who routinely saw their grand designs for spatial order thwarted. Out of this crucible—out of the transformation of border culture—came some of Catholicism's most effective strategies for reinventing itself both before and after 1800.

1

Holy Place and Sacred Territory in the Age of Revolutions

Was God a refugee?

As bizarre as this question might seem, it proved seriously vexing to Citizen Resch, the French government's central commissioner in the southern Alsatian department of Haut-Rhin. In a printed letter from April 1796, published in both French and German and addressed to all state officials and inhabitants of the department, Resch deplored what he viewed as the superstitious and counterrevolutionary impulses that mobilized many of his fellow citizens. By going on pilgrimage to the Swiss shrine of Mariastein, Alsatian Catholics "allow themselves every day to leave the Republic . . . as though the deity had fled to the Canton of Solothurn and as though it was impossible to worship at home, freely and each in his own way!"[1]

The commissioner's words suggest that he was wrestling with the relationship between territory and place. Territory had become both self-evident and immensely precious. In writing about pilgrims who left "the Republic" rather than the *territory* of the Republic, Resch took for granted the idea that in some sense the French Republic *was* its territory. This simple equation between a polity and its space worked to naturalize the new ideal of the territorial nation-state. Place, meanwhile, was harder to pin down. Describing God as "the deity," Resch raised the issue of whether people really even needed particular places to worship this abstract, either ubiquitous or placeless being. Why seek special encounters with the divine at a shrine such as Mariastein, an abbey quite close to the southern fringes of Alsace yet, from Resch's perspective, irremediably distant due to its location outside of France? Why not pray at home instead? Most of this book is dedicated to showing how pilgrims in the age of revolutions answered this question—primarily through practices of border-crossing devotion—and why their answers mattered. For these discussions to make sense, however, we first need to understand the meaning and urgency of the question itself. To build such an understanding, this chapter surveys revolutionary-era notions of holy place and sacred territory. It follows up a brief intellectual history with a case study that shows how those two notions mattered on the ground, in the borderland setting of Luxembourg.

I argue that Catholic elites in the age of revolutions worked hard to reconfigure pilgrimage places, not least by embedding them in new or shifting territories of Marian patronage. Far from seeking merely to halt the erosion of a traditional status quo, these Catholics were busy reorienting pilgrimage.[2] To be sure, they did not do so spontaneously. They were responding to enlightened attacks on the core idea that legitimized pious journeys, namely the belief that God's special grace was more accessible in certain places than in others. While undermining the Baroque concept of holy place, the Enlightenment also valorized territorial space, and some French revolutionaries went so far as to explicitly sacralize territory. These developments fueled the transformation of border culture: since territory was (and is) conceived of above all as "a bounded social space," reimagining territory necessarily involved reimagining boundaries, too.[3] Yet, as I noted in the introduction, border culture was reshaped not just by enlightened intellectuals, statesmen, and bureaucrats but by many other people as well, including pilgrims and pilgrimage promoters. Indeed, Catholics actively transformed the links that connected holy places to reimagined territories and redrawn borders.

Much of this chapter addresses the case of devotion to Our Lady of Luxembourg, which can illuminate these processes of challenge and renewal especially well. Around 1800, Luxembourg was a (mostly) German-speaking borderland par excellence.[4] What is more, the Luxembourgian example suggests just how dramatic the need to reorient pilgrimage could be with regard to both place and territory. Before the revolutionary era, Luxembourg's Marian pilgrimage was run by the Jesuits, fostered by the Virgin's status as patroness of the Duchy of Luxembourg, and centered on a widely known suburban chapel. All three of these pillars came crashing down within less than twenty-five years: the Jesuit order was suppressed in 1773, the duchy conquered and dissolved by the French in 1795, and the chapel demolished in 1796. Yet the pilgrimage survived and even thrived with little interruption. Its promoters helped ensure this continuity by giving Our Lady of Luxembourg a new, ultimately permanent home in the city's central parish, as well as by forging departmental and diocesan variations on the theme of territorialized Marian patronage. Before turning to this case study, however, let us first explore the more abstract debates that changed the way Catholics in German-speaking Europe and beyond thought about place, territory, and the sacred.

Sacred Space: New Meanings and New Conflicts

In the Gospel according to John, a Samaritan woman encounters Jesus while drawing water from a well. They start a conversation, and the woman soon becomes convinced that Jesus is a prophet. So, she encourages him to reveal where people ought to go to properly worship God—to Mount Gerizim, as the Samaritans assert? Or rather to the temple in Jerusalem, where God dwells according to the Jews? Jesus's enigmatic answer subverts the choice between the two pilgrimages suggested by the Samaritan: "Woman, believe me, the hour cometh, when ye shall neither in this mountain, nor yet at Jerusalem, worship the Father." Jesus elaborates on this remark by saying that "the hour cometh, and now is, when the true worshippers shall worship the Father in spirit and in truth."[5] The Catholic pilgrims at the center of this book almost always sought to reach specific holy sites, performing what Dee Dyas has termed "place pilgrimage."[6] How should clerical authorities justify or condone this kind of endeavor if Jesus's words were taken to mean that true worship must not be indebted to the particularities of place at all? Moreover, would the Catholic notion of sacred space lose much of its power if the secular space of state territory—the kind of space that Citizen Resch and so many others fought to valorize after 1789—were to take on stronger hues of the sacred itself?[7] Pondering these two questions will help us understand why enlightened elites in France and Catholic parts of the Holy Roman Empire largely viewed pilgrimage as transgressive.

As for the first question, the one about worship in spirit and truth, it is important to acknowledge that the theological vulnerability of pilgrimage dates back much further than the eighteenth century, further even than the rise of Protestantism. To grasp the historical depth of this vulnerability, we must take a look at Late Antiquity. Since the 1980s, much brilliant scholarship has argued that Christian pilgrimage did not grow organically from a preexisting, indeed timeless soil of "natural" or "popular" religiosity.[8] Instead, sometime around the fourth century CE, early Christianity turned from a religion that had been quite hostile to the very idea of holy place into one with an elaborate and cherished sacred topography. The tombs of martyrs, in particular, came to serve as places connecting Earth to the heavenly realm and consequently attracted large numbers of pilgrims.[9] Yet the rise of Christian pilgrimage never led to a full-fledged, confident theology of place. As historian Sabine MacCormack noted, "in Christian eyes holiness was not inherent in a place." Places could only be sanctified by "a human impact," such as the activity and death of a saint or "the unfolding of sacred history"; in short, the sanctity of place was derivative rather than primordial.[10] The numerous medieval and early modern critics of pilgrimage thought they were merely taking the problem to its logical conclusion when they accused pilgrims of superstition for trying to localize the divine.[11]

Even when theologians accepted *in practice* that some places were holy, they remained wary of embracing the *theory* that God's presence was durably bound to specific sites. They therefore had trouble making sense of the apparent fact that miracles kept happening time and again in the same locations, most notably at martyrs' tombs. Consider a well-known letter that Augustine wrote between 401 and 403 to the clergy and the faithful of his diocese. This letter was important to erudite early modern Catholics who defended pilgrimage against Protestant criticism. Most notably, the German Jesuit Jacob Gretser used the letter to support the case for pilgrimage that he made in his treatise *De sacris et religiosis peregrinationibus* (1606, translated into German in 1612).[12] Yet Augustine's appraisal of holy place was more ambiguous than Gretser would have cared to admit. Discussing the "sanctity of the place where the body of the blessed Felix of Nola is preserved," Augustine explicitly claimed not to understand why pilgrims experienced healings there: "who can scrutinize His judgment, through which these miracles occur in some places and not in others?" Augustine also prefaced these remarks with a theological caveat that referred to the passage I have quoted above from the Gospel of John, reminding his readers that "God, who made everything, is everywhere and is not contained or enclosed in any place, and it behooves His true worshippers to worship Him in spirit and truth."[13] The key example of Augustine shows how, already in late antique Christianity, the Johannine phrase "in spirit and truth" was connected to the notion of God's omnipresence, and thus to a certain bafflement at why special divine graces clustered in a few select places.

Whereas Gretser, following Augustine, bracketed this bafflement and accepted that miracles mysteriously occurred at shrines "by virtue of God's hidden judgment," a much more skeptical line of reasoning would gain traction in the Catholic Aufklärung.[14] Its champions drew a different conclusion from the doctrine of divine omnipresence: if the all-loving God is always present everywhere, then it is absurd and indeed blasphemous to assume that He might show Himself to be more benevolent in some places and less so in others. Therefore, place pilgrimage made no sense. To drive home this point, enlightened German Catholics made especially frequent use of the biblical verses about worship in spirit and truth. Church historians have piled up evidence of such usage, not least for the southwestern borderlands of the Holy Roman Empire.[15] To be sure, enlightened clergymen were displeased with many other aspects of pilgrimage, too, from the danger of sexual excesses on overnight trips, to the impious pushing and shoving and gawking among crowds at shrines, to the sheer multitude of annual pilgrimages by many communities that took away much time from work at home and in the fields. Yet such "abuses," as clerical writers and preachers usually called them, could be remedied.[16] By contrast, the claim that place-bound worship conflicted with worship in spirit and truth aimed at the very heart of pilgrimage—at the hope that God, Mary, and the saints might answer one's pleas for divine grace and healing more readily in some places than in others.[17]

Even a rather moderate Catholic enlightener such as Johann Michael Sailer (1751–1832) related divine omnipresence and worship in spirit and truth directly to the futility of pilgrimage in his main early work, the *Lectures in Pastoral Theology*. Although Sailer lived in Bavaria and published the first two editions of the *Lectures* (1788/9; 1793/4) in Munich, he wrote at the time as a protégé of the last archbishop of Trier, Clemens Wenceslaus, who was also bishop of Augsburg.[18] Much of Luxembourg, including the duchy's eponymous capital, belonged to the Archdiocese of Trier, so Sailer's arguments mattered, however indirectly, in this region as well.[19] Sailer placed his critique of pilgrimage in the context of the cult of saints. In his opinion, the clergy should deemphasize the external, sensory aspects of veneration—touching relics, looking at images—and exhort laypeople to take the virtues of faith and love more seriously instead.[20] This shift in focus implied combatting "coarse conceptions according to which the adoration of God and His answers to our prayers are tied to specific places." Against such mistaken assumptions, pastoral instruction needed to insist that "this omnipresent God is spirit and truth, and looks for worshippers who worship Him everywhere and always in spirit and in truth." This insight would help extinguish the "infatuation with pilgrimage" in which people indulged mostly because they confused the essential "value of trust" in God with the dubious "value of place."[21]

Polemical discourse in and around revolutionary-era Trier suggests that the focus on worship in spirit and truth had become sufficiently prominent to preoccupy the champions of Counter-Enlightenment, too. Most notably, the Augustinian friar Ernst Kronenberger pondered the biblical passage repeatedly in his *Polemical Sermons on the Aberrations of Reason and the Terrible Situation of Our Times*, published in 1798. This work implicitly continued the author's quarrel with two Catholic enlighteners from the region of Trier, the parish priest Johann Jakob Stammel and the self-identified Kantian Catholic Johann Kaspar Müller.[22] The latter had published a sharply anticlerical treatise in Luxembourg City in 1797, using the passage from the Gospel of John to clarify and legitimize his idea of what "the religion of Jesus" was and what Christianity accordingly ought to look like: a "divine, venerable, pure, simple, admirable religion free from ceremonies" such as Mass and pilgrimage festivals.[23] Kronenberger responded to this argument by using the same Johannine passage as the theme for no fewer than three of his roughly two dozen *Polemical Sermons*.[24] The opponents of ceremonial worship, he argued, "seem to want to forget that we consist not only of a spiritual soul but also of flesh and blood that must be led back by means of sensory objects to the pure spirit that is God." Hence, Jesus's admonition to the Samaritan woman meant only that external, embodied forms of worship must *relate* to belief in God and in church doctrine, not that belief should *replace* embodiment.[25] On this basis, Kronenberger could defend the corporeality of miraculous healings and the associated practices of pilgrimage to shrines, "those places of grace of Catholic Christianity."[26]

Summing up this glimpse into the history of a key quote from the Bible, we may say that the link between place and grace in Christian theology was enigmatic, fragile, contestable—and, indeed, sharply contested in the later eighteenth century. Place-making at shrines is a social, embodied, material process through and through. Does the ideal of worship in spirit and truth delegitimize the sacrality of such places because the word "spirit" refers to the *human* spirit in this case and thus to "the interiority of human beings where the real worship is to take place"? Answers to this question continue to vary widely in modern exegesis, among both Catholics and Protestants.[27] Knowing that these disagreements persist in the present can help us take Kronenberger's position seriously: he was not simply fighting a rearguard skirmish against an inherently more valid reading of the Gospel. Yet his defensive polemical posture signals how seriously the religious Enlightenment and the French Revolution had undermined the Baroque theological foundations of sacred place.

When enlightened Catholic critics of pilgrimage doubted the value of place, they were participating in a much broader tendency of early modern and nineteenth-century European thought. As philosopher Edward Casey has argued, by the eighteenth century, most "Western philosophers and scientists" accepted the idea that "places are merely momentary subdivisions of a universal space quantitatively determined in its neutral homogeneity."[28] To put it a little more simply, space had ontological priority as an empty container that God had filled in his act of creation. While drawing some criticism, most notably from Leibniz, this abstract way of thinking about space ultimately bolstered the idea that matter was just the content of space, a content that could be rearranged without genuinely changing the container.[29] Working under these assumptions, philosophers concluded that places, too, were ultimately just place*holders* for moveable contents on the grid of space, or, in Casey's words, an "unlimited set of simple locations."[30]

By taking into account this increasing focus on space as a container, we may better understand why Sailer and his fellow Catholic enlighteners held such a different view of divine presence than Gretser and other earlier writers. It would be misleading to try to answer this question by asserting that the protagonists of the Catholic Enlightenment denied immanent divine presence altogether. To be sure, they cautioned against credulously accepting unverified reports of miracles, but most of them did not reject the possibility of miracles per se.[31] Nor did they doubt the Catholic doctrine of transubstantiation, according to which the real and bodily presence of Christ in the Eucharist opened a sacramental conduit of divine grace.[32] More broadly, while the deists and atheists among the French philosophes as well as many revolutionaries roundly rejected such teachings, Catholic enlighteners affirmed—rather than ruptured—the theological tradition of their Church. That is why, as much recent scholarship has insisted, "Catholic Enlightenment" and "enlightened Catholicism" are not contradictions in terms to begin with.[33] In other words, we ought not to interpret the difference between Gretser and Sailer as a chasm between an "orthodox" and a "heterodox" conception of God's omnipresence and God's grace. Instead, it seems that Sailer and other Catholic enlighteners had accepted a wider philosophical tendency to homogenize or flatten place into mere location. Once they had integrated this flattening into the doctrine of divine omnipresence, the idea of God singling out "places of grace" slipped, for them, from the realm of mystery into the domain of the absurd and the impossible.[34]

Meanwhile, the philosophical appeal of space as a container was also filtering into politics, a trend that speaks to the core of the second question—the one about sacred territory—that I outlined at the beginning of this section. Considering that, at the level of the cosmos, space appeared to have primacy over the things with which it was filled, should not an analogous principle obtain at the level of the polity as well? If so—and French statesmen in particular took this conclusion for granted by 1700—then territory was bound to receive vastly increasing attention as the spatial container of the state.[35]

Historians have long understood that early modern territorialization was a pervasive and momentous process, but scholarship undertaken since the cultural and spatial turns has made the point with renewed vigor and has generated many new insights. To be sure, territory and borders already mattered a great deal in the Middle Ages, largely due to the ways in which the Church and legal cultures evolved. After the fall of the western Roman Empire, medieval dioceses turned into new laboratories of territorial organization and delimitation.[36] Fourteenth-century commentators of Roman Law came to define *territorium* as the space to which temporal jurisdiction applied, thus strengthening the spatial alongside the personal dimension of rulership.[37] Early modernity, however, did bring crucial new factors into the equation. After the Reformation, the principle *cuius regio, eius religio* based upon the Peace of Augsburg (1555) propelled the territorialization of confessional belonging in the Holy Roman Empire—although recent research has rightly emphasized the extent to which this process remained incomplete.[38] France under Louis XIV was another key arena of sharpened territorial imagery and practice: a coherent state territory defined by securitized borders (the *pré carré*) came to serve as both a powerful marker and a primary object of sovereignty.[39] In the German lands, with their famous "patchwork" of imperial Estates, this kind of spatial cohesion remained unattainable for most princes. Yet here, too, cameralist scholars and bureaucrats were eager to give theoretical primacy to state territory and to exalt bordering as the cornerstone of effective rule.[40]

Political elites in the seventeenth and, especially, the eighteenth century took another decisive step by developing the ideal of natural frontiers and attempting to anchor the shape of territories in what they idealized as Nature itself. Again, France has long figured as the paradigmatic case in this respect. Already in Richelieu's time, the goal of tying French territory to natural frontiers—primarily rivers and mountain ranges—oriented diplomatic and military action in tangible ways. Under Louis XV and Louis XVI, French administrators and diplomats concentrated more on turning the territorial discourse inward, that is to say, on imagining—though not actually implementing—a more homogenous division of provinces. But they also redoubled their efforts to delimit external state boundaries ever more precisely, eliminating a slew of territorial enclaves and exclaves and often insisting on following natural boundaries in the process. Finally, during the French Revolution, the objective of reaching the left bank of the Rhine as a new natural boundary justified French expansion into the borderlands with which this book is concerned.[41] In the eighteenth-century Holy Roman Empire, jurists, geographers, and philosophers of history also embraced the ideology of natural boundaries more and more. German as well as French and Swiss writers identified Nature as an orderly, legible source of eternal norms—which made natural boundaries appear as the most self-evident and stable guardrails of territory.[42] In short, enlightened elites further raised the prestige of territory and borders by naturalizing them.

These processes culminated after 1789, when French revolutionaries designated state territory as a genuinely sacred space. Although the phrase *territoire sacré* had come into usage shortly after 1700, before 1789 it remained confined to scholarly literature and almost exclusively referred to the haram area of Mecca.[43] The revolutionaries innovated by beginning to call France itself a *territoire sacré*. For example, the expression appears eight times in the records of speeches given and letters read at the National Assembly between August 1791 and late 1793.[44] The first of these eight instances occurred after Louis XVI had attempted to flee the country (in late

June 1791) and been stopped by citizens in the town of Varennes, not far from the French border with the Austrian Netherlands. In the climate of escalating suspicion that developed after this incident, deputies from the Parisian Poissonnière section addressed the National Assembly on August 14. They speculated that revolutionary France's likely enemies might prove "savage or barbaric enough to dare violate the sacred territory of liberty"—in which case the French army would, of course, inflict a crushing defeat on them.[45] Here, as in the other recorded cases, the sacredness of territory was emphasized precisely because foreign "despots" and their troops seemed to be threatening it.

This explicit sacralization was a way for protagonists of the Revolution to try to ground its accomplishments—and their own identity—in the soil of the *patrie*.[46] Members of the assembly used the expression less frequently (twice) than did section deputies or local revolutionary clubs (six times), which suggests that the turn of phrase resonated among ordinary supporters of the Revolution both in Paris and in the provinces. In 1799, as evidenced by the letter from Alsace that I cite at the very beginning of this book, the notion of the Republic's sacred territory remained available and plausible to local revolutionaries in France's eastern borderlands.

Yet while the revolutionaries undoubtably sacralized territory in new ways, early modern Catholicism had preceded them in endowing territorial space with a sacred aura. Marian patronage and pilgrimage to provincial, dynastic, or "national" Marian shrines played a paramount role in this process. Catholic elites across Europe proclaimed and promoted Mary as heavenly patroness and protectress of Catholic territories, and clergy as well as rulers and magistrates poured immense efforts into tying this patronage to popular pilgrimage destinations. These efforts yielded impressive results in many different lands, including France, Bavaria, Poland-Lithuania, the Spanish province of Aragon, Bohemia and other central European lands under Habsburg rule, and the southern Low Countries to which the Duchy of Luxembourg belonged.[47] Long before the French Revolution, Catholics—and especially promoters of pilgrimage—routinely deployed what Olivier Christin has termed "the double movement of sacralizing territory and territorializing the sacred."[48]

Perhaps the best-known case in the Holy Roman Empire concerns sixteenth- and seventeenth-century Bavaria, where the champions of Counter-Reformation turned Our Lady of Altötting into an icon of Pietas Bavarica.

Today the most famous pilgrimage place in all of southern Germany, Altötting acquired notoriety as a site of miracles and Marian devotion around 1490. Under Duke Albert V (r. 1550–1579), who launched the Counter-Reformation in Bavaria, members of the ruling House of Wittelsbach began making regular pilgrimages to this shrine situated roughly fifty miles east of Munich. Albert's successor, William V (r. 1579–1597), also founded a confraternity consecrated to Our Lady of Altötting whose membership rapidly grew into the thousands and whose main tasks included the organization of annual pilgrimages. A picture of territorial integration emerged, at least in the minds of elites, as Bavarian dukes (and later electors) kept going on pious trips to Altötting alongside ordinary subjects not just from Munich but, crucially, from all over the duchy—although Altötting attracted pilgrims from other territories as well.[49]

The central European lands under Habsburg rule offer many similar examples, above all Mariazell in northern Styria. To this day Austria's most-visited shrine, Mariazell began attracting pilgrims in the early fourteenth century. The shrine's political significance grew very pronounced in the early modern period, once the Catholic Reformation got underway and the Austrian Habsburgs developed a specific, Baroque style of devotion, the Pietas Austriaca. Emperor Ferdinand II (r. 1619–1637) and several of his successors dedicated their dynasty to the Virgin of Mariazell. Yet already by the later Middle Ages, legends had firmly tied devotion to her to a military exploit of King Louis I of Hungary (r. 1342–1382) against the Ottomans and credited one of Bohemia's foremost saints, the tenth-century duke Wenceslas, with having played a crucial role in the shrine's founding. Therefore, early modern Catholic writers glorifying the Habsburgs had little difficulty claiming that the history of Mariazell foreshadowed and symbolized the joining of Austria, Hungary, and Bohemia under Habsburg rule. This interpretation appeared palpable and extended its social reach thanks to the persistently massive influx of pilgrims from all these lands to Mariazell (an exceptionally high number of 370,000 devout visitors was recorded in 1757). Josephism mostly dismantled the Pietas Austriaca in the 1780s, but Mariazell remained an important imperial shrine and gradually morphed into the national shrine of both Austrians and Hungarians in the nineteenth and twentieth centuries.[50]

To sum up, renewed and intensified territorial imaginaries did affect place-making around shrines but did not simply spell the decline of Catholic holy places, let alone of Europeans' sense of place in general. There is no Heideggerian zero-sum game in which any gain in the perceived power of space (territorial or otherwise) would entail a corresponding loss in the perceived power of place.[51] Rather, historians need to ask how Europeans came to think about place differently as territorializing states and confessionalized churches ramped up their efforts—if not always their real capacity—to reshape spaces and literally put people "in their place."[52] For example, the reception history of the biblical passage about "worship in spirit and truth" shows on the one hand how the Catholic Enlightenment questioned the link between divine grace and holy place. On the other hand, the counter-enlightener Ernst Kronenberger's sermons hint at a competing, more place-friendly interpretation of "spirit and truth." Similarly, by valorizing, naturalizing, at times even sacralizing state territory, secular French revolutionaries directly defied the Catholic Church's claimed monopoly in identifying and cultivating sacred space. Yet this exaltation of territory strangely echoed a Catholic culture of spatialized patronage, which had enshrined the status of prominent holy places—especially Marian pilgrimage sites—as "territorial poles" for states and provinces in the Ancien Régime.[53] Overall, the challenges to pilgrimage were serious at the levels of both place and territory, but Catholics who favored pilgrim practice had powerful resources on which to draw in response.

Tying Place to Territory: Our Lady of Luxembourg

I now want to add depth to these reflections on place, space, and grace by zooming in on Luxembourg as a city and a territory. Far from present-day associations with finance, wealth, and openness toward Europe and the world, early modern Luxembourg was a poor and highly militarized province of the Habsburg Netherlands. It was also staunchly Catholic, not least due to the intense pastoral activities of Jesuit priests.[54] In the 1620s, the Jesuits opened a new chapter in the duchy's religious history: they built and began managing a Marian chapel, just outside Luxembourg City, which soon turned into a regionally important pilgrimage destination. Our Lady of Luxembourg attracted countless devotees from neighboring northern Lorraine, from the area around Trier, and above all within the Duchy of Luxembourg itself. The turbulences of Enlightenment reform could not leave such a major expression of piety unaffected, but the ensuing power struggles wrought transformations rather than decline. In particular, a closer look at events of the 1770s and 1780s shows how lay Catholics, clergy, and authorities constructed a territorial sense of place—and a place-bound sense of territory—through the devotion to Our Lady of Luxembourg.

This devotion bore all the hallmarks of early modern Catholicism, from laypeople's keen interest in sacred images to the importance of Marian patronage to the powerful impulses given by the Jesuits. They ran a college in the duchy's capital between 1594 and 1773, and they initiated the Luxembourgian devotion to Mary as Consoler of the Afflicted (the Consolatrix afflictorum) in 1624. The chapel consecrated to her, built on the slopes outside the fortress walls of Luxembourg City, developed into a major pilgrimage place by 1640, as the Consolatrix quickly gained fame for interceding effectively with God and procuring miraculous cures to those who prayed to her.[55] How quickly and how far did knowledge of these miracles spread across the region? That is hard to tell, but we do know that, after 1650, the Jesuits propagated the cult of the Consolatrix during their missionary excursions into the Luxembourgian countryside.[56] In 1651/2, they also founded a confraternity in her honor. Between the 1650s and the 1790s, roughly ten thousand people registered their names in this confraternity's membership book, thus placing themselves under Mary's protection.[57] While this aspect of the devotion blended individual and collective Marian patronage, political authorities added another layer in 1666: the governor of Luxembourg, the provincial council, and the city magistrate solemnly proclaimed the Consolatrix patroness of Luxembourg City.

From the very start, Mary's patronage over Luxembourg was inextricably intertwined with the issue of territory. In hindsight, the declaration of 1666 easily appears as a prelude to 1678, the year in which the provincial estates consecrated the duchy as a whole to Our Lady of Luxembourg.[58] Less teleologically, the decisions of both 1666 and 1678—and indeed the entire early history of devotion to Our Lady of Luxembourg—can be embedded in one overarching context of extended and interlocking crises. In the middle decades of the seventeenth century, climate-related famines, outbreaks of the plague, and nearly continual warfare compounded each other's devastating impact on much of the world's population. Luxembourgers were by no means spared in that situation, notably due to the persistently looming specter of French territorial expansion.[59] Already in 1659, the Habsburgs had ceded the southernmost parts of the Duchy of Luxembourg to France in the Treaty of the Pyrenees. Both in 1666 and in 1678, provincial authorities justified their recourse to Marian patronage particularly by pointing out the threat of French invasion and takeover.[60] That menace proved real soon enough: through the War of the Reunions (1683/4), Louis XIV obtained the rest of the duchy, although the Habsburgs reversed this result in the Peace of Ryswick (1697). Between 1684 and 1697, while the cult of the Consolatrix continued to function as a provincial devotion within Catholic France, Louis XIV's famous military engineer Vauban expanded the fortifications of Luxembourg City and treated Luxembourg as a sensitive piece of the *pré carré*, the thoroughly territorialized image of France as a spatial container.[61]

While kept apart from high politics, the duchy's population probably began to perceive the Consolatrix's patronage as a distinctly territorial relationship as well, even outside the city of Luxembourg itself. For one thing, after 1678, all parishes in the duchy celebrated a feast of Our Lady of Luxembourg as *patrona patriae* on the fourth Sunday after Easter.[62] The local importance that this feast could take on over the decades emerges most clearly in a case—so seemingly odd, yet so typical of early modern border complexity—in which a Luxembourgian village in the Eifel mountains, Malberg, belonged to a parish whose seat, Kyllburg, was situated on *trierisch* territory. The parish priest of Kyllburg refused to celebrate the feast of Our Lady of Luxembourg for the people of Malberg—even in the early 1770s, when a replica of the Consolatrix in the chapel of Malberg Castle acquired a reputation as a miracle-working image and began attracting pilgrims.[63] In this situation, both the seigneurial family and the commoners of Malberg protested by insisting that "we are no less Luxembourgian than those who reside close to the capital."[64] What is more, in the eighteenth century, the chapel in Malberg was just one of a handful of smaller shrines on the duchy's easternmost fringes where pilgrims came to pray before replicas of the Consolatrix.[65] This strong and proliferating presence of Our Lady of Luxembourg effectively marked the border with the Electorate of Trier, thus tying Marian patronage to territorial consciousness.

After 1770, territorial issues of parish and province also became more salient at the center of the duchy, where devotion to Our Lady of Luxembourg had originated. The main event that catalyzed this trend in Luxembourg City was the suppression of the Jesuit order—the favorite enemy of enlightened Catholic reformers—in 1773.[66] As a result, representatives of Empress Maria Theresa disbanded and dispossessed the Jesuits everywhere in the

Habsburg lands. In Luxembourg, the state took over the Marian chapel just outside the fortress walls as well as the church of the Jesuit college near the city center.[67] The latter church traditionally played a major role in the calendar of Marian pilgrimage: the statue of the Consolatrix was transported there from the chapel once a year for a duration of eight days, in the fifth week after Easter. During this period known as the Muttergottesoktav, the main pilgrimage festivals and the annual renewal of the vows of Marian consecration took place. To be sure, the new administrators of the two holy sites had little interest in diminishing the religious splendor—and the economic windfall—of the Oktav. As they noted in 1774 shortly before Easter, "it matters as much to the administration of the city and to the interest of its burghers as it does to the piety and edification of the people that this festivity not be affected by the suppression of the Jesuits."[68] Yet the fact remained that both key places of Marian devotion in Luxembourg now faced an uncertain future, as they came under the provisional care of state bureaucrats.

This uncertainty manifested itself in two concrete ways—first in the attempt to keep the parish clergy of Luxembourg City from taking control of the devotion to the Consolatrix, and later in a proposal that put the riches of the pilgrimage chapel on the chopping block. The first of these issues came up before the Oktav of 1774, not least because the church of the Jesuit college was located in the territory of the city's main parish, Saint Nicholas. The president of the Luxembourgian provincial council, François-Chrétien Gerden, acknowledged this fact, but he also persuaded the government that the ecclesiastical management of the Oktav should stay with the priest who had been serving as chaplain at the suburban shrine since long before the suppression of the Jesuits. After all, Gerden claimed, "the service of the Oktav is merely a consequence of the service that occurs all year long at the chapel outside the city, where the parish priest of Saint Nicholas has no jurisdiction because the chapel is situated inside the parish of Hollerich," a nearby village.[69] Gerden's proposal prevailed and seems, at first glance, to have simply ensured a maximum of continuity after the end of the Jesuit order.[70] Yet by refusing to cede responsibility for the pilgrimage and the Oktav to an established ecclesial institution such as the parish, Gerden was in fact perpetuating the provisional regime of administration created in 1773. What, for example, would happen once the ex-Jesuit chaplain died? How would continuity of pastoral care for pilgrims be ensured then? These questions remained unresolved as Gerden used territorial arguments to avoid transferring authority over the pilgrimage and its two main places of devotion.

In 1777, another possible consequence of continued state administration loomed on the horizon, as the government pushed for solutions to the financial problems it faced in managing the Jesuit legacy. In Luxembourg, an inquiry coming from the Conseil privé in Brussels prompted the overseer of the ex-Jesuit estate, Jean-Baptiste Leonardy, to suggest consolidating the possessions of the chapel and the church of the former college. Among other things, he asked for permission "to sell those possessions of the chapel that are entirely useless for the service of said chapel, such as hearts and other similar objects made of silver."[71] These valuable objects would in most cases have been donated by devotees as tokens of gratitude for the Virgin's protection and intercession.[72] The quantity as well as the quality of those hearts, crosses, and rings reflected Mary's honor and power, so their sale might very well have appeared as a deliberate attempt to undermine the devotion to Our Lady of Luxembourg. That said, Leonardy's plan almost certainly did not come to fruition. Just a few months after his exchange with the Council, jurisdiction over the pilgrimage chapel fell to the parish of Saint Nicholas after all, by virtue of a decree issued in Brussels in the empress's name.[73] It is tempting to speculate that the parish priest Paul Feller, and possibly other influential devotees of Mary in Luxembourg, had lobbied for this decree precisely to avert the realization of Leonardy's proposal.

In any case, the government did Feller and his parishioners a favor by granting them public, communal stewardship of the Marian shrine. In 1774, Gerden had claimed that, "this devotion having been introduced, supported, and grown by the Jesuits, who do not exist anymore, it is exclusively at Your Majesty's [that is, the empress's] disposal."[74] Through this argument as well as the territorial one I analyzed earlier, Gerden had imposed the view that the parish clergy of Saint Nicholas had no jurisdiction over the chapel of Our Lady and the Oktav. By contrast, the empress's decree of 1777 redefined the chapel as "a public oratory, funded by the piety of the faithful, and entirely independent from the possessions of the said Society [of Jesus], which only had rights of simple administration."[75] This change of status from a Jesuit chapel to a public oratory empowered the community of Luxembourgian Catholics—the wider "public" devoted to Mary—and in particular the parish community of Saint Nicholas, led by the *curé* Feller. The decree also stipulated a territorial adjustment to reinforce the overall shift in power: Maria Theresa declared the pilgrimage chapel annexed and united in perpetuity to the parish of Saint Nicholas.[76] Moreover, in April 1778, the government tied the Consolatrix's second major holy place firmly to the parish of Saint Nicholas: Brussels agreed to let the bishopric of Trier turn the church of the former college into the new parish church of Saint Nicholas, now rededicated to Saints Nicholas and Theresa in the empress's honor.[77] Ultimately, the challenges of the 1770s led to a realignment that bound together place, territory, and urban community more consistently than before around Our Lady of Luxembourg.

The following decade continued this development while taking it in a slightly different direction, as the theme of *provincial* territory took center stage again. In 1781, once the dust had settled after the sweeping changes of 1777/8, tens of thousands of Luxembourgers belatedly celebrated the centenary of the duchy's consecration to the Consolatrix. Secular and ecclesiastical authorities deployed a monumental iconographical program. Ephemeral architecture, paintings, and accompanying inscriptions and booklets all contributed to juxtaposing the Virgin and the province. Artists visualized its territorial extension by depicting the coats of arms of the duchy's fifteen towns prominently in various places, including inside the church of Saints Nicholas and Theresa, and by personifying the three main rivers flowing through the province (the Mosel, Sauer, and Alzette).[78]

Between 1786 and 1790, however, Emperor Joseph II's desire for enlightened religious reform threatened the very existence of the Oktav. In particular, an edict of May 1786 restricted the number of processions in any given parish of the Austrian Low Countries to two per year, entirely banned processions on Sundays, and forbade people from carrying along any statues or other images.[79] This legislation incidentally delegitimized the entire framing of the Luxembourgian Oktav. Both its opening and closing processions took place on Sundays. Above all, the point of those processions was to transport the miraculous statue of the Virgin, publicly and with honor, from the suburban pilgrimage chapel to the church of Saints Nicholas and Theresa and (a week later) back again. As a result of the emperor's edict, the processions seem to have ceased between 1787 and 1789.[80]

While this partial dismantling of the Oktav did not go uncontested, the emperor's counselors in Brussels remained distinctly unimpressed by the petitions that the provincial estates of Luxembourg sent in this matter in December 1786 and March 1787.[81] Nicolas Dufour, the ecclesiastical counselor responsible for issues of pilgrimage and processions, adhered strictly to the principles of Josephist reform.[82] What this ideal meant for the devotion to Our Lady of Luxembourg became clear in his response to the grievances voiced by the provincial estates in 1787. Dufour claimed that Luxembourgers' trust in the Consolatrix "reaches the point of superstition" and that the influx of pilgrims during the Oktav degraded social "mores" by leading to "all the little disorders that are inevitable in large crowds."[83] With this rationale, he roundly rejected the estates' plea to have the opening and closing processions of the festival exempted from the emperor's ban on Sunday processions. What is more, in a draft of his opinion on the petition, he questioned not only the Oktav week but also the emplacement of the Consolatrix's statue in the pilgrimage chapel during the rest of the year: "the image will remain in the chapel where it currently stands until the restructuring of parishes and church service."[84] Although he eventually decided against including this sentence in his opinion, the reforms he hoped to implement threatened to sever the ties that linked holy places and territories of Marian patronage in Luxembourg. For Dufour, pilgrimage to Luxembourg City was ultimately incompatible with "worship in spirit and truth."[85]

At the same time, however, the protest of the provincial estates made those ties explicit and reasserted their importance against Josephism. In their first and most detailed petition—the one of December 1786—the estates exalted the Oktav as a "religious festivity of such special importance to this capital city and this entire province of Luxembourg."[86] The petition echoed the emphasis that the belated centenary of 1781 had already put on the province and its territory as a space of Marian patronage. For one thing, the estates highlighted the provincial consecration of 1678 much more thoroughly than the urban one of 1666. Above all, in order to circumvent the emperor's edict of May 1786, which seemingly applied to *parish* processions, the petitioners let their argument culminate in the claim "that what we are dealing with is not a pious ceremony established by a particular parish, but rather a devotion solemnly dedicated to the Holy Virgin by all the orders and all the inhabitants of a vast province."[87] In the 1770s, as we have seen, the Consolatrix's devotees had solved the issue of the Jesuits' legacy by pulling Luxembourg City's Marian sites into the territorial and communal framework of the parish. In their petition of 1786, by contrast, the provincial estates downplayed that very framework. Acting as the foremost defenders of the Oktav vis-à-vis the government, they were able to present the territory of the duchy as the crucial space of reference for the Marian patronage and devotion to which they were attached.

While these protests had no effect in the short run, the overall failure of Josephist reform in the Austrian Netherlands became obvious within a few years. Widespread opposition to the emperor's policies escalated into the Brabant Revolution of 1789/90. By early 1790, the Austrian commissioner Cobenzl was busy reestablishing the status quo ante in Luxembourg, the Low Countries' only province still under Habsburg control at that moment. Cobenzl retracted the edict on processions along with other pieces of legislation, enabling Luxembourgers to celebrate the Oktav of 1790 in full splendor again.[88]

In the previous two decades, the champions of devotion to Our Lady of Luxembourg had achieved a new synthesis of place, territory, and Marian patronage. They reacted to challenging developments by respatializing this patronage in various ways. Thus, pilgrimage promoters spun an elaborate, increasingly cohesive devotional web. It connected remote border villages to the capital city, the suburban pilgrimage chapel to the church in the city center of Luxembourg, and the duchy's parishes to the province as a whole. Moreover, even for the late 1780s, quantitative evidence suggests that the Oktav continued to draw huge crowds (despite the lack of formal opening and closing processions), and that more than ten thousand pilgrims visited the suburban chapel during the rest of the year.[89] All that said, more radical challenges lay ahead for devotion to the Consolatrix and pilgrimage to Luxembourg, as another revolution was just gathering steam in neighboring France.

Renewal without Rebuilding

Less than a year after the French conquest of Luxembourg, its new administrators sealed the fate of the region's most famous pilgrimage chapel. In their session of March 13, 1796, they considered a letter from Luxembourg's new chief engineer, who demanded that the chapel of Our Lady be razed to the ground, as it stood excessively close to the city's outermost western fortifications.[90] The members of the departmental administration agreed "that no special motive can outweigh that of the interest of the Republic, which imperiously commands the demolition of said chapel."[91] By mid-June, most of the building had been taken down and its materials auctioned off.[92] To be sure, Marian pilgrimage to Luxembourg did not end then and there, and neither did devotion to Our Lady of Luxembourg more broadly. Yet things had definitely taken a drastic turn—not just because the chapel was gone but also because the territory consecrated to the Consolatrix in 1678, the Duchy of Luxembourg itself, had officially ceased to exist at the moment of French annexation in 1795.

Hence the last question I want to answer in this chapter: to what extent were Luxembourgian Catholics able to resituate the Virgin within the radically altered spaces they now inhabited? The answer, in a nutshell, is renewal without rebuilding. The Napoleonic years brought many disappointments, particularly to those who hoped to reconstruct the pilgrimage chapel after the end of the Revolution. French rule also, however, enabled those who either retained or developed an attachment to the Consolatrix to ground her in new imperial and diocesan territories.

Just as Luxembourg, the city and the province, had been far from unique as spaces of Marian patronage in early modern Catholic Europe, so did the demolition of the pilgrimage chapel in 1796 resemble many other acts of pillaging, destroying, or repurposing shrines. In the next chapters, we will repeatedly encounter shrines that suffered heavy damage from French revolutionary troops. While some of these places—Tholey in the Saar region, for instance—never recovered as pilgrimage destinations, others did so rather quickly, most notably Einsiedeln in Switzerland. In between those two extremes, we may situate Luxembourg's second famous pilgrimage event, the so-called Hopping Procession (Springprozession) of Echternach, today a border town in eastern Luxembourg. In 1797, after forcefully disbanding the monks of Echternach Abbey, French administrators proceeded to sell off the monastery buildings, including the church that had housed the relics of Saint Willibrord and served as the goal of the great annual pilgrimage procession.[93] While the pilgrimage continued, with processions now culminating at the town's parish church, the old abbey church fell into ruin and was only rebuilt in the late 1860s.[94] Countless other examples would work equally well to support the point that the French Revolution entailed dramatic displacements of the sacred, both in France and in the many regions its armies conquered after 1792.[95]

In Luxembourg, these displacements occurred amid wider social and political tensions provoked by French conquest, occupation, annexation, and introduction of revolutionary policies. The French army controlled most of the Luxembourgian countryside by late 1794, but warfare in the region dragged on until June 1795, when Luxembourg City surrendered after more than six months of siege. Together with the rest of the former Austrian Netherlands, Luxembourg transitioned from an occupation regime to formal incorporation into the French Republic rather quickly: a decree to this effect signaled the official demise of the old duchy on October 1, 1795. The French hastily introduced the Revolution's entire legal and administrative regime in their new departments. The local population might have appreciated the advantages of this regime—for example, the use of the metric system—if they had not been accompanied by various adjustment issues and perceived iniquities. Luxembourg's old elites felt snubbed as men from the interior of France swooped in to occupy many key positions of regional state authority. These newcomers made few friends and rarely hesitated to line their pockets, whether in the market for secularized former church property (the *biens nationaux*) or by other, at times unsavory means. Meanwhile, rural communities grumbled because their tax burden rose quickly even as they had to find new ways to materially support their priests: the Republic had abolished almost all tithes and declined in 1795 to compensate the parish clergy for their resulting losses.[96]

In October 1798, a peasant insurrection known in Luxembourgish as the Kleppelkrich revealed the profound mingling of religious and secular grievances. The Coup d'État of Fructidor an V (September 1797) had entailed a resurgence of state-sponsored anticlericalism across the French Republic. As a result, many Catholics in Luxembourg came to believe that their Church faced a fundamental threat. Many insurgents in the fall of 1798 invoked the urgency of defending their faith. Yet, what actually triggered the revolt as well as similar ones in present-day Belgium was a French law on military conscription. The mixture of religious resentment and draft refusal calls to mind the most famous of all antirevolutionary uprisings, the Vendée insurrection of 1793 that had escalated into a protracted and extremely bloody civil war in western France.[97] By contrast, the Kleppelkrich lasted only a few weeks: the poorly armed and disorganized peasant troops were quickly defeated, never having managed to take the fighting far beyond the epicenter of the revolt in present-day northern Luxembourg. The Kleppelkrich did, however, signal the new regime's severe lack of popularity in the region.[98]

For Marian devotion in Luxembourg, the most difficult years stretched from the Fructidor coup of 1797 to Napoleon's Brumaire coup of November

1799. After Fructidor, Catholic parish clergy were obligated to swear an oath of hatred of royalty and anarchy if they wanted to continue their work and keep their parish churches open.[99] Jean-Baptiste Käuffer, the *curé* of Saint Nicholas, swore the oath but in doing so alienated the majority of his parishioners—especially the most fervent Marian devotees—who resented his apparent commitment to revolutionary ideas. These Catholics appropriated the statue of the Consolatrix and, in early May 1798, attempted to celebrate a clandestine Oktav centered on another, officially closed church in the city. The urban police commissioner witnessed the large, illegal, and thus defiant opening procession that, according to his report, included several oath-refusing priests and 250 children carrying white candles. The following night, he intervened and even had the Marian statue removed from the church, a harsh measure that almost led to an outbreak of violence between frustrated Catholics and the police.[100] There seemed to be, quite literally, no place for Our Lady of Luxembourg anymore.

Religious tensions began to decrease, however, after Napoleon's coup d'état and especially after April 1802, when the new Concordat between the French Republic and the papacy went into effect.[101] In Luxembourg City, the first state-authorized Oktav since the French conquest was promptly celebrated in May 1802, and the underlying initiative seems to have come mainly from the parishioners of Saint Nicholas. Eighty-seven of them signed a successful petition to the mayor to obtain permission for their *curé* to lead the customary opening and closing processions through the city streets. In favor of the Oktav, the petitioners pointed out that "the entire former province had an interest in it thanks to the spiritual consolations as well as the material help" that it had procured for more than a century. They acknowledged that the post-Concordat reorganization of parishes had barely begun, but they proceeded to brush aside this issue with an astonishing claim: their existing parish "has always exclusively possessed the right to carry out this festivity, hence why it is neither a novelty nor a favor infringing on the rights of other, not-yet-existing parishes."[102]

Moreover, in a parallel petition to the prefect, two churchwardens of Saint Nicholas, Jean-François Baclesse and François Röser, wrote that "in this department, the Holy Virgin is honored as protectress of the land" and that her statue had stood in the parish church "since the demolition of the chapel of this patroness of Luxembourg." Crucially, the grammar of their French letter makes it clear that by "Luxembourg" they meant the old provincial territory rather than the city alone.[103] The Duchy of Luxembourg had officially vanished, but the prerevolutionary spatial links between Mary as patroness and her Luxembourgian devotees were reemerging nonetheless. With regard to the parish of Saint Nicholas, the parishioners' petition now even backdated these links to time immemorial even though they were barely twenty-five years old, as I have shown above.

This textbook case of inventing a tradition did not, however, mean that the Consolatrix's devotees were simply hoping to stabilize what was left of Luxembourgian sacred space after the loss of the suburban pilgrimage chapel. On the contrary, they soon proceeded to try to regain an exclusively dedicated *chapelle de Notre-Dame*. The most influential spokesperson of this cause vis-à-vis the government was the new bishop of Metz, to whose diocese Luxembourg City and the surrounding region—called the Forêts Department since 1795—belonged after the Concordat. By late 1802, Bishop Pierre-François Bienaymé (1737–1806) seemed, as state administrators put it, "convinced that the interest of religion demands that the special veneration formerly given to Our Lady of Luxembourg be reestablished, and he considers it necessary to assign to that end one of the city's churches."[104] Specifically, Bienaymé had decided to turn the parish church of Saint Nicholas into a church of Our Lady that would "replace the former chapel of that name" and would no longer serve as a parish church but would instead "come under the direct jurisdiction of *monsieur* the bishop."[105] Most likely inspired by Luxembourgian Catholics—who else would have drawn his attention to the Consolatrix in the first place?—Bienaymé was, in other words, working to replace the old, destroyed pilgrimage chapel with a much bigger, more centrally located one. Of course, this plan would only come to fruition if he could simultaneously allocate a different church to the parish community of Saint Nicholas.

Bienaymé failed in this undertaking, even though he sought to exploit the opportunities created by the revolutionary secularization of many convents and monasteries, whose churches now appeared as potential new parish churches. Until the early spring of 1804, the bishop tenaciously fought the prefect of the Forêts and the local engineering corps, who had appropriated the former convent church of the Recollects for military purposes, primarily as a storage space. Here again, local laypeople played a major role in prodding the bishop to action: already in September 1802, some one hundred members of the Saint Nicholas parish (soon to be rebaptized Saint Pierre) had petitioned him to annex the Recollects' church to their parish.[106] The city's lay Catholic elite also seems to have supported Bienaymé's overall plan, even though episcopal jurisdiction over the projected new chapel of Our Lady would have disempowered the parish community to an extent. At least, Baclesse and two other municipal counselors of Luxembourg City sent a declaration to the bishopric in March 1803, explaining that they had hoped to officially endorse the option of turning the Recollects' church into the parish church of Saint Pierre. Prefect Lacoste, they complained, had responded by unilaterally suspending the session and preventing a vote on the matter.[107] The bishop's abundant correspondence, too, suggests that the key reason he failed to desecularize the Recollects' church was Lacoste's insistence on confirming the military engineers and the artillery in their possession of the building.[108] In this affair, Luxembourg's status as a fortress town trumped its role as a place of Marian devotion.[109]

The same conflict between piety and artillery yielded an analogous result in the following years, after Luxembourgian Catholics and the bishopric of Metz embraced an alternative plan, that of reconstructing the chapel in its former location. Between the spring of 1804 and the fall of 1809, numerous civil and ecclesiastical elites—from local and regional to diocesan authorities—repeatedly tried to get the government in Paris to authorize this rebuilding project. Whether addressed to the ministers of the interior and of *cultes* or to Napoleon himself, all these requests ultimately came to nothing because the minister of war categorically opposed the construction of any building as close to the fortress walls as the old chapel had been.[110] Eventually, the chapel was not rebuilt until the 1880s, in a slightly different spot and after the dismantling of Luxembourg City's fortifications that occurred after 1867.[111] Yet, the petitions and debates of the Napoleonic years are worth dwelling upon because, once more, they raised and intertwined the key issues of place and territory.

First, a thicket of disparate arguments grew around the question of why rebuilding the chapel in its exact previous location mattered. Indeed, why not carry out the reconstruction project outside the no-man's-land radius defined by a law of 1791, as the war ministry suggested in 1804?[112] Did Luxembourgian Catholics hold the belief, discussed in the first section of this chapter, that the holy manifested itself only in certain places and not in others? Gaspard-Jean-André-Joseph Jauffret (1759–1823), Bienaymé's successor as bishop of Metz, suggested as much in late 1809 when writing to the minister of *cultes*: "Although it seems that God and the saints can be honored equally well in all places, it is important to preserve the worship given to them by an inherently religious people in the same place where it has pleased God to receive homages and where the people have been accustomed to offering them."[113] Jauffret here ascribed a belief—or a religious instinct—to ordinary Catholics while tentatively distancing himself from it. We need to take his assertion with a pinch of salt, not least because other, older arguments also existed against the site proposed by the war ministry. In 1807, either Jauffret himself or his Luxembourgian vicar-general, Henry Neunheuser, had claimed that the more removed terrain was too agriculturally fertile and thus too expensive to be purchased for a building project. Moreover, unlike the fortress's glacis where the old chapel had stood, the alternative spot was inconveniently far from the city and unsuitable as a gathering place for large crowds of pilgrims, who would constantly trample on surrounding fields.[114] Rhetoric shifted and, perhaps, so did understandings of place.

Above all, judging by the timeline, the idea of rebuilding the pilgrimage chapel in its former location constituted a mere plan B rather than an expression of some overriding, immutable religious instinct. All the available evidence suggests that the bishopric of Metz and Luxembourg's Catholic notables first tried to turn the parish church of Saint Pierre into a new, gigantic chapel of Our Lady of Luxembourg. As we have seen, this attempt failed in 1803 because the engineering corps and the prefect resisted the rededication of the former Recollects' church as a seat for the Saint Pierre parish. Only in 1804, once the Recollects' church appeared as a lost cause, the local and departmental assemblies of Luxembourgian notability began voicing the ambition to have the Marian chapel rebuilt on the glacis. In other words, if Bienaymé had managed to realize his initial plans, the campaign to reconstruct the old chapel on the glacis might never have been launched, or at least it would not have taken on nearly as much urgency as it did in 1804–9. All the while, as Neunheuser put it, the parish church of Saint Pierre continued to "represent" the chapel of Our Lady.[115] Luxembourgian elites did want more than a mere representation, and the same may have been true for nonelite Catholics, although we lack source material recording their views on this matter. Yet having a chapel at all, setting *some* proper place of worship apart for the Consolatrix, mattered more than recovering the sacred in a single, "original" location. In that sense, place-making efforts remained flexible.

The debates over a new chapel of Our Lady also had a strong territorial component because they foregrounded "phantom borders," an aspect of border culture that marks the aftermath of dramatic territorial changes. Defining phantom borders as "former, usually political boundaries or territorial formations that continue to structure space even after being abolished institutionally," scholars of modern Eastern European history and culture have pioneered the study of this phenomenon.[116] Perhaps the most famous European phantom borders to emerge from the revolutionary era are those of Poland-Lithuania, the continent's largest republic, partitioned and eventually wiped off the map by Russia, Prussia, and Austria in 1772, 1793, and 1795. Pilgrims played a significant role in shaping the resulting spatial phantom of "Poland" through their trips to the extremely well-frequented shrine of Our Lady of Częstochowa, recognized as "Queen of Poland" since the seventeenth century. Beginning in the 1770s, the traditional pilgrimages to Częstochowa evolved into transimperial transgressions, quickly perceived and treated as such especially by Josephist Austria.[117] Considering this fascinating case that involved one of Europe's most important shrines, why not also apply the concept of phantom borders to German-speaking Europe in the revolutionary era? After all, armies and diplomats redrew borders and erased territorial entities at a staggering pace in those decades, as I noted in the introduction.

Luxembourg City exemplifies the local shifts—and phantoms—that this overarching geopolitical process created. In Napoleonic times, the city no longer constituted a major borderlands fortress of the Habsburg empire but rather a strategically less interesting provincial center, removed from France's new external borders. Yet that previous borderland location continued to mark Luxembourg City, whose status as a fortress could, after all, hardly disappear overnight. Napoleonic military authorities struggled to manage the vast fortifications and downsize the garrison without wrecking the urban economy and thereby testing Luxembourgers' loyalty.[118] Phantom borders account for military engineers' persistent hold on the space of Luxembourg City, and thus help explain the failure of plans to create a new special place for the Consolatrix—whether those projects involved the former Recollects' church or the suburban glacis.

Yet phantom borders also played into the Catholic discourse on why such a special chapel was still needed at all, even after the disappearance of the Duchy of Luxembourg, whose patroness the Consolatrix had been since 1678. We have already seen how local notables exalted Our Lady of Luxembourg as protectress of the former province and the Luxembourgian lands in 1802, when pushing for a revival of the Oktav processions. From 1804 to 1806, in their reports and letters to the government, the deliberative assemblies of the Forêts Department kept making the same point. A session of the department's general council in 1806 offers the most intriguing instance of this tendency to articulate a postprovincial Luxembourgian identity—and thus to invoke the phantom borders of the old duchy, which largely coincided with those of the Forêts Department.[119] Specifically, the council members advocated "the reconstruction of the chapel of Our Lady, patroness of the former province."[120] In order to better speak for the entire population of the Forêts, they must have felt it appropriate to refer to a space of Marian patronage that went beyond Luxembourg City. The old Duchy of Luxembourg thus had a devotional afterlife. Though no longer visible on new maps and in French institutions, it still existed as a Marian territorial phantom.

Beyond these echoes of a vanished province, the Napoleonic years also witnessed a new variation on the theme of the Consolatrix's spatialized patronage. During the Oktav of 1807, Bishop Jauffret visited the church of Saint Pierre and consecrated the Diocese of Metz to Our Lady of Luxembourg. He did so first in a sermon on Thursday, April 30. As he noted in his diary, "I was moved. I spoke with force and vehemence. I finished by invoking the Holy Virgin, patroness of the Luxembourgian land, placing the bishop of Metz and his diocese under her protection."[121] Framed in this way, the new diocesan consecration appeared as a direct extension—not an erasure—of the old provincial patronage. This approach probably made sense because most of the pilgrims Jauffret encountered on this occasion came from places that had belonged to the old Duchy of Luxembourg. The bishop himself, at any rate, claimed in his subsequent report to Paris that "an immense multitude" of people from all over the Forêts Department as well as neighboring areas took part in the Oktav festivities. According to him, on the final Sunday of the Oktav, when he repeated the diocesan consecration in a more solemn format, thirty to forty pilgrim processions converged on the city, amounting to an influx of "more than fifteen thousand visitors" on a single day.[122] Jauffret may have exaggerated, but other evidence supports the assumption that, in those years, a five-figure number of pilgrims visited Luxembourg City annually during the Oktav.[123] In sum, this festive week continued to attract a great number of pilgrims from Luxembourgian lands who most likely still considered Mary their patroness, and Jauffret built on this attachment while adding a new spatial layer to the Consolatrix's patronage.

Intriguingly, the bishop embedded the diocesan consecration of 1807 within a broader strategy of integrating a "German" space into the French Empire. After the Concordat, the Diocese of Metz was one of the largest in France, covering the Moselle Department in northern Lorraine and the Ardennes Department to the west in addition to the Forêts. Devotion to Our Lady of Luxembourg had become widespread in the northernmost parts of Lorraine since the seventeenth century,[124] so the Consolatrix's diocesan patronage may have made perfect sense to local Catholic populations there. Moreover, most people in the Moselle department's northern and eastern parts spoke German dialects, as did the vast majority of inhabitants in the Forêts. Jauffret himself distinguished the "German part" of his diocese and treated Luxembourg City as its center.[125] The diocesan consecration served as a strong signal to that effect.

At the same time, worried that the inhabitants of the Forêts were opposed to "anything that comes from France," Jauffret developed plans to Frenchify them gradually.[126] Specifically, he wanted future generations of clergy and schoolteachers to teach French even to poor and rural speakers of German.[127] In the seminaries that he founded in Luxembourg City and other regional centers of his diocese, he envisioned bringing together the French and Luxembourgian "races" to engender a new, bilingual, and more unified clerical elite.[128] Napoleonic rule in Luxembourg did not last long enough for these far-reaching ambitions to unfold. In 1807, however, they formed the key context in which Jauffret created a new space of patronage for Our Lady of Luxembourg. Through the Marian consecration, he sought to present his diocese as a territory that united old and new French subjects, German- and French-speaking Catholics—in short, as an arena of beneficent imperial Frenchification.

Overall, the conflicts and developments regarding the Consolatrix in the Napoleonic era reflect how Catholics continued to try to forge new links between holy place and territory. In the Luxembourgian case, many of these efforts failed, largely because the French military had little patience for the Christian sacred and approached the space of a fortress town such as Luxembourg City accordingly. That said, the struggles I have analyzed generated opportunities for elites to tie new territorial units, such as the Forêts Department and the Metz diocese, into the older tradition that viewed Mary as patroness of the Luxembourgian lands. Such strategies, moreover, only made sense because many thousands of pilgrims from across the region continued to pay homage to Our Lady of Luxembourg year after year. These aspects have received little attention in Catholic and Luxembourgian historiography, which instead emphasizes a later "revival" of the Oktav in the 1840s—conveniently preceded by the independence of the new Grand-Duchy of Luxembourg in 1839.[129] From the perspective of the Consolatrix's devotees, the 1790s and early 1800s undeniably brought many setbacks. Yet for that very reason, Catholics searched all the more intensely for new solutions, new ways to anchor the sacred both in places and in territories.

Reorienting Pilgrimage

The crisis of Catholic pilgrimage in the revolutionary era had multiple facets and many different consequences. This chapter has focused on one particularly important aspect, namely the destabilized relationship between place and territory. Devout travel to shrines orders and orients spaces, centering them on special, holy places. Viewed from this angle, the manifold challenges that pilgrims and pilgrimage promoters faced in the decades around 1800 were challenges of disorientation. Enlightened Catholic writers questioned the very concept of holy place; diplomats and revolutionaries changed spatial arrangements drastically, by redrawing borders across western and central Europe and valorizing state territory to an unprecedented degree; anticlerical, iconoclastic, and secularizing politics led to the destruction of numerous shrines, including the Marian chapel on the glacis of Luxembourg City's fortress. In order to overcome the resulting disorientation, the defenders of pilgrimage had to come up with new strategies for place-making and for relating sacred spaces to territorial borders—whether those of the parish, the province, or the state.

The case of Luxembourg highlights the flexibility with which Catholics went about the task of reorienting pilgrimage. Confronting first the suppression of the Jesuits and, later on, Josephism, the French conquest of 1795, and the destruction of the Marian chapel in 1796, Luxembourgers found multiple ways to secure and reimagine the "territorial bond" of patronage that tied them to the Virgin.[130] Adapting their tactics and discourses to various new situations, the devotees of Our Lady of Luxembourg reasserted her function as urban patroness by integrating her holy sites into the territory of the city's main parish. They also kept reasserting her importance as protectress of the Luxembourgian province. After 1795, when this territorial entity had disappeared, they kept projecting its phantom borders onto reorganized state and diocesan spaces: they represented Mary as though she was now the patroness of the French department of Forêts, and they saw the Diocese of Metz officially consecrated to her in 1807. Marian devotion and pilgrimage to Luxembourg City evolved and persisted even as the chapel of Our Lady turned out to be irretrievably lost. In sum, rather than fixate on one crucial location of the holy, promoters of this pilgrimage experimented with new links between various places and territories of devotion. As the following chapters will show, similarly dynamic repertoires of place-making and territorial practice emerged in the age of revolutions among the pilgrims themselves.

2

Shifting the Confessional Frontier

The churchwardens of Tholey were aghast when the wrath of the Church struck their parish community. After a pastoral visit in 1770, the bishop had issued an ordinance prohibiting a number of pilgrimage processions to the shrines of Tholey Abbey, Blasiusberg, and Sankt Wendel, all situated within a few miles of each other in the Diocese of Trier and the present-day German province of Saarland. The parish of Tholey had obtained a partial exemption from this measure in early 1771. "But soon," the churchwardens complained in their petition of May 1772, "we saw with surprise that a supposed contravention was being punished, targeting our royal mayor who was sentenced to three days in jail." Therefore, as the next pilgrimage season was approaching, the petitioners asked the bishop to forestall any further unpleasant surprises by reconsidering his ordinance.[1]

Among the main reasons they invoked to get him to withdraw the ordinance altogether was the "decency" of the pious spectacle these processions represented. As the authors of the petition asserted, the splendor of these rituals had edified and impressed spectators so much "that many Jews and Protestants [*autres Religionnaires*], penetrated by the devotion of the faithful, have abjured in order to embrace the Roman Catholic religion." Now, by contrast, Catholics in and around Tholey were becoming the objects of mockery because of "a shocking contradiction": while the parishes covered by the episcopal ordinance of 1770 were forbidden from going to Sankt Wendel, the burghers of that town were still allowed and even expected by diocesan authorities to continue their annual processions to Tholey! The churchwardens of Tholey deplored the "disagreeable mixture" that was thus emerging "in the exercise of the Catholic religion." They also could hardly stress enough "how much our adversaries and neighbors [*nos adversaires voisins*] in the Duchy of Zweibrücken and the Principality of Nassau exploit this to ridicule the sudden changes and divergences of that sort."[2] Both Zweibrücken and Nassau-Saarbrücken were nearby territories inhabited mostly by Protestants.[3]

This chapter shows that enlightened religious reform and Revolution reshaped how rural and small-town Catholics in the borderlands perceived their Protestant *adversaires voisins*. Catholic laypeople used pilgrimages to Sankt Wendel, Tholey, and Blasiusberg to perpetuate the logic of confessional enmity—even against the wishes first of their own enlightened Church hierarchy and later of French revolutionary authorities. After all, the auxiliary bishop whose ordinance the parish leaders of Tholey questioned in their petition was none other than Johann Nikolaus von Hontheim (1701–1790). Also known as Febronius, Hontheim was one of the first and most brilliant representatives of enlightened Reform Catholicism.[4] My story focuses on a series of transformative conflicts between the 1770s and 1790s to explore the growing importance of laypeople's confessionalist impetus. These moments of conflict signal a departure from a previous era that had lasted from roughly the late sixteenth to the mid-eighteenth century. During that time, Catholic rulers as well as their lay and clerical subjects had fostered pilgrimage as one of the most effective demonstrations of Catholicity against neighboring Lutherans and Calvinists.

Yet the story of Sankt Wendel, Tholey, and Blasiusberg also reveals continuities and resonances—not just confrontations—between Baroque piety and Enlightenment reform of worship. Uncovering these resonances means challenging a historiography that has assumed a simple binary opposition between Baroque and Enlightenment and has often imagined a sequence in which enlightened tolerance superseded early modern confessionalism.[5] By contrast, I argue that lay Catholics and their allies among the local clergy held authorities to account by insisting that enlightened reforms of pilgrimage could prove counterproductive. Practitioners and defenders of pilgrimage were able to drive home this point because Baroque and enlightened Catholicism *shared* certain ideals against which to measure the success of a given reform measure. Especially along borders and on the confessional frontier, these shared ideals included enshrining a harmonious territorial order and ensuring that Catholicism looked respectable rather than ridiculous. By complaining about Protestant mockery and about a "disagreeable mixture"[6] in the spatial parameters of worship, voices from Tholey and elsewhere did not simply *resist* reformist or revolutionary projects. Instead, they *reflected* enlightened anxieties over spatial heterogeneity and the supposed inferiority of rural Catholic culture.[7]

Pilgrims, the Baroque, and the Making of Confessional Frontiers

To understand how and why Baroque and enlightened Catholicism got entangled with each other through pilgrimage, we must take a step back in time and grasp the extent to which pilgrims had embraced the Baroque in the first place. Three points are worth elaborating upon in this section. First, the early modern period saw the spectacular rise of a new, processional, and decidedly communal type of pilgrimage, often called *Wallfahrt* in German.[8] From the Age of Reformation onward, this collective religious practice lent itself to the ostentatious assertion of Catholic identity and power. Hence, my second point is that *Wallfahrt* became an effective way of marking—and occasionally pushing—confessional boundaries wherever Protestant communities lived near Catholic pilgrimage places or pilgrimage routes. Third, to make these historical phenomena more palpable by way of example, I will demonstrate how important pilgrimage, confessional difference, and territorial boundaries were in and around Sankt Wendel, Tholey, and Blasiusberg before the crisis of the early 1770s.

The word "pilgrimage" is a big tent. It gathers a bewilderingly diverse array of practices that can loosely be defined as forms of spiritually charged travel, both within and beyond Christianity.[9] Pilgrims may take a single day or several years to accomplish their trips. They go by themselves, in small bands often composed of family members and friends, or in larger groups led by a guide or a member of the clergy. To get to their destinations and back home, they may walk, go aboard ships, or use any other available and affordable means of transportation; indeed, they may even stay at home and use only their minds to embark on interior pilgrimage as a kind of imagined, mystical travel. They may go on their journeys as a matter of individual choice or to meet an obligation defined by religious authorities. In their hearts—and in their ways of talking or writing about their actions—pilgrims may foreground any number of motivations, such as the desire to get better spiritually and physically, the need to do penance or fulfill a vow, the hope to please God (or other transcendent beings), the will to make a political statement, or sheer curiosity about foreign lands and extraordinary places. Moreover, they may visit one or many such special places in the course of a single pilgrimage, and just what makes each destination special may be defined by one or several religious traditions or in more secular terms. This vast spectrum of pilgrim practices, rationales, and goals raises the question of how to put into sharper relief the particular variety of pilgrimage that we may call *Wallfahrt*.

Corporate belonging and liturgical order defined a pilgrim group on *Wallfahrt*, distinguishing it from a mere crowd that would form organically when many individual pilgrims converged on the same shrine at the same time.[10] From confraternities to parishes to urban citizenries, different kinds of corporate communities could organize a *Wallfahrt* and encourage or even oblige their members to participate in it. Timing and rhythm followed the church calendar, which fixed the feast days of Mary or any particular saint that the community set out to venerate at a shrine, usually once a year and based on an ancestral vow. To publicly honor this vow and thereby cultivate their tie to the saint as a powerful heavenly benefactor, community members—men, women, and children, sometimes led by one or several priests and sometimes without any clerical company—marched across the countryside in processional order, praying the rosary together for extended stretches of time. To be sure, they did not always keep this order in practice, especially on their way back home from the shrine. Yet at significant points of the journey, when entering a town or village, for instance, or when approaching the shrine, pilgrims tended to project as much liturgical splendor and discipline as possible: they would sing church songs, raise their parish or confraternity banners, and display the large candle that they intended to leave as an offering at the shrine. Many *Wallfahrten* were short-distance trips, so the pilgrim group would depart in the early morning and return before sunset, but somewhat longer, overnight *Wallfahrten* also occurred, frequently triggering clerical concerns about nocturnal sexual excesses among pilgrims.

Although the processional variety of pilgrimage gradually emerged in the late Middle Ages, it only became prominent in the early modern period—a trend that is indissociable from the anti-Protestant mood of Baroque Catholicism.[11] Early modern pilgrims came to understand *Wallfahrt* as a *demon-*

stratio catholica, a show of force designed to intimidate, impress, and distinguish themselves from the "heretical" other. To be sure, other motives also played important roles, such as the desire to honor collective vows or simply the quest for a communal form of leisure, a break from the drudgery and narrowness of everyday life.[12] Yet, the confessional overtones of *Wallfahrt* could hardly escape anybody's attention—especially after the Peace of Westphalia (1648). While overtly religious rationales for warfare began losing importance at this time, ordinary people experienced Catholicism and Protestantism ever more deeply and instinctively not just as competing theological options but as starkly opposed and overdetermined identities.[13] In this context, *Wallfahrten* functioned as effective "rites of distinction."[14] They were public, collective, and fairly pervasive, particularly in the eighteenth century, when many shrines in German-speaking Europe attracted dozens of large processions each year. Many parish communities undertook more than a handful of *Wallfahrten* annually, and most Catholic dioceses boasted at least one shrine visited by more than fifty thousand—or even more than one hundred thousand—pilgrims per year.[15]

In the territorially fragmented, pluriconfessional spaces of the Holy Roman Empire and the Old Swiss Confederacy, these pilgrims often performed their rites of distinction in especially confrontational ways: after all, in these parts of Europe, many Catholics lived in close spatial proximity to Protestant communities. The churchwardens of Tholey, quoted at the outset of this chapter, were hardly alone in perceiving Protestants as both rivals and neighbors. Hence, early modern Germany and Switzerland were full of shrines to which Catholics flocked in a kind of confessional "frontier pilgrimage."[16] For example, two of Westphalia's most popular destinations of Marian pilgrimage, Telgte and Vinnenberg, were situated just a few miles west of the border between the Catholic Prince-Bishopric of Münster and the Lutheran Duchy of Ravensberg. In the Catholic parts of the confessionally mixed Grisons (southeastern Switzerland), Capuchin priests exalted local shrines as so many ramparts "on the frontier against heresy."[17] On their journeys toward holy places, too, pilgrim communities often marched along—and across—the countless borders that ran between Catholic and Protestant territories.[18] In short, Baroque pilgrims routinely mapped spatial and confessional boundaries onto each other when engaging in *Wallfahrt*.

Some people transgressed both of these kinds of boundaries, as pilgrimage intersected with the thorny issue of conversion. As a highly public rite of confessional distinction, pilgrimage was a meaningful practice for individuals who had recently converted to Catholicism and who sought to demonstrate their allegiance to their new faith. Moreover, in confessionally mixed regions such as Upper Swabia, Jesuits and other Catholic clergy tended to frame *Wallfahrt* as an especially promising form of proselytism. On their way from the town of Kaufbeuren to Ottobeuren Abbey or from Augsburg to the famous shrine of Andechs, for instance, Catholics were supposed to display exemplary pious behavior not only for their own benefit but also in order to sow the seeds of conversion in potentially impressed Protestant witnesses.[19]

In all likelihood, however, mutual provocations and violence ensued more frequently than did conversions when Catholic pilgrimage processions overstepped territorial and confessional borders. Take the example of the Eichsfeld, today a region divided between the *Länder* of Lower Saxony and Thuringia, back then a northern exclave of the Archbishopric-Electorate of Mainz—a Catholic outpost surrounded by Protestant principalities. Here, pilgrimage processions repeatedly made ostentatious little detours across the territory of Calvinist Hesse on their way to the frontier shrine of Hülfensberg, situated on the southern edge of the Eichsfeld. As historian Christophe Duhamelle argues, the villages carrying out these *Wallfahrten* aimed to boost their sense of collective honor and identity by daring to make incursions into the space of the confessional other.[20] When such territorial transgressions led to run-ins with irritated local Protestants, tensions frequently escalated—in the Eichsfeld and in many other regions—as communities traded insults, engaged in mass brawls, or even fired guns in each other's direction.[21] A particularly serious incident took place in western Franconia in 1781: the Protestant burghers of Wertheim violently attacked a defiant procession of Catholic pilgrims who were returning from the famous shrine of Walldürn. The prince-bishop of Würzburg reacted by sending troops to the County of Wertheim, and it took an intervention by one of the two highest imperial courts, the Reichskammergericht, to stop the conflict from degenerating into a minor regional war.[22] Although the Wertheim affair represents an extreme case, it clearly signals the salience of *Wallfahrt* as a confessional frontier practice.

The examples of Franconia and the Eichsfeld also point to another important aspect: the diverse and large group of frontier shrines included both exceptionally popular ones such as Walldürn and lesser-known ones such as Hülfensberg.[23] Indeed, the overwhelming majority among the thousands of Catholic pilgrimage sites in the Holy Roman Empire was composed of small or midsized shrines, which drew between a few and a few dozen *Wallfahrten* a year, plus vastly varying numbers of individual pilgrims.[24] Despite the merely local or regional fame of these smaller shrines, their very ubiquity meant that they—and the *Wallfahrt* communities that visited them—played a significant role in the Holy Roman Empire's spatial and confessional order. To get a more granular sense of that order, let us take a closer look at the cluster of three relatively modest shrines that included Sankt Wendel, Tholey, and Blasiusberg, highlighting the status they held as Catholic beacons on the confessional frontier.

Sankt Wendel was the most important of the three sites. Today a district capital of about twenty-five thousand inhabitants, it was a bustling but small town of fewer than 1,500 in the late eighteenth century.[25] It had received its name from Saint Wendelin, an early medieval saint whose most influential hagiographer, Nikolaus Keller, was a man of the late seventeenth and early eighteenth centuries. Keller's life of Saint Wendelin, first published in 1704, described the saint as a Scottish prince who had abandoned the splendors of his royal home to become first a pilgrim, then a miracle-working shepherd, hermit, and missionary, and, eventually, the abbot of Tholey in 597 before passing away in 617.[26] The legend thus linked the sacral topographies of Sankt Wendel and Tholey, but even within the town and on its immediate outskirts, holy sites abounded. The impressive parish church, the so-called Wendalinusdom built in the fourteenth and fifteenth centuries, probably drew the biggest pilgrim crowds. In addition, three chapels—the Magdalenenkapelle, the Annenkapelle, and the Wendelsbrunnenkapelle—were frequently visited by both individual pilgrims and entire processions.[27]

Although even rough estimates of total annual visitors are impossible to obtain for the eighteenth century, we do know that the cult of Saint Wendelin reached the height of its flourishing at that time. Rural Catholics held Wendelin in particular esteem as a patron saint of livestock.[28] Moreover, as a description of the region noted in the 1770s, the local population depended heavily on income from raising and trading livestock, both cattle and sheep.[29] It makes sense, then, that many parish communities went on *Wallfahrt* to Sankt Wendel each year in order to honor him. Others organized extraordinary pilgrimage processions when deadly diseases circulated among the cattle and peasants urgently needed Wendelin as a heavenly intercessor.³⁰ Overall, we may plausibly assume that Sankt Wendel received more than ten thousand pilgrims per year on the eve of the French revolutionary period.

Located some ten kilometers west of Sankt Wendel, Tholey Abbey is primarily known as one of Germany's oldest monasteries, and its early modern appeal as a holy site on the confessional frontier owed much to its power as a big Benedictine convent. Though repeatedly pillaged in the wars of the seventeenth century and drowning in debt at the end of the Old Regime, the abbey continued to shape the lives of surrounding rural populations.³¹ It held a vast array of seignorial and tithe-related rights on a regional scale. Many of the villagers tied to the abbey by these legal relationships also accomplished annual processions to Tholey in honor of Saint Maurice, the patron saint of the abbey, whose relics constituted its main spiritual treasure. More precisely, a list from 1454 names fifty parishes obligated to go on these processions, and such obligations remained largely intact in this region until the revolutionary era.³² Tholey did not have an extended *Wallfahrt* season—unlike Sankt Wendel, where multiple feast days punctuated the months of May through October. Rather, all processions converged on Tholey Abbey on the same day each year (the Friday after Pentecost), and this spectacle could rival the main pilgrimage festivals celebrated in Sankt Wendel.

Finally, perched atop a hill just west of Tholey, a chapel under the patronage of Saint Blaise attracted numerous annual processions from the surrounding area as well. The Blasiuskapelle stood under the jurisdiction of Tholey Abbey and was rebuilt in 1716 in the Baroque style. Two or three hermits lived next to the shrine, took care of it, welcomed visiting pilgrims, and collected their offerings. Most processions came here on either February 3 (the saint's feast day) or April 25 (Saint Mark's Day, a fixture in the processional calendar of Catholic communities). On both days, the crowds would attend first a solemn mass and then an annual fair on the hilltop—an occasion to buy or sell livestock but also to quench one's thirst. According to a document from 1775, some two thousand liters of wine and beer were served during the Blasiusberg fairs of that year, so pilgrims presumably numbered in the thousands. They came from up to fifty different villages and hamlets.³³ Together, Sankt Wendel, Tholey, and Blasiusberg formed a powerful cluster of well-frequented holy sites in the second half of the eighteenth century.

A multitude of ecclesiastical and civil borders ran around this cluster in 1770, creating something that looked like spatial disorder to the enlightened beholder (see map 2). Within the Diocese of Trier, both Sankt Wendel and Tholey belonged to the Deaconry (Landkapitel) of Wadrill. Many of the communities in this deaconry, including Sankt Wendel, also found themselves under the temporal jurisdiction of the archbishop: they formed part of the Electorate of Trier. By contrast, Tholey and nine other parishes (numbered 1 through 9 on map 2) in the same deaconry belonged to the Bailliage de Schambourg in the Kingdom of France (in Lorraine before 1766). The archbishop's General Vicariate at Trier exercised spiritual authority over the parts of the deaconry situated in the electorate, but this control did not extend to the French part. As protectors of the Gallican Church, the kings of France sought to limit the influence of foreign prelates, and Habsburg rulers of the Austrian Netherlands took a similar stance. Therefore, the archbishops had to designate auxiliary bishops such as Hontheim to manage spiritual affairs in the French and Luxembourgian parts of the diocese—under the constant watch of secular authorities in Nancy, Luxembourg, and beyond.[34] This splintering is a classic feature of early modern border regions and of the early modern Holy Roman Empire.[35] It explains why, in 1770, Hontheim was responsible for the Schambourg parishes and could target only these parishes in his ordinance against processions to Sankt Wendel, Tholey, and Blasiusberg.

The map also shows that an intricate web of borders between different territories of the Holy Roman Empire surrounded Sankt Wendel and Tholey. The parish of Sankt Wendel, which included the town itself as well as a handful of surrounding villages, had constituted a Catholic outpost since the sixteenth century. It bordered mostly on the Lutheran County of Nassau-Saarbrücken in the south and on the primarily Calvinist Duchy of Pfalz-Zweibrücken in the north and the east. A bit farther north, the parish of Bleiderdingen (today Hoppstädten-Weiersbach) formed a French, Catholic exclave surrounded by two Protestant territories—Pfalz-Zweibrücken and the Lower County of Sponheim. East of Sankt Wendel and south of the *zweibrückisch* town of Kusel, another smattering of Catholic communities dotted the map, notably the parishes of (Glan-)Münchweiler and Kübelberg. While Münchweiler belonged to the Imperial Counts von der Leyen, Kübelberg was situated on the western fringes of the Electoral Palatinate (Kurpfalz). This important principality had served as a beacon of

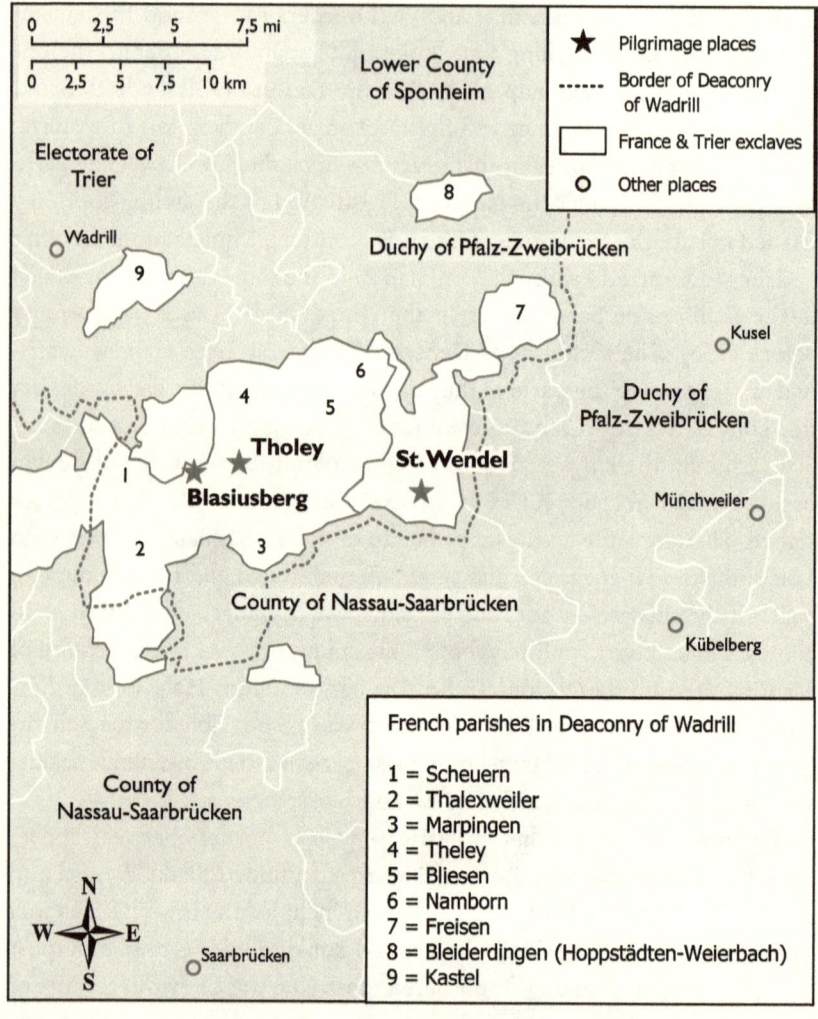

MAP 2. Territories of the region around Sankt Wendel and Tholey in 1770. (Adapted from Irsigler, *Geschichtlicher Atlas*, vol. 5, fasc. 1, and Zimmer and Noack, *Archiepiscopatus Trevirensis*; adjustments reflecting the situation of 1770 based on information from BA Tr, Abt. 40, Nr. 71, and Fabricius, *Erläuterungen zum Geschichtlichen Atlas*)

Calvinism between the second half of the sixteenth century and the late seventeenth century. In 1685, however, the electoral dignity fell to a Catholic prince, Philipp Wilhelm of Pfalz-Neuburg. King Louis XIV of France disputed Philipp Wilhelm's succession, which triggered the so-called Nine Years' War of 1688–97, but Louis XIV also hoped to foster the Catholicization of the Palatinate. Due to French diplomatic pressure and against the provisions of the Treaties of Westphalia (1648), the new Treaty of Ryswick (1697) enshrined large legal openings for Catholics to settle and conduct public worship in this territory.[36] For example, in the eighteenth century, a new Catholic parish community of Kübelberg went on annual processions to Sankt Wendel, apparently resuming a tradition that the rise of Calvinism had disrupted.[37]

Such processions repeatedly gave rise to conflict in the mid-eighteenth century as they crossed through Protestant territory on their way to Sankt Wendel or Tholey. In 1752, Christian IV of Pfalz-Zweibrücken decreed that processions from Bleiderdingen to Tholey and from Kübelberg to Sankt Wendel—both of which traversed the *zweibrückisch* district of Nohfelden— should be allowed to continue. They must, however, lower their parish banners and abstain from loud chanting or praying when passing through Protestant villages.[38] Catholics did not consistently respect these conditions. In 1764, the new parish priest of Kübelberg reported to the Palatine government in Mannheim that, some years prior, several of his parishioners had been injured in a brawl with Protestants during a procession from Kübelberg to Sankt Wendel. Still, the priest added, the inhabitants of Kübelberg wanted not only to keep going on this annual procession but also "to sing and to chant while passing through any settlements, as is customary among Catholics."[39] A similar violent clash during a procession had occurred in 1758 or 1759 between the Catholics of Bleiderdingen and their Protestant neighbors—probably the inhabitants of Nohfelden, a village located between Bleiderdingen and Tholey. As a result, Bleiderdingen's annual communal visits to Tholey Abbey ceased.[40] Finally, in 1767 and 1769, the Catholics of Münchweiler—in processions led not by their priest but by a lay churchwarden—caused further outrage in the Protestant community of Ohmbach by ostentatiously marching through this village on their way to Sankt Wendel, in a deliberate departure from their usual itinerary.[41]

All these incidents, largely driven by laypeople rather than priests on the Catholic side, fit the broader pattern of confessional provocations and violence in the eighteenth-century Holy Roman Empire. By 1750, Baroque pilgrimage processions had become a major way for rural Catholics to practice and showcase the special features of their confessional identity—from public praying of the rosary and loudly proclaimed trust in the saints as intercessors to the rituals of penance and Mass that *Wallfahrt* participants frequently attended at shrines. *Wallfahrt* thus became a key arena in which ordinary people could both draw and occasionally overstep confessional boundaries. It mattered especially in regions where Catholic and Protestant communities existed in close proximity to each other, as was the case in the empire's territorially and confessionally fragmented southwestern borderlands. There, *Wallfahrt* developed into a frontier practice almost by necessity, involving rites of distinction and sometimes attacks on the honor of the confessional other, including acts of physical violence. The shrine cluster of Sankt Wendel, Tholey, and Blasiusberg exemplifies these phenomena well. Just as importantly, its history also illustrates how Catholics reacted to the attempted enlightened reform of *Wallfahrt*.

Provocative Processions, Shocking Reforms

Decades before anti-Catholic revolutionaries and Napoleonic prefects struggled to police the mobility and religious practices of pilgrims, Enlightenment reform presented a serious challenge to pilgrimage. As I have shown in chapter 1, this challenge flowed largely from theological doubts about the very notion of sacred place, as well as from elites' desire to homogenize and containerize state territories. Against this backdrop, two further questions arise, beyond the issues of place-making and territorial flexibility that proved crucial in the case of Luxembourg. First, how did rural or small-town Catholics respond when reforms began affecting their *Wallfahrt* practices in concrete and radical ways? Second, how did Catholic–Protestant differences and tensions inform the resulting conflicts between local communities and parts of the clerical hierarchy? Combining my answers to these questions, I argue, in a nutshell, that Catholics around Tholey and Sankt Wendel beat reformers at their own game in the early 1770s. They did so by foregrounding fears of Protestant mockery and the danger of eroding Catholic uniformity across their home region.

A larger, confessionalized spatial order was at stake in this conflict, even though it directly affected only ten parishes situated on the southeastern margins of the diocese and on the confessional frontier. Indirectly, however, the confrontation involved a larger regional panorama structured around the three pilgrimage places, and spatial limitations were not simply a given but rather a *problem* on which the protagonists reflected. As one local parish priest wrote to Hontheim in 1771: "If your ordinance was general"—that is to say, if it covered the entire region instead of just those ten parishes visited in the spring of 1770 — "there would be no opposition to it at all."[42]

From within the hierarchy of the Catholic Church itself, this ordinance systematically targeted pilgrimage processions in the region. On what basis did Hontheim write it? In early 1770, he had entrusted Johann Augustin Lauxen with the task of visiting the ten French parishes in the Deaconry of Wadrill on the bishop's behalf. As parish priest of Theley, Lauxen had seized the occasion of the last pastoral visit, in 1760, to submit a lengthy complaint about the abuses he considered prevalent at pilgrimage festivals: around the shrines, pilgrims offended God and ruined their own souls by "gourmandizing, dancing, getting into fistfights, whoring, and so on," sometimes "even at the same time as Mass is celebrated."[43] Lauxen's accusations were not entirely baseless. Most notably, on St. Mark's Day in 1756, pilgrims at Blasiusberg had beaten each other with lashes or sticks, to the point of leaving one man dead and two others dangerously injured.[44] Hontheim may have delegated the visit in 1770 to Lauxen because this pastor would most likely put together as devastating a dossier as possible against the "abuses" perpetrated by pilgrims.[45]

After all, in that period, Hontheim worked to implement enlightened reforms in the religious life and liturgy of the diocese more broadly, as the work of Andreas Heinz and Gilbert Trausch has shown.[46] Either Hontheim or Lauxen himself even modified the questionnaire for the pastoral visit of 1770, adding suggestive questions such as: "Aren't processions led to places where there are public markets, where wine and brandy is generously served" and where festivities degenerate "into bloodshed, maimings and killings, immodesty, blasphemy, fornication, and other kinds of public scandal?" Furthermore: "Are such processions apt and made to appease the divine Being, moving It to take pity, spare, and bless us? Or rather to produce the very dreadful opposite of those desirable effects?"[47] In short, Hontheim and Lauxen were putting the three pilgrimages on trial.

And indeed, Lauxen's visit provided more than enough evidence to justify a radical intervention by the auxiliary bishop. According to Lauxen's report, eight of the ten parishes had major issues with their annual pilgrimage processions. Parish priests generally complained that their flocks did not stick to processional order on their way back from shrines such as Tholey and Blasiusberg. Many lay churchwardens admitted that pilgrimages to these places could foster excessive behaviors and promised that they would submit to an episcopal ordinance directed against those abuses. To be sure, for some parishes such as Kastel and Exweiler, Lauxen wrote that "the churchwardens were divided" on the issue at hand. Others were allegedly afraid to speak out, as in Tholey, where one powerful local inhabitant profited from the pilgrimage festivals of Tholey and Blasiusberg because he held a royal monopoly allowing him to sell wine and liquor on these occasions every other year.[48] Yet the overall picture clearly confirmed what Lauxen had already asserted in 1760: "It would be much better not to go on pilgrimage at all than to go on pilgrimage with this kind of fervor."[49]

Intriguingly, the fraught relationship with Lutheran neighbors also came into view as part of the problem. The Catholics of Marpingen went on annual processions to Illingen, an exclave of the Electorate of Trier surrounded by *saarbrückisch* territory. On their way through various Lutheran villages situated between Marpingen and Illingen, these pilgrims "are not only insulted but often assailed with threats as well, provoking serious dangers of deadly clashes," according to the visit notes.[50] Hontheim reacted to this information in his *ordinata* of August 23, 1770, by including the procession to Illingen in his general ban on pilgrimage processions from any of the ten French parishes to Sankt Wendel, Tholey, or Blasiusberg.[51] This part of the decision seems puzzling at first glance. To the auxiliary bishop, what the inhabitants of Marpingen experienced on their way to Illingen apparently did not constitute a legitimate Catholic grievance to be addressed between Trier and Saarbrücken. Instead, he chose to discipline his diocesan subjects by abolishing their procession to Illingen, even though Lauxen framed the Lutherans as the primary aggressors in this case. Why, in short, did hostile Protestant reactions to *Wallfahrt* seem less problematic to Hontheim than did *Wallfahrt* itself?

The answer to this question lies in Hontheim's personal quasi-ecumenic leanings and, more broadly, in what some historians have described as a confessional "inferiority complex" that haunted Catholic reformers in the eighteenth century.[52] Published under the pseudonym of Febronius, Hontheim's crucial treatise *De statu ecclesiae* of 1763 explicitly aimed at paving the way for reconciliation between Catholics and Protestants by arguing that papal power needed to be curbed significantly. While Hontheim never wavered from his belief in the truthfulness of Catholic doctrine, he did seek to deescalate confessional animosity.[53] By 1770, he may have also been affected by the ideological theme of Catholic inferiority that pervaded the

German Aufklärung. Catholic elites at the time grew increasingly worried that their confession was becoming a laughingstock due to the commonly alleged backwardness of Catholic German states. In particular, the territories ruled by prince-bishops—including the Electorate of Trier—were supposedly less prosperous, less well organized, and less able to curb superstition than the empire's Protestant cities and principalities.[54] Therefore, protagonists of Reform Catholicism such as Hontheim had a strong interest in clamping down on any "popular" practices that smacked of Baroque laziness, shocked enlightened sensibilities, and provoked Protestants' disdain.[55]

As decreed in August 1770, these restrictions radically questioned the ways in which Catholic communities near Sankt Wendel and Tholey built and maintained a regional, religious sense of place. For one thing, judging from Lauxen's notes about his pastoral visit, the ten parishes had no other noteworthy pilgrimage destinations. In part because the surrounding territorial patchwork included many Protestant principalities, the density of shrines was lower here than in many other parts of the Diocese of Trier. So, would-be pilgrims had fewer nearby options to choose from, which may have made their loss of Sankt Wendel, Tholey, and Blasiusberg all the more sensitive. From Hontheim's perspective, the only acceptable replacement consisted in short and modest, separate processions within the confines of each parish—no more festive gatherings, no more encounters with prestigious relics.[56] And even beyond the ten French parishes, the veneration of Saint Maurice (the patron saint of Tholey Abbey) and Saint Wendelin would take a serious hit. By abolishing the procession from Tholey to Sankt Wendel, Hontheim effectively amputated the ceremonial structure that literally brought the two saints together: every year on the Wednesday after Pentecost, the procession from Tholey to Sankt Wendel carried the relics of Saint Maurice with it, so all the pilgrims coming to Sankt Wendel on that day could honor Maurice and Wendelin at the same time. Then, on the following Friday, the parishioners of Sankt Wendel conversely carried Wendelin's relics to Tholey, enabling another solemn meeting between the two saints. Now, however, Hontheim had forbidden the first of these two important processions in which Catholics from across the region could—as the prior of Tholey Abbey explained in a letter to Hontheim—celebrate the protection afforded them by their two "patrons of the land."[57]

The scope of the disruption explains why Catholic villagers chose to contest Hontheim's decision. At the start of the next pilgrimage season, right after Saint Mark's Day in 1771, Lauxen informed Hontheim that the parishioners of Exweiler, Marpingen, and Bliesen had undertaken their usual processions to Blasiusberg anyway—against the will of their own parish priests and "to the extraordinary scandal of the other parishes."[58] Hontheim responded with vigor. He complained in turn to Pascal-Joseph de Marcol, *procureur général* of the Sovereign Court at Nancy that had given the French state's confirmation to Hontheim's episcopal ordinance. De Marcol promptly had the *bailli* of Schambourg throw the mayors of Exweiler, Marpingen, Bliesen, and—for good measure—Tholey into jail for three days.[59] This harsh measure only fanned the flames of the conflict. On May 28, Lauxen claimed that he barely dared leave his house these days, given how much "the imprisonment of the four mayors has alarmed people throughout this region."[60] As the pilgrimage season of 1771 ended, the struggle remained unresolved, and after the lay parish leaders of Tholey sent their second petition in May 1772, Hontheim reinvestigated the affair through different commissioners.[61]

No longer influenced or subdued by Lauxen, local clergy and parish notables now openly defended their customary communal pilgrimages. In doing so, they inverted the themes of social conflict and religious scandal that Hontheim and Lauxen had initially mobilized against the processions. For example, the churchwardens of Bliesen admitted that "some boisterousness" had occasionally marred the parishioners' devotional visits to Blasiusberg, Tholey, and Sankt Wendel in the past. Yet the "general uproar" triggered by the *ban* on these processions was much worse, and the measures had thus proved counterproductive, these laymen suggested. The churchwardens and priest of Freisen deployed a very similar argument.[62] The new commissioner Demerath also warned in his report to Hontheim: "Most churchwardens want to resign from their office, and not without good reasons; they, after all, are blamed in almost all the villages for the abolition of the processions—a great slander that they can no longer bear."[63] In short, these statements painted a somber picture of tears running through the social fabric of the villages affected by the ban, which threatened to paralyze parish life and leadership.

Yet the pressure that produced these tensions was not simply generated internally among Catholics: it also resulted from conflicts that flared up between Catholic villagers and nearby Protestant communities. The parish leaders of Bleiderdingen recalled the extreme discontent caused in their community when they had had to discontinue their annual pilgrimage to Tholey years ago due to the violence with which nearby Protestants had allegedly disrupted the procession. Now that Hontheim's ordinance had raised the issue again, these parishioners were hoping to recover their right to go on this pilgrimage.[64] The uproar described by the churchwardens of Bliesen, meanwhile, continued, "especially here at the frontiers with the Lutherans and Calvinists." They added, "We would hope to God that our true Christian Catholic religion did not receive too much mockery and dishonor" from these consequences of Hontheim's ordinance.[65] The petition from Freisen struck an even more dramatic tone. By the ban on processions, "especially in our region, such uproar was created among the heretics who live barely fifteen minutes away from our village that no Catholic who passes through their localities gets away without the greatest religious reprimand; and so we have already suffered very much that affects our conscience." Thus, the petitioners begged Hontheim "to most graciously allow to reestablish the previous splendor of our tottering religion for the heretics' sake."[66]

A spatial disjuncture mediated and amplified the sense of confessional humiliation that these petitions articulated. To grasp this point, we need to recall that the ten French parishes were far from the only ones to go on annual pilgrimage processions to Tholey, Blasiusberg, or Sankt Wendel. Other villages—and the town of Sankt Wendel itself—belonged to the Electorate of Trier and therefore stood not under Hontheim's spiritual authority but under that of the General Vicariate. In 1771, the General Vicariate had allowed these other communities to continue their pilgrimages and merely admonished them to keep the processional order not just while headed toward the shrines but also on their way back home.[67] I quoted above the parishioners of Tholey who claimed that this "shocking contradiction" was used by Protestant communities in the region to ridicule Catholicism.[68] Demerath similarly explained the "very great scandal for the non-Catholics who live extremely close to us": they seized on the absurdity that he had to stay home with his parishioners on the Wednesday after Pentecost even though his parish (Exweiler) was only a few miles away from Tholey, while processions from much more distant parts of the diocese passed through Exweiler on their way to the abbey.[69] In short, far from reinforcing a homogenous spatial order by containing the processions of each community within its respective parish boundaries, Hontheim's ordinance had created spatial heterogeneity and even chaos.

Confessional scandal stemmed from Protestants' ability to deride this heterogeneity as a sign that Catholics were deviating from their own, most basic standard of universality. The commission report drafted by the dean of the Wadrill *Landkapitel* made this point explicit. The dean propounded four reasons in favor of withdrawing the episcopal ordinance. His fourth argument, which he flagged as the most important one, stated that "the Catholic religion" might become "rather ridiculous" in the eyes of neighboring Protestants if the customary pilgrimage processions could no longer take place. Indeed, he asserted, "according to reliable information, a Lutheran preacher at the chancel already said that *the Catholics would soon resemble them* [Lutherans], *there was no unity among them* [Catholics] *anymore, even though they referred to unity as a principal feature of their religion.*"[70] This mockery speaks to the impact of Counter-Reformation apologetics, which had appropriated universality, a traditional criterion of doctrinal truth expressed in the Greek adjective *katholikos,* for the Roman Church—against the splintering of "false" Protestant doctrines and churches.[71] So, according to the dean, Catholics were becoming nervous that Hontheim's ordinance might suddenly degrade their social status from proudly Catholic to would-be Protestant, exposing them to humiliation at the hands of their neighboring confessional enemies.

In this regard, again, the case of the Saar region resonates with the broader situation prevailing after 1750 in German-speaking Catholic areas: many of them were abuzz with laypeople's fears of being turned Lutheran by their own ecclesiastical and state hierarchies. As historian Peter Hersche has argued, expressing such fears was an accepted and widespread way for Catholic subjects to protest enlightened policies of religious reform. In addition to restrictive measures targeting *Wallfahrten* and other processions, such policies included reducing the number of holy days, promoting the use of German over Latin in the liturgy to make its verbal content intelligible to laypeople, shutting down remote chapels as supposed hotbeds of superstitious activities, and enforcing the use of new church songbooks that omitted anti-Protestant song texts. Taken together, these reforms seriously undermined the Baroque liturgical and social life that generations of Catholics had come to accept as normative and appropriated as markers of their local and confessional identities.[72]

Crucially, laypeople's protests reveal not just a frontline between Baroque and Enlightenment, but at the same time a common ground, defined by concern for spatial order and Catholic respectability. To clarify this point, it is worth summarizing and reflecting on the arguments between Hontheim and the various parish communities that I have detailed above. The auxiliary bishop sought to create homogenized, disciplined parochial spaces by insisting that these communities must replace their *Wallfahrten* with shorter processions. Yet, as petitioners pointed out to him, the preexisting complexity of the borderlands thwarted his attempt to arrange Catholic territories in such a homogenous manner. Spatial confusion *increased* instead, as only the ten French parishes of the region were affected by his ordinance. Moreover, as Hontheim's decision to abolish the processions from Marpingen to Illingen suggests, he also targeted *Wallfahrt* in order to diminish the scandal and contempt that Baroque religious practices might trigger among Protestants. Again, however, petitioners from Tholey and surrounding villages made the case that the ordinance had actually produced the opposite of its intended effect: it only gave *more* ammunition to Protestants who were keen to mock their confessional rivals.

The auxiliary bishop gave way eventually. He may very well have realized that his initial measures had backfired in this instance. Though strongly committed to advancing the cause of enlightened reform, Hontheim was neither a stranger to realpolitik nor unwilling to craft pastoral compromises.[73] Thus, through a new ordinance drafted in September 1772, he allowed the ten French parishes to reinstitute their yearly communal pilgrimages to Sankt Wendel, Tholey, and Blasiusberg. While insisting on processional discipline and strict schedules, he also recognized that his decision of 1770 had caused "very great discontent among the people," that "parishioners' trust" in their churchwardens and priests was eroding, and that "all of this inflames the scorn of neighboring non-Catholics."[74] In other words, Hontheim accepted and echoed the arguments with which petitioners and commissioners had confronted him throughout the previous months.

This episode signals a remarkable shift in the roles that various social groups—the clergy and the laity, governing authorities and village communities—played in the making of confessional boundaries. In the sixteenth and seventeenth centuries, Counter-Reformation elites had largely led the way in setting, enforcing, and continually reinforcing those boundaries. Then, in the eighteenth century and especially during its second half,

Catholic and Protestant elites both deconfessionalized themselves and hoped to deconfessionalize the people, too, in the name of a broadly Christian Aufklärung.[75] By that point, however, rural communities had thoroughly appropriated confessional identities and stereotypes. This development explains why the Catholics of Tholey and nearby villages fought for their *Wallfahrten* by embracing a leading role in reasserting the value and distinctness of Catholicism. They channeled that confessional impulse into a contest over public, spatially salient worship. Crucially, they persuaded Hontheim that his initial ordinance had proved counterproductive when measured against the larger ambition of Reform Catholicism itself. They succeeded by speaking *to* rather than *against* the preoccupations of the Enlightenment.

From Crisis to Crisis

Beyond the events of 1770–72, Catholics devoted to Saint Wendelin kept cultivating a Catholic frontier spirit, and, in the 1790s, they exploited new spatial ambiguities on the edges of expanding France. I will demonstrate the continuity of the confessional impulse first by discussing how the initial conflict resonated across the next twenty years, when Reform Catholicism reached its apogee in the Electorate of Trier. Subsequently, pilgrims in and around Sankt Wendel envisioned the challenge of the French Revolution through lenses that overlaid older anti-Protestant sentiments with antirevolutionary ones. As both officials and lay Catholics continued asking how to organize spaces of collective worship in the most appropriate and dignified way, these lenses magnified Catholics' desire to protect pilgrimage and impress those who might feel tempted to mock it.

Despite such elements of continuity, the Revolution also caused the frontier of Catholicism to shift again. In a certain sense, the frontier simply heated up because the dynamic of mockery and pride accelerated. While secular revolutionary administrators steered a far harsher course against "superstition" and even religious "fanaticism" than ecclesiastical reformers had done, Catholic pilgrims defiantly came together in large, long, and urgent processions. The confessional frontier also changed in terms of how it interacted with specific territorial boundaries. Most crucially, the border between France and the Holy Roman Empire now mattered no longer as an obstacle to uniform Church administration as it had done in the 1770s but instead as an unstable territorial edge of revolution. During the 1790s, uncertainty abounded as to where exactly France ended in the Saar region. In this situation, pilgrims created openings for a new type of mobilization: they mapped confessional enmity onto the challenge posed by a secular state that aspired to the methodical policing of worship.

In the twenty years before the French Revolution arrived in Sankt Wendel and Tholey, pilgrimage remained a sensitive issue. Local authorities worked autonomously to enforce discipline and processional order around the annual pilgrimage festivals, perhaps with additional vigilance after the conflict of the early 1770s. Thus, in 1778, the parish council of Sankt Wendel slapped twenty-three male and ten female parishioners with fines for having failed to join or only belatedly joined the most recent communal procession to Tholey on the Friday after Pentecost.[76] More crucially, however, beginning in 1785, parts of the region were affected by more general restrictive measures that effectively prohibited almost all *Wallfahrt* activities in the Electorate of Trier. This ban was enacted by the last archbishop-elector, Clemens Wenceslaus of Saxony, who supported enlightened Reform Catholicism in the mid-1780s.[77] On November 29, 1784, he published a decree banning longer processions because they lured people away from "true devotion" and made them "wander around in idle swarms, without any edification or any expectable spiritual benefit."[78] From then on, processions must not take longer than an hour—scarcely enough time for *Wallfahrt* communities to reach any except the nearest holy sites. Hence, the change signified a considerable hit to the more popular shrines, the ones that had attracted processions from far and wide.[79]

The reform put a stop to processions from Sankt Wendel to Tholey between 1785 and 1790, but it did not go uncontested. Across those years, a steady stream of grievances against the decree flowed from the parish community and municipal representatives of Sankt Wendel to the ecclesiastical and civil authorities in Trier and Koblenz, respectively.[80] Meanwhile, the French parishes were not targeted by the restrictions because they belonged to the Diocese but not to the Electorate of Trier. In the rest of the Wadrill *Landkapitel*, no major protest seems to have erupted either, although the silence of sources on this region might mean that local populations and authorities simply ignored—rather than accepted—the decree of November 1784. The reinforced restrictions on *Wallfahrt* did, moreover, trigger serious dissatisfaction and local struggles in other parts of the territory. For instance, the burghers of Trier petitioned Clemens Wenceslaus to reverse his decision because the reduced influx of pilgrims into the city was impairing local consumption and thus the urban economy as a whole (see chapter 5). Above all, in the Moselle Valley, several village communities repeatedly flouted the ban on *Wallfahrten* to the widely known shrine of Eberhardsklausen between 1784 and the mid-1790s.[81] In short, the grievances coming out of Sankt Wendel after 1785 were not unique.

They are remarkable, however, in echoing several themes that had dominated the conflict of the early 1770s. The town deputies in 1788 were mainly trying to point out the disruption that local economies were suffering due to the partial collapse of pilgrimage festivals in the area. But in doing so, they did not fail to mention that among the people who enjoyed going to these festivals and spending money at them were "even Protestants, eager to watch the solemn entry and departure" of processions.[82] According to these town notables, far from epitomizing Catholic economic backwardness, the pilgrimages enhanced the material as well as the spiritual benefits of Catholic religious practice, attracting even the confessional enemy. Moreover, the parish council of Sankt Wendel decided to explicitly remind the General Vicariate of the earlier conflict of 1770–72 and to emphasize that Hontheim had only been able to resolve those tensions by revoking his restrictive measures.[83] This time it took five years of tenacious complaints, but in April 1790, the General Vicariate and the archbishop-elector's government decided to reallow the annual pilgrimage procession from Sankt Wendel to Tholey.[84]

Soon thereafter, the French Revolution and the War of the First Coalition began seriously impacting both the lives of this region's inhabitants and its shrines. Although France had ceded the Bailliage de Schambourg to the Duchy of Pfalz-Zweibrücken in an exchange treaty of 1786, the First French Republic "reunited" this *bailliage* to its territory in early 1793. Therefore, Tholey bore the full brunt of French religious policy in the Revolution's most radical phase, about which I will go into detail in chapter 3. Tholey Abbey was pillaged by French troops in 1793 and secularized by the state in July 1794. Although local inhabitants managed to acquire the former abbatial church as their parish church in 1806, and although a community of monks reestablished Tholey Abbey in 1950, the Church of Saint Maurice never recovered as a pilgrimage destination after the events of 1793/4.[85] Meanwhile, Sankt Wendel, its main church, and its chapels suffered from pillages and forced war contributions as well. Of the town's three chapels, only the Wendelsbrunnenkapelle survived the 1790s.[86] Yet unlike Tholey, Sankt Wendel belonged not to French but rather to French-occupied territory until the full absorption of the left-bank Rhineland into Napoleonic France in 1802.[87] As a result, Sankt Wendel experienced a belated and incomplete implementation of French policies. Once more, the border mattered, as the Revolution effectively eclipsed only one of the two religious centers in the region (Tholey). The other one (Sankt Wendel) not only maintained its status as a pilgrimage place but even strengthened that cachet through the crisis of 1796.

This environmental crisis hit much of western and central Europe but may well have had particularly dire consequences in the Saar region, which constituted a theater of war at the same time. The bad harvest of 1794, terribly cold winter of 1794/5, and consequent famine of 1795 had already wrought havoc among the poor in Thermidorian France and beyond.[88] In addition, an epizootic had broken out across eastern France in 1794/5, killing much of the livestock that fulfilled several crucial functions in the peasant economy by providing manure and serving as plough animals.[89] By 1796, the epizootic reached its height and ravaged not just Lorraine and Alsace but also the regions of Luxembourg, Trier, Sankt Wendel itself, and indeed much of southern German-speaking Europe. In many of these places, previous or ongoing warfare and occupation compounded the damage because passing armies had been requisitioning large numbers of cattle for years.[90] Frantically, Catholics turned to Saint Wendelin as an intercessor now because they recognized him as a major patron saint of peasants and livestock. The epizootic of 1796 thus favored the flourishing of this devotion in many regions including Swabia, Franconia, Alsace, and northern Lorraine.[91]

In particular, the events that transpired throughout German-speaking Lorraine in that summer of 1796 show how serious upheaval and political tensions could arise from such a crisis. As a slightly later pastoral inquiry shows, many rural communities in northern Lorraine had already adopted the cult of Saint Wendelin a long time ago, for example by turning him into the secondary patron of their parish churches.[92] Now, in July 1796, Catholics' despair over the epizootic drove them to improvise many dozens of processions that contravened the recent French legislation on *police du culte* (the policing of worship). This legislation included most notably the law of 7 vendémiaire an IV (September 29, 1795), which banned all religious ceremonies taking place outside of churches and thereby targeted *Wallfahrten* alongside other kinds of processions.[93] Refractory priests led and blessed some of these processions. In response, state administrators in the Moselle Department sent in the gendarmerie and even the regular military to disperse the "fanatical" crowds and arrest any identifiable ringleaders and clergymen. Many of these regional administrators also alerted the Ministry of General Police in Paris to what the revolutionary bureaucracy and government came to call "a religious insurrection of some sort."[94] In short, the summer of 1796 threw the region into a state of panic and rebellion that largely took the form of pilgrimage processions.[95]

Many of these processions were headed for Sankt Wendel, to implore help from the patron saint of livestock in the town that possessed his relics, the place of both his grave and his hermitage (at the Wendelsbrunnenkapelle). It is impossible to say anything precise about the number of pilgrims who went to Sankt Wendel in 1796, but the available sources do signal a major spike, an influx of many thousands. In early August, the director of the postal service in French-occupied Saarbrücken informed the government in Paris about "processions composed of between two hundred and two thousand people, crowds which thus make their way in part to Sankt Wendel (in the conquered lands) and in part to a chapel near Saint-Avold."[96] At that time, the French occupying administration decided to intervene and ordered the municipality of Sankt Wendel to keep the church doors locked except for regular parish worship, so *Wallfahrt* groups would not be able to enter the church anymore.[97] Did this measure prove effective in curbing pilgrimage to Sankt Wendel that summer? I have my doubts. After all, pilgrims might not learn about the closing of the church until they got there, and even then, they could still redirect their processions to the Wendelsbrunnenkapelle, located just outside of town and not targeted by the occupying administration.[98]

Moreover, Catholic communities going on *Wallfahrt* could not only circumvent but also confront and selectively appropriate the new spatial order created by the Revolution, as a report from Saarbrücken suggests. In the summer of 1796, a troop of French soldiers stationed there dispersed a procession of several hundred pilgrims coming from northwestern Alsace and headed for Sankt Wendel. In the occupied region to which Saarbrücken belonged, holding a procession was not illegal in 1796. So, to better justify their arrest, the administrative inspector Le Lièvre asked the leaders of the *Wallfahrt*—seven laymen—whether they had obtained passports before leaving the territory of the Republic. Their answer was striking: "They thought they were still in their own homeland [*leur pays*]."[99] What did this reply mean? The majority of participants in this *Wallfahrt* came from the former County of Saarwerden, absorbed into the French Bas-Rhin Department in 1793 but previously a foreign enclave within France, part of the County of Nassau-Saarbrücken (and, to a lesser extent, Nassau-Weilburg).[100] Were these Catholics implying that they saw the environs of Saarbrücken as part of their homeland because they *refused* to recognize the territorial changes the Revolution had brought? On the other hand, their reply might actually *affirm* French expansion: why, they might be suggesting, would they need a passport for a trip "abroad" if their home villages, Saarbrücken, and Sankt Wendel were all part of France now, whether formally integrated or durably occupied? The ambiguity may be the point here.[101] Catholic pilgrims probably hoped to evade scrutiny or punishment by the state thanks to the spatial uncertainties that pervaded revolutionary border culture.

Read from a different angle, the *Wallfahrt* dispersed outside of Saarbrücken also reflects the ways that the course of the Revolution caused many Catholics in the Saar region to grow even more hostile toward their Protestant neighbors. The members of that procession had intended to march right past or even through the Saar region's main center of Lutheranism.[102] We may plausibly assume that they had hoped to impress and perhaps provoke the Protestant burghers of Saarbrücken through this public manifestation of Catholic belonging—and that pilgrims' resolve was partly born from resentment at perceived revolutionary anti-Catholicism. For example, in the parts of the Saar region that had already belonged to France before 1793, Catholics claimed that they had suffered much more at the hands of radical revolutionaries in 1793/4 than their Lutheran and Calvinist counterparts had.[103] In addition to the epizootic, this resentful attitude may have added to the desperation that drove Catholic crowds to march past or through Protestant communities despite the risks associated with such ostentatious acts.

In at least one instance, this renewed drive toward religious confrontation expressed itself in violence against Jews. Catholics participating in a procession assaulted two Jewish men who were traveling on the road between Sarralbe and Sarreguemines and who failed to remove their hats in deference when encountering the procession.[104] This incident resonates with a broader history of how pilgrimage enforced Christian supremacy vis-à-vis the Jews, both in the Saar region and elsewhere in central Europe.[105] At the outset of this chapter, I quoted the churchwardens of Tholey who asserted that the spectacle of *Wallfahrt* enabled the conversion of Jews as well as Protestants to Catholicism. Such conversions were probably rare but not unheard of in the area: in March 1773, the General Vicariate at Trier authorized the parish priest of Sankt Wendel to baptize two Jews.[106] In other German regions, *Wallfahrten* and other processions entailed a temporary—but no less deliberate—erasure of any Jewish presence. In the Prince-Bishopric of Würzburg, for instance, Jews were forbidden from going out into the streets whenever a public procession was taking place.[107] Moreover, the Tholey churchwardens were not unique in blending anti-Jewish and anti-Protestant impulses. Take the example of Deggendorf (Bavaria), whose much-frequented pilgrimage was based on a late medieval host desecration libel. In the late eighteenth century, parishioners there accused the priest responsible for the shrine of being a crypto-Protestant after he decided to omit a Judeophobic litany (*Judenlitanei*) from local *Wallfahrt* liturgy.[108]

Among the inhabitants of Sankt Wendel itself, too, the pilgrim influx of 1796 also triggered an attempt to reaffirm confessional boundaries for the benefit of the Catholic faith. In July 1797, Johann Steininger, a burgher of Sankt Wendel, asked the General Vicariate for permission to publish a new and revised edition of the legend of Saint Wendelin. Steininger gave two main reasons why this publication was necessary. First, due to the recent spike in pilgrimages to Sankt Wendel, demand for such a book of hagiography and prayer had increased. This remark offers additional confirmation that the epizootic had indeed brought new fame to Sankt Wendel as a pilgrimage place. Second, the most recent edition of the legend had been produced by a "Protestant printer in Saarbrücken, with a fake place of publication," who had not hesitated to omit "several phrases that were not to his liking."[109] By proposing a new edition not despite but *because of* the revolutionary crisis, Steininger was claiming to reestablish Catholic control over the story of Saint Wendelin and the prayers recommended to his devotees. In other words, Steininger represented his project as a straightforward move to reconquer lost literary terrain on the confessional frontier.

A closer look at a 1783 edition of the Wendelin legend, however, complicates Steininger's story decisively. According to the frontispiece, the version from 1783 was published in Saarbrücken by the Lutheran court printer Hofer. This fact resonates at first glance with Steininger's assertion about a recent Protestant takeover of the legend, except that Saarbrücken was the overtly named (rather than concealed) place of publication. More importantly, however, the 1783 edition follows Keller's original hagiography of 1704 quite faithfully.[110] Notably, the 1704 and 1783 editions use the same partisan language to describe events said to have taken place in 1540, "when the Lutheran heresy was rampant" and Luther's followers tried to get into Sankt Wendel under the cover of night to conquer the town: "Saint Wendelin, however, protected his town so powerfully that the heretics did not have the slightest success and were unable to even fire a single shot, but instead had to retreat in embarrassment and disgrace."[111] By contrast, Steininger's edition featured telling changes to the text here, not least by presenting 1540 much more neutrally as "the time of Luther's reformation."[112] Contrary to what Steininger implied in his letter to the General Vicariate, his publication actually toned down the confessionalism that had characterized this part of the saint's legend previously.

Overall, the 1797 edition offered a complicated and innovative perspective on the confessional frontier, combining Baroque and enlightened Catholicism as well as anti-Protestant and subtly antirevolutionary commentary. As for the injection of Enlightenment ideas into Baroque hagiography, aside from the hint at tolerance toward "Luther's reformation," the reedition distinguished itself through a verbose new preamble. Almost fifty-five pages long and probably penned by Sankt Wendel's new, pro-Enlightenment parish priest Johann Castello, it presented the reader with characteristically enlightened injunctions on how to pray to God and the saints.[113] For example, true Catholics should worship God not with external exuberance but with internal sincerity, "in spirit and truth"—a trope of the Catholic Enlightenment that I discussed in chapter 1.[114] True Catholics should also follow the enlightened moral compass by praying "for virtue and righteousness, for a proclivity for goodness, for the power to do good," rather than for something as Baroque as a miracle.[115] Moreover, the part of the book that contained prayers to Saint Wendelin alternated abruptly between Enlightenment and Baroque discourse.[116]

While none of these additions truly erased the condemnation of "heresy" for which parts of the saint's legend continued to provide a vehicle, the 1797 edition changed the thrust of this condemnation by blending it with covert criticism of the French Revolution. In particular, the text reimagined the menace of the confessional other as a result of foreign occupation. Unlike the editions of 1704 and 1783, the one from 1797 named a specific enemy—"the Swedes"—as the group that had besieged Sankt Wendel in 1540 and attempted to "poison it with their heresy."[117] Projecting the traumatic events of the Thirty Years' War back onto the sixteenth century, the text connected the problem of "heresy" less directly to Luther than to an invading army. Moreover, pushing the reader to draw a parallel between Swedish occupiers and French revolutionaries, the editor—perhaps Steininger himself—proceeded to praise Saint Wendelin for ensuring that the town's church had "remained free from all heretical poison until several years ago."[118] Again, the contrast with the 1704 and 1783 editions is especially illuminating. In 1783, this passage had still proclaimed, as it had done in 1704, that Wendelin's church "has remained free from all heretical poison up to the present day."[119] What changed between 1783 and 1797? In late 1783, Clemens Wenceslaus decreed limited toleration for Protestants who wished to settle in the electorate, but his decision was never publicized.[120] Hence, readers of the 1797 edition would have been most likely to associate the recent intrusion of "heresy" with the expanding Revolution, not least because French soldiers had destroyed the church bells of the Wendalinusdom in January 1794.[121]

The conclusion to the book's hagiographical part pursued this way of thinking further, in three new paragraphs on the pilgrim influx that had occurred due to the epizootic. In 1796 and 1797, "people from the entire region went on pilgrimage to Sankt Wendel in greater numbers than in any other year of the century, and were deterred neither by the tumult of war nor by the insecurity of the roads, neither by mockery nor by other obstacles."[122] The text does not specify whose disdain Catholic pilgrims had to confront most acutely—that of their Protestant neighbors or that of French soldiers and revolutionary authorities? Perhaps a combination of both. In any case, a form of Catholic pride emerged once more from the spatial practice of *Wallfahrt*. It drew humiliating responses from outsiders *and* created an aura of power and perseverance around the humility of the pilgrims themselves, who implored Saint Wendelin in their hour of despair.[123]

To summarize, pilgrims sought help from Saint Wendelin when facing the terrible epizootic of 1796 and repositioned Sankt Wendel as a Catholic outpost in the process. The town and its holy sites now attracted those hoping to outmaneuver a new other—agents of the French state such as Le Lièvre, who fought to enforce a revolutionary policing of both territory and worship. On the one hand, the resulting conflicts did not involve Franco-German hatred in the way that people would begin to conceive of it in the nineteenth century; as the 1797 reedition of the Wendelin hagiography suggests, local Catholics who resented the Revolution viewed the French primarily as heretics rather than as national enemies.[124] On the other hand, the expansion of the French Republic made a difference in the Saar region, by drawing pilgrims into a new round of struggles over spatial and specifically territorial (dis)order.

In addition, the evidence discussed here confirms that revolutionary *police du culte* reshaped—and by no means replaced—older religious rivalries and hostilities in and around Sankt Wendel.[125] Most pilgrims probably continued to view Protestants as the primary religious other, but the incident of anti-Jewish violence on the road to Sarreguemines offers the most poignant reminder of the weight that the distinction between Catholics and non-Catholics continued to carry. In some ways, this weight even increased, as old confessional resentment and new hostility to the secular state's policing of worship quickly came to loop into each other.

Moreover, the wider historical context of the 1790s and the early nineteenth century suggests that a closer look at other places may very well yield stories commensurable (albeit certainly not identical) to the one I have just told. As we saw earlier in this chapter, the theme of *Wallfahrt* as confessional confrontation runs through the history of many German-speaking lands in the decades before the French Revolution. But what about the decades after 1789? How unique to the case of mid-1790s Sankt Wendel is the way that Catholic pilgrims renewed and reoriented that confrontational theme as they faced redrawn borders and intensified policing of worship? Existing scholarship cannot offer a fully fleshed-out answer to this broad comparative question. That said, across the Rhineland, the French Revolution obliterated "the delicate confessional balance established by the Peace of Westphalia," as Michael Rowe argues, and thus prompted a resurgence of interconfessional tension.[126] More generally, the dramatic shifting of borders in Napoleonic and post-1815 western Germany turned millions of Catholics into subjects of Protestant rulers, whether in the Kingdom of Württemberg, the Grand Duchy of Baden, the various Hessian states, or the Prussian

Rhine Province. In all these territories, governments pursued an enlightened *Religionspolicey* (the German word for *police du culte*) that tended to challenge Catholic practices of public worship and specifically pilgrimage.[127]

Therefore, in the early decades of the nineteenth century, pilgrims in these different states faced similar conundrums and quite possibly used similar tactics to those of Catholics in the revolutionary Saar region. In Württemberg, for example, the ministry of the interior issued a blanket ban on pilgrimage abroad in 1811. Catholics did not always respect this prohibition or other restrictions on *Wallfahrt*; in particular, many processions from Württemberg continued to visit the famous shrine of Walldürn, which now belonged to Baden. Crucially, pilgrims' disobedience of their new, Protestant ruler did not go unnoticed by authorities bent on implementing *Religionspolicey*. In situations of conflict with these authorities, Catholics presented a variety of arguments to justify their practices, and a recent analysis by Amelie Bieg highlights their subversiveness. For one thing, they insisted on the continued validity of pilgrimage vows and customs stemming from pre-Napoleonic times—when their hometowns and villages had not yet belonged to Württemberg but rather to smaller, Catholic territories that had not survived the sweeping territorial consolidations of *Mediatisierung* and *Säkularisation*. In other words, without going so far as to question Württemberg's territorial expansion as such, they did contest some of its concrete legal consequences. Additionally, pilgrims sometimes made the explosive claim that the end game of *Religionspolicey* in majority-Protestant Württemberg was to turn Catholics into Lutherans.[128] This example suggests that, during the decades after 1789, issues of territorial complexity and Catholic defensiveness kept feeding into the everyday politics of *Wallfahrt*—not just around Sankt Wendel and Tholey but also elsewhere in German-speaking Europe.

Wallfahrt and the Transformation of Border Culture

At the height of enlightened reformism and at the dawn of the revolutionary era, *Wallfahrt* was a salient medium of confessional conflict in the religiously diverse western borderlands of the Holy Roman Empire. Enlightened and revolutionary elites often scorned this kind of pilgrimage as out of place, as a disturbing residue of the confessionalism that they hoped to have overcome in theory. In practice, however, *Wallfahrt* participants and promoters forced state and church authorities to contemplate the unintended outcomes of their own battles against alleged spatial disorder, superstition, and religious violence.

The case of the Saar region shows, then, that "elite" and "popular" conceptions of confessional, political, and spatial order did not simply collide in the same way that an unstoppable force clashes with an immovable object. Instead, pilgrims and Catholic communities repeatedly *took up* the themes propounded by reformers and revolutionaries, trying to catch them in their own contradictions. First, consider the problem of confessional ridicule. In the early 1770s, communities from the area of Tholey compelled Hontheim to rethink and ultimately withdraw his ban on pilgrimage processions. He conceded that these restrictions had ended up reinforcing the stigma of Catholic inferiority by giving nearby Protestants great opportunities to lampoon their confessional rivals. The second key theme, that of spatial coherence, directly ties in here because everybody agreed that confessional disorder and border trouble went hand in hand, especially when it came to pilgrimage. Catholic communities built on this shared assumption very effectively in their petitions to Hontheim. Later, French revolutionary leaders conjured up the ideal of natural boundaries as a pillar of rational statehood to justify the Republic's expansion to the left bank of the Rhine (see chapter 1). But the chaos of war and occupation meant that, far from finally making the borderlands legible, the revolutionary state was merely reorganizing spatial illegibility on its territorial edges.[129] Pilgrims on their way to Sankt Wendel embodied this illegibility and tried to benefit from it by acting as though they were simply and innocuously wandering through "their own *pays*."[130]

Ultimately, local practitioners and defenders of *Wallfahrt* made two significant contributions to the transformation of border culture. For one thing, they changed the confessional dimension of this culture by taking ownership of it at the grassroots level, even as clerical and civil elites were growing much more interested in erasing that same dimension or at least smoothing out its rougher edges. Pilgrims not only appropriated an agenda of confessional boundary-setting which, in the Holy Roman Empire, intersected pervasively with the complexities of territorial borders; they also reoriented the confessional frontier by overlaying Catholic–Protestant conflict with the clash—and the less obvious resonances—between Baroque and Enlightenment. Second, in the 1790s, *Wallfahrt* came to serve as a powerful conduit for many Catholics to integrate yet another challenge, that of the expanding French Revolution, into the mental framework of the Catholic frontier. They did so by conflating revolution with heresy and by resisting the radicalized attempt to confine Catholic religious practice spatially. To be sure, these developments did not predetermine the fate of nineteenth-century German or European Catholicism. Yet, as a matter of fact, both contributions made by the champions of *Wallfahrt* proved durable, as both of them fed into the anti-Protestant, antirevolutionary mass politics of ultramontanism.[131]

3

Inventing Transnational Pilgrimage

This chapter focuses squarely on the relationship between borderland pilgrimage and the French Revolution, an issue whose importance the story of mid-1790s Sankt Wendel has already suggested. Like most of the Saar region, however, Sankt Wendel belonged to the Holy Roman Empire, not to France, at the end of the Old Regime. To gain a fuller picture of how pilgrims faced the Revolution on the western edges of German-speaking Europe, we must also look toward places that had become part of the Kingdom of France long before 1789. Above all, we must look toward Alsace. This mostly Germanophone region was annexed under Louis XIV but was never fully integrated by the Bourbon monarchy, which left political, cultural, and ecclesiastical entanglements between Alsace and the Holy Roman Empire—and between Alsace and Switzerland—largely intact.[1] In the years after 1789, by contrast, Alsatians not only turned from subjects into citizens but also confronted for the first time the full implications, warts and all, of belonging to France.[2] How, then, did Alsatian Catholics work out these implications, in particular when going on pilgrimage across borders as so many of them had been wont to do for centuries?

Answering this question means shedding light, I argue, on a process in which lay Catholics, clergy, and agents of the state together invented transnational pilgrimage. At least in Alsace, the age of revolutions and the 1790s in particular mark the fulcrum of this process, its key moment of acceleration and breakthrough as a significant issue in the history of piety and state-building. The French revolutionaries attempted to bring about a congruence of nation, state, and territory—a closed circuit in which any of these three terms would necessarily evoke the other two. As a result, forbidden border-crossing mobility could evolve from a merely territorial transgression into a national one. This double transgression soon found its emblematic figure in the émigré.[3] As the revolutionary politician Merlin de Douai put it in September 1793, "if anyone is guilty of the crime of violating the nation, it is certainly the émigrés."[4] This chapter will show that pilgrimage and emigration intersected in the 1790s. I do not mean to describe emigration as some kind of "forced pilgrimage," although a prominent French émigré did just that at the time.[5] Rather, I ask how—and with what consequences—revolutionaries came to perceive Catholic pilgrimages to Switzerland as a kind of emigration.

The resulting slippage between border-crossing and national betrayal reveals how the transnational implied the national and vice versa; the transgression and the transgressed frame were mutually constitutive. Therefore, my notion of transnational pilgrimage departs from broad definitions of transnational history as the study of all cross-border flows and activities regardless of whether the border in question was that of a nation-state. I prefer instead to reserve the term "transnational" for an approach that challenges internalist, self-referential national narratives while still recognizing that "going beyond the nation is not just stepping above it, dismissing it" but rather studying it critically.[6] Along these lines, I will explore how Alsatian Catholics came to recognize French nationhood and national politics as a significant and, at times, even crucial ingredient of what it meant to go on pilgrimage abroad. By the early nineteenth century, pilgrimage from northeastern France to Switzerland was no longer the same kind of devotional act it had been a few decades prior. Pilgrims began to move between nationally distinct religious climates, enabling themselves to see revolutionary France in a transnational mirror through their visits to shrines abroad.

My account thus highlights that negative or ambiguous attitudes toward the Revolution—and not just full-blown patriotism—could entail greater "national awareness," that is to say, a politically relevant sense of one's own national belonging.[7] To be sure, the leaders and supporters of the French Revolution set the stage in a crucial way by positioning the nation, rather than the king, as the sovereign source of authority.[8] They practiced nation-building as a radical political program on a much vaster scale than their Old Regime predecessors had done.[9] The Revolution's royalist enemies, meanwhile, rejected the notion of national sovereignty. Yet, they developed their own, very pronounced vision of what the French nation was and what it should be, as a response to the vision created by revolutionaries. This point, skillfully made by Pierre Nora, has not received sufficient recognition among historians, presumably because the Revolution, with its sprawling and fascinating set of national symbols, eventually found itself on the winning side of history.[10] The nonelite Catholics on which this chapter focuses were hardly royalists, but neither were most of them happy with the Revolution and particularly with its politics of religion. Yet, through pilgrimage to Switzerland, these Catholics learned to navigate patriotism and helped nationalize border culture in eastern France, powerfully and often painfully, sometimes with their very lives on the line.

Although there is some evidence of conflict developing around pilgrims who crossed the Rhine, the famous Swiss shrines of Einsiedeln and Mariastein constituted by far the most important destinations of pilgrimage abroad for Alsatians in the 1790s.[11] I will therefore begin by introducing these two Marian shrines and discussing how pilgrims from France related to them until 1791, when the Revolution's religious policies started to provoke massive repercussions in Alsace. A closer look at five dramatic destinies will reveal the variety of ways in which individual pilgrims faced the radicalization of the revolutionary struggle and the policing of the Franco-Swiss border in the years after 1791. In addition, at the more collective level of political culture, I will examine how pilgrimage, emigration, and nation-building intersected in the case of revolutionary-era Alsace.

Hardly French

Alsatian Catholics in the 1790s did not create transnational pilgrimage ex nihilo. Under the definition that I have outlined, transnational pilgrimage is a distinct variety of pilgrimage across borders, one whose meaning is shaped decisively by pilgrims' national origin. On the way to distant shrines such as Rome, Loreto, or Santiago de Compostela, pilgrims from central Europe have crossed state borders ever since they came into being. What is more, in the early modern period, the hospice of Santa Maria dell'Anima in Rome and the Opera pia germanica in Loreto had the explicit mission of giving shelter to "German" pilgrims, that is, people coming from the Holy Roman Empire of the German Nation. That said, both institutions also welcomed Dutch and Swiss pilgrims as well as those from Habsburg

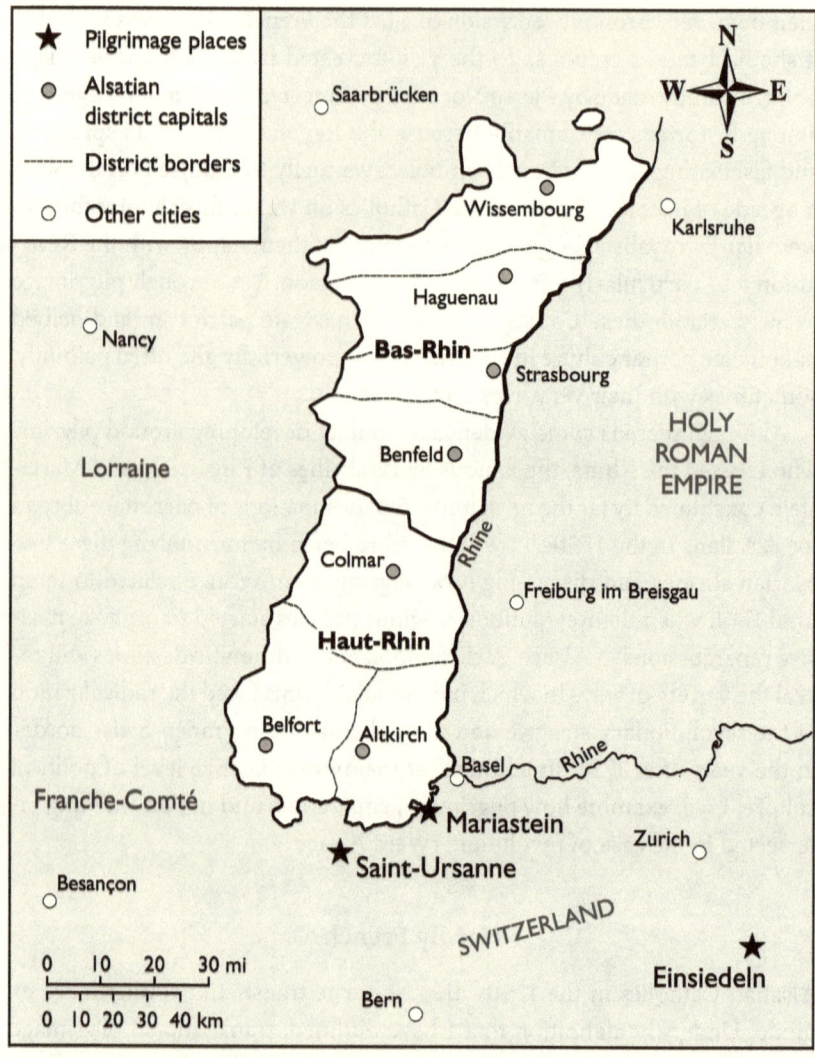

MAP 3. Alsace in 1790 and the shrines across the border. (Adapted from Wisniewski and Droux, "Carte administrative," modified and complemented with information from the departmental maps available online at https://numistral.bnf.fr/ark:/12148/btv1b102233129 and https://numistral.bnf.fr/ark:/12148/btv1b10223313r)

possessions outside the empire, such as Croatia and Slavonia.[12] People's "German" background mattered only vaguely and to a limited extent in these instances. Early modern pilgrims going from France to Switzerland, I argue, cared little about either the state borders they crossed or their own status as subjects of the French king—even though those borders and that status did take on increasing weight in the eighteenth century. Only in the heated political and religious climate of the early Revolution did pilgrimage abroad begin to look like a distinctly national transgression.

The relationships between Mariastein, Einsiedeln, and present-day northeastern France predate the invention of transnational pilgrimage by several centuries. According to later legends, the miracle that founded the reputation of Mariastein took place in the late fourteenth century: a child fell from a promontory into the abyss but survived and even suffered no injury, thanks to the Virgin's intervention. By the time of the Council of Basel, in the mid-fifteenth century, a pilgrimage chapel existed on the promontory. After the uncertain years of the Reformation, the Benedictine monks of nearby Beinwil took on the spiritual direction of the pilgrimage in 1636 before relocating the monastery itself to Mariastein in 1648. The shrine flourished in the seventeenth and eighteenth centuries, with fifty to sixty thousand annual pilgrims at the height of the Baroque. Many thousands of Alsatians were among these pilgrims each year—unsurprisingly so, given that Mariastein was situated in a northern exclave of the Swiss Canton of Solothurn, partly surrounded by the episcopal principality of Basel but also right on the border with the southernmost region of Alsace, the Sundgau. Aside perhaps from Trois-Épis near Colmar, no shrine enjoyed greater popularity among southern Alsatian Catholics than did Mariastein.[13] Alsatian pilgrims, moreover, visited Mariastein not just as a holy destination in its own right but also as a station on the way to Switzerland's most famous shrine, Einsiedeln.[14]

The Benedictine abbey of Einsiedeln in the central Swiss Canton of Schwyz traces its origins to Saint Meinrad, an early medieval hermit (*Einsiedler* in German) whose way of religious life gave the place its name.[15] According to later chroniclers and several medieval and early modern papal bulls, the founding miracle occurred on September 14, 948: when Conrad I, bishop of Constance, arrived to consecrate a chapel built by Meinrad's successors, Christ appeared, surrounded by angels and saints and insisting on performing the consecration rite himself. In addition to the holy chapel, Einsiedeln has had a second object of pilgrimage, a miraculous Black Madonna. From the later Middle Ages onward, this statue steadily gained in prominence compared to the chapel in which it stood.[16] Especially in the seventeenth and eighteenth centuries, copies of both the chapel and the statue proliferated across Catholic Europe, not only in Switzerland but also in Alsace, Lorraine, Franche-Comté, Savoy, Baden, Bavaria, Vorarlberg, Tyrol, and as far away as the Moselle Valley, the Lower Rhineland, Bohemia, and Hungary.[17] This process, driven largely but not exclusively by rulers and elites of these different regions, both reflected and amplified the far-reaching fame of Einsiedeln in the Baroque era.

An equally impressive pilgrim movement to Einsiedeln Abbey developed in the later Middle Ages and reached a first apogee in the century before the French Revolution, when an average of about 150,000 pilgrims per year visited the shrine.[18] Large groups came from all of Catholic Switzerland as well as from many other regions, such as Baden and Vorarlberg.[19] Late medieval sources also document an early influx of Alsatian pilgrims to Einsiedeln.[20] This pilgrim movement persisted throughout the early modern period.[21] In Franche-Comté, devotion to Our Lady of Einsiedeln (Notre-Dame des Ermites) became popular in the fifteenth century but reached far bigger proportions in the seventeenth.[22] Similarly, Catholics in southern and eastern Lorraine viewed Einsiedeln as one of their favorite pilgrimage destinations from the seventeenth century onward.[23] In short, from the shrines of Mariastein and Einsiedeln, many far-flung links stretched across and beyond Switzerland—especially into Alsace. To understand how some of these links became conduits of conflict and mobilization in the age of revolutions, we must first look at Old Regime royal policy.

Pilgrimage across borders could be an illicit and risky undertaking in early modern Europe. As far as French subjects are concerned, the seventeenth century—the time when Alsace was annexed by France—marks a meaningful point of departure on this issue: under Louis XIV and his successor, Louis XV, relevant royal pronouncements became stricter and more numerous. A total of five edicts (issued in 1665, 1671, 1686, 1717, and 1738) established the permissions any would-be pilgrim to, say, Santiago de Compostela or Rome would have to obtain from both the local bishop and royal authorities in order to travel legally. The edict of 1717 even prohibited pilgrimage abroad completely, threatening contravening men with a one-way ticket to the galleys and women with different forms of corporal punishment.[24] Such obstacles, diminished in practice because the state lacked means of control and enforcement, did not deter many people from their pious undertakings: in the eighteenth century, Santiago even seems to have received a *growing* number of French pilgrims.[25] Yet by the late Ancien

Régime, pilgrims had developed a veritable *politica peregrinesca,* as one of them called it in his personal narrative.[26] These politics encompassed, among other things, the forging of paperwork and the tricks of traveling incognito to avoid trouble with local inhabitants and authorities who did not see pilgrims but instead, increasingly, saw suspect strangers.

These suspicions embedded pilgrim mobility on the margins of France in a broader context, where controlling all kinds of border crossings became a critical security issue in the fever pitch of eighteenth-century state-building efforts. Such security concerns usually reached a climax in times of war, a tendency reflected in the making of the most severe royal edict against pilgrimage abroad. In 1717, when the War of the Spanish Succession had barely ended, a local military commander in southwestern France complained that the local *lieutenant du roi* had issued passports to ten thousand pilgrims within the last year alone. This policy "is very harmful to the service of the king because they are arrested in Spain and recruited" by force into the Spanish army.[27] A bureaucrat at the War Ministry named Le Gendre confirmed that "a prodigious quantity of pilgrims" crossed the Pyrenees each year to visit Santiago and the Catalonian shrine of Montserrat. Crucially, "the passage of all these vagabonds fosters a spirit of desertion on the frontier" as French soldiers sometimes decided to join groups of pilgrims. Hence, Le Gendre successfully recommended "absolutely forbidding these kinds of travels, in which devotion is mostly founded on libertinage."[28] On France's northeastern territorial margins, too, the triple specter of emigration, desertion, and smuggling haunted police forces, generals, and administrators even in peacetime.[29] Against this backdrop, state officials quickly attached a gamut of negative associations to border-crossing pilgrimage, constructing the figure of the pilgrim as a culpable, truly transgressive traveler long before the revolutionary era.

In the Alsatian borderlands, some local elites made intermittent and partial efforts to enforce the royal edicts against pilgrimage abroad, but laypeople seem not to have reconsidered the meaning of their pious journeys as a result.[30] In the 1740s, for instance, the parish priest of Réchésy in southwestern Alsace repeatedly refused to lead his parishioners on an annual pilgrimage across the border to the Church of Saint-Ursanne, in the episcopal principality of Basel. While the priest legitimized his refusal by pointing to the royal edicts on pilgrimage, the lay community of Réchésy simply ignored this rationale in their complaints against him.[31] Moreover, insofar as being French mattered at all during cross-border pilgrimages, it did so in the limited and rather practical sense of avoiding language barriers between pilgrims and those who welcomed them: when pious visitors from Alsace or Lorraine knelt in the confessional, when they listened to sermons at Einsiedeln, they could be either "French" or "German" depending on their mother tongue. In this respect, the category of "German" pilgrims included most people from French-ruled Alsace, much as the category of "French" pilgrims referred to speakers of French—some of whom came from areas outside of France, such as the Canton of Fribourg.[32] As we will see, it took a revolution to shake up this narrowly linguistic understanding of pilgrims' Frenchness or lack thereof.

That said, pilgrims may have been growing more aware of links between Einsiedeln and Counter-Enlightenment ideology by the 1780s. The first potential element here is the cult of Benoît Labre, the most famous pilgrim of the eighteenth century. This Frenchman died in Rome in 1783 and immediately became an object of popular veneration in Italy and France—as well as an icon of counter-enlightened propaganda. Einsiedeln counted among the shrines Labre had repeatedly visited in the 1770s, and this information probably spread as fast as all the other stories that quickly coalesced into a hagiographical whole after 1783.[33] Moreover, starting in the late 1770s, pilgrims listening to sermons at Einsiedeln would often hear about the spiritual dangers posed by freethinkers and other Enlightenment monstrosities, as distinct from the traditional enemy, the Protestant. Today, the abbey's archives preserve the texts of eight sermons preached in the 1770s and 1780s at Einsiedeln's main pilgrimage festival, the Engelweihe. Only one of these eight texts does *not* feature any explicit polemics against the Enlightenment. The others mock "our present-day enlighteners" who prided themselves on turning simple folk into "true worshippers in spirit and truth," or deplore the "dangerous times" in which "so many freethinkers, possessed by the bad spirit of philosophy, do their utmost to discredit holy places and pilgrimages, in fact anything that is holy and venerable."[34] In short, Einsiedeln was a site of Counter-Enlightenment in the 1780s, even though some of the monks there had begun engaging open-mindedly with Enlightenment thought in the years around 1770.[35]

In the last years of the Old Regime, the Einsiedeln monastic community also started to promote a certain idea of France, not least with regard to Marian devotion and pilgrimage. This idea referred not to the France of the skeptical, anticlerical Enlightenment but to a France which stayed true to its special role as the oldest daughter of the Church—especially in the face of a hostile zeitgeist. The monks expressed their commitment to the French monarchy publicly in 1787 by dedicating a thoroughly revised edition of their abbey's chronicle to Louise de France (1737–1787), a Carmelite nun and aunt of Louis XVI. Unlike its predecessors, this new *Chronique d'Einsidlen* was no longer a devotional book jammed with hundreds of miracle stories for pilgrims to devour but primarily an erudite rebuttal of enlightened critics who targeted pilgrimage rituals and legends surrounding the divine consecration of the holy chapel.[36] Along these lines, the dedicatory epistle addressed to Louise de France spoke *about* pilgrims rather than *to* them: "We still see the Christian people excited about coming from everywhere, and especially from the depths of the Most Christian Kingdom [of France], to this holy place."[37] As a whole, the new *Chronique d'Einsidlen* attempted to embed pilgrimage from France to Einsiedeln in a clear-cut ideological context for the first time.

While these pre-1789 commitments matter, much more sweeping new trends came to the fore once the Revolution had broken out. Its politics of religion reached a major turning point in late 1790, when the Constituent Assembly decided to require an oath of allegiance to France's new constitution from all parish priests. The legislators thereby aimed specifically to enforce adherence to the Civil Constitution of the Clergy, a law passed on July 12, 1790. The Civil Constitution amounted to a sweeping reform of the Gallican Church. Bishops and parish priests turned into salaried and elected state servants. The law suppressed large parts of the ecclesiastical body—for example, canon chapters and most religious orders—while conceding modest state pensions to these supposedly less useful priests, monks, and nuns. Another far-reaching innovation redrew diocesan boundaries to make them conform exactly with those of the recently created departments. This measure particularly affected the edges of French territory, where many dioceses, including that of Basel, had straddled not just departmental but state borders. The reforms stunned and divided French Catholics, not least because the majority in the legislature ostentatiously neglected to consult the papacy on these issues. In particular, Timothy Tackett's work shows how the oath crisis filtered the multiform regional differences within France's religious culture into a sharp polarization between nonjurors and jurors. This polarization escalated into "the last French war of religion" in the 1790s, and its traces endured far into the twentieth century, in the form of a difference between fervently Catholic and religiously more detached French regions.[38]

Tackett's overview also confirms that a clear majority of Catholics in Alsace, the Franche-Comté, and German-speaking parts of Lorraine quickly rejected the oath, even as the national percentage of jurors hovered around 50 percent. These provinces had fallen to France so recently that their clergy and broader religious culture had not turned fully "Gallican" and had instead forged closer ties to "ultramontane" (that is, Roman and papal) models and networks. Many Catholics in these regions also read the Civil Constitution of the Clergy through the lens of preexisting confessional rivalries, as a new form of heresy. After all, Protestants constituted an influential minority in Alsace and had a strong presence right across various borders, in northwestern Switzerland (Basel, Neuchâtel) and the southwestern Holy Roman Empire (for example, Saarbrücken, Montbéliard). In Alsace and northern Lorraine, the language barrier may also have added to "profound popular suspicion and incomprehension of the Civil Constitution."[39]

In addition, however, different receptions of the ecclesiastical oath *within* Alsace play an equally important part in the story of how pilgrimage to Mariastein and Einsiedeln changed for French citizens in the 1790s. In southern Alsace (the Haut-Rhin Department), many parish priests did swear the oath in 1791—40 percent, according to Tackett, or more than two-thirds, according to Dominique Varry and Claude Muller. By contrast, in the Bas-Rhin, barely one in ten parish priests took the oath.[40] How to explain this divergence? In the eighteenth century, the Diocese of Strasbourg had developed in a more ultramontane direction and had remained more aloof from the Enlightenment than the Diocese of Basel, whose territory included almost the entire southern half of Alsace.[41] Moreover, the Old Regime's last auxiliary bishop for the French part of the Diocese of Basel was none other than Jean-Baptiste Gobel, who would go on to become one of the most prominent and popular figures of the Constitutional Church.[42] Whatever the precise factors that combined to produce the relatively high oath-taking rates in southern Alsace, the Civil Constitution of the Clergy clearly had many supporters among Catholics there, especially in the Districts of Altkirch and Belfort on the Swiss border. Hence, unlike in the Bas-Rhin, where refractory unanimity was the norm, many parish communities in the Haut-Rhin were torn apart as strong pro- and anti-oath factions formed among

Catholic laypeople.[43] As we will see, the resulting local conflicts interacted decisively with the issue of the Swiss pilgrimages.

Already in 1791, revolutionary leaders, administrators, and the recently elected bishop of the Haut-Rhin, Arbogaste Martin, took various steps to construct a link between pilgrimage to Mariastein or Einsiedeln and threats to the Revolution. After the king's failed flight to Varennes on June 20 and 21, the National Assembly quickly passed several laws that penalized emigration and introduced stricter passport requirements for travel abroad.[44] Referencing these laws, the central administration of the Haut-Rhin wrote to the districts of the department in September 1791, singling out pilgrimage abroad as a particularly insidious form of "emigration." In fact, the letter stated, pilgrims did *not* emigrate permanently but instead came back home and spread the "bad principles" that ill-intentioned priests inculcated in them in Switzerland.[45] Around the same time, Bishop Martin issued a pastoral letter condemning pilgrimage abroad for the same reason. His correspondence with the Ecclesiastical Committee of the French National Assembly shows that Mariastein and Einsiedeln were the places he had in mind.[46] Interestingly, to further justify their interventions, both the bishopric and the civil administration at Colmar also alluded to the seventeenth- and eighteenth-century royal edicts on pilgrimage.[47] In this way, Alsatian revolutionaries explicitly built on Old Regime foundations even as their campaign against pilgrimage abroad unfolded within a profoundly transformed political context.

Far from merely *registering* polarization around the issue of pilgrimage, this campaign actually helped to *produce* such a polarization in the first place. In particular, many proconstitutional pilgrims continued to go to Einsiedeln after the oath crisis began. At their destination, they had tense encounters with a community of monks who had mostly come to abhor the Revolution. As Joseph Thomas Fassbind (1755–1824), a clergyman and historian from Schwyz, wrote sometime between 1808 and 1823, "pilgrims from Alsace caused regrettable clamor because at Einsiedeln they did not obtain absolution for adhering to the French constitution"—the Civil Constitution of the Clergy, as is clear from a corroborating remark in Abbot Beat Küttel's diary for the year 1791. "This affair was publicized by a newspaper," Fassbind added, though without specifying the name of the paper or the time of publication.[48] This evidence suggests, on the one hand, the role that the Einsiedeln monks played—alongside prorevolutionary Alsatian authorities—in forcing the ecclesiastical oath onto pilgrims' agenda. On the other hand, laypeople's actions also mattered: some proconstitutional Catholics contested the monks' spiritual directives so overtly that the resulting tensions spilled into the ebullient public sphere of the revolutionary press.[49] In 1791, while Bishop Martin and others were insisting that pious journeys to Switzerland equaled the rejection of the Revolution's religious policies, laypeople's positions on this issue were not that clear-cut—at least not yet.

On the whole, before the 1790s, the border-crossing pilgrimages around which this chapter revolves did not amount to a transnational practice in the sense of something that transcends but also implies the nation. During the Old Regime, devotional preferences and mother tongues tangibly shaped how pilgrims going to Einsiedeln or Mariastein related to the holy place, while their status as French subjects did not. And yet, we cannot understand the breakthrough of transnational pilgrimage in the revolutionary decade without acknowledging the various relevant elements that already coalesced in the Old Regime. Military commanders and royal bureaucrats conflated pilgrimages abroad with forms of vagabondage and emigration-as-desertion. What is more, right in the years before 1789, the monks and preachers of Einsiedeln tied "their" Black Madonna increasingly to the French monarchy and the Counter-Enlightenment. In the crucible of the French Revolution and the conflicts it triggered over church reform, these elements began interacting in new ways with pilgrims' struggles.

Five Tales of Transgression

After 1791, Alsatians' and other French people's trips to Mariastein and Einsiedeln turned into illicit and often dangerous adventures. To be sure, most border-crossing pilgrims were never caught or punished, despite the revolutionary campaign against pilgrimage abroad that aimed to halt the flow of many thousands of Catholics per year toward shrines situated outside of French territory. As a rule, we glimpse these pilgrims only indirectly, through the eyes of eager local revolutionaries who denounced these pious—and sometimes recalcitrant—travelers. For example, in late April 1795, an Altkirch district official reported to Colmar about two unnamed villages he had just visited. "Within two hours," he wrote, "I saw between two and three hundred men, women, and children, all French citizens, on their way back from Mariastein; they marched in groups of forty to fifty, loudly singing Marian hymns." Even worse, "trustworthy citizens told me that, sometimes, up to a thousand of them passed through here each day."[50] In short, it seems safe to assume that large streams of pilgrims continued to cross the Franco-Swiss border during the 1790s. Yet the revolutionary struggle over this mobility had serious consequences, as the rest of this chapter will show. To begin with, a look at five life-altering episodes will enable us to understand the risks that pilgrims ran, their highly diverse motivations, and the terrible price that some of them paid.

Joseph Bürr and his wife, Anna Libis, fled France in August 1793 to avoid arrest, an escape which earned them émigré status. Until then, they had lived in the Alsatian village of Bettlach, right across from the Mariastein enclave.[51] Already in May 1793, the cantonal justice of the peace heard thirteen witnesses who gravely incriminated Bürr and Libis. Both had called the Constitutional Church a new expression of Lutheran heresy.[52] Bürr had made a pilgrimage to Einsiedeln in July 1792, allegedly to avoid having to participate in the civic oath ceremony that capped the Revolution's second Fête de la Fédération. Most strikingly, Blaise Rey, a cobbler from the nearby village of Fislis, recalled an episode in which he, André Rey, and Bürr sat in a tavern in Basel and were asked by the innkeeper whether they were good French patriots. Bürr "first replied that he would rather be *Bâlois* than of the [French] nation, and that, since [Blaise Rey] is a patriot, he should change his ways and go to Mariastein and confess his sins there."[53] For a Catholic as embittered by the Revolution and the "sins" of patriots as Bürr was, a clear relationship had emerged between the Swiss pilgrimages and French national belonging: the former served to signal one's contempt of the latter. Bürr and Libis's story exemplifies how political polarization could progress and crystallize around the issue of pilgrimage after 1791.

The revolutionary measures against pilgrimage disrupted not just individual lives but also the larger fabric of devotional ties that connected Einsiedeln or Mariastein to the Catholic communities of Alsace. On May 13, 1793, the district administrators at Altkirch interrogated Christine Beller, a thirty-nine-year-old woman from Dangolsheim in northern Alsace and recently arrested on her way through Habsheim near Mulhouse. She had "no profession" but instead went to Einsiedeln "as often as her capacities allowed her to do."[54] Remarkably, she had transported and intended to hawk a panoply of pious objects, so her arrest and later deportation affected a large number of potential customers who were attached to Einsiedeln yet too busy or too scared to go there themselves. In her bags, the local authorities found not just various letters and hagiographic pamphlets on the recently guillotined Louis XVI but also a box that contained six rosaries,

> 24 sticks of yellow wax, plus three sticks of white wax, and a small one of yellow wax, plus forty-nine earthenware Virgins, plus six rolls of fine wax, plus two images of the Virgin, and a small painting representing the same object, another thirty-five rosaries, plus two figures made of lead and representing the Virgin, a small wooden cross, a small rosary, and four splinters of fir wood, another rosary, another rosary with a medal of the Virgin, and three small cases with Virgins inside, plus eight skulls sculpted from [animal] bone, plus a small silver Christ, plus twenty small wooden crosses, plus six tin crosses and some medals made from the same metal, plus several small Virgins, plus a dozen lead crosses, plus nine images of the Virgin, plus a book titled: *Geistliches Trostbrünnlein* [Spiritual fountain of consolation], plus a bottle containing an altar and the figure of a priest topped by a small wooden cross, plus two framed Virgins, plus a book titled: *Pilgerstraß* [The pilgrim's road], plus sixteen printed prayers to the Virgin.[55]

Although the hagiographic writings on Louis XVI linked Beller to the Counter-Revolution, the multifarious materials she was transporting reflect her economic and devotional—rather than merely political—concerns. As she explained to her interrogators, she had been entrusted with some of these objects at Einsiedeln as gifts for specific individuals, and she had bought the other pieces in the hope of reselling them for a profit back home. In other words, she eked out a living as a proxy pilgrim for Catholic communities that wished to stay in touch with faraway Einsiedeln through her. She had thus been serving as a conduit through which the exceptionally rich material culture of devotion to Our Lady of Einsiedeln would have reached Alsatian Catholics even in the troubled times of revolution.[56] Moreover, Beller's activities were not unique. For example, women—and more rarely men—accomplished regular proxy pilgrimages to Einsiedeln for communities in the Franche-Comté well into the nineteenth century.[57]

Regardless of pilgrims' individual political stances, they faced the greatest danger at the height of the radical Revolution. In the spring and summer of 1794, three pilgrims even lost their lives under the guillotine after returning from Einsiedeln to France. One of them came from southern Alsace:

Bernard Meyer, a twenty-five-year-old weaver from Muespach, publicly executed in Colmar on June 28, 1794.[58] His case, however, is much less well documented than that of Anne Dausson, age twenty-eight, from the village of Docelles east of Épinal (Vosges Department), arrested on May 3, 1794, by Sergeant Laneuve of the French army.[59]

Laneuve ran into Dausson while he was patrolling the Franco-Swiss border between Basel and the Alsatian town of Saint-Louis, renamed Bourglibre under the First Republic in order to efface the memory of royalty and Christian sainthood. He took her to the Passport Surveillance Bureau of Bourglibre, whose officials interrogated and searched her.[60] The only things she carried on her were "a crucifix, an *Ange conducteur* [Guiding angel] full of images, a confession certificate dated Einsiedeln, 1794, and a very mystical prayer book." Anne Dausson declared that she had left Docelles thirteen months prior, "that she had been at Einsiedeln since then, and that she had only left France to travel to Switzerland and work there." In other words, she had been traveling purely of her own volition and had not transported any letters to émigrés or refractory priests, as she would later clarify before the criminal tribunal of Mirecourt in the Vosges.[61] But why, the inspectors at Bourglibre asked her, had she come back? Surely, she knew that the death sentence awaited émigrés caught returning into French territory? She "said that she has returned to France because she is tired of her existence [*ennuyée d'exister*] and the only mercy she asks for is to not be brought back to her relatives."[62]

Anne Dausson died on the guillotine in Mirecourt, around noon on May 18, 1794. A court official (*huissier*) certified in writing that "the execution was accompanied and followed by repeated cries of 'Long live the Republic!'"[63]

Revolutionary authorities gave Dausson's case publicity even beyond her execution, again contributing to the wider politicization of pilgrimage. In line with the major anti-émigrés law of March 28, 1793, communities across the Vosges Department were required to put up printed copies of the judgment that pronounced her death sentence. This judgment explained that she had been arrested as "a person without passport, carrying different objects and signs of fanaticism," and that she was "strongly suspected to have carried letters and money to émigrés in Switzerland."[64] Other potential pilgrims to Mariastein and Einsiedeln would know, based on the example of Dausson, that the state would treat them as border-crossing fanatics. In fact, it is implausible that she should have acted as a messenger within counterrevolutionary networks, even though around two thousand refractory French clergymen and other émigrés visited Einsiedeln at some point between 1791 and 1798.[65] When the surveillance agents at Bourglibre searched Dausson, they did not find any *return* letters from French émigrés to supposed contacts in the Vosges. Moreover, it would not make sense for such a messenger to spend over a year at Einsiedeln between her outward and homebound trips.[66] So, more likely, Dausson had been a pilgrim, a migrant worker, and a runaway all at the same time, and she had returned because she had grown weary of life. But the agents of the revolutionary state publicly cast her journey—and, by extension, similar pilgrim travels—as a counterrevolutionary act, deserving of capital punishment. Later, Catholic writers of the nineteenth century instrumentalized her story as well, presenting her and the two other guillotined pilgrims of 1794 as especially pious Christians and even as "martyrs."[67]

Even after the fall of Robespierre and the end of the radical Revolution, and even when pilgrims did not travel alone as Beller and Dausson had done, they could still face life-threatening situations. Johann Georg Homatt, a miller from the southern Alsatian village of Bartenheim, knew the risk when he moved back across the border from Switzerland into France on the evening of February 2, 1795: both he and one of his four fellow travelers carried guns. They were prepared for a showdown. Did they sense, at some point, that somebody was following them as they snuck through the woods on their way home? At any rate, when four French customs officers of the Bettlach brigade finally decided to confront the group, Homatt loaded his rifle and took aim. The leader of the customs brigade, Lieutenant George, "saw the action coming and fired his rifle, hitting the leg of that malefactor who fell down before he could execute his project of destruction." The brigade members then proceeded to arrest Homatt and his four companions.[68]

Unable to count on the cooperation of local authorities in Bettlach, Lieutenant George and his men abandoned their posts to personally transfer the four men in the group to the district jail in Altkirch, about fifteen miles northwest of the border. By contrast, the only woman in the group, the wife of one of the men, "has been released upon a suretyship oath by the national agent of the Commune of Bettlach." The customs officers seized the two guns, of course, but also a number of other items, including "some small rolls of candle wax, three rings, and a bottle of water—presumably holy water." According to the customs inspector who reported the incident a few days later, these objects "prove that the five people in question were coming back from la Pierre."[69] In other words, they had gone on pilgrimage to the shrine of Notre-Dame de la Pierre, as Mariastein is called in French.

While the pilgrimages that ended badly left the biggest paper trails, a fifth and final tale, from the fall of 1795, illustrates how much a border-crossing pilgrimage could mean to an individual when it succeeded. Instead of being arrested on the way back from a shrine, Joseph Erb went the other way around, turning from a prisoner into a pilgrim. A native of Haguenau in northern Alsace, punished by the revolutionary state for reasons he did not care to specify, Erb managed to escape on August 23, 1795, somewhere on the western outskirts of Strasbourg. After climbing a wall, he jumped down twenty-three feet into the Bruche River without injuring himself. He ascribed his good luck to "providence and to his strong trust in the most blessed Virgin, Our Lady of Einsiedeln"—and decided to thank her by undertaking a pilgrimage to her shrine. Upon arriving at Einsiedeln roughly two weeks later, he wrote down a short description of the special grace he had received and handed the piece of paper over to the monastery, in whose archives his story has survived.[70]

Alongside Einsiedeln, Mariastein as a border shrine played an intriguing role in Erb's escape. According to him, after getting out of the river safe and sound and heading south toward the Swiss border, he "made it past all guards without any incidents, all the way to Mariastein."[71] At first glance, it seems surprising that he would have used Mariastein as a waystation. After all, since the spring of 1793, when the French Republic had annexed the northern parts of the episcopal principality of Basel, Mariastein and the surrounding villages had formed an enclave completely surrounded by the French departments of Haut-Rhin and Mont-Terrible.[72] Therefore, to get from Mariastein to Einsiedeln, Erb first had to cross back into French territory. Did he consider the risk of multiple border-crossings worth taking because his devotion to Mary also extended to her manifestation at Mariastein? In addition, perhaps, he had somehow become aware of the enclave's reputation as a place where people could get passports more easily than elsewhere. In the mid-1790s, these passports enabled many local inhabitants as well as strangers to move more smoothly through a borderland rife with smuggling, pilgrimage, and agitation against the French Constitutional Church.[73]

From Joseph Bürr to Joseph Erb, the tales I have told here constitute a wide gamut of dramatic—and partly tragic—experiences of territorial transgression. Rather than cast them as somehow representative of pilgrimage from France to Switzerland in the 1790s, I want to foreground the ambiguities of gender and politicization that these different experiences reflect. The revolutionary repression of pilgrimage abroad spared neither men nor women. Especially when traveling alone, marginalized women ran terrible risks on their way back from Einsiedeln, as the cases of Christine Beller and Anne Dausson suggest. At least after the end of the so-called Terror in 1794, however, women gained wiggle room for local religious and political action as the state grew less interested in holding them criminally accountable—a tendency reflected in the fact that the sole woman in Homatt's group got off the hook with relative ease.[74] Meanwhile, levels of politicization clearly varied from individual to individual: some, such as Bürr, used pilgrimage explicitly to perform their rejection of the Revolution and its religious policies, whereas others, such as Dausson, most likely had little interest in politics altogether. Yet, each of the five tales indicates how powerfully individual pilgrims' fates could reverberate through the wider social and devotional landscape in which they were embedded. On this basis, I want to reiterate the central questions animating this chapter: How did that landscape become transnational? How did pilgrims going from Alsace to Switzerland transcend—but also refer to—the French revolutionary project of nation-building?

Dangerously French

In answering these questions, I contend that many Alsatian Catholics in the 1790s faced the nation most poignantly when they envisioned the danger of being labeled émigrés. By conflating pilgrimage abroad with the crime of emigration, the revolutionaries placed a sword of Damocles above the heads of all devout border-crossing travelers. To be sure, both during and after the age of revolutions, there were numerous other ways in which ordinary villagers engaged in "the apprenticeship of republicanism" and helped more or less willingly to construct the national political frame.[75] Relevant practices included celebrating revolutionary festivals, voting, joining the army, and appropriating new symbols such as the tricolor cockade in 1790s France—a repertoire that nineteenth-century local nation-builders continued to use and expand.⁷⁶ Especially on the nation-state's territorial margins, however, this well-known repertoire reflects only part of the story. Where people kept moving in and out of the national frame in a concrete, spatial sense by crossing a nearby border, we must look beyond the interplay of locality and nation to integrate *trans*national aspects such as pilgrimage abroad.⁷⁷ This section therefore explores how pilgrims quite literally walked into the intersection of piety and emigration in 1790s Alsace, and how they attempted to cope with the consequences. In addition, I will consider briefly how the resulting conflicts reverberated beyond the end of the revolutionary decade.

While the French revolutionary state never criminalized pilgrim mobility as such, Alsatian authorities effectively treated pilgrimage to Switzerland as a punishable activity by casting it as a form of emigration.⁷⁸ As we saw earlier, this process began in the fall of 1791. It escalated after the beginning of the war with Austria and the overthrow of Louis XVI in 1792. In this context, a French law of July 29, 1792, acquired particular importance. It forbade municipalities from issuing passports for trips abroad. Crucially, it also stated that anyone who left French territory without a valid passport must be considered an émigré and treated accordingly if they dared reenter the country.⁷⁹ On January 8, 1793, the district directory of Altkirch issued an order calling on municipal officers and police agents to enforce the law of July 29 more rigorously. This order specifically targeted "the great number" of people in the district who allegedly acquired counterrevolutionary attitudes and propaganda on their "frequent trips to Mariastein and other shrines outside the territory of the Republic."⁸⁰ Subsequently, Anne Dausson, Christine Beller, and many others were arrested, accused of emigration, and punished on this legal basis.⁸¹ To be sure, between the end of the Terror and the left-wing, anticlerical Coup d'État of Fructidor (September 1797), regional administrators backed away from the position that treated pilgrims as émigrés even if they had left France for only a day or two to go to Mariastein.⁸² Yet, after Fructidor, departmental administrators and the police ministry promptly renewed the strident demand that Mariastein pilgrims, in particular, be prosecuted "in accordance with the laws on émigrés."⁸³

Revolutionary authorities framed border-crossing pilgrims as émigrés partly because they doubted the loyalty of nonelite, German-speaking borderland inhabitants toward the French nation. Such doubts first became acute when, as I have noted, most priests of the Strasbourg diocese refused to swear an oath on the Civil Constitution of the Clergy. In the Haut-Rhin, revolutionary elites appealed to the "vigilance of officials in a border department where the people, due to the difference of language, are misled more easily and enlightened less quickly."[84] In early 1794, this generalized suspicion culminated in an oft-quoted report by the radical deputy Bertrand Barère, who claimed that the use of Breton, Basque, German, and (in Corsica) Italian had been "perpetuating the reign of fanaticism and superstition, assuring the dominance of priests, nobles, and conmen, [and] preventing the revolution from penetrating nine important departments" on France's peripheries. Concerning Alsace in particular, Barère thundered that "emigration and hatred of the Republic speak German."[85]

In fact, while most French émigrés were either members of the clergy or the nobility or domestic servants belonging to noble households, Alsace presented a very different picture. Most notably, Austrian troops invaded the north of the region in October 1793 but had to retreat before the French army two months later. This turnabout prompted roughly twenty-five thousand to thirty thousand local inhabitants—overwhelmingly peasants and other members of the former Third Estate—to flee across the Rhine rather than risk being accused of having collaborated with the Austrians. Many thousands of these fugitives ended up on the French state's lists of émigrés.[86] The treatment of pilgrims as émigrés represents a similar phenomenon, further underscoring the specificity of the borderland context.

The criminalization of pilgrimage abroad posed a serious danger to the thousands of Alsatians who went to Mariastein or Einsiedeln each year, even though only a small fraction of them got caught.[87] Focusing my quantitative analysis on the population of the Haut-Rhin, I found documents on 181 individuals who were arrested on their return from a Swiss shrine. Fifty-nine of them were declared émigrés, a measure that usually led to deportation but in one case (that of Bernard Meyer) to a death sentence. Tables 1 and 2 offer additional information on this group.[88]

This information enables us to discern the group profile of affected pilgrims and the evolution of the risk these Catholics ran across the revolutionary decade.[89] The near-perfect gender balance of the group has to do with the often-familial character of *Wallfahrt* in early modern German-speaking Europe. This finding also dovetails with recent research that has cautioned against casting the adventurous young man as the ideal-type of the pilgrim.[90] While all three guillotined individuals were returning from Einsiedeln, the

TABLE 1. Numbers of Haut-Rhin pilgrims arrested in the 1790s

Gender	Male	Female	Unknown
	80 (44.2%)	83 (45.9%)	18 (9.9%)
District of origin	Altkirch	Belfort	Colmar
	123 (68.0%)	13 (7.2%)	45 (24.9%)
Pilgrimage destination	Mariastein	Einsiedeln	Both	Unclear (but in Switzerland)
	146 (80.7%)	11 (6.1%)	2 (1.1%)	22 (12.2%)

TABLE 2. Haut-Rhin pilgrims jailed and declared émigrés, 1792–1797

Year	No. detained temporarily	No. added to the list of émigrés	Total no.
1792	1	0	1
1793	21	34	55
1794	44	21 (incl. 1 guillotined)	65
1795	33	0	33
1796	23	1	24
1797	0	3	3
Total (1792–97)	122	59	181

overwhelming majority got into trouble after going to Mariastein, whose abbot and monks were condemning the Revolution, though less overtly and radically so than those of Einsiedeln.[91] These statistics on pilgrimage destination align with the prominence of the district of Altkirch, the southeasternmost of Alsace, in terms of the pilgrims' places of origin: many of them embarked on short-distance *yet border-crossing* trips. Information on the socioprofessional standing of the pilgrims remains scarce, but it suggests that almost none of them had risen above the station of peasant, vigneron, or rural artisan. Many of them were poor servants or dependent agricultural workers; the group includes only two priests and two nuns. Finally, the radical revolutionary years of 1793 and 1794 mark the apex of state repression. Yet the risk of arrest remained palpable through 1796, and after the Fructidor coup of September 1797, the Haut-Rhin Department added three more pilgrims to the list of émigrés.

The punishment of border-crossing pilgrims sometimes resulted directly from the local conflicts that had broken out across southern Alsace over the ecclesiastical oath in 1791. This dynamic is well illustrated by the case of the single-largest group of pilgrims who were declared émigrés and deported out of France during the Terror. The deportation of nineteen citizens of Brunstatt took place on January 16, 1794, based on an *arrêté* of the Departmental Revolutionary Commission of the Haut-Rhin, which in turn reinforced a previous *arrêté* of the District Directory of Altkirch.[92] The pilgrims had left for Mariastein on December 24, 1792, which suggests they rejected the Christmas celebrations led by a constitutional priest in the parish church of Brunstatt.[93] Right after the pilgrims' return, the municipality of Brunstatt slapped them with a fine, but the fault line running through the community was so massive that most members of the group refused to pay and appealed against it to Altkirch.[94] This tactic backfired spectacularly and led to their deportation. At least some of them obtained permission to return in late 1794 and others in early 1795.[95] In the interim, "a small municipal hatred" had continued to rage between Brunstatt's comité de surveillance and the miller Jean Schultz, to whose extended family about half of the deported group belonged.[96] The Brunstatt case thus shows how the issue of pilgrimage to Mariastein connected local enmities to trenchant revolutionary decisions on who belonged to—and within—the emerging territorial nation-state and who did not.

In this situation, Catholic Alsatians began to consider border-crossing pilgrimage and the French Constitutional Church in terms that bound together nation and territory. While we already glimpsed this trend in the witness testimony given against Joseph Bürr, petitions shed even more light on the issue. On May 30, 1794, for instance, thirty-six Mariastein pilgrims from the villages of Friesen and Hindlingen were arrested at the border and jailed. The district administrators of Altkirch turned to their superiors in Colmar: should they treat all these people as émigrés and thus either deport them or send them before a revolutionary tribunal at the height of the Terror? Nobody wanted to make this tough decision—neither the departmental administration, nor the National Convention's representative on mission Foussedoire, nor the Convention itself. Only in mid-October 1794, during his second mission to Alsace, would Foussedoire finally release these prisoners.[97] In the meantime, seven members of the group conceded in a petition to the district directory that they had gone on "a pilgrimage that priestly deceit had suggested to them" but insisted that they had never even thought about "renouncing their fatherland."[98] These captive Catholics from Friesen and Hindlingen grasped the stakes clearly: to avoid being cast as émigrés, they needed to contest the assumption that pilgrimage to Mariastein meant voting against France with their feet.

Other petitioners engaged in the same rhetorical maneuver to try to redraw the line between devotion and treason that the revolutionary struggle had blurred. Writing in early 1794, Sebastian Galliath from Bergholtzzell implored the Haut-Rhin departmental administration to remove his daughter Anne-Marie from the list of émigrés. Against his wishes, she had gone on pilgrimage to Mariastein to fulfil a vow and recently been punished with deportation. Her father had, as he insisted, "always given splendid proof of patriotism, manifested ever since the beginning of the Revolution." For him, moreover, there existed "a great difference between a momentary absence motivated by a false religious opinion, such as his daughter's pilgrimage to Mariastein on neutral territory, and an emigration, which constitutes a malicious desertion of one's fatherland."[99] Galliath's wish was granted, unlike a similar petition by a young woman, Elisabeth Boll. She had formerly lived in Wittenheim (today a suburb of Mulhouse) but had been declared an émigré while making a pilgrimage to Einsiedeln and thus prevented from returning home. Boll claimed to have acted as a proxy pilgrim for her father, a French soldier, who had promised a pilgrimage to Our Lady of Einsiedeln in 1792—hoping that Mary would intercede "for the success of the Republic's army"![100] We will never know just how patriotic these pilgrims and their families truly were, but the point is that they embraced the new language of patriotism. In doing so, they contributed to constructing pious travel to Switzerland as a transgression of the French national frame.

The practices of diplomacy, too, helped turn pilgrimage to Mariastein and Einsiedeln into a challenge to this territorialized frame. Between 1792 and 1797, the embassy of France in Switzerland repeatedly alerted the government in Paris about politically suspicious events and visitors at both major Marian shrines.[101] Moreover, this embassy cooperated with the departmental administration of the Haut-Rhin and the passport surveillance agency at Bourglibre to police the mobility of French citizens traveling through Switzerland or hoping to return from Swiss into French territory.[102] What this could mean for pilgrims is illustrated in a letter the *citoyenne* Ferniot sent to the minister of justice in the summer of 1796. Ferniot explained that she was languishing in prison in Besançon after going on pilgrimage to Einsiedeln and being arrested in Basel—a frequent waystation for Einsiedeln pilgrims and also, at the time, the seat of the French embassy.[103] "In Basel," she wrote, "I went to Citizen Barthélemy in order to get a passport, I couldn't find him, I presented myself at the first entrance [of the embassy?], the officer led me to the agent who told me he was going to send me to my department to see if I wasn't an émigrée."[104] Ferniot's adventurous spelling suggests she did not belong to the social elite, and yet she had known that her "devout travel" (as she called it) might get her in trouble unless she could get the right paperwork from the ambassador Barthélemy himself.[105] She ended up spending four months in prison until the Doubs Department decided to release her instead of adding her name to the list of émigrés.[106]

Diplomatic tensions between France and the Swiss cantons rose after the Coup d'État of Fructidor, and matters came to a head in the spring of 1798, when French troops invaded Switzerland to help accomplish the Helvetic Revolution. They thus created another one of France's sister republics, the Helvetic Republic, which would exist until Napoleon's Mediation Act of 1803.[107] On March 14, 1798, French soldiers arrived at Mariastein, where civil commissioners were already busy creating an inventory of the monastery's seized assets; only in 1802 would the abbot of Mariastein get the chance to reacquire the convent buildings. Einsiedeln Abbey, a hotbed of resistance to the new Helvetic regime, underwent thorough pillage in early May 1798. The holy Marian chapel within the abbey church was dismantled and would not be rebuilt until 1817, long after the Mediation Act formalized the reestablishment of the convent. In May 1798, most of the monks fled at the eleventh hour, but like their counterparts at Mariastein, they still managed to hide the miraculous statue of the Virgin.[108] They placed a copy of the statue above the altar, and the French general Schauenburg mistook that copy for the original. He triumphantly reported to the War Ministry that one of his officers would bring to Paris "the famous Virgin of Einsiedeln, whose transport into France will undoubtably be the most astonishing as well as the last of her miracles."[109] Schauenburg was wrong. Although 1798 marks an interruption in this story, the breakthrough of transnational pilgrimage would prove irreversible.

Indeed, when Switzerland's two most famous statues of the Virgin returned to Einsiedeln and Mariastein in 1803 and 1804 respectively, tensions around these pilgrimage places soon reemerged in a new, Napoleonic context.[110] As early as June and July 1803, the prefect of the Haut-Rhin, Félix Desportes, rang the alarm bell about "a great number of inhabitants of the

Departments of Bas-Rhin and Vosges" who were passing through southern Alsace on their way to Einsiedeln. As Desportes asserted, "the ignorant and fanaticized class of my *administrés*" was resuming this habit of pilgrimage as well. While the remark about fanaticism sounds as though Desportes wanted to tie "popular superstition" to political danger, he mostly mobilized political economy to condemn this religious practice: pilgrims wasted their time and harmed the French economy by spending their money abroad.[111] Interestingly, the police commissioner at Colmar who had first alerted Desportes to the issue also invoked two of the old royal edicts that had severely restricted pilgrimage abroad.[112] On the whole, these civil authorities saw enough reasons to denounce the renewed pilgrimage activity to the government in Paris as well as to the responsible bishoprics in Strasbourg and Nancy.[113]

In response, the Napoleonic-era bishop of Strasbourg, Jean Pierre Saurine, promised to reinforce the national territorial frame while depoliticizing it ostensibly. Right after the Concordat of 1801 between France and the papacy, Saurine was working hard to move past the violent conflicts of the recent past by reconciling Alsatian Catholics with each other and with the French state.[114] In a letter to Paris, he claimed that the people "absolutely need these objects of devotions; it is not possible to dissuade them" from the practice of pilgrimage. He therefore proposed reducing the attractiveness of Einsiedeln to French Catholics by revitalizing well-known shrines located *within* France's borders, especially Marienthal near Haguenau.[115] Indeed, throughout his episcopate, Saurine attempted both to foster pilgrimage to Marienthal and to impose his personal oversight over that shrine.[116] In his reply to Prefect Desportes, he made a similar case for offering domestic pilgrimage destinations as alternatives to the incurably superstitious *peuple* instead of choosing repressive means in the name of Enlightenment principles: "This is not exactly the job of the Christian as a philosophe, but rather that of the Christian as an administrator."[117]

The intersection between Frenchness and contested pilgrimage became truly salient again when Napoleon—in his relentless quest for European hegemony—fell out with Pope Pius VII in 1807, had him taken prisoner, and annexed the Papal States in 1809. Already in 1808, a pilgrimage sermon preached at Einsiedeln exhorted believers to pray that God would send an angel to "comfort Pius VII and restore him to his faithful people in the esteem that befits his eminent dignity."[118] In March 1809, the dean of the monks' chapter reminded his fellow *patres* that a penitent's nationality was one of the things they might need to take into account when hearing confession.¹¹⁹

A new crisis of transnational pilgrimage finally threatened to erupt in early 1810, when Auguste Talleyrand, Napoleon's plenipotentiary in Switzerland, complained to the Swiss government about Einsiedeln Abbey. As Talleyrand alleged, preachers there were conveying propapal propaganda to the "great number of inhabitants of the Jura, the Vosges, the Meurthe, and the Haut-Rhin" Departments that came to Einsiedeln as pilgrims.¹²⁰ In response, Abbot Konrad Tanner insisted on his own innocence and that of his monks. Referencing the Gospel, he asserted that they had all been "striving to admonish French pilgrims to give to the Emperor what belongs to the Emperor."¹²¹ We can never know exactly whether the conversations held between monks and penitents about Rome and France skewed Gallican or rather ultramontane. Yet we can say with some certainty that many such conversations did take place and that pilgrims' Frenchness mattered, to the point of sparking diplomatic tensions between Paris and Bern.¹²²

Einsiedeln thus continued to represent a major transnational reference for eastern French Catholics in the Napoleonic era and even beyond. Pilgrims might have tense exchanges with their confessors at Einsiedeln about how the Gallican Church related to the imperiled papacy of Napoleon's later imperial years. They might listen to an 1817 Engelweihe preacher who reminded them of how, in the 1790s, "it took the incitement of the most powerful nation to satanic fanaticism" to bring about the destruction of the old holy chapel.¹²³ To add just one more example from the Restoration era, upon hearing (false) news that the pope was going to visit Einsiedeln, they might immediately start planning a pilgrimage to this shrine, as many inhabitants of Strasbourg apparently did in the fall of 1828.¹²⁴ Long after the Revolution, Einsiedeln remained a place where Catholic Alsatians could weigh and connect the national, transnational, and Roman components of their faith.¹²⁵

Looking into the Swiss Mirror

This chapter has shown how Swiss shrines functioned as places of power and peril for Catholics from Alsace and, to a lesser extent, Lorraine and Franche-Comté. Old Regime royal edicts, Enlightenment, and Counter-

Enlightenment already brought into play many of the elements that would shape the rapidly shifting situation in the 1790s. Then, pressured by both revolutionaries and counterrevolutionaries—by administrators in Colmar, Altkirch, and elsewhere as well as by the monks of Einsiedeln and Mariastein—French Catholics began to envision border-crossing pilgrimage in a new way. Alsatian pilgrims in particular endowed the border with a strong political and religious charge. They came to consider trips to Mariastein or Einsiedeln as a form of resistance to the Civil Constitution—and frequently even to the overall course of the Revolution. Overall, they inflected border culture in the region by turning a centuries-old tradition of religious mobility into a transnational transgression, in many cases a very risky one.

Through this transnationalized practice, they also grasped and rethought France as the *patrie*. That rethinking became necessary because the French revolutionaries territorialized the nation and nationalized territory. A chasm opened up between pilgrimage abroad and adherence to the revolutionary national community. Sooner or later, many Catholics confronted that chasm in a number of different situations—when a monk hearing their confessions at Einsiedeln told them that adherence to the French Constitutional Church equaled a fall into heresy; when a revolutionary soldier or customs agent arrested them near the border; when they faced deportation; when they learned about the public execution of Anne Dausson. The Franco-Swiss border came to acquire new weight and meaning for pilgrims: by crossing it, they risked becoming émigrés, and the radicalizing Revolution made them increasingly aware of that risk. Emerging from the crossfire of Revolution and Counter-Revolution, the category of the émigré signaled that leaving French territory for the wrong political and religious reasons meant undermining French revolutionary nationhood. In this sense, pilgrims-as-émigrés became truly transnational travelers. They turned Mariastein and Einsiedeln into a Swiss mirror, in which competing visions of national belonging appeared sharply for everyone to see.

Other opportunities to confront the contours and stakes of these visions existed, but to Catholic Alsatians, few mirrors may have offered as much clarity as this transnational one. It reflected the concerns with border security that intensified around the outbreak of the revolutionary wars; the church schism that ran deep between and within local communities; the radical politics that cast emigration as national treason; and, as a result, the immense postrevolutionary scar tissue at which so many committed Catholics kept picking throughout the nineteenth century. Much about this story might be unique in the context of western and central Europe around 1800, given the specificities of France turning into a revolutionary nation-state as early as 1789 and inventing the category of the émigré. Yet the general problems of transnational pilgrimage would come to resonate strongly in the later nineteenth century.[126] Lourdes, for instance, the site of modern Europe's most famous Marian apparitions, was a place not only of self-consciously national pilgrimage for French Catholics but also of transnational pilgrimage for Germans, including Alsatians between 1871 and World War I.[127] The crucial issue of Marian apparitions, however, also deserves separate scrutiny, as we will see in the next chapter.

4

Mary's Overflowing Presence

Toward the end of the French Revolution, pilgrims no longer risked being guillotined. As this chapter will show, however, pilgrimage continued to trigger transformative conflicts. The year 1799 became pivotal in this respect for the Franco-German borderlands. Starting in March, Marian apparitions and sacred water gave hundreds of thousands of Catholics a sense of access to divine grace. Women and children stepped forth with claims that bathing in well water had immediately cured them from disease and incapacitation. Printed reports of Mary's appearances and miracles circulated throughout the region. Countless pilgrims traveled by foot from far-flung places such as Luxembourg, Trier, central Alsace, Mannheim on the right bank of the Rhine, and even Cologne to pay visits to the Good Well, the main apparition site situated in German-speaking Lorraine. They prayed and experienced the spectacle of a great religious gathering. As a result, "This place resembles a great fairground, more than fifty shops have been set up, as well as guinguettes on the plain and in the woods."[1] Yet the atmosphere was not always this cheerful. When state officials planned to interfere, lay Catholics who heard about these threats reportedly "dared to say that no matter what armed forces will be sent against them, it won't prevent them from going on pilgrimage to the Virgin's well."[2] In the crisis-ridden summer of 1799, devotion and defiance once again mingled in the borderlands.

In this chapter, I argue that the pilgrims of 1799 effectively subverted the efforts of French revolutionary authorities to control both devotion and territory. In the process, a new type of apparition space emerged—a type distinguished by its ephemeral, fluid, and expansive qualities. By quickly impeding access to the Good Well near Hoste that constituted the initial source of apparitions, revolutionary administrators, gendarmes, and soldiers involuntarily encouraged pilgrims to elect secondary sacred sites wherever they could at least transport bottles of water from that well. In the process, Catholics aptly navigated the instability and vulnerability of borderland spaces, a vulnerability heightened by the broader political and religious turmoil of the last months before Bonaparte's coup d'état. The apparitions around Hoste exhibit some features that evoke early modern precedents. Yet pilgrims were also inaugurating a devotional and political pattern of overflow that would often recur in later decades. In that sense, the events of 1799 shed light on how Marian apparitions could come to mobilize millions of Catholics during and after the revolutionary era.

This interpretation challenges the dominant narrative in the historical study of Marian apparitions that has produced much outstanding scholarship but has also neglected the revolutionary era. Classic work on Lourdes by Ruth Harris and on Marpingen by David Blackbourn has shown that spectacular apparitions did not simply take place in modern times more often than before; rather, they were profoundly *of a piece* with modern Catholic ways of thinking about divine grace and the body, as well as with modern socioeconomic realities and politics of mass mobilization.[3] Scholars have developed this insight while concentrating on the especially numerous and influential apparitions of the mid- to late nineteenth century. As a result, the events of La Salette in 1846 have come to serve as a convenient starting point for those trying to discern a modern model of Marian apparitions, in sync with notions of midcentury religious renewal that have by and large shrouded the earlier, momentous changes of the revolutionary era.[4]

Moreover, the focus on fixed, emblematic apparition sites—La Salette, Lourdes, Marpingen, Fátima, and so forth—has tended to obscure the pattern of spatial overflow that pilgrims first enacted in 1799 by taking their encounters with the Virgin beyond any single place, even one as powerful as the Good Well near Hoste.[5] Far from "always" producing a "fixation of place" as Alphonse Dupront claims in his seminal work of historical anthropology, modern apparitions often came in waves, spilled across boundaries, and thus created a *fluid plurality* of places.[6] The pilgrims of the revolutionary period pioneered precisely that fluidity and tapped into its mobilizing potential.

The apparitions of 1799 are not easy to trace in the historical record.

Intriguing police dossiers on Hoste and the other pilgrimage places exist, but these sources report on pilgrims' actions in lopsided, hostile, and condescending ways. They convey little sense of what the pilgrims' own perspectives might have been. Only a few individuals emerge distinctly from these materials; even the seers who first reported a Marian apparition near Hoste in March 1799 remain anonymous. Other, highly relevant documents burned in Metz during World War II. Mere glimpses into those riches are preserved in a local church-history publication that appeared in the early twentieth century.[7] Only thorough and wide contextualization can mitigate the silences of what either has been lost or was never recorded in the first place. This chapter begins accordingly by showing that the apparitions of 1799 constituted a final, spectacular subseries of miraculous interactions between Mary and European Catholics that had already been proliferating for years from Italy to the Rhineland. Only then do I zoom in to elucidate how devotion, border culture, and politics intersected specifically in and around Hoste to create spatial and spiritual overflow. In turn, the final section of the chapter situates this pattern against broader historical vistas, emphasizing that it recurred in the nineteenth and twentieth centuries whenever Catholic–secular conflict reached its highest pitch.

Revolutionary Expansion and the Thirst for Miracles

Let us return for a moment to the Swiss abbey at Einsiedeln, the largest of the pilgrimage destinations I discussed in the previous chapter. Sometime in the summer of 1796, the monks of Einsiedeln added a summary of recent miraculous events in Italy to their capitulary acts. Inside the Cathedral of Ancona, a city on the Adriatic Sea, statues of Mary as well as Saint Anne and Saint Cyriacus had come alive, according to this report. Specifically, Mary and the two saints had opened their eyes, glancing lovingly at their local devotees but also at foreigners, including skeptical Frenchmen. Soon, inhabitants of Rome, other cities of the Papal States, and Naples began telling of similar wonders occurring in their own neighborhood churches. As the report stressed, "there is no more room to doubt the truth of the miracle, as the matter has been closely inspected and subjected to thorough examination." The text went on to praise the "prodigious" amelioration of morals among the populations that witnessed the events.[8] By August 1796, Abbot Beat noted in his diary, stories about them had also been "spread and recounted here in Switzerland" for the benefit of anxious Catholics who were facing "these most dire times."[9]

From the abbot's perspective, the times were dire primarily because revolutionary France was becoming a Grande Nation, extending itself across the Alps as well as solidifying its control over the left bank of the Rhine. In the process, local populations suffered the hardships of warfare and fiscal-military exploitation. The economic pressure and violence had many aspects, going far beyond the rapidly increasing tax burdens and the frequent requisitioning of cattle that I have mentioned in previous chapters. Administrators of occupied territories such as the Rhineland levied huge sums of money as ad hoc contributions and forced civilians to labor for the purposes of fortification works, road-building, and transport. Soldiers engaged in looting and frequently harassed the families in whose homes they were billeted. Members of the most undisciplined troops perpetrated beatings and rapes with impunity. Around the same time, moreover, the new pro-revolutionary states imposed religious policies that many Catholics viewed as shockingly restrictive, even sacrilegious—not least because the French soldiers they encountered were among the most anticlerical segments of revolutionary society.[10]

In this tense situation, individual laypeople's miraculous experiences had massive social and political ripple effects, often unleashing a dynamic of repeated and collective encounters with Mary. Such dynamics responded to key moments of French expansion, whether in the Papal States during Bonaparte's Italian campaign of 1796 or in the northern Rhineland when French administrators tried to introduce most revolutionary policies there in 1798. In other words, by ramping up efforts to redraw borders in western Europe and Italy, the French Directorial government of 1795–99 produced many frontiers of revolution, and miracles easily proliferated on these frontiers as local inhabitants faced radical political and cultural challenges. Occurring across the borderlands that included Lorraine, Luxembourg, and southern parts of the occupied Rhineland, the apparitions of 1799 thus capped off a yearslong sequence.

In drawing attention to this sequence, I connect the issue of Catholic resurgence in Directorial France to a larger European landscape of religious panic associated with French territorial expansion. Several historians working on the mid- to late 1790s have revealed the scope of resurgence even for central French regions strongly affected by de-Christianization in the year II (1793/4), such as northwestern Burgundy, the northern Île-de-France, and Limousin. For example, Catholic villagers in the Yonne Department organized *messes blanches* (lay rituals substituted for the Mass in the absence of clergy) and religious riots to claim and achieve greater freedom of worship after the Terror.[11] Even when revolutionary officials returned to heavier repression of "superstition" and Catholic claims to public space after the coup of Fructidor an V (September 1797), this "second Terror" could not stifle dissident worship altogether.[12] Two obstacles have made it difficult to link these observations to scholarship on other parts of late-1790s Catholic Europe. First, that other scholarship is dispersed across multiple national historiographies—those of Belgium, Germany, Switzerland, Italy, and so forth. Second, the classic synthesis of the field, Jacques Godechot's work on the Grande Nation, deprioritized the issues of changing religious practice and conflict. Godechot emphasized instead the spreading of "new notions" such as "*laïcité*" and "tolerance," as well as what he considered the relative self-restraint of French anticlericals in freshly conquered regions.[13]

Italian, Rhenish, and Swiss examples show, however, that many areas of French territorial expansion during the Directorial period became zones of intense encounters with the supernatural. For a short time, but in spectacular numbers, pilgrims would flock to the sites of these encounters.[14] The most important phenomena of this kind created turmoil in the Papal States in 1796/7, precipitated or at least shaped by the pressure that Bonaparte's campaigns were putting on northern and central Italy. On June 25, 1796, a Marian image at the Cathedral of Ancona opened her eyes and smiled, according to testimony first given by a few women and children but quickly corroborated by large swaths of the city's population and by the clergy. Soon, people from dozens of communities were reporting smiling or crying Marian images in their home parishes or local chapels, too. Waves of miracles swept through the Papal States and triggered "a veritable migratory flow of pilgrims from the countryside to the places where the extraordinary events were transpiring," according to historian Massimo Cattaneo. Unlike in Lorraine in 1799, urban "epicenters" played a decisive role in 1796—not just Ancona but also Perugia and above all Rome, where more than a hundred images suddenly showed miraculous features and movements.[15] Moreover, as northern Italy made further experiences of revolution during the late 1790s, Marian miracles generated much counterrevolutionary excitement in Venetian cities (Vicenza, Verona) and in Lombardy as well.[16]

The miracles in the Papal States impressed and inspired Catholics far beyond Italy. I have described how these events resonated at Einsiedeln. Cattaneo himself mentions not only a whirlwind of letters on the miracles circulating throughout the Papal States but also a pamphlet printed as far away as London in 1796 and entitled *Evenemens miraculeux etablis par des Lettres autentiques d'Italie*.[17] The French title suggests that this publication was specifically aimed at the large French émigré community that resided in the English capital at that time. Most intriguingly, there is a handwritten account of the events of Ancona and Rome "sent from Italy to the internuncio who is in Münster and who will forward it to Cardinal Montmorency," the nonjuror émigré bishop of Metz to whose diocese Hoste belonged.[18] We know from instructions and authorizations given by Cardinal Louis-Joseph de Montmorency-Laval (1724–1808) that he kept in touch with clergymen who carried out clandestine pastoral work in the Diocese of Metz during the Directorial period.[19] To be sure, no direct link seems to exist between Ancona and Hoste. I cannot prove that the Italian miracles became a topic of conversation between refractory priests and parishioners in the Moselle Department, or between the monks of Einsiedeln and pilgrims coming from Alsace and Lorraine. Yet, given how fast and far news of these miracles traveled in 1796, they may very well have heightened the attention that Catholics across revolutionary Europe would pay to Mary's supernatural action in the world.

The central Swiss region around Einsiedeln offers another example of how religious effervescence—and Marian devotion in particular—developed in response to French military advances. In early May 1798, French troops under General Schauenburg invaded the Catholic cantons south of Zurich that had refused to accept the constitution of the new Helvetic Republic. In the course of this campaign, the French not only pillaged and closed Einsiedeln Abbey (see chapter 3) but also won several skirmishes against hastily formed, ill-coordinated Catholic peasant armies.[20] Some of these armies carried Marian banners before them into battle. In the Canton of Nidwalden, according to some testimonies, a Marian apparition occurred in these weeks of desperate defense against an overwhelmingly strong adversary. Part of what drove Catholic populations to alarm and resistance was a new, counterrevolutionary propaganda against an equally new form of republicanism, denounced as alien and godless. Sermons preached at Einsiedeln during a time of great pilgrim influx there formed a crucial element of that propaganda.[21] The Swiss example thus illustrates—much as the Italian one does on a bigger scale—that the pressures resulting from expanding French republicanism created remarkably dynamic, politicized religious frontiers where Catholics experienced urgent interactions with the Virgin.

In the French-occupied Rhineland, a similar frontier opened up in the spring of 1798, in this case largely due to a change of administrative regime that revolutionized these borderlands. Until the end of 1797, the military had governed this region, ruthlessly pursuing economic exploitation but otherwise ruling pragmatically and unsystematically. Then, however, the French commissioner Rudler introduced regular departmental administrations and gradually published French law: based on the Treaty of Campoformio (October 17, 1797), the Directory considered France's possession of the left-bank Rhineland secure enough to prepare its definitive annexation.[22] In this moment, anticlerical hard-liners such as Anton Dorsch, commissioner to the central administration of the Roër Department, lobbied for the introduction of a more restrictive *police extérieure du culte*. The government had put such a policy in place by 1795 in France's then-existing departments, as I discussed in chapter 2. The explicit goal was to prevent processions and pilgrimages through which Catholics might assert and perpetuate "superstitions" as well as counterrevolutionary attitudes. "The impressions of fanaticism must have taken root in a country where the people are naturally good, but stupid," as Dorsch wrote.[23] Yet "fanaticism is fortified by persecution," his fellow administrator L. P. Caselli cautioned.[24]

Indeed, around Easter of 1798, miraculous events only multiplied and attracted more believers in response to the rigorous repressive measures that Dorsch had pushed through precociously in the Roër.[25] Pilgrims flocked not only to the statue of Our Lady of Kevelaer, the most important shrine in the Lower Rhine region since the seventeenth century, but also to freshly miraculous sites. For instance, an image at a chapel in Heinsberg and a crucifix near Geilenkirchen "have for some time become very famous and often attract more than ten thousand pilgrims on a single day," as Dorsch claimed on June 1, 1798.[26] One year later, in the early summer of 1799, he had to admit that Heinsberg and Geilenkirchen were again (or still) witnessing numerous "*rassemblements fanatiques*": his uncompromising approach had proved ineffective and perhaps even counterproductive.[27] On the other side of the struggle, the defiant attitude of lay Catholics is further exemplified in an episode of the summer of 1800, at a later stage of the Rhineland's occupation crisis. Near Aldenhoven—just a few miles southeast of Geilenkirchen—the gendarmerie stopped a procession of chanting pilgrims and "pointed out to them that one could not sing prayers in public like that." The pilgrims reacted: "Instead of singing, they started shouting" those same prayers.[28] In sum, whether to the north or to the southeast of Lorraine, the instability of France's new borders correlated with a profusion of the miraculous toward the end of the revolutionary decade. The events of Hoste and beyond belong in this broader, transregional context.

In Hoste, initially undisturbed by the revolutionary state apparatus, lay Catholics—including women and children in prominent roles—"made" the Good Well as an apparition site and pilgrimage place largely on their own terms. A miracle report was soon authored or at least distributed by a layman, a local schoolteacher named Paul Spaeth.[29] According to him, the Virgin appeared on March 24, 1799, to "six innocent children, twelve to thirteen years of age."[30] Above all, stories of several miraculous healings helped attract more and more Catholics to Hoste. The report mentions two such healings in some detail, both concerning anonymous women. One of them had been mute for four months and regained her voice upon placing her foot in the well water, and the other, possessed by a demon, was delivered from her convulsions when the people who had transported her to the Good Well succeeded in having her swallow a sip of the water.[31] A later gendarmerie report identified a third miraculously cured woman, Gertrude Derving, said to also have recovered her voice on June 2 after no fewer than fourteen years of muteness.[32] We do not know when the other two healings had happened, but by the time revolutionary officials began taking notice, namely in early May, miracle reports must have already been circulating for a while.[33]

These miracles drove a pilgrimage whose remarkable scope is confirmed by both existing scholarship and revolutionary authorities. On June 1, 1799, "indeed at least six thousand souls were gathered at this well" according to a gendarmerie lieutenant stationed at Sarreguemines.[34] Another lieutenant, from Pont-à-Mousson in the Meurthe, reported even higher numbers ten days later: "It is not an exaggeration to say that, across the meadow where this well is located, I have seen more than twelve thousand people whose fanatical enthusiasm is beyond the imagination of any reasonable human being."[35] Another two months later, the Directorial commissioner at the cantonal administration of Bascharage (present-day Luxembourg) still complained that "apparently the Moselle Department has only taken half-hearted measures: otherwise, these gatherings of thousands of fanatics would no longer exist."[36] Thus, a swelling chorus of republican patriots alerted the government in Paris about the unusual dimensions of this pilgrimage. More recently, historians Joachim Bouflet and Philippe Boutry have characterized the Marian apparition of Hoste as the most important one among those that occurred in France during the revolutionary decade.[37]

As the reputation of Hoste spread and pilgrims journeyed back home with water they had bottled at the Good Well, other sites of Marian miracles cropped up throughout the summer of 1799 (see map 4). Among the first of these emergent secondary sites was the parish church of Bacourt (about halfway between Nancy and Saint-Avold), where pilgrims hoped for further miraculous healings thanks to the well water that a female resident of Bacourt had brought home in a bottle from a trip to Hoste. On

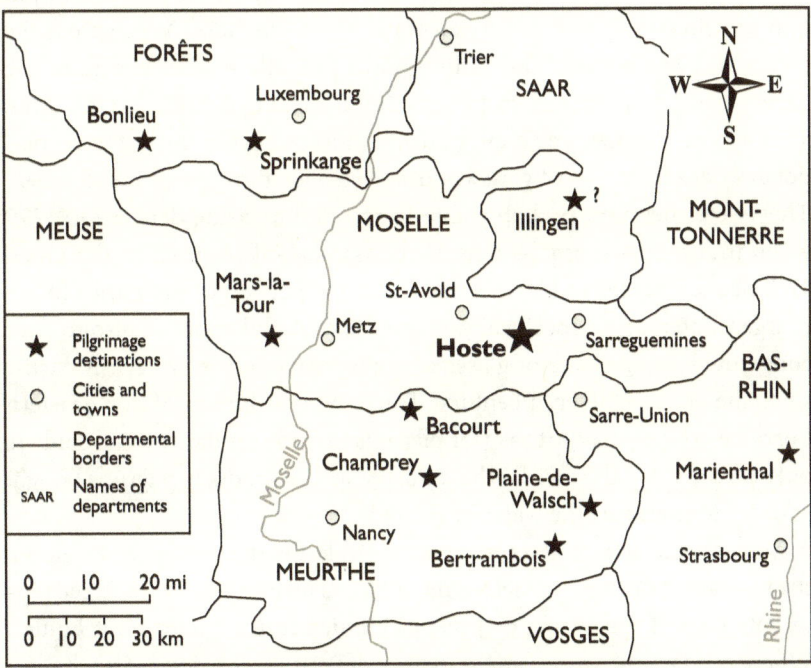

MAP 4. Hoste and connected pilgrimage sites in the summer of 1799. (Adapted from Poirson, *Carte de l'Empire*; departmental borders simplified)

some days, several thousand pilgrims crowded through the village at the same time.[38] Countless Catholics also flocked to other places in the Meurthe Department that reported sightings of the Virgin and miraculous healings, including Chambrey, the Rehtal well near Plaine-de-Walsch, and Bertrambois.[39] A little later, in late July or early August, local and departmental authorities in the Bas-Rhin began noticing a spike in travel to the regionally well-known chapel of Marienthal. They radically disincentivized this movement by having the chapel doors walled up.[40] Yet the region kept teeming with new miracles in places where pilgrims had transported well water from Hoste: Mars-la-Tour in the western part of the Moselle, Sprinkange and another, unidentified site in the Canton of Bascharage, and the woods north of Virton in present-day Belgium.[41] Finally, there is a potential link between Hoste and the village of Illingen in the French-occupied Rhineland, where local inhabitants constructed a "Marian fountain" (*Liebfrauenbrunnen*) around a well precisely in 1799.[42] This dynamic only died down in September or October, as the pilgrimage season ended.

The regional economy of Lorraine facilitated this multiplication of pilgrimage sites as Catholics carried water from the Good Well across the region in glass bottles.[43] Lorraine—and especially its German-speaking parts—had been one of Europe's great glassmaking regions for centuries. This as well as other regional industries took a severe hit in the revolutionary decade, but most glassworks stayed alive throughout the decade.[44] They were therefore probably able to respond to rising demand in 1799 when thousands—perhaps tens of thousands—of pilgrims to the Good Well needed bottles to fill with their personal portion of the miraculously charged water. More specifically, Plaine-de-Walsch happened also to have constituted a major site of glassmaking industry in the eastern Meurthe since the early eighteenth century. Thus, the vast forests of northeastern Lorraine not only made it easy for pilgrims to elude gendarmes and soldiers but also provided the fuel for the industry whose products pilgrims bought in order to transport the water of Hoste.[45]

Widespread use of glass made it possible for this water to develop a strong—albeit fleeting—religious potential, as many pilgrims could see representations of the Virgin or Jesus swimming in the transparent bottles. Where gendarme Rapin from the district of Pont-à-Mousson (Meurthe) reported about a simple figurine slipped through the bottleneck by the former schoolteacher and "charlatan" Spaeth, many faithful Catholics were prone to think that further genuine apparitions were occurring. As Rapin added, "The inhabitants of the bigger part of my district have gone on pilgrimage. They have returned persuaded that they had seen the Virgin and several miracles."[46] Bottles containing devotional figurines had become a very popular item in the material culture of eighteenth-century pilgrimage—perhaps a precedent on which to draw for the Catholics who saw bottled apparitions in 1799.[47] At Chambrey, Bacourt, and Mars-la-Tour as well as near Virton, such bottles containing Mary even became the principal objects attracting thousands of pilgrims.[48] For example, either in Chambrey or in Bacourt (the sources are unclear on this point), the bottle "contained extremely dirty and thick water. A little cork swam in it, wrapped in a piece of plainsong paper with letters and notes of different colors, which, through the thickness of the water, people took at times for the Virgin and at other times for baby Jesus," according to revolutionary officials.[49] Later in the summer, at Mars-la-Tour, people stopped coming after they learned that the representation of the Virgin had dissolved in the bottle.[50] The visual qualities of glass and muddy water both enhanced and destabilized pilgrims' perceptions of the miraculous: north of Virton, if a Virgin appeared in the bottle brought there from Hoste, she did so only "momentarily."[51] In short, these perceptions were ephemeral but highly dynamic. They bolstered the logic of proliferation.

To sum up, the apparitions of 1799 continued and heightened a tidal wave of miracles that had been accompanying French revolutionary expansion across large parts of Catholic Europe since 1796. Important differences existed between events playing out in various regions. In Italy, pilgrims converged not on remote wells and villages but on urban power centers including Rome, endowing devotional actions with more immediate visibility. In the Papal States, moreover, Catholics saw moving and crying Marian statues rather than apparitions in water, and in the Rhineland, not all the miraculous phenomena of 1798/9 even involved Mary. Yet an equally important pattern binds together these episodes: miracles triggered more miracles along with spontaneous pilgrimages on the margins of the Grande Nation's expanding territory, according to the vicissitudes of war. Were pilgrims thus mobilizing against the Revolution? Based on the work of the historians who have explored the relevant Italian, Swiss, and Rhenish contexts, the answer seems to be yes. To be sure, apparitions and individual Catholics' quests for miraculous healing or deep spiritual experience cannot be reduced to political movements. Neither, however, can we bracket politics as extraneous to people's encounters with Mary, especially in a time and place as tumultuous as France in the 1790s.[52] Therefore, the next section will probe how the Marian apparitions and pilgrimages of Hoste and beyond intersected with revolutionary politics and border culture.

Marian Devotion and the Politics of 1799

Indeed, the pilgrims of 1799 encountered and occasionally incorporated politics in their quest to experience the holy at the Good Well and other apparition places. The evidence is tricky to handle because, once again, it comes overwhelmingly not from the pilgrims themselves but from those who either promoted the apparitions or denounced them to the police. Yet these very attempts to exalt or (more frequently) excoriate pilgrimage to Hoste and other sites invariably suffused the events with the sharply polarized politics of the moment. France was traversing another severe crisis of warfare and government in the spring and summer of 1799, during those last months before Bonaparte would seize the reins of power as First Consul and begin dismantling the Republic. By the end of the revolutionary decade, moreover, both lay Catholics and clergy had learned how to benefit from the various quirks of regional bordering processes around Hoste—more specifically, how to practice forms of mobility that disrupted revolutionary *police du culte*. The pilgrimages of 1799 thus constitute spectacular and effective transgressions against the religious policies and the left-leaning agenda of the late Directory. And while some Catholics tried to combine enthusiasm about these apparitions with assent to the Revolution, the virulent anti-"fanatic" discourse of French state officials and anticlericals ended up erasing any political ambiguities.

While the Marian miracles of 1796–98 had coincided mostly with French military successes, the apparitions in and around Hoste took on political meaning in part because of French setbacks, as the tide of military fortune seemed to turn. In the winter of 1798/9, European monarchies including Great Britain, Austria, and Russia had formed the Second Coalition against the revolutionary republic. In the following spring, French armies suffered grave defeats in present-day southwestern Germany (Battles of Ostrach and Stockach in late March) and northern Italy (for example, Battle of Magnano, April 5). After a decade of mutual radicalization between Revolution and Counter-Revolution, French republican leaders and officials recognized in these struggles another, particularly strong and concerted effort of Europe's counterrevolutionary forces.[53] In response, national and neo-Jacobin sentiment was gaining ground not just in Parisian politics but across the country.[54] Patriots may thus have been more eager than ever to suspect and denounce fifth-column activities—especially in France's eastern regions, which were most exposed to the military threat. What is more, enlightened Francophone revolutionaries had long been classifying Alsatians and German-speaking Lorrainers as backward, fanatical, and politically unreliable.[55] Against this backdrop, the apparitions of 1799 gave Catholic pilgrims, antirevolutionary clergy, and anticlerical republicans ample opportunity to link devotion to politics.

In northern Lorraine, moreover, the proximity of the border with the French-occupied left-bank Rhineland had enabled both laity and clergy to enact politically subversive crossings throughout the 1790s. As the French state policed religious life much less heavily in the occupied lands, thousands of Lorrainers chose to undertake religious excursions across the border. We encountered a major instance of those crossings in chapter 2: among many others, Catholics from Lorraine went on pilgrimage to the shrine of Saint Wendelin, a famous patron of livestock, in the Saar region during the devastating epizootic of 1796. In addition, a recent analysis of Church records from the 1790s for just five parishes on the "German" side of the border found 731 baptisms and 510 marriages of Lorrainers.[56] So, after the ecclesiastical oath of 1791 had met with overwhelming rejection in German-speaking Lorraine,[57] the inhabitants of this region developed border-crossing mobility to keep in touch with a clergy who seemed more legitimate to most than the jurors.

In turn, certain members of the clergy did not hesitate to accomplish the same movement in the opposite direction—incursions into "old" France from the relatively safe areas that had belonged to the Holy Roman Empire.[58] The most notorious of these priests was Jean Chavant, nicknamed "the local pope" (le Pape du Pays) and author of the counterrevolutionary pamphlet *Te Deum in Gallos*.[59] What is more, an enclave of French-occupied territory persisted within the Moselle Department throughout the 1790s. This enclave of Rouhling and Lixing lay less than ten miles northeast of Hoste. From there, a priest and former monk named Jean Prost made excursions into "old" French territory to spread "the venom of fanaticism" in 1796.[60] In sum, new forms of clandestine religious activity had emerged and begun affecting border culture in the region around Hoste long before the apparitions began.

Then, in 1799, refractory clergymen and nuns probably established a discreet presence in the woods around the Good Well after the initial apparition and the spectacular healings had triggered a great influx of pilgrims. The evidence is admittedly delicate to handle in this respect. Revolutionary officials easily convinced themselves that priests were secretly orchestrating the pilgrimage all along, yet none of the contributors to the various police dossiers ever succeeded in identifying any clergymen involved in organizing the apparition place. Priests probably kept a prudent distance from the public spectacle *at* the well, in which gendarmes, army officers, and administrative commissioners intervened frequently. For example, exorcisms at the Good Well were performed not by clergymen but by Paul Spaeth or another former schoolteacher.[61] That said, the wooded and swampy surroundings certainly made it possible for priests to hide and hear pilgrims' confessions *near* the well. Saulnier, the Directory's commissioner to the Meurthe Department, made a plausible case for this possibility when he noted that pilgrims were proclaiming the necessity of "confessing to a *bon prêtre* (we know what that word means in counterrevolutionary language)." Otherwise, the pilgrims asserted, one could neither perceive the miracles occurring at the well nor be healed oneself. Saulnier concluded from these stories "that *bons prêtres* still exist, especially around the well."[62]

Even stronger evidence comes from a denunciation of the Hoste pilgrimage that Marie Anne Mangin, a patriotic inhabitant of Dieuze in the Meurthe Department, sent to the Directory in early August 1799. As Mangin explains in her letter, she struck up a conversation with a group of returning pilgrims while tending to her garden. Feigning excitement about the miracles of Hoste, she asked these pilgrims whether she might get an opportunity to confess her sins to a *bon prêtre* near the Good Well. They replied that they themselves had done so in one of the woods north of Hoste but also that these priests were disguised as peasants to avoid arrest. Upon further questioning from Mangin, the pilgrims told her about "a female religious who was present" as well and who "assured us that the night before, God and the Holy Virgin had spoken to them, that He had said that we needed a king." The exchange ended there, as Mangin tried unsuccessfully to alert her husband, the *adjoint communal* of Dieuze, so he would get the pilgrims arrested. To be sure, anticlerical exaggeration shaped how Mangin framed her letter: she insisted on "the villainy of priests" and warned the government that "if you don't clean up there, it could become a Vendée."[63] Yet this caveat need not lead us to suppose that she falsified the specific information she had received from the group of pilgrims. While nonjuring clergy could not control the events of Hoste, many a lay Catholic may well have sought contact with them to bestow additional, sacramental power on the pilgrimage.

Pilgrims also encountered subtle political commentary alongside exultation of miracles in the report written or at least disseminated by the local schoolteacher Spaeth. This pamphlet was exuberantly titled *An extraordinary and very singular miracle, knowledge of which has already spread into this land and which occurred on March 24 of the present year 1799, helping the just to persevere and inviting sinners to repentance and penitence*. Printed copies of the German original of this miracle report circulated "by the thousands" (according to one source) in the spring and summer of 1799; the handwritten French translation that made it into the Directory's police dossiers came from the departmental administration of the Bas-Rhin.[64] Interestingly, the pamphlet suggests specific prayers that Catholics should consider saying while on pilgrimage to Hoste. Where revolutionary officials saw "*des écrits fanatiques*,"[65] the historian discovers an intricate web of devotional and political references. The last few lines of the prayer, for instance, echo, on the one hand, the ending of the Hail Mary, while, on the other hand, the appeal to the Virgin as "protectress of France" hearkens back to the Bourbon monarchy, to Louis XIII, who consecrated the Kingdom of France to Mary in 1638: "Oh Mary our Mediatrix, protectress of France, always mother, do not abandon us, oh Mary mother of mercies, now and at the hour of our death. Amen."[66] New political struggles intertwined with old devotional formulas as Catholics flocked to Hoste in 1799, in "these alarming times" of revolution, as the author of the pamphlet called them.[67]

Among the secondary apparition places, the Bonlieu chapel in the forest north of Virton presents a possible case of deliberate political overtones directed against the expanding Grande Nation. To be sure, when eleven pilgrims were arrested by an army detachment in the woods and interrogated by a judge in the nearby town of Habay-la-Neuve, they struck no political notes at all. For instance, echoing all of his fellow pilgrims, a man named Charles Thiry declared that the group had simply "been hearing people saying for some time that miracles were occurring at the Bonlieu" and had decided "to go say their prayers in that place."[68] These pilgrims presumably understood that it would have been unwise to talk about politics if they wanted the judge to close the proceedings against them—which he did.[69] Yet they likely knew that the Virton forest had been the main gathering point for rebels in an anti-French insurrection that had rocked this western part of the Forêts Department in the spring of 1796, mere months after the French annexation of the Austrian Netherlands.[70] They may also have known that the order to demolish the old Marian chapel of Bonlieu had come from a special departmental commissioner sent from Luxembourg to quell that insurrection. Many other pilgrims probably learned about this fact at the pilgrimage place, seeing the recent ruins in which believers now gathered around a bottle with well water from Hoste.[71] In this context, by reappropriating Bonlieu in the summer of 1799, pilgrims implicitly enacted defiance on the Belgian frontier of the Grande Nation—especially after new, more serious and widespread insurrections had shaken the region very recently, in the fall of 1798.[72]

A clearer instance of politicized resistance related to the Hoste affair occurred in late July 1799 in Trier. There, two processions on a single day animated the city streets and exasperated local French officials. The first one formed after "a woman, who claims she was miraculously healed at the well of Hoste, went to the Church of Our Lady, gathered a great crowd there and especially women and children." She formed the center of this procession, "carrying before her a religious image." The second one was led by a man named Karl Kaspar Kirn and featured a child "that was allegedly also miraculously healed."[73] While the lone source offering information on this episode does not mention any bottles filled with well water, the far-flung impact of the Hoste events does emerge clearly. After all, over sixty miles separate Trier from Hoste, which had never belonged to either the Diocese or the Electorate of Trier. Crucially, moreover, Kirn was gaining prominence at the time as lay leader of a group of committed Catholics belonging to the city's Marian civic sodality (Bürgersodalität). This group repeatedly challenged the occupiers by using pilgrimages, processions, and petitions to mount an expressly politicized religious resistance to the new, French rulers over Trier.[74]

The Hoste affair had a few less confrontational facets as well. For one thing, the village priests of Chambrey and Bacourt, who solemnly installed bottles with apparitional water from Hoste on the altars of their parish churches, had sworn the oath on the Civil Constitution of the Clergy in 1791.[75]

In other words, they belonged to what had become the ex-constitutional French Church by the time of the Directory: a struggling but vigorous ecclesial community under the indefatigable leadership of Henri Grégoire, which still sought to reconcile Catholicism and revolutionary republicanism.[76] The role played by those two *curés* contradicted blanket assumptions, so frequent in high-level revolutionary discourse, that "suspicious" religious practice must be driven by *refractory* clergy. Perhaps even more intriguingly, a resident of Puttelange and ardent promoter of the Hoste miracles called Jean Guerber claimed in the summer of 1799 that pilgrims had actually seen a "patriotic" Virgin in blue, white, and red in the depths of the well.[77] This description evoked the tricolor flag, one of the symbolic keystones of France's new political culture. While antirevolutionary and (in annexed and occupied areas) anti-French sentiment clearly informed much place-making around Hoste, the affair was complex enough to allow for a measure of political ambiguity.

The reactions of anticlerical patriots, however, erased this ambiguity in a discourse that associated the apparitions directly and exclusively with the Counter-Revolution. We have glimpsed this discourse in the letters by Saulnier and Mangin, but two further examples may help to clarify this point. Warning the government about Bonlieu in late August 1799, a group of Luxembourgian republicans asserted that "fanatics and royalists converge massively on this place."[78] The central administration of the Moselle reflected at greater length on what they saw as the political geography of the initial apparition. In an *arrêté* of June 22, 1799, the administrators described "the topographic situation of the well of Hoste, considered from a political angle." They noted its proximity to the Meurthe and Bas-Rhin Departments as well as to the occupied left-bank Rhineland: because pilgrims were coming from these other regions, a territorial spillover was occurring through which the phenomenon was already exceeding the limits of competence and responsibility set for the Moselle administration. Worse still, according to the *arrêté*, the well was also "surrounded by forests that, on one side, stretch into the interior through the Departments of Meurthe and Vosges, and on the other side, toward the Rhine, where bandits were only waiting for our enemies to throw some minions onto the left bank and deliver the expected ammunition." For good measure, the administrators expressed their conviction that the pilgrims' movements were "directed by royalists, by agents of Austria and England"—in sum, that outside forces were threatening to "turn this Department into a new Vendée."[79] Administrators thus mobilized territorial thinking to explain how pilgrimage to Hoste was linked to all the other dangers besetting the Republic. In the process, they integrated the Moselle Department into a bigger picture of France's imperiled borders.

Yet in practice, agents of the state needed primarily to navigate the details of this picture in order to carry out effective administrative measures, and the devil was in those details. Internal, that is departmental, borders retained a dazzling complexity throughout the region, as my mention of the Rouhling/Lixing enclave has suggested. This complexity continued mainly because Lorraine, the Austrian Netherlands, and various other parts of the Holy Roman Empire each became absorbed into France at different moments in time. Departments created in different years thus necessarily inherited highly irregular border lines, as those lines had subsisted—at each step of French expansion—between the territory of the First Republic and different parts of the Holy Roman Empire.

This process happened to produce, among many other unintended effects, an unusual clustering of internal borders right around the area of Hoste and Sarreguemines (see map 4). Here, the Moselle Department narrowed into a thin territorial strip, sandwiched between the German-speaking part of the Meurthe Department in the south and the left-bank occupied lands in the north.[80] The northern borderline, between the Moselle and Saar Departments, was especially complex, despite late–Ancien Régime attempts to regularize this part of the border between France and the Holy Roman Empire.[81] Furthermore, just south of Sarreguemines, the County of Saarwerden, an old imperial enclave within France, had turned in 1793 into a northwestern salient of the Bas-Rhin Department (colorfully called the Alsace bossue, or Alsatian Hunchback), adding another internal border that ran quite close to Hoste.[82] In short, departmental boundaries had multiplied around what became the apparition place in 1799—and these were above all boundaries *for* revolutionary administrators, boundaries of their respective competence.

Therefore, as soon as pilgrim movement to Hoste outgrew its small-scale origins, the complexity of departmental borders hampered the coordination of state responses to the events. Relatively early on, the departmental administration of the Moselle gave guidance on reinforcing passport controls to those of its subordinate cantonal administrations which were responsible for the region surrounding Hoste. But some of these seats of cantonal authority, such as Morhange, were in fact farther away from the Good Well than Saarbrücken in the Saar Department or Sarre-Union in the Bas-Rhin, and there is no evidence that the administration of the Moselle ever reached out horizontally to the authorities of either of those departments.[83] It preferred to report vertically to the Ministry of Police—which, however, did not always act as an effective coordinating hub. For example, when the zealous cantonal commissioner of Bascharage (Forêts) reported directly to Paris, skipping his departmental administration at Luxembourg, the Ministry responded by writing a letter to the central administration of the Moselle rather than to that of the Forêts. Why? It seems that the Parisian police bureaucrats failed even to recognize that Bascharage was situated quite far (almost seventy miles) from Hoste and in a different department.[84] Furthermore, by July 10, when the Ministry finally got around to alerting the departmental administration of the Bas-Rhin, this authority had already begun taking measures spontaneously.[85] If the revolutionary state had great difficulties controlling and repressing pilgrim movement to Hoste, they were due in part to how badly leading officials handled the complex administrative geography of France's northeastern territorial edge.

In particular, the weak official response in the Bas-Rhin held great significance to the Hoste affair because of the special politico-religious climate that prevailed in this Alsatian department. In the religious history of the French Revolution, the Bas-Rhin is well known for having the highest percentage of refractory priests among all French departments in 1791, the year of the oath on the Civil Constitution of the Clergy. Though far from being the only causal factor here, border complications contributed their fair share to this situation. The Diocese of Strasbourg was a border-crossing territory, straddling French Alsace and the southwestern Holy Roman Empire. Operating from his remaining stronghold on the right bank of the Rhine, the last Old Regime bishop, Cardinal Rohan, had ample opportunity to sway his clergy against the Civil Constitution.[86] The ensuing religious troubles were compounded in 1799 by the military defeats I have discussed, and the miracles of Hoste catalyzed a fusion of these two crises, notably in the Alsatian Hunchback area. In late June, the fortress commander at Saarlouis, Sauveton, commented on the high desertion rates in the Bas-Rhin—especially "around Bouquenom [part of Sarre-Union], a canton bordering on that of Puttelange, where an allegedly miraculous Virgin attracts a considerable influx of fanatics."[87] Already in early June, local officials in Puttelange had noticed the arrival at the Good Well of "unknown people, suspected to be émigrés or draft-dodgers or deserters."[88] In other words, as France's military front moved west toward the Rhine, pilgrimage to Hoste helped destabilize both eastern Lorraine and Alsace on the exposed margins of the Republic.

In sum, the Good Well and several secondary apparition sites became political rallying points in 1799 for Catholics who held little formal authority but boasted great strength in numbers across the region. Politically either ambiguous or subversive, this massive mobilization eluded revolutionary officials' attempts to classify or to control it. German-speaking populations easily gathered around the Good Well; then again, the areas of Virton, Mars-la-Tour, Chambrey, and Bacourt were French-speaking, and Lieutenant Rapin reported from the Francophone region of Pont-à-Mousson that the Good Well "attracts today the idiots, the simple-minded, the fanatics of all the communes of my district."[89] While Paul Spaeth's miracle report about Hoste gave an oblique royalist tip of the hat to Louis XIII's Marian vow, Jean Guerber sought to improve the reputation of the Good Well by celebrating a tricolor Virgin. Moreover, the process of French expansion had created a complicated landscape of internal borders in the northeast, and revolutionary officials repeatedly lost their bearings while navigating this landscape to try to halt pilgrim movement toward the Good Well. Yet, as I will show next, repressive measures did have significant effects—albeit mostly unintended ones, as pilgrims responded to policing efforts by pioneering new patterns of devotional movement.

Writing Hoste into the History of Apparitions

The apparitions of 1799 constitute one of the most overlooked twists in the long history of Marian apparitions. That history abounds with surprises and contingencies. Yet we can hardly apprehend it without considering the one aspect that has drawn by far the greatest attention among scholars and the wider, indeed global public—namely, the extraordinary appeal of apparitions in Roman Catholicism since the nineteenth century. Dupront, for instance, wrote with verve about "the apparitions of the Virgin, this great fact of the sacred in the modern period."[90] Summarizing a very complex phenomenon as effectively as possible, we can say that a powerful combination of four features accounts for this modern prominence of apparitions in the Catholic world: the public charisma of individual seers; the poignancy of

Mary's messages; the high stakes of confrontation with hostile state authorities; and the fluidity of proliferating holy places. In the story of Hoste and its secondary apparition sites, public focus on seers and messages from Mary play no discernible role. The other two features, however—confrontation with the state and fluidity of place—appear crucial. What is more, they represent the genuine and innovative contribution of revolutionary-era Catholics to that longer, complex history of apparitions. Pilgrims in 1799 experimented with fluidity and created effects of spatial overflow—not least in response to passport issues and heavy-handed revolutionary *police du culte*. As a comparative look at Marian apparitions in modern Europe reveals, these spillover effects went on to become a central trait of Catholic mobilization, most notably during the *Kulturkampf* of the 1870s and again in the 1930s.

The challenge is to situate the events of 1799 in the history of Marian apparitions without misconstruing them as a point on a supposed pathway leading step by step toward modernity. To begin meeting this challenge, it makes sense to point out elements of long continuity—three characteristics that have recurred time and again in apparitions at least since the late Middle Ages. First, whether in the fifteenth and sixteenth or the nineteenth and twentieth centuries, the seers were disproportionately often children. Medieval Christians as well as later Catholics often believed these seers, viewing childhood innocence and simplicity as qualities that would naturally make Mary prefer to appear and speak to young boys and girls. In the case of Hoste, Spaeth's miracle report did not fail to mention that the Virgin first appeared on March 24, 1799, to "six innocent children, twelve to thirteen years of age."[91] Second, the importance of wells and sacred water—so central to the apparitions of 1799—may have grown since the events of Lourdes in 1858, but already in many earlier apparitions, seers reported that Mary designated wells or springs as the special places she had come to sanctify.[92] Early modern holy wells were often consecrated to Our Lady, and Spaeth's pamphlet echoes Baroque publications in emphasizing entanglements of Marian and aquatic symbolism.[93] Finally, the promise of miraculous healing constitutes a third feature of the *longue durée*, drawing countless pilgrims to Marian apparition places ever since medieval times. As my earlier discussion of Gertrude Derving's and other women's spectacular healings at the Good Well indicates, this aspect applies to the pilgrimages of 1799 as well.

Yet some things did change over the centuries, albeit often in a nonlinear manner, and consequently modern apparitions stand out in the four significant ways to which I already alluded. In the fifteenth through seventeenth centuries, apparitions usually "took place offstage." Even where they sparked a new pilgrimage, they remained private experiences, often unmentioned in the historical record until years or even decades later. By contrast, the famous modern apparition cycles of Lourdes, Fátima, or Medjugorje have unfolded as public dramas, as seminal encounters between seers and pilgrim crowds both during and after the moments of apparition.[94] In modern times, seers also took on a new role as transmitters of poignant divine messages with far-reaching implications. Around 1500, Mary might admonish a local community to repent and request that a chapel be built at the apparition site; at Fátima in the pivotal year of 1917, she announced little less than an imminent global apocalypse.[95] As the messages grew more urgent and provocative, so did the politics surrounding apparitions and resulting pilgrimage movements. This development came to a head in the 1870s, when the devoutly Catholic and proudly liberal forces of the time collided with unprecedented force and state-sponsored anti-Catholicism peaked. Millions of pilgrims then turned established as well as brand-new apparition places in republican France and Bismarck's Germany into politically explosive sites.[96] Finally, as I discuss in detail below, these clashes of the modern era tended to provoke a spatial spillover of the holy.

What I am arguing here is *only* that many of the most famous apparitions from La Salette onward combined all four of these characteristics and that this combination was new in the mid-nineteenth century. I am *not* arguing that *all* great apparitions after those of La Salette evinced all four features, as if they formed a tight bundle or "package" of elements indispensable to apparitional "modernity."[97] For example, Mary reportedly did not convey any verbal message when appearing to villagers in Knock, Ireland, in 1879. This silence has not prevented Knock from becoming a pilgrimage place almost as well-known and well-frequented as Fátima.[98] Nor am I claiming that each of the four features, considered separately, only came into existence in the mid-nineteenth century. The history of early modern apparitions is not devoid, for instance, of seers who became charismatic public figures quickly, while continuing to report encounters with Mary over extended periods. One of these earlier charismatic seers, the shepherdess Benoîte Rencurel from Le Laus in the French Alps, experienced apparitions from 1664 until her death in 1718.⁹⁹ In other words, there is neither a stable apparition "package" nor a singular point of origin for its components. Rather, each apparition draws on multiple currents that emerged at different moments and that have combined, shifted, and recombined continually. The revolutionary decade matters in this story as one of the moments in which new currents first formed.

The events of 1799 do not evince all of the four characteristics I just outlined. The copious police dossiers on Hoste never mention the initial six seers to whom Spaeth alluded only briefly and without giving any names in his miracle report. These children did not become public personalities, let alone living saints. They resembled the Spanish village seers of the decades around 1500 much more than Bernadette Soubirous of Lourdes or Lúcia dos Santos and the other two seers of Fátima. Moreover, Mary seems not to have uttered any verbal messages in 1799, unlike in La Salette, Lourdes, Fátima, and other more recent apparition places. These observations make it impossible to embed the apparitions of Hoste and beyond easily within the history of modern Marian apparitions. That said, the sequence of 1799 is chronologically removed from early modern predecessors as well: eighteenth-century Catholic Europe before 1789 had witnessed extremely few apparitions and none of them had generated much attention.¹⁰⁰

The impact of a hostile state and pilgrims' responses to that hostility shaped the events of 1799 in a way that likewise sets them apart from early modern apparitions. To be sure, war, invasion, and political upheaval had often fostered Marian effervescence among Catholics for centuries. Famous cases include the devotion to Our Lady of Guadalupe in early colonial Mexico and the miracle stories about how the Polish fortress and Marian shrine of Częstochowa withstood a Swedish siege in 1655.¹⁰¹ Yet within these contexts of general crisis, the specific issue of state-sponsored repression did not move to center stage. Even in Protestant parts of Europe, measures against travel to holy wells and other pilgrimage places were by no means as systematic or harsh as one might assume. German Lutheran elites left space and legitimacy for some religious practices tied to visits of "miracle wells" (*Wunderbrunnen*). English Puritans also did not radically curb place-making efforts at such wells but rather recoded these efforts in a medical, balneological, theologically sanitized key.¹⁰² By contrast, a new level of intensity and new dynamics of politicization characterize the severe policing of worship to which the agents of the revolutionary French state aspired in the 1790s.¹⁰³

Legitimized in terms of *police du culte*, the various measures of state repression ended up weakening the initial pilgrimage to Hoste. The municipal administration of Puttelange made a first attempt to stop the gatherings of pilgrims at the well by sending a commission of three officials accompanied by five gendarmes from Sarreguemines, as decided in an *arrêté* of May 5, 1799.[104] After a brief lull around Pentecost, it became clear that the pilgrimage continued stronger than before, so on May 22, the departmental administration weighed in, deciding to ask the commander of the Third Military Division at Metz, General Morlot, to provide "armed forces sufficient" to block access to the apparition site.[105] It took Morlot almost two weeks to delegate this request to the commander of the fortress of Saarlouis (called Sarrelibre at the time), who finally dispatched thirty hussars to Puttelange on June 6.[106] The soldiers were not only somewhat late but also failed to effectively cut pilgrims off from access to the well water, preferring instead to monopolize and monetize that access: as the gendarmerie lieutenant Rapin reported, the hussars sold the water to pilgrims "at five to six *sols* the bottle."[107] Little wonder that the commissioner of the departmental administration, Legoux, sent them back immediately when he arrived on the scene a few days later—accompanied by a second, much larger detachment of two hundred infantrymen and two cannons. Legoux succeeded in disbanding the crowds around the apparition site, and he had the well blocked with rocks. After he and the soldiers left, new pilgrims kept arriving throughout the summer, but their numbers slowly dwindled.[108]

A stable sense of sacred place was thus almost impossible to achieve for pilgrims, especially when they tried to move the focus of their activity from the watery, forested margins to established parochial centers of worship. The main police dossier on the affair contains a report about two processions leading from the well to the parish church of Hoste in a single day. The first aimed to transport a bottle in which the Virgin seemed to appear to the church, but two gendarmes intervened, confiscating the bottle and disbanding the procession. The second accompanied Gertrude Derving to the parish church to celebrate her miraculous recovery of speech after fourteen years. Here, too, the gendarmerie stepped in, arresting both Derving and two of her male family members.[109] In Chambrey and Bacourt, after pilgrims had brought bottles containing the Virgin or Jesus back home from Hoste, the parishioners formed processions led by their local priests (*curés*), who solemnly placed these bottles on the altars of the respective parish churches.¹¹⁰ Yet pilgrimages to these two villages lasted only a few weeks, not least because parish churches were relatively easy targets for the revolutionary state: "The bottles displayed for the veneration of citizens in the temples of Bacourt and Chambrey have been removed and the temples have been closed without opposition," as departmental administrators soon noted.¹¹¹ These episodes show how difficult revolutionary officials made it for pilgrims to balance the place-making fluidity facilitated by the water with a measure of stability. Indeed, the proliferation of short-term pilgrimage places in the summer of 1799 suggests that Catholics, unable to ensure that stability, resorted all the more readily to fluid place-making and spatial overflow.

But the struggle between pilgrims and agents of the state did not just unfold at apparition sites and churches; it also played out along the innumerable routes the pilgrims took to reach their destinations across the region. Passport surveillance by gendarmes and local administrative or military authorities gained a crucial role in this respect. The Directory had inherited some passport legislation from the late Thermidorian Convention. A law of 10 vendémiaire an IV (October 2, 1795) stipulated that no French citizen could travel outside of their home canton—a remarkably small territorial unit—without a passport signed by the members of the respective urban municipality or cantonal administration. Another law of 28 vendémiaire an VI (October 19, 1797) added the requirement that the travel destination be noted on each passport.¹¹² In early June 1799, when the pilgrim movement toward Hoste was peaking, revolutionary officials decided to stimulate the enforcement of these legal dispositions in the Canton of Puttelange and the surrounding region. In a circular letter to nine cantonal commissioners, the central commissioner of the Moselle admonished them: "Give the strictest and clearest orders to the national gendarmerie, to garrisoned troops if there are any in your canton, or to the mobile column in order to have seized, arrested," and brought before the justice of the peace any strangers "heading toward Hoste without passports."¹¹³

This reminder had limited effect, as French authorities found it much harder to control pilgrims on the move—and the sacrally charged water they transported—than to crack down on any one specific site of worship. A departmental gendarmerie report from late June included a note that the brigade of Morhange, more than twenty miles southwest of Hoste, had arrested an atypically large number of individuals (thirty-seven men) traveling without passports and apparently on their way to the Good Well.¹¹⁴

Already in May, the brigade of Sarreguemines had arrested fifteen citizens without passports at the apparition place itself. But the judicial branch of the revolutionary state had then proved utterly uninterested in punishing these pilgrims.[115] Nor did the national guards collaborate well with the gendarmerie on this point.[116] In sum, administrators and gendarmes mounted a noticeable effort of using the territorial technique of passport surveillance in order to get a handle on the pilgrimage, but this effort may not have produced a major impact.[117]

The impact was rather small not just because the gendarmerie could not control every road and trail in the region but also because pilgrims had been familiarizing themselves with the world of passports for centuries before the Revolution. As early as the fifteenth century, pilgrims grappled routinely with the need for travel documents, at least if the destination was far from home (for example, Rome for those living north of the Alps).[118] In the eighteenth century, passports often circulated among individuals moving in the interstices between pilgrimage and vagabondage, and pilgrims turned to a wide variety of civil and ecclesiastical authorities in order to obtain the documentation they needed to face border and other territorial controls.[119] Indeed, for the particular case of Hoste, the sparse available evidence suggests that a vast majority of pilgrims did succeed at getting passports, even relatively late in the summer of 1799, when most authorities in the region had grown aware of this religious phenomenon.[120] Above all, we have a telling set of numbers from a Sarreguemines gendarmerie lieutenant who accompanied an expeditionary force of one hundred dragoons to the Good Well in late July. These soldiers managed to seize some two hundred pilgrims, "sleeping in rooms, granaries, stables, and even cellars, of all ages and sexes." They shepherded the crowd into the parish church of Hoste and then ordered people to come back out one by one for individual passport controls. Of the two hundred, "only twenty-seven" did *not* have a passport on them.[121] In other words, based on this acceptably random and sizeable sample, almost seven-eighths of all pilgrims—across boundaries of age and gender—made sure to get passports before heading toward Hoste. Catholics thus proved adept at taking the techniques of a hostile territorial state apparatus into account while contributing to the making of a sacred space.

What is more, the French revolutionaries had reorganized the border between Lorraine and neighboring regions in ways that facilitated the passport game for Catholics wishing to go on pilgrimage to Hoste. France annexed the Austrian Netherlands in 1795 and, beginning in late 1797, gradually promulgated the laws of the Revolution in the occupied left-bank Rhineland, as I mentioned above. Therefore, by 1799, inhabitants of these two regions only needed internal passports to cross legally into Lorraine—as opposed to the external passports they would have to obtain if they wanted to cross *national* borders.[122] On the terms of the law of 10 vendémiaire an IV (October 2, 1795), the bureaucratic hurdles for obtaining internal passports remained relatively low and local, as municipal or cantonal administrations were responsible for issuing certificates of this kind. Some cantonal commissioners in the Forêts and Saar Departments did grow wary when an increasing number of people demanded passports for travel to the Cantons of Puttelange or Saint-Avold.[123] Yet it is plausible to suspect that many more municipal administrations remained quiet and kept issuing passports to hopeful pilgrims—not least because, as the Ministry of Police itself recognized, no clear legal foundation existed for making the issuance of internal passports contingent on proof that a citizen's motives for travel were pressing and respectable from a patriotic viewpoint.[124] Thus, pilgrims had the upper hand in terms of the mobility that constantly enabled spatial overflow of sacred water, while hostile state authorities did manage to disrupt Catholics' attempts at stabilizing their apparition places.

The timing of the secondary apparitions also suggests that pilgrims stayed one step ahead of the police by practicing spillover rather than stability and rapidly valorizing new holy places when necessary. For example, in the first half of a letter sent to the Ministry of Police on June 15, 1799, the departmental administrators of the Moselle congratulated themselves on having reestablished public order at the Good Well with the help of Special Commissioner Legoux and two hundred soldiers. Now, "we hope there will no longer be any question of this gathering on our territory." Yet immediately thereafter, the second part of the letter announced that the pilgrimage might not have disappeared so much as shifted its destination: "We are informed that [the gathering] has re-formed in a commune of the Meurthe Department."[125] And indeed, on June 22, confirmation came from Nancy, *chef-lieu* of the Meurthe, in a letter from commissioner Saulnier notifying the Ministry of Police that pilgrims were now flocking by the thousands to a newly established holy site in his department. A few weeks later, Saulnier informed the government in turn that, on the one hand, his administration had effectively counteracted pilgrim gatherings not only in Bacourt but also in Chambrey and Plaine-de-Walsch, two other villages of the Meurthe. On the other hand, "the allegedly miraculous Virgin," now "chased away" from both the Moselle and the Meurthe Departments, "has just escaped to a well in the Bas-Rhin," probably Marienthal, where she was "still attracting a following of thousands of pilgrims."[126]

The pilgrims of 1799 thus inaugurated a logic of spatial overflow that would serve Catholics well in later, critical moments of heightened state pressure on religious practice. The fluid, ephemeral, and sharply contested place-making of 1799 presents striking similarities with the especially frequent apparitions of the 1870s, another decade of great upheaval from the Franco-Prussian War to the *Kulturkampf*.[127] Numerous apparitions occurred during the same decade in the Franco-German borderlands. This time, borders had just shifted to the disadvantage of France, with the German annexation of Elsass-Lothringen in 1871. Across the annexed province, Catholics reported recurring Marian apparitions near the Alsatian village of Neubois (1872) but also in L'Hôpital (less than ten miles northwest of Hoste; 1872), Bettviller, Diding, Guising, Reipertswiller, Rixheim, Sarreinsberg, Walbach, and Wittelsheim (all in 1873). In the case of Neubois, Catholics even reported offshoot apparitions that recall the secondary pilgrimage sites of 1799.[128] Finally and most spectacularly, in 1876, Mary appeared to several children near the village of Marpingen, situated in the Saarland about thirty miles north of Hoste. This event sparked a genuine mass mobilization of pilgrims.[129] Heavy-handed repressive measures only accelerated the currents of Catholic enthusiasm and made them more elusive—much the same effects as those produced in 1799 around Hoste.

Likewise, just when the newly proclaimed Second Spanish Republic seemed to embark on an anti-Catholic agenda in 1931, countless women and children reported apparitions of Mary and drew pilgrims to dozens and perhaps hundreds of villages, first in the Spanish Basque Country and then across northern and central Spain.[130] Later in the 1930s, pilgrims responded subversively to anti-Catholic crackdowns in Nazi Germany by seeking out numerous new and old apparition places—most notably Heede, Dittrichswalde (present-day Gietrzwałd), and again Marpingen.[131] In short, pilgrims returned to the spillover pattern whenever political crisis and state pressure reached a higher pitch.[132]

Therefore, the events of 1799 ultimately represent a moment of structural innovation. To be sure, there is no genealogical connection to later apparitions because Hoste never gained national fame as a place of Marian devotion and was indeed no longer a well-known pilgrimage place by the time of the famous apparitions in Paris (rue du Bac, 1830), La Salette (1846), and Lourdes (1858).[133] But the apparition waves of the 1790s, 1870s, and 1930s show how, in moments of crisis, Catholics repeatedly engaged in a particular type of transgressive place-making—rhizomatic, fluid, enacting a logic of spatial spillover. More specifically, around Hoste in 1799, they faced a revolutionary, highly restrictive *police du culte* and responded by creating a powerful network of ephemeral holy places.

The Fleeting Sacred

Today, a tiny chapel hides among the ponds, woods, and meadows that characterize the landscape around Hoste. The Chapel of the Good Well (chapelle de la Bonne Fontaine) is a modern edifice, and local erudition reports that earlier, nineteenth-century efforts to build one at this site foundered against an episcopal veto. In that period, devout Catholics hoping for a miraculous healing sometimes came here, and a few of them left votive offerings either on the spot or at the parish church of Hoste.[134] Yet the nineteenth century never saw a massive influx of pilgrims to the chapel, and today this place is nearly forgotten outside the community of parishes Saint-Jean de Neuwiese, to which Hoste now belongs.[135]

The village itself, too, has all the qualities of a small, peripheral place unlikely to attract much attention. Its population has been dwindling rapidly for years. In 2020, it amounted to little more than six hundred, a figure that includes the inhabitants of a neighboring hamlet.[136] The Autoroute de l'Est passes nearby, but only occasionally do trains stop at the closest railroad station in Farschviller, several miles to the north. In short, Hoste remains on the spatial margins between French- and German-speaking Europe, as it did at the end of the eighteenth century. That very marginality, however, not only conditioned but in some ways even fostered Hoste's momentary prominence as the most notable place of Marian apparitions in revolutionary Europe.

Believers joined in the making of a sacred space with an extraordinary energy that reflects the depths of anxiety generated by the French Revolution's religious policies. Ironically, attempts by revolutionary administrators and gendarmes to stymie this energy only heightened its dynamics in the short run. Many pilgrims reacted defiantly to the threat of an encounter with gendarmerie and regular troops. Above all, when agents of the state effectively disrupted place-making at Hoste, these interventions encouraged Catholics to switch to a plurality of *other* places in which to celebrate the miraculous qualities of the water. Pilgrims adjusted their perceptions of the miraculous, heightening their sense of its fluidity as they exploited the potential of the well water to bring a sacral charge to other places across the region. In this way, the revolutionary situation helped give birth to a new type of devotional space: ephemeral, volatile, elusive, increasingly diffuse, and polycentric. In 1799, Catholics in Lorraine and neighboring regions thus responded creatively to the modern state's policing of worship on the destabilized territorial margins. This pattern would recur in those same regions in the 1870s, following the German annexation of Alsace-Lorraine and during the *Kulturkampf.* Therefore, the apparitions of Hoste and beyond underscore the formative nature of religious change around 1800—as well as the contribution that Catholic pilgrims made to border culture under the pressure of the Revolution.

5

The Making of an Imperial Mass Pilgrimage

Sometime in 1799 or 1800, Karl Kaspar Kirn sent a short and provocative letter to the municipal administration of French-occupied Trier, his hometown. We have encountered Kirn in the previous chapter, as a confraternity leader who celebrated the miracles of Hoste by leading a procession through the streets of Trier in July 1799. On many other occasions, too, he flouted restrictions that the new authorities had imposed on public demonstrations of Catholicism. After receiving a warning from the administration, he penned his letter, beginning with the words, "Praise be to Jesus Christ." Even though he called himself the "most devoted servant" of the municipality, he stated that he would obey its order only "insofar as it does not contradict the will of God and His highest honor." He added a rather irreverent postscript: "N.B. I reserve the right to give a real response on this matter later."[1] A fervent Catholic and organizer of controversial pilgrimages—as we will see in the first section of this chapter—Kirn embodied a direct challenge to the same repressive, late revolutionary policing of worship that pilgrims encountered around Hoste and the other apparition sites in 1799.

Kirn's activities contrast starkly with the event that truly makes Trier stand out in the history of revolutionary-era pilgrimage. Between September 9 and 27, 1810, over two hundred thousand people converged on Trier Cathedral to see a relic called the Holy Coat (heiliger Rock), a garment said to be the seamless robe worn by Jesus at the time of his crucifixion. Apart from the emperor's coronation in 1804, the scope and significance of this pilgrimage dwarfed those of any other religious event in the Napoleonic period. Catholics journeyed to Trier in September 1810 from the city's immediate hinterland but also from other parts of the Rhineland, Luxembourg, and Lorraine. It was a gigantic show of piety, deeply embedded in an imperial context, officially planned and presided over by the French bishop of Trier, Charles Mannay, who served as one of Napoleon's foremost ecclesiastical counselors.[2] Pilgrim participation exceeded all expectations, surprising the bishop and unsettling state officials. Unlike Kirn's provocations a decade earlier, however, the showing of the Holy Coat did not produce any severe tensions between pilgrims and police, or between Catholic clergy and the government. Such relative lack of conflict is by no means obvious: after all, pilgrimage was "constantly at the center of the Napoleonic administration's malevolent attention."[3] Moreover, the pope had excommunicated Napoleon and been kidnapped by the French in 1809, just one year before the great pilgrimage to Trier. How could this showing of the Holy Coat even take place, let alone turn into a mass spectacle and a peaceful triumph of Catholicism in the imperial borderlands?

In answering this question, I will show that pilgrims and pilgrimage organizers ensured the postrevolutionary reassertion of their faith not only by resisting the empire but also by *using* it to their advantage.[4] In other words, they harnessed the empire's power, adapted to its structural features, and exploited its loopholes. These strategies did not amount to anything like the full-fledged rejection of Napoleonic takeover and reform that drove the postrevolutionary renewal of Catholicism in Italy and Spain.[5] North of the Alps and the Pyrenees, anti-imperial resistance occurred on a much smaller scale, making it easy to overlook Napoleonic-era stirrings of Catholic renewal in that relatively peaceful, well-assimilated "inner empire" or "imperial core" that included most of France and Rhenish Germany.[6] Looking for major flashpoints of popular Catholic resistance, and finding none in these regions, historians of Napoleonic Europe have tended to move on quickly. The showing of the Holy Coat merits attention because it pushes us to complement this focus on resistance and crisis by analyzing the usable empire. But the great pilgrimage of 1810 also allows us to assess how border culture evolved once the revolutionary decade was over.

More specifically, I argue that pilgrimage to Trier benefited in three ways from what Napoleonic elites could and could not accomplish in their efforts to expand and manage France's borders.[7] First, by establishing the Rhine border and thus splitting the old Archbishopric-Electorate of Trier that had straddled the river, the French forced a reckoning over *trierisch* relics. As a result, Bishop Mannay managed to retrieve the Holy Coat for the episcopal city after it had spent most of the preceding 150 years on the other side of the Rhine. Second, the bishop responded aptly to the Napoleonic imperative of order, including spatial order, by using the boundaries of his diocese as a territorial frame to legitimize the pilgrimage of 1810. Yet who would enforce those boundaries, and what did public order mean in practice during the showing of the Holy Coat? Indeed, a third major aspect is that lay Catholics made massive use of loopholes to shape the contours of the pilgrimage in their own ways. Most notably, around one hundred thousand pilgrims came unauthorized, from outside the diocese, especially because its new territory largely did not coincide with the areas whose Catholic populations had regarded Trier as a holy city for centuries.

The making of mass pilgrimage in 1810 thus reveals the ambiguities of border culture in Napoleonic times. French imperial hegemony over continental Europe meant that the territorial revolution continued. Moreover, an authoritarian border regime was establishing itself, building on the foundations laid by late French revolutionary governments. As historian Michael Rowe has suggested, many a repressive nineteenth-century border policy was inspired by the Napoleonic "step-change in the development of institutions to police borders." This development ranged from customs agencies to complicated passport rules that even affected mobility across internal, administrative boundaries such as those of cantons and departments.[8] Yet the great pilgrimage of 1810 shows that unruly mobility continued to matter as an essential ingredient of border culture, even when people did not express any hostility to Napoleonic rule and its "hegemonic borderscape."[9] The pilgrims of September 1810 and Bishop Mannay, who organized the event, acted much less subversively than Kirn and his fellow confraternity members had done a decade prior. From another perspective, however, they all belong to the same story—the story of Catholics' persistent quest to access and remake holy places in the borderlands. To grasp the full significance of this quest, we first need to follow Trier's trajectory as a holy city through the late eighteenth-century crisis that culminated in Kirn's clashes with local authorities.

Pilgrims and the Struggle over Holy Trier

Toward the end of the eighteenth century, pious visitors encountered Trier as a place with a glorious past—but also as a struggling city for which pilgrimage was becoming a critical answer to mounting challenges. The regional politics and religious reforms of the decades before and during the French Revolution seriously undermined Trier's status as both the capital of the eponymous archbishopric-electorate and a pilgrimage center. As the situation escalated toward 1800, lay pilgrims got increasingly used to acting independently and defying military, civil, and ecclesiastical authorities if necessary.

In early modern times, Trier had been one of three European "pilgrimage capitals" alongside Rome and Cologne, because the city combined the assets of a great pilgrimage place and a territorial center.[10] Aside from the increasingly rare showings of the Holy Coat (none occurred at the cathedral between 1655 and 1810), Trier's best-known pilgrimage site was the suburban St. Matthias' Abbey, well frequented since the twelfth century as the only place north of the Alps that contained the tomb of an apostle.[11] Over seventy confraternities devoted to St. Matthias organized annual pilgrimages, typically across large distances because most confraternities were located in towns of the northern Rhineland. From there, it took pilgrims between four days and a week to walk all the way south to Trier. At the height of the season, right before Pentecost, more than ten thousand people would visit the abbey in a single week, at least in busy years.[12] Overall, more than fifty thousand pious visitors per year came to the city.[13] This devotional influx massively shaped and supported the topos that had first appeared on Trier's municipal seal in the central Middle Ages and epitomized the city's reputation ever since: Sancta Treveris, Holy Trier.[14]

Thus, at the dawn of the revolutionary age, Trier was regionally important and even famous, but that fame had more to do with a glorious past than with contemporary dynamism. The city had been a major Roman imperial residence in Late Antiquity, and when a strong hagiographical tradition developed there in the tenth to twelfth centuries, it easily connected the presence of major relics to imperial glory. Saint Helen, the mother of Constantine the Great, had allegedly offered the early Christian community of Trier many of the treasures she had discovered during her journey to the Holy Land—including the Holy Coat, the bones of the apostle Matthias, and one of the nails from Jesus's crucifixion.[15] The archbishop-elector of Trier also governed a vast diocese and—as a temporal ruler—a sizeable territory of the Holy Roman Empire, from the confines of Luxembourg down the Moselle Valley to Koblenz and on to the right bank of the Rhine (see map 1). Parts of the diocese, however, were lost due to the Protestant Reformation, and neighboring France's wars hit Trier hard in the seventeenth century. The city struggled economically and demographically. Around 1695, fewer than three thousand people lived inside its walls. A quick recovery ensued in the first half of the eighteenth century, but in the decades after 1750, the number of inhabitants stagnated again, this time at around eight thousand.[16]

Even within the Electorate of Trier, the episcopal city was ceding ground to its main rival, Koblenz—a trend reflected in the history of the Holy Coat. Located more centrally within the Holy Roman Empire and less exposed to French military incursions, Koblenz served as the main residence of the archbishop-electors in the eighteenth century. The last archbishop, Clemens Wenceslaus (1768–1802), showered particular attention on Koblenz while treating Trier as a backwater.[17] His predecessors, to be sure, had sponsored several prestigious projects in Trier, not least a magnificent Baroque chapel dedicated to the Holy Coat and built between 1687 and 1710 within the choir of the cathedral. But the large and highly visible reliquary in the front of that chapel remained empty.[18] Except in the years 1759–65, the electors now kept the relic at their fortress Ehrenbreitstein, on the right bank of the Rhine opposite Koblenz. Moreover, Archbishop-Elector Johann Philipp von Walderdorff (1756–68) organized the eighteenth century's only public showing of the relic right after its return to Ehrenbreitstein, on May 4, 1765. Many thousands of pilgrims rushed to catch a glimpse of the Coat and have their personal objects of devotion—rosaries, pious images, and so on—touch the powerful relic.[19] This event showed just how tenuous Trier's status as a pilgrimage capital had become.[20]

The crisis of Sancta Treveris reached the next level in the mid-1780s and prompted the municipality and lay burghers to step up, responding to the more general restrictive measures enacted by Clemens Wenceslaus that I discussed in chapter 2. Nobody could stop lay Catholics from going on less official, individual or small-group trips to Trier around the traditional feast days, and indeed, many pilgrims still came to the city—but probably not nearly as many as before the electoral decree of 1784.[21] The burghers of Trier even claimed in a petition to the elector that his move to restrict pilgrimage processions was reducing the income of the city's merchants and artisans by a whopping total of thirty thousand *Reichstaler* each year.[22] The assembled burghers (*Bürgerschaft*) also pressured Clemens Wenceslaus via a petition addressed to the cathedral chapter in August 1789. Among other things, they asked him specifically to reinstate the yearly solemn procession that led from the cathedral to St. Matthias' Abbey on the feast of the Nativity of Mary (September 8) and that had fallen victim to the 1784 decree as well. The government acquiesced quickly.[23] Moreover, in January 1790, Clemens Wenceslaus instructed the General Vicariate to allow all pilgrimage processions to the cathedral as well as to St. Matthias to take place again.[24] Laypeople's initiatives in defense of pilgrimage processions and related festivals clearly paid off in this case.

After the French conquest of the region in 1794, events of 1797 to 1800 intensified the battle over occupied Trier as a holy place.[25] A small but extremely vocal and active group of burghers fought this battle openly, defying the French occupying military as well as administrative authorities. That group was known as the Burghers' Marian Sodality (Marianische Bürgersodalität), a confraternity of devout laymen founded by Jesuits and brought under the direction of the Augustinian friars after the papacy had suppressed the Society of Jesus in 1773. The sodality boasted a large membership of nearly three hundred in the later eighteenth century.[26] Its spiritual director, a friar named Ernst Kronenberger, had been preaching along Counter-Enlightenment lines since around 1790, most notably when the sodality gathered at the Jesuits' church on Sundays. In the later 1790s, his published sermons exalted "Trier! holy Trier!" as a "German Jerusalem," proud and splendid but now castigated by war and occupation, and more durably and radically threatened by freemasons as well as other forces of false Enlightenment.[27] In 1797 and 1798, he also engaged in an escalating polemic against local champions of the Catholic Enlightenment who were questioning pilgrimage practices, the belief in miracles, and the authenticity of Trier's foremost relics—including the Holy Coat and the Holy Nail.[28]

Kronenberger's public presence should not obscure the fact that lay members of the Marian sodality—far from serving as mere marionettes—pulled most of the strings themselves. After April 1798, when Kronenberger fled eastward to escape arrest and deportation by the French police, the lay leaders of the Marian sodality only intensified their struggle.[29] Above all, they carried out frequent, spectacular, and illegal processions through the streets of Trier and south to St. Matthias.[30] In August 1799, the French Directory itself intervened with a decree that placed Kirn, the most prominent of these radical lay Catholics, under municipal surveillance.[31] Even in 1797, when Kronenberger had still been in Trier, Kirn had already drawn attention as someone who actively and successfully placed demands for frequent public processions on the city's clergy, such that the General Vicariate admonished him not to encroach on clerical prerogatives.[32] Some laymen such as Kirn poured so much energy into defending their ideal of a truly Catholic Trier that they alarmed not just the French occupying forces but even the local ecclesiastical authorities.

Not content to try to embody this ideal through processions *within* Trier, the group around Kirn also tied pilgrimage *to and from* the city into their struggle. As members of a Marian sodality, they consistently preferred shrines known for their miraculous statues of the Virgin. Before the Revolution, they had made an annual procession to Igel in the Duchy of Luxembourg, a village whose church featured one of the oldest copies of Our Lady of Luxembourg. This trip to Igel had fallen victim to the decree of November 1784, but as soon as restrictions loosened in 1790, the sodality petitioned successfully for the reinstatement of their *Wallfahrt*.[33] Later on, in the conflict-ridden years of 1798 to 1800, Kirn organized visits to the region's most important Marian shrines, Beurig and Klausen.[34]

The conflict with French authorities escalated in 1800 on the weekend of Pentecost, when the sodality timed a trip to Klausen to coincide with the usual influx of pilgrims to Trier. In the northern suburbs, Kirn and up to one hundred fellow confraternity members returning from Klausen placed themselves in the lead of a procession joined by hundreds of these other pilgrims. They marched to the city's central market square, near the cathedral, and Kirn led a public prayer session with clear political overtones. He especially invoked the Sacred Heart of Jesus, that master symbol of Counter-Revolution in the 1790s. Eventually, the gendarmerie used physical force to stop the spectacle and disperse the crowd, arresting Kirn and eight other pilgrims, including two women.[35] This escalation demonstrates just how critical pilgrimage had become to the religiously grounded sense of place that Trier provided as a holy city to many Catholics. Clemens Wenceslaus had confronted that development in 1789/90; the French, too, confronted and galvanized it ten years later. The more the upheavals of Enlightenment and Revolution challenged that sense of place, the more saliently lay Catholics would pursue—whether in somber silence or loud and defiant prayer—the pilgrim's quest for the holy-in-place.

"The Nudity and Misery of My Church"

By using pilgrimage to revalidate the notion of the holy city, Catholics in and around Trier initiated a strategy that they would eventually deploy on a much vaster scale in 1810. Ordinary pilgrims, however, could not bring back the most prestigious of all *trierisch* relics, the Holy Coat. Instead, Bishop Mannay was able to carry out this feat, as turmoil ended up providing new opportunities on the level of high politics, too. Specifically, the bishop succeeded in retrieving the Holy Coat in 1810 largely because preceding shifts of borders favored his ambition in crucial ways. Napoleonic imperial hegemony played a complicated role here. French expansion to the Rhine destroyed the Old Regime Archbishopric-Electorate of Trier, and thus the pillars on which the city's cachet had rested. Yet among the places with a plausible claim to the Holy Coat, Trier was now the only one situated in French imperial territory. Thanks to this geopolitical accident, Mannay could gain a decisive edge in the race for the relic by mobilizing French power. His success helped reverse the previous, decades-long downward trend in Trier's spiritual prestige.

Only governing elites had enough leverage to retrieve the Holy Coat, this cloth with which "to cover the nudity and misery of my church," as Bishop Mannay put it in early 1810.[36] His plaintive words reflect how difficult Catholic rebuilding remained in Trier and its hinterland even after 1802, the year the Concordat between Napoleonic France and Rome came into effect and Mannay became bishop of the revamped French Diocese of Trier. As France restructured its new Rhenish borderlands, Trier turned from the capital of an ecclesiastical electorate and one of Europe's most prestigious archbishoprics into a minor episcopal see. Moreover, Clemens Wenceslaus and his cathedral chapter had hidden away countless precious diocesan possessions—including the Holy Coat—east of the Rhine in the early 1790s.[37] Mannay's interest in retrieving the Coat and organizing a spectacular pilgrimage stemmed in part from this sentiment of loss and lack.

By setting their sights on the relic, Mannay and his local confidants identified an opportunity within the crisis provoked by revolutionary turmoil and French expansion. The redrawing of boundaries in Napoleonic Europe furnished that opportunity by bringing to the forefront the questions of where the church of Trier really was and where the Holy Coat truly belonged. While the left-bank parts of the electorate fell to France, the ones on the right bank—including Ehrenbreitstein—were absorbed into the Imperial County of Nassau-Weilburg (which would become part of the Duchy of Nassau in 1806) on the basis of the Treaty of Lunéville and the Final Recess of the Imperial Deputation (Reichsdeputationshauptschluss, 1803).

By contrast, the right-bank part of the archdiocese subsisted, and Clemens Wenceslaus retained his spiritual jurisdiction there.[38] Did this rump archdiocese form a more immediate legal successor to the old Archdiocese of Trier than the new Diocese of Trier governed by Mannay? Might the princes of Nassau have a stronger claim to the secularized treasures of the old electorate and cathedral chapter than the French government? Indeed, in 1803/4, Clemens Wenceslaus and the former cathedral canons accepted the transfer of nearly the entirety of these riches to the treasury of Nassau-Weilburg.[39]

Against stiff competition from actors on the other side of the French border, it was by no means self-evident for Mannay to reestablish Trier as the true home of the Holy Coat.[40] Already in 1802 and 1803, the burghers of Ehrenbreitstein had claimed the Holy Coat for their parish church in petitions to their vicar-general and to Clemens Wenceslaus, who hid the relic in his castle near Augsburg.[41] The vicar-general himself, meanwhile, tried to convince Clemens Wenceslaus to transfer the relic to the main church of Limburg, envisioned as the cathedral of a soon-to-be-erected separate diocese.[42] The archbishop-elector came under even greater pressure from the regency of Ehrenbreitstein, a branch of the Nassau government whose agents grew increasingly frustrated that Clemens Wenceslaus was withholding the prestigious relic from them.[43] In early July 1810, when the Holy Coat was already secretly on its way from Augsburg to Trier, the Ehrenbreitstein regency was still deliberating on what strategies and arguments to use in order to enforce Nassau's claims to the relic.[44]

French hegemony proved an important factor in determining the return of the Holy Coat to Trier in the summer of 1810. A key piece of the puzzle was Clemens Wenceslaus's unwillingness to have the relic transferred to any place other than Trier. In addition, however, the old archbishop needed some reassurance that his decision against Nassau-Weilburg would not ignite a diplomatic scandal. Louis-Marie de Narbonne-Lara, then French ambassador to Bavaria, implied as much when he wrote that Clemens Wenceslaus required meetings with French diplomats to "eliminate certain difficulties created by the pretensions of the Nassau princely regency." In particular, the archbishop obtained a guarantee that the French government would handle any protests he might receive from Nassau. "Our responsibility in this respect is unlikely to be an embarrassing one," Narbonne finished smugly.[45] In other words, the French knew that they could precipitate a decision about the relic without risking a damaging public backlash. In Napoleonic Europe, the Duchy of Nassau represented a minor player within the Confederation of the Rhine created and controlled by France. Prince Friedrich Wilhelm of Nassau-Weilburg fumed with anger when learning that he had been outmaneuvered by Mannay, but he did not dare to protest openly.[46]

So far, the picture offered here mostly corroborates historians' established understanding of church–state collaboration under Napoleonic rule—except that the initiative in this case proceeded from the ecclesiastical rather than the civil side. Mannay seems to have brought up the subject of the Holy Coat for the first time in August 1808, in a letter to the French minister for foreign affairs, Jean-Baptiste Nompère de Champagny. The bishop drew Champagny's attention to the issue and asked him to compel Nassau-Weilburg to renounce the old *trierisch* cathedral treasure, including its most prestigious relic. Mannay also provided the minister with various arguments he might need to employ in this diplomatic endeavor, specifically citing the Final Recess of 1803.[47] Later, Mannay mobilized his close friendship with Talleyrand, who had preceded Champagny as minister for foreign affairs. In late 1809, Talleyrand retained enough influence to convene a decisive meeting with Mannay and the Nassau-Weilburg diplomat Hans Christoph von Gagern in Paris. On this occasion, Mannay and Talleyrand coaxed Gagern into promising that the Ehrenbreitstein regency would not take any active steps to prevent the extradition of the Holy Coat from Augsburg to Trier.[48] Therefore, I suggest the value of flipping the dominant perspective on church–state collaboration, which calls for exploring "to what ends Napoleon instrumentalized religion."[49] Mannay's actions exemplify, conversely, how a churchman used the power of formal and informal French diplomacy in his quest to revalorize his episcopal see.

Overall, the return of the Holy Coat to Trier illustrates the ambiguous consequences of territorial revolution in the Napoleonic age. On the one hand, innumerable thorny questions arose as French expansion sounded the death knell for the Holy Roman Empire. The parallel existence of a rump Archdiocese of Trier on the right bank of the Rhine and a new, French Diocese of Trier figured among those issues, and the race for the Holy Coat exemplifies what was at stake. On the other hand, Napoleonic continental dominance helped decide such conflicts in favor of French interests—in this case, in favor of the city of Trier and its new bishop.[50] On the revolutionized map of Europe, Trier could reemerge as a great pilgrimage site during the Napoleonic era in part simply because the city was situated on the "right" side of the new border. Yet the relic did not return to Trier automatically. The Coat's fate remained undecided until 1810, when Mannay's interventions ended up bearing fruit. In short, this ambitious and well-connected prelate used the empire's diplomatic resources to great effect.

The Imperial Smokescreen: Planning a Mass Pilgrimage

"Pilgrimages are morally dangerous, and I can barely recognize the bishop of Trier in all this foolishness." These exasperated marginalia were penned by Pierre-François Réal, *conseiller d'état* at the Ministry of Police and former radical Jacobin, a few days after the showing of the Holy Coat had ended on September 27.[51] Réal's note touches on two important facets of the event. First, his surprise at Mannay's involvement in "foolishness" reveals how the bishop had used his wiggle room as a pilgrimage organizer in a way that was anything but foolish. Mannay understood that he needed permission from state authorities to realize his projects for a public showing of the Coat. He knew that he could only obtain this permission by presenting the planned pilgrimage as a tightly controlled event under the auspices of *police du culte*, the policing of worship key to securitizing revolutionary and postrevolutionary France.[52] Therefore, he promised to deliver a policeable pilgrimage by framing it as a form of mobility that would avoid the transgression of departmental and diocesan boundaries. But the promise was illusory, not least because French expansion had created some highly irregular territorial subdivisions in the borderlands.

Second, Réal's frustration reflects not only the police's failure to predict or effectively contain pilgrim mobility around Trier but also that Napoleonic elites held severely hostile views on pilgrimage, as their pro-Enlightenment predecessors had done for decades. I have discussed these views in previous chapters: pilgrims supposedly formed raucous, even dangerous crowds, wasted their time instead of performing useful work, indulged in superstition, and undercut the spatial stability of parish worship.[53] In the French Rhineland, such perceptions gained even greater purchase when relationships between Paris and the papacy broke down in the years before 1810.[54] The understanding reached by Bonaparte and Pope Pius VII in 1801 had always appeared fragile. The French consul and later emperor treated the pope as a junior partner whose interests deserved minimal consideration, whether in interpreting and implementing the Concordat of 1801 or at the imperial coronation in 1804: Pius VII duly presided over the ceremony, but Napoleon famously crowned himself. The power struggle escalated as the imperial juggernaut of war and expansion rolled on, leading the French to dismantle and annex the Papal States in 1808/9.[55] Even though few Catholics north of the Alps dared to protest these developments, tensions were rising inexorably.[56] Therefore, the making of the great pilgrimage to Trier is remarkable in part because of how the hostility of anticlerical French administrators was mitigated just enough by Mannay's promise of territorial containment and by the general tranquility of the imperial core.

After securing the Holy Coat for Trier Cathedral, the bishop and other local authorities took steps to orchestrate and control the pilgrimage down to the detail. They began to encourage public devotion to the Holy Coat in July, when Mannay's vicar-general, Anton Cordel, returned to Trier after having retrieved the relic at Clemens Wenceslaus's castle near Augsburg.[57] On August 22, in a printed pastoral proclamation (*exhortation aux fidèles*), Mannay followed up by announcing his plan to show the Coat in the cathedral the next month. He emphasized collaboration between the Church and the Napoleonic state, noting that the French government itself had "resolved to add its powerful support" in helping to return the relic to its rightful place in Trier.[58] The bishop projected a strictly regimented pilgrimage: from among the nineteen days between September 9 and 27, he allocated two days to each canton of the Saar Department whose territory coincided with that of his diocese. On either of these two days, the inhabitants of a given canton would be allowed to come to Trier—in processional order and escorted by parish clergy, who must lead the processions back out of the city as quickly as possible, within two hours after their visit to the cathedral.[59] Prompted by the prefect, the mayor of Trier likewise publicized elaborate orders and "special police measures" to enforce "public order" in the city during the time of the pilgrimage.[60] In this way, a state apparatus that appreciated disciplined devotion seemed to join forces with a bishopric that was trying to resanctify the city and episcopal see of Trier.

These top-down planning efforts perhaps appeared all the more promising because, far from being unprecedented, they followed tried-and-true Baroque methods of mobilizing large numbers of Catholics for pilgrimage events. When Archbishop-Elector Karl Kaspar von der Leyen had organized the last public showing of the Holy Coat at Trier Cathedral in 1655, he had already designated specific pilgrimage days for each region from which he expected many thousands of pilgrims.[61] More generally, Catholicism in the seventeenth and eighteenth centuries had fostered a predilection for giant pilgrimage festivals at which processions served to symbolize both splendor and order. In 1754, for instance, when the prince-bishop of Münster in Westphalia invited the Catholics of his territory to come celebrate the centenary of the renowned Marian chapel at Telgte, he issued elaborate rules and schedules for processions. These festivities attracted between sixty and eighty thousand pilgrims within two weeks.[62] Closer to Mannay's own time and place, the clergy of Luxembourg had been experimenting at least since 1804 with procession timetables for the main annual pilgrimage week in Luxembourg City, the Muttergottesoktav that we encountered prominently in chapter 1.[63] Mannay sojourned in Luxembourg more than once, even though it now belonged to the Diocese of Metz and no longer to that of Trier. In May 1810, invited by the bishop of Metz, Mannay even celebrated the final Mass of the Oktav and took part in a procession through the streets of Luxembourg together with thousands of pilgrims.[64] In short, Mannay and his collaborators at the bishopric of Trier could build on a strong Baroque legacy—including a direct Luxembourgian model of urban pilgrimage—as they organized the showing of the Holy Coat.

Mannay skillfully reworked that legacy to adapt to the new, postrevolutionary situation. Above all, he gave a promise of territorial containment to fit the pilgrimage event within the legal frameworks that constrained him as a bishop in imperial France. Napoleonic policies discouraged the processional form of pilgrimage (*Wallfahrt*; see chapter 2) that had become popular in early modern Catholic Germany. After 1802, no procession beyond the boundaries of the home parish could take place in the Saar Department without the bishop's explicit permission and the prior knowledge of the prefect or subprefect.[65] But by the same token, the bishopric and the prefecture together did have the authority to project the department as a legitimate space for exceptional pilgrimage processions to Trier. Therefore, when writing to the French *ministre des cultes*, Bigot de Préameneu, on August 27, Mannay did not bother to ask the ministry for permission to carry out the showing of the relic. Rather, he confronted Bigot de Préameneu with the fait accompli of a decision already made in accordance with the prefect of the Saar and the general who commanded the armed forces in the department.[66] Moreover, while the official pilgrimage timetable incorporated the likelihood that some Catholics from the peripheries of neighboring departments would join the processions that departed from nearby cantons of the Saar, Mannay mentioned this scenario only to the prefect and not to Bigot de Préameneu.[67] In other words, Mannay claimed to keep the pilgrimage within the bounds of legality by keeping it within the limits of the diocese and the department.

This claim ignored persistent territorial irregularities in the borderlands. French administrators inherited from the Old Regime a long and complicated boundary between the Forêts and Saar Departments (see map 1) and failed to introduce major simplifications.[68] In his statistical and topographical yearbook for 1810, C.-H. Delamorre even asserted that "in the entire [French] Empire, there is not a single department that is as misproportioned as that of the Saar."[69] Stretched thin along a north–south axis, riddled with enclaves and territorial salients, this department hardly lent itself as an effective spatial container for a pilgrimage that might bring to Trier "a quarter of the population of the surrounding regions in a radius of thirty to forty [French] miles," as the prefecture suspected by early August.[70]

Dead ends and chaotic moments in correspondence between Trier, Paris, and Luxembourg only aggravated those issues of territorial containment that agents of Church and state found especially intractable—once again—in the borderlands. Bigot de Préameneu never responded to the bishop's letter of August 27.[71] Nor did the prefect of the Saar Department receive any instructions from the Ministry of Police when he wrote—as early as August 6—to inform the ministry of Mannay's plans and to ask whether all pilgrims should be required to obtain individual passports for their trip to Trier.[72] The ministerial bureaucracy reacted with concern and emphasized in an internal note that the pilgrimage could cause "regrettable scenes" and that, more generally, "these pilgrimages could at the very least foster laziness and serve as pretexts for vagabondage."[73] The emperor's police council was supposed to discuss this issue on August 24.[74] Yet Mannay's plan to show the Holy Coat does not appear in any of the versions of Napoleon's daily police bulletin that I was able to consult, and the Ministry of Police lost sight of the pilgrimage until late September, when it was almost over.[75] For once, Napoleon had a hard time "making order reign" in his empire when his own police apparatus perceived clear risks yet failed to inform him beforehand of what would become one of the biggest mass events of his time.[76]

At the Bishopric of Trier, too, organizing the pilgrimage proved less straightforward than Mannay's self-confident letter to Bigot de Préameneu might suggest. On July 17, Mannay sent a letter on this topic to Franz Richard Gattermann, a local judge who had helped navigate the negotiations between Trier and Ehrenbreitstein over Jesus's Coat and other relics. The bishop announced to Gattermann that "I have finally received the Holy Coat. To respond to the pious eagerness of the population, I would like to exhibit [the relic] for just one day."[77] This plan would have yielded a pilgrimage similar to the short showing that had occurred at Ehrenbreitstein in 1765. Within weeks, Mannay changed his mind and opted for a much grander, nineteen-day showing. But, as his vicar-general, Cordel, noted in his diary, the last days before the start of the pilgrimage brought great hesitations. Afraid that "things might go badly," and well aware that the central government had at no point given the bishopric or the prefecture permission to go ahead with their plans, the local authorities considered calling the whole event off at the last minute.[78] They eventually decided not to—realizing perhaps that such an about-face would only further imperil "public order" by creating confusion and resentment among the faithful.

Mannay also vacillated on what to do about pilgrims coming to Trier from other departments and dioceses. By the end of August, he realized that people's interest in visiting the city and seeing the relic was going to exceed his initial expectations dramatically, thus jeopardizing the logistics of channeling processions to, through, and from Trier according to schedule. At the same time, he received news that Catholics in the neighboring Forêts Department were spontaneously planning to send processions to Trier between September 10 and 27. Alarmed at the prospect of disorder that would arise if too many pilgrims per day rushed to see the Holy Coat, the bishop wrote to Luxembourg (the capital of the Forêts) and announced that he was going to prolong the showing by six days—specifically for pilgrims of that department, so their processions would not clash with those from within the Saar Department.[79] The Bishopric of Metz applauded this change of plan.[80] The prefect of the Forêts, however, decided in early September to prohibit any and all processions from within his department to Trier on the occasion of this pilgrimage, and he ordered the gendarmerie to enforce this ban.[81] Ultimately, the Catholics of the Forêts cared neither about their prefect and gendarmes nor about Mannay's modified timetable: by mid-September, they were already pouring into Trier by the thousands. On September 14, therefore, Mannay retracted his decision to extend the showing by six days and only asked that larger pilgrim groups from the

Forêts "be accompanied by clerics, to maintain good order and ensure that everything happens in an edifying manner."[82] In short, the bishop found himself forced to compromise repeatedly on what constituted that elusive "good order" and on how to enforce it.

In addition to the Forêts, other neighboring prefectures took restrictive measures and eventually sent messages of alarm to Paris after the pilgrimage had begun. The departmental administration of Rhin-et-Moselle, based in Koblenz, had been developing a hard-line antipilgrimage stance for several years—in part because the eastern border of this department, the Rhine, also constituted the border of the empire, and the prefect suspected that pilgrims who visited right-bank shrines often engaged in smuggling.[83] The old rivalry between Koblenz and Trier also fed into this restrictive approach. As the Rhin-et-Moselle prefecture complained to the Ministry of Police in June 1810, authorities at Koblenz fought an uphill battle against religious "prejudices" as long as the administrators of the Saar Department welcomed pilgrims "in order to favor the city of Trier."[84] Therefore, the prefecture at Koblenz reacted with a mix of vigor and frustration when confronted with the news that large crowds of pilgrims from the Rhin-et-Moselle were leaving for Trier to see the Holy Coat. A circular letter sent on September 12 instructed all mayors in the Rhin-et-Moselle to conduct rigorous controls and send back home any pilgrims who had failed to obtain passports.[85] But this measure probably did not disrupt many people's pious travels. In October, the prefecture sent two plaintive and disillusioned reports to Paris, depicting the pilgrimage to the Holy Coat as a "torrent" that had broken the dam erected against superstition and had brought about "a great step backward in popular reason."[86]

The prefect of the Moselle Department, Vincent-Marie de Vaublanc, displayed the same impotent anger after he learned that many of his administrative subjects had decided to go and see the Coat as well. In late September and early October, he began bombarding the Ministry of Police with a series of reports that emphasized the chaos and dangers of this mass mobility. He claimed, for example, that "entire communities were spending the night in the fields or in the middle of the road" and that "there may be brigands among these numerous pilgrims who traverse a wooded countryside on their way to Trier."[87] But Vaublanc did not give any concrete orders to halt pilgrimage processions before September 24, so these measures could hardly be implemented by local administrators and police forces before the showing of the relic ended.[88]

If the prefectures of the Moselle and Rhin-et-Moselle faced the pilgrimage as an unpleasant surprise, it was because the Ministry of Police had not informed them beforehand, let alone taken any steps to coordinate various departments. Might the transition from Fouché to the less competent minister Savary in June 1810 have disturbed some relevant bureaucratic mechanisms? In any case, the imperial government would hardly have treated the subject with such negligence if Mannay and his diocese had not enjoyed a favorable reputation in Paris to begin with. Already in 1806, Bigot de Préameneu's predecessor Portalis had described the Diocese of Trier as "perfectly calm" to Napoleon.[89] The prefect's *mémoire* on the state of the Saar Department in 1809 characterized its inhabitants as "naturally good and peaceful," and even prone to "apathy"—not exactly the stuff of a police minister's nightmares.[90] To be sure, in the autumn of 1809, a rebellion of national guards had affected large parts of the department, leading to some pillaging and to the execution of ringleaders after the army had crushed the revolt and brought many of its participants before a special military tribunal. That said, as Roger Dufraisse noted, many such short-lived "local tumults" erupted in 1809, even in parts of pre-1792 France. In the Saar, Mannay was in fact able to shine by obtaining the emperor's pardon for more than a dozen of those condemned by the military tribunal.[91] The situation calmed down quickly: the Saar prefecture's reports on the first two trimesters of 1810 praised the *esprit public* and the "most perfect union" in which "the ministers as well as the faithful of the various confessions" coexisted in the department.[92] In short, Trier and its diocese belonged firmly to the imperial core, and this comfortable position made the empire quite manageable for Mannay in his planning of a mass pilgrimage—despite theoretical state hostility to such religious spectacles.

Ultimately, seen from above, the pilgrimage of 1810 did look rather messy, as the police approached it reactively rather than proactively. About two weeks after it ended, the Ministries of *cultes* and Police sent letters of rebuke to Mannay and the prefect of the Saar. Yet, in their respective responses, the bishop and the prefect simply asserted that pilgrims had not violated public order and had instead displayed great "tranquility" and "moderation."[93] Indeed, had not the state been justified in paying little attention initially, considering that the pilgrims behaved just as peacefully as one could expect from well-adjusted residents of the inner empire? While I will turn to pilgrims' actions in the following section, one thing should already be clear: despite some hesitations about pilgrims from the Forêts, Mannay had deftly navigated the parameters of imperial territory. He had done so by promising to produce an orderly pilgrimage via police regulations and above all via spatial containment using departmental borders. In this sense, the smokescreen of an imperial hegemonic borderscape proved crucial in the making of mass pilgrimage in 1810.

Pilgrim Tactics in and around Trier

The top-down picture of uneven concern and contrived claims to control raises the question of what the pilgrims themselves did, given that they could not be policed as tightly as state authorities would have liked. In this section, to illuminate the pilgrims' own practices and especially their transgressions of borders, I begin by surveying their numbers and regions of origin. The pilgrims of 1810 overwhelmingly came from places where the imaginary of Trier as spiritual center resonated through a centuries-old tradition. This tradition inserted the Holy Coat in a broader recognition of Trier's holiness, nourished by a history of archiepiscopal and temporal power, the presence of Saint Matthias's relics, and a more recent flourishing of Marian devotion. Moreover, the evidence allows some glimpses into how pilgrims tried—often successfully—to deflect or overcome the challenges of being policed. Tactics in this regard ranged widely, from sheer disobedience to evasion to the gendered and classed self-presentation as honorable and harmless *dévotes*. For ordinary pilgrims, too, the empire proved usable, or at least manipulable. They seized the opportunity Mannay created, and many of them did so in ways that the official, strictly territorialized framework of the pilgrimage had not stipulated.

Based on close analysis of contemporary estimates and pilgrim registers kept by the bishopric, more than 220,000 Catholics went to see the Holy Coat in September 1810, and at least 95,000 of them came from outside the Saar Department.[94] In other words, at least 43 percent of them did not come from the territory for which Mannay had officially intended the showing. We thus need to question the idea of a pilgrimage event carefully and successfully organized and controlled from above, a notion curated by the bishopric itself and perpetuated by most of the few modern historians who have researched the showing of 1810.[95] A remarkably great number of uninvited pilgrims participated, and conversely, a large minority of Catholics living within the Diocese of Trier failed to do so. In a nutshell, Catholics tended to participate massively in the pilgrimage of 1810 only if they held preexisting religious attachments to Trier. Many from the northern parts and some other cantons of the Saar Department had never developed such ties, and this lack corresponds to the low participation rates recorded in the pilgrim registers for these cantons, although physical distance from Trier also mattered. By contrast, remarkably large numbers of pilgrims came from regions *beyond* the borders of the department. The evidence from the registers corroborates Vicar-General Cordel's impression that these regions most notably included Luxembourg, Lorraine, and the hinterlands of Koblenz and Cologne.[96]

In these regions, Catholics cultivated centuries-old relationships to Sancta Treveris, based partly on practices of pilgrimage and long-distance procession and partly on Trier's former status as archiepiscopal see and capital of an imperial principality. The eastern and southern parts of Luxembourg were not only geographically close to Trier but had also belonged to its Old Regime archdiocese. Before the French Revolution, moreover, the dioceses of Lorraine had been part of the metropolitan church province of Trier, and in the Napoleonic era, pilgrimage processions from Lorraine continued to pour into Trier year after year on the feast day of St. Peter.[97] The environs of Koblenz had belonged to both the Archdiocese and the Electorate of Trier since the Middle Ages, and the Moselle River valley served as a natural infrastructure connecting Koblenz with Trier. Additionally, the left-bank Rhenish areas near both Koblenz and Cologne featured a high density of St. Matthias confraternities, whose members were used to making pilgrimage to Trier annually.[98] Overall, against the misproportioned territorial container of the Saar Department, which served as the official frame for the 1810 pilgrimage, actual pilgrim participation reveals the contours of a different, devotional borderscape. These contours derived from older Rhenish pilgrimage patterns, the "phantom borders" of the old electorate, archbishopric, and metropolitan province, as well as from sheer geographical proximity.[99]

Devotees to Saint Matthias, for instance, most likely built on their confraternal pilgrimage traditions in deciding to go and venerate the Holy Coat in September 1810. In the early modern period, the Matthias pilgrimage confraternities had been led by laymen, the Brudermeister, and had guarded almost complete independence from the clergy.[100] After 1802, Mannay saved the church of the secularized St. Matthias' Abbey by repurposing it as a parish church. Both parish archives and printed pilgrim booklets suggest that the apostle's tomb continued to attract many Rhenish Catholics in subsequent years.[101] Pilgrimage processions from all over the Rhineland offered large votive candles to St. Matthias during the Napoleonic era.[102] To be sure, the number of visitors per year may have declined somewhat during that time, as suggested in 1814 by Viktor Dewora, the parish priest of St. Matthias and Enlightenment-inspired author of the new pilgrim booklets. Some confraternity members disapproved of Dewora's overt rejection of devotional customs that he considered superstitious.[103] On the whole, however, the evidence demonstrates that the confraternities remained effective as organizers of pilgrimage to St. Matthias throughout the late eighteenth and early nineteenth centuries.[104]

What is more, pilgrims had connected the devotions to Saint Matthias and to the Holy Coat long before 1810. Pilgrimage guidebooks of Matthias confraternities typically contained prayers or songs that honored the Coat and indicated Trier Cathedral as the pilgrimage groups' last significant stop before St. Matthias' Abbey. The guide reprinted in 1808 for the Matthias confraternity of Anrath, for instance, instructed pilgrims to sing "Ist das der Rock Herr Jesu Christ," the most famous of early modern songs about the Coat, while entering Trier.[105] Likewise, pilgrimage coins from the seventeenth and eighteenth centuries sometimes showed Saint Matthias on the front and the Holy Coat on the back.[106] By putting Trier prominently on the pilgrim's mental map and keeping it there long after the 1655 showing of the Coat had faded from living memory, devotion to Matthias factored into Catholics' decision to visit Trier for the showing of 1810.

Pilgrims also connected the showing of the Holy Coat with their devotion to Mary, whom the song "Ist das der Rock Herr Jesu Christ" presented as the weaver of the sacred garment.[107] On Sunday, September 9, the first day of the showing, Trier was overrun by crowds of pilgrims who had acquired the habit of visiting the city each year on September 8 to witness the great procession of the Nativity of Mary. The origins of this annual urban procession from the cathedral to St. Matthias and back lay in 1675, when Archbishop Karl Kaspar had first organized it to offer thanks for a retreat of the French army from the Rhineland during the Franco-Dutch War of 1672–78.[108] Thus, the weekend of September 8 and 9 saw a seamless transition from a highlight of Marian devotion to the adoration of Christ.

What is more, since 1697, the cathedral had been home to a Marian statue whose reputed miraculous powers had become a pilgrimage attraction in its own right over the course of the eighteenth century. Within the cathedral, the chapel that housed this statue was located on the south side of the choir, relatively close to the chapel of the Holy Coat.[109] Even in the years 1794 to 1802, when French occupying troops sequestered the cathedral building and used the Marian chapel as a stable for their horses, Mary's devotees could still pray in front of the statue because it had been transferred to the neighboring Church of Our Lady (Liebfrauenkirche).[110] Perhaps, alongside the Matthias confraternities, this Marian devotion provided the second main element of continuity in pilgrimage to Trier across the two decades of French rule. At least, when the mayor of Lutzerath denounced the persistence of that pilgrimage in May 1810, he described the city as home to a prestigious image of Mary.[111] For this Marian element, too, the producers of pilgrimage coins had long forged a relationship to the Holy Coat: a coin from the year 1698 shows Trier's miraculous statue of the Virgin on one side and the Coat on the other.[112]

During the pilgrimage of September 1810, this connection became manifest in the sacred healing of Elisabetha Klein. At the age of fifty-two, this widowed mother of five had been suffering from fevers and gout for three years, to the point of near-total incapacitation. Although she consulted doctors from ten different towns including Sankt Wendel, Birkenfeld, and Trier, none of them could help her find relief. So, when she learned about the upcoming pilgrimage, she decided "to let herself be transported to the Holy Coat."[113] Friends and family members placed her on a cart and dragged her from her home village Nunkirchen (in the Saar Department) across the Hunsrück mountains to Trier, roughly thirty miles. They arrived on the evening of September 18. At seven thirty on the morning of September 19, she entered the cathedral. Her guides obtained permission to lead her right through one of the regular processions so she could kneel and pray individually in front of the Holy Coat for almost ten minutes. Then "she left, now holding the hands of her guides: they no longer needed to hold her under her arms."[114] Yet instead of stopping there, Klein took a turn toward Mary, going to the Church of Our Lady and saying more prayers there. Next, she returned to the cathedral, still holding her guides' hands, and paid a visit "to the Chapel of the Mother of God, where she knelt on the naked floor, stood up by herself, and let herself be guided to the Holy Coat once more even though she felt strong enough to go there by herself."[115] By noon on

September 20, when she told her story to the vicar-general, she was able to walk all by herself, although she suffered from great fatigue.

Klein's journey demonstrates how one woman could pursue her quest for healing amid a pilgrimage event that, at first glance, left space only for mass processions. Even as a resident of the Saar Department, Klein was not beholden to the schedule and instructions given by the bishopric—a point that applies far beyond her individual experience. For example, official rules prescribed that each procession, upon leaving the cathedral after passing in front of the Holy Coat, "shall be led out of the city immediately and must not reenter it."[116] But in practice, as almost all processional envoys openly acknowledged, pilgrims took several hours to get some rest and perhaps make small purchases of pious objects and food while still in the city, and many thousands stayed in Trier overnight.[117] We cannot know how many of them seized the opportunity to pray in the Church of Our Lady or in the cathedral's Marian chapel, as Klein did, or how many added a detour to St. Matthias. At any rate, individual pilgrims could connect various strands and sites of devotion, thus activating a broader imaginary of Holy Trier in which Jesus's Coat played a critical but by no means isolated role.

That said, Klein's story sheds light not only on pilgrims' religious culture but also on the spatial tactics they used to navigate the hegemonic borderscape and its policing strictures. The liberties Klein took with the strict processional order at and around the cathedral exemplify low-stakes obstinacy, the first of the three major tactics discernible in the sources. Whether due to a desperate quest for healing or out of simple impetuousness, many pilgrims pushed the boundaries of public order without blatantly breaching them. For instance, pilgrims from Luxembourg "behaved more rashly," according to Cordel: "when their patience for waiting was exhausted, they jostled more vehemently into the queues in front of the church."[118] Similarly, a local parish priest admitted that "many soldiers always needed to ensure order; for there was frequently an enormous pushing and shoving among the people."[119] Behind the facade of well-planned, orderly mass devotion, the overwhelming influx from Luxembourg and other regions outside the Saar Department created tensions as pilgrims tried to outbustle each other as well as the police.

Tens of thousands of pilgrims also disobeyed restrictions on mobility, thus deploying a second tactic that verged on what we might call "resistance." The situation in the Rhin-et-Moselle Department was especially delicate because—as I mentioned above—the prefecture of this department had taken a harsh stance against pilgrimage in general. Yet the resulting difficulties were not insurmountable. Sometime in the spring of 1810, for example, "a troop of pilgrims, having reached the Rhine, obtained at a local *mairie* free passage to the right bank of this river, after having been rejected at other neighboring *mairies* due to their lack of passports for a trip abroad."[120] Other scholarship shows that many pilgrims in Napoleonic Europe did have recourse to passports.[121] For those unable or unwilling to pay passport fees or to ask potentially hostile authorities for passport visas related to pilgrimage, however, there were still ways of escaping the control systems that shaped the Napoleonic borderscape. At least in theory, these systems did apply to the pilgrimage of 1810 because, since the mid-1790s, passports had also been required for domestic trips within France (see chapter 4). Moreover, leaving for Trier from places of residence in the Roër or Rhin-et-Moselle Departments meant violating a recent ban by the Bishopric of Aachen on pilgrimages exceeding the boundaries of that diocese.[122] Against this backdrop of state and Church restrictions, many of the pilgrims of September 1810 were marching according to a mental map that stood directly at odds with the hegemonic borderscape of the time.

Not all pilgrims crossing departmental boundaries, however, needed either passports or a good plan for avoiding passport controls. Some relied on their elevated social status—at least in 1810, pilgrimage was by no means a purely "popular" form of devotion—to keep them aloof from such pesky bureaucratic and policing issues. For example, among the few people from the city of Metz who journeyed to Trier to see the Holy Coat, the majority were "devout women and priests," according to the mayor who sent the prefecture a list of about a dozen ladies, *demoiselles*, and *abbés*. These pilgrims were heading to Trier without passports, but such lack of documentation hardly mattered, given that "this list contains only people who are honorable and well known in Metz."[123] It seems that women of a certain social standing, especially when accompanied by clergy, could pass as obviously unproblematic travelers and thus simply afford to care little about the official mobility regime. For these women, the empire proved usable thanks to its postrevolutionary reinforcement of social hierarchy.

To sum up, pilgrim movement in September 1810 undercut the hegemonic borderscape without genuinely challenging public order. Prefect Vaublanc's reports to Paris best encapsulate this ambiguity. On September 28, he wrote that, according to hearsay, pilgrims had "proffered ill-considered remarks about the pope and about religious affairs." In other words, they were criticizing Napoleon's detention of Pius VII since 1809.[124] Yet four days later, Vaublanc claimed that "the biggest part of those from my department who have gone on this trip would not have done so" if they had not believed the rumor that the government had officially authorized the showing of the Holy Coat.[125] These rumors probably spread far and wide.[126] They, too, instrumentalized the empire by deriving their plausibility from the Napoleonic principle that authority always came from above. How, indeed, could a three-week public showing of a famous relic, under the auspices of the local bishop, be taking place *except* with the knowledge and assent of the emperor and his government? Yet, as we have seen, Napoleon had actually not been informed, and the Ministries of *cultes* and Police had not managed—or bothered—to make a decision about the pilgrimage. Their inaction did not erase the norm of public order but did render it muddled and malleable. For the pilgrims who went to Trier in 1810, the opportunity to reassert their faith arose from this ambiguity.

Trier, Napoleon, and the "Great Awakening of Pilgrimage"

Just as one swallow does not make a summer, one pilgrimage does not amount to large-scale religious revival—but, zooming out from the case of Trier, I suggest that the spectacularly successful showing of the Holy Coat in 1810 was not an isolated phenomenon. On the geographical level, historian Michael Broers's distinction between the inner and outer empire again proves meaningful here. In the outer empire, as Broers himself has argued through the example of central Italy, traditional Catholic practices such as pilgrimage to local shrines gained powerful new meaning and appeal as vehicles of resistance to the French. In the process, previously skeptical clergymen and upper-class city-dwellers discovered new common ground with remote rural communities, and the resulting alliance unleashed sufficient energy for a durable devotional resurgence.[127] For another, similar example, consider Montserrat Abbey, Catalonia's foremost place of Marian pilgrimage. In the Spanish wars that erupted in 1808, the monastery quickly proved attractive to Catalan militias (*somatenes*) whose members sought both material support and the Virgin's protection. Although French troops sacked the abbey in the late summer of 1811 and again in July 1812, the statue of Our Lady of Montserrat survived and thus provided a focal point for continued popular attachment to the shrine and to Mary herself.[128]

At the same time, pilgrimage also proved alive and kicking in much of the imperial core, not least in the Rhineland and neighboring borderlands, even though little clear-cut anti-imperial resistance existed to fuel religious devotion in these parts of the empire. Two decades ago, Jacques-Olivier Boudon even discerned a "great awakening of pilgrimage" in Napoleonic France.[129] He did so on the basis of limited evidence from Lorraine and the Diocese of Soissons, but a glance at other regions substantiates his assertion. In Alsace, Bishop Saurine amplified state officials' worries that too many French Catholics kept crossing the border with Switzerland to visit the shrines of Einsiedeln and Mariastein. Yet Saurine did so not in order to combat pilgrimage per se but rather to promote Alsace's own shrines, particularly the one in Marienthal over which the bishop was trying to gain direct control (see chapter 3). In Aachen, local clergy felt encouraged by Napoleon's fascination with the city of Charlemagne and consequently revivified the great septennial Heiligtumsfahrt in 1804. This mass pilgrimage had been interrupted by Enlightenment reformism and French revolutionary occupation for roughly two decades.[130] In the sparsely populated Luxembourgian region, too, the annual pilgrimage festivals of Luxembourg City and Echternach reemerged in full force after 1799.[131]

While these successes have little to do with resistance, they do not appear as results of straightforward church–state collaboration either. For one thing, they built implicitly on the legacy of Karl Kaspar Kirn, his fellow confraternity members, and the many thousands of other Catholics whose actions I have discussed in previous chapters—the pilgrims who had practiced and defended devout mobility in ways that did amount to overt resistance. Moreover, the case of Trier confirms that many Napoleonic state administrators held hostile views about pilgrimage. Yet this hostility was neither consistent nor intense enough to keep clerical leaders or lay Catholics from further reasserting pilgrim practice while drawing on both the empire's strengths and its weaknesses. Thus, by mobilizing French imperial diplomacy, Bishop Mannay managed to secure the Holy Coat for Trier Cathedral in 1810. Next, he tapped into the departmentalized territorial regime to create the vision of a well-bounded, strictly orchestrated pilgrimage. The pilgrims themselves, in turn, exploited the limitations of the imperial spatial order just as effectively as Mannay had exploited its powers. Napoleonic state officials read the pilgrimage disapprovingly through the lens of public disorder, but the half-heartedness of their response signals that they did not seriously perceive pilgrims as resisters. In short, Catholics in the imperial core discovered that they had much leeway to pursue religious renewal whenever the empire turned out to be neither glorious nor abhorrent, but simply usable.

Finally, these findings should inflect how we approach the larger story of nineteenth-century Catholic renewal in both France and Germany. As I noted in the introduction of this book, the revolutionary and Napoleonic era have often been omitted from this story by scholars who heavily emphasize the rise of a new "populist" and extremely effective generation of ultramontanist clerical leaders between 1830 and 1850.[132] At least for western Germany, such a periodization does make sense at first glance. Throughout the early decades of the nineteenth century, the Catholic Enlightenment in these regions retained its intellectual hold on the clergy, many of whom therefore approached pilgrimage and related practices with skepticism or even contempt.[133] Without a doubt, the demise of the Catholic Enlightenment after 1830 constituted a turning point. Yet this observation does not settle the issue of how much was genuinely new about the ultramontane style of devotion, for which the next showing of the Holy Coat in 1844 marked a breakthrough in the Rhineland.[134] Intriguingly, the organizers of that later pilgrimage drew heavily and explicitly on the model created in 1810, in ways ranging from urban policing to timetables for cantonal processions.[135] My interpretation of the pilgrimage in 1810 suggests, more broadly, how the Napoleonic-era revival may have mattered in the long run. Life under Napoleon taught both clergy and laypeople a lesson that would remain valuable throughout the century: how to make mass pilgrimage work by dealing successfully with the powers and quirks of the territorial state.

Conclusion

"Men's ideas about the merits of pilgrimage have truly changed," the Chevalier de Jaucourt asserted in his entry on pilgrimage for the *Encyclopédie*, that centerpiece of the Enlightenment. No longer did sensible and responsible people "visit distant places" to obtain special divine grace. Only some "rascals" still insisted on going to Loreto or Santiago de Compostela "out of superstition, laziness, or licentiousness."[1] In short, writing in the 1760s, Jaucourt declared pilgrimage dead, and he was happy to dance on its grave. One hundred years later, however, not just France but all of Europe was in uproar over the recent birth of what would become the continent's most emblematic modern pilgrimage—Lourdes. Today, pilgrimage keeps flourishing within Christianity as well as in many other traditions.[2] Jaucourt was a bad prophet when he implied that pilgrims would have no place in a more and more enlightened future.

He was also wrong to presume the quaint irrelevance of their religious practices in his own time. Through decades of Enlightenment reforms, revolution, and Napoleonic authoritarianism, pilgrims tenaciously visited and revisited their regional and local shrines in western central Europe, from the Swiss Alps to the Eifel Mountains. And far from merely sticking around in times of crisis, pilgrimage proved a potent, transformative experience as Catholics trod new paths of devotion and politics.

Pilgrims and their allies participated in many different ways in the great political upheavals of the revolutionary era. Catholic elites refashioned the ties that embedded holy places within sacred territories. Laypeople reoriented their confessional pride. National awareness grew among pilgrims while its political implications shifted. Subversive encounters with Mary proliferated. An imperial model of mass pilgrimage emerged. In all these cases, pilgrimage destinations turned into focal points of political struggles and transformations, whether at long-established shrines such as Einsiedeln in Switzerland or at ephemeral apparition sites such as Hoste in Lorraine. In the process, pilgrims sometimes—not always—came to present their transgressions as resistance, which is to say that they articulated an explicit stance against changes wrought by the Enlightenment and the French Revolution. More broadly, pilgrims' actions might seem to express merely stubborn adherence to traditions inherited from early modern times. But when Catholics encountered obstacles or felt threatened by an enlightened or revolutionary reform measure, they often responded by innovating.

What is more, rather than merely adapt pilgrimage, they made it politically relevant by engaging with major themes and ideals that reformers and revolutionaries themselves were promoting. Supposed Catholic inferiority was one such theme that preoccupied enlightened clergy by the mid-eighteenth century as well as revolutionary elites in the 1790s. On this front, lay villagers and townspeople defended shrines as sites of confessional distinction, insisting that abandoning such outposts would weaken Catholicism's ability to inspire respect rather than ridicule. French revolutionaries also hoped to fuse national identity and territorial security by criminalizing emigration, casting departures as betrayals of the fatherland. Alsatian Catholics adopted this national lens while also subverting it when they reinvented their traditional pilgrimages to Switzerland as decidedly transnational acts. And in 1810, more than two hundred thousand pilgrims saw the Holy Coat of Jesus in Trier, almost one hundred thousand of them coming unauthorized—all under the cover of what pilgrimage organizers touted as public order, that keyword of Napoleonic ideology. In other words, pilgrims did not isolate their religious practices from such urgent issues as national identity, new notions of confessional balance, or Napoleon's bid to resolidify authority from the top down. Catholic pilgrimage regularly led to strong, politically charged interventions on those issues—especially in the context of what I have conceptualized as the transformation of border culture.

This transformation produced radically new problems and contexts for pilgrimage while being shaped in turn by this religious practice. Diplomatic and intellectual elites of the revolutionary era valorized borders as frontlines of securitization, guarantees of cohesion for the territorial state, and spatial markers of national identity. At the same time, France as well as several other continental powers expanded and clashed massively, not least in the borderlands with which this book has been concerned. As a result, borders paradoxically appeared both more important and more unstable than ever before. The mix of extreme significance and fragility, of ever-tightening control and ever-new loopholes proved "empowering as well as dangerous," in particular to borderland inhabitants.[3] Indeed, ordinary people rarely affected the bigger political picture more strongly than they did by crossing borders in more or less illicit ways—whether as vagabonds or smugglers, deserters or draft-dodgers, emigrants or pilgrims.

As this book has shown, pilgrims and pilgrimage promoters found many different ways of transgressing borders or speaking out about them. Devotees to Our Lady of Luxembourg worked throughout the age of revolutions to match shifting territorial boundaries with the contours of the sacred space of patronage that underpinned pilgrimage to Luxembourg City. During the apparition wave of 1799, pilgrim politics involved crossing departmental borders, switching rapidly from one site of Marian presence to the next, in order to stay a step ahead of hostile regional agents of the state. Catholics also attached new meanings to territorial boundaries by helping to nationalize the Franco-Swiss border through their trips to Mariastein and Einsiedeln. In sum, pilgrims and pilgrimage promoters were bound to get drawn into the transformation of border culture at every turn, and they often managed to put distinct and powerful Catholic twists on that transformation.

Thus, with each new challenge that appeared between the 1770s and the Napoleonic period, Catholics rethought their religious practices and enriched their political repertoire in ways that would deeply inform successive developments. Historians of nineteenth-century Germany have relied too heavily on the idea of rupture when treating the mid- to late nineteenth-century heyday of Catholic mobilization as a revival—the very notion of which implies prior death or at least languishing. These scholars either have ignored the late eighteenth and early nineteenth centuries altogether or have claimed that while changes did occur within Catholicism during that time, they did not make much of a difference in the long run. To be sure, not everything that pilgrims did in the decades around 1800 was new or inventive. They still traveled first and foremost to experience the sacred and receive special divine grace, as their predecessors had done for many centuries.

Now, however, they also began to confront Catholic inferiority complexes, partake in transnational demonstrations of their faith, circumvent state-sponsored anticlericalism, and manipulate intensified regimes of territoriality. All these aspects would remain central to the politics of German and European Catholicism for a long time to come.

Both during and after the age of revolutions, some holy sites and pilgrimage events also combined several of those themes, which the chapters of this book have kept largely separate for the sake of analytical clarity. For example, given long-standing confessional tensions in Alsace and the proximity of Einsiedeln and Mariastein to the Protestant cities of Zurich and Basel, respectively, the issues of transnational and confessionally militant pilgrimage overlapped there.[4] The famous 1844 showing of the Holy Coat in Trier illustrates the point even more clearly. Within fifty days between mid-August and early October 1844, more than five hundred thousand Catholics visited the cathedral of Trier to catch a glimpse of the relic. This genuine mass pilgrimage had regional as well as transnational dimensions. Sympathetic observers at the time hailed the event as a great gathering of Rhenish Catholics. Many commentators were equally keen to note that pilgrims came by the tens of thousands from Luxembourg—which was beginning to turn into a separate nation-state after achieving independence in 1839— and France, a few even from the Netherlands and Ireland.[5] Meanwhile, the pilgrimage sparked a firestorm of criticism by bourgeois liberals who used the flourishing press to denounce the devout masses as superstitious, reinvigorating the discourse about Catholic backwardness.[6] A closer look at what people did while on pilgrimage reveals, however, that they pursued their own itineraries and interests much as they had done in 1810 under Napoleon, instead of being utterly constrained by state control and clerical manipulation.[7]

Moreover, imperial resonances exist between the Napoleonic era and later, extra-European politics of pilgrimage. During the Egyptian campaign of 1798, Bonaparte had already proclaimed the intention to apply the enlightened and revolutionary principles of policing worship to Islam.[8] As European colonialism engulfed more and more of the Arab world over the course of the nineteenth century, the French put many facets of that program into practice. Among other things, they often tried to prevent Algerian Muslims from going on the *hajj* to Mecca. As historian Valeska Huber has argued, these antipilgrimage measures were grounded in "fears of contagion, not only of disease, but also of political ideas"; in response, Muslims developed tactics of clandestine mobility that involved forging passports and deviating from prescribed travel routes.[9] Hence, we would need to reach beyond histories of Germany, Europe, or Catholic Christianity to fully account for the revolutionary era's legacy in terms of policed and politicized pilgrimage.[10]

Ultimately, I suggest that pilgrims have encountered and influenced the modern world above all through the dialectics of place and mobility. Since the age of revolutions, cultural order has appeared perpetually up for grabs. Thus, "whatever political, social, ecclesial structures we aspire to have to be mobilized into existence" in the postrevolutionary "Age of Mobilization," as philosopher Charles Taylor puts it.[11] In other words, any attempt to either forge a new order or reestablish an old one would become a project to remold society. Sense of place—that great, ambivalent promise of order—had never been self-evident. But in a revolutionary and postrevolutionary world, people perceived order as destabilized for good, and place-making became an increasingly arduous quest, a goal for which to mobilize.[12] As a result, sense of place and mobility have complemented and even implied each other to an unprecedented degree. Pilgrimage may appeal against this backdrop because it combines a heavy emphasis on the fullness, indeed the sacrality of special places with an equally strong insistence on the value of wandering and boundary-crossing.[13] Although pilgrimage has existed for millennia, it features a deep affinity with modern predicaments.[14] Hence, we may understand more easily just why it has remained such a widespread, adaptive, and politically salient practice in Europe and beyond while many other traditional patterns of religious life have disintegrated.

Even in the twenty-first century, although the potential for specifically Catholic politicization seems greatly reduced across western Europe, I quickly encountered the themes of my research when going on a little pilgrimage of my own. On the early morning of April 22, 2019, I set out from Trier to visit the shrine of Our Lady of Girsterklaus. This shrine of medieval origin, located since 1815 inside the Grand-Duchy of Luxembourg, previously belonged to an exclave of the Electorate of Trier and then the French Saar Department (see map 1). After crossing the border between Germany and Luxembourg, just outside of Rosport, I came across a little monument erected in 1989 to celebrate the 150th anniversary of Luxembourgian national independence. At Girsterklaus itself, a Luxembourgian flag was waving in front of the chapel. And when I came back to Girsterklaus in July, leafing furtively through the open book in which visitors record their thoughts or prayers, I noticed that somebody had composed a little eulogy for Jean, Grand Duke of Luxembourg, who had died on April 23. Visiting Our Lady of Girsterklaus meant experiencing a specific, nationally tinged Marian climate, one that has earned the grand duchy the nickname of "Marienland Luxemburg."[15]

Girsterklaus remains a confessionally marked place, long after the breakthrough of modern ecumenicism around 1960. In fact, a second flag was flying above the little cemetery that surrounds the chapel, and its colors—yellow and white—were those of the Vatican. Inside the shrine, the sacred statue of Our Lady of Girsterklaus above the main altar attests to the Catholicity of the devotion encouraged and practiced here, and so do the representations of saints such as Walburga and Joseph. Moreover, the perception of a new, threatening religious other had seeped into the makeup of this place. On a pinboard near the entrance of the chapel, a magazine cutout from almost three years prior presented a picture of the French priest Jacques Hamel, who was "assassinated on July 26, 2016, inside the church of Saint-Étienne-du-Rouvray by Islamist terrorists," as the cover page of the magazine read. This hint at present-day Catholic martyrdom provided something like a distant echo of earlier confessional ages.[16]

Girsterklaus is not an apparition site, yet it connects the attentive pilgrim to some of modern Europe's major places of Marian apparition, illustrating the logics of fluidity and proliferation that help make those places powerful. About a hundred feet from the chapel, Marian devotees will find a replica of the Lourdes grotto, one of thousands in the Catholic world today. This replica includes a small statue of Bernadette, kneeling down, dressed in a white headscarf and a red robe, looking up toward Our Lady. The sculpture of the Virgin is framed by the lush green of ivy, distinctly mimicking the moss and leaves that surround the famous statue in the Massabielle Grotto at Lourdes. Inside the Girsterklaus chapel, on the same notice board that proclaimed the death of Jacques Hamel, someone had attached a rosary with a place-name carved into the wooden cross that dangled beneath the beads: "MEĐUGORJE." A majority-Catholic village in present-day Bosnia and Herzegovina, Medjugorje is home to several men and women who have reported daily meetings with Mary since 1981. Having passed through the violent disintegration of Yugoslavia and much controversy around the authenticity of the apparitions, Medjugorje constitutes the most celebrated and most hotly politicized place of Marian presence to have emerged in the last fifty years.[17] Together, the Lourdes replica and the Medjugorje rosary reveal how Catholics have tied the medieval shrine of Girsterklaus into contemporary transnational networks of faith galvanized by apparitions.

Girsterklaus also greeted me in April 2019 with a reference to the kind of mass pilgrimage that characterizes modern Catholicism not only in Trier, the home of the Holy Coat, but in countless other cities as well. A banner showing Our Lady of Luxembourg, Consoler of the Afflicted, leaned against a pillar inside the chapel. This reminder of Mary as national patroness fit the season. Only a few weeks later, in mid-May, Luxembourg City hosted the celebrations of the Muttergottesoktav, whose participants—including the grand-ducal family—continue to perform an elaborate public confluence of urban, national, and Catholic identities year after year.[18] Some twenty-five miles northeast of Luxembourg City, the banner showcased at the Girsterklaus chapel presented a faint but discernible reflection of this performance.

Finally, Girsterklaus remains a border shrine even though it is no longer situated in an enclave. The Sauer River that today separates Luxembourg from Germany in this area passes only a quarter mile northeast of Girsterklaus. On my way back to Trier, I crossed a pedestrian bridge that connects the Luxembourgian village of Moersdorf on the west bank of the Sauer and the German community of Metzdorf on the east bank. A plate informs the curious passerby that a bridge has existed in this place since 1987, as both an element and a symbol of the unsurveilled, unproblematic border between two mutually friendly countries. The border thus still had a place in the political imaginary, though now as a privileged place of peaceful encounters within a united Europe rather than as a barrier between nation-states. Then again, crossing the Sauer suddenly became less easy one year later, in April 2020, when governments all over Europe and the world were sealing borders as part of pandemic response plans.

Even aside from COVID-19, border regimes remain deeply interwoven with pilgrims' hopes and experiences. Today, no Catholic shrine in the world attracts as many pilgrims as the Basilica of Our Lady of Guadalupe, situated on the Hill of Tepeyac in northern Mexico City. For the main feast of Guadalupe on December 12 alone, several million gather and celebrate there each year. Regardless of whether they are Mexican citizens or Mexican Americans, they tend to perceive the Virgin as a distinctly national figure around which people from both sides of the US–Mexican border can rally. Among the poorer pilgrims from within Mexico, some implore Mary to help them with their plans for immigration to the United States. Many others ask her to protect family members and friends who have already made the dangerous journey north in search of a better life. From their perspective as well as from the Chicanx one, the pilgrimage is an integral part of border culture.[19] Considering the extreme securitization and racialization of the US southern border, Our Lady of Guadalupe also reveals poignantly what Our Lady of Girsterklaus suggests subtly: the political history of Catholic pilgrimage continues.

NOTES

ABBREVIATIONS

AAEB	Archives de l'ancien Évêché de Bâle (Porrentruy, Switzerland)
ADBR	Archives départementales du Bas-Rhin (Strasbourg, France)
ADHR	Archives départementales du Haut-Rhin (Colmar, France)
ADioc Lux	Archives diocésaines de Luxembourg
ADipl	Archives diplomatiques (La Courneuve, France)
ADM	Archives départementales de la Moselle (Saint-Julien-lès-Metz, France)
ADV	Archives départementales des Vosges (Épinal, France)
AEA	Archives de l'État à Arlon (Belgium)
AGR	Archives générales du Royaume (Brussels, Belgium)
AM Lux	Archives municipales de Luxembourg
AN	Archives nationales (Pierrefitte-sur-Seine, France)
AN Lux	Archives nationales de Luxembourg
AP	*Archives parlementaires de 1787 à 1860. Recueil complet des débats législatifs et politiques des chambres françaises* (Paris: Paul Dupont/CNRS, 1867–)
BA Tr	Bistumsarchiv Trier (Rheinland-Pfalz, Germany)
BnF	Bibliothèque nationale de France (Paris, France)
DAL	Diözesanarchiv Limburg (Rheinland-Pfalz, Germany)
Hémecht	*Hémecht: Zeitschrift für Luxemburger Geschichte/Revue d'histoire luxembourgeoise*
KAE	Klosterarchiv Einsiedeln (Switzerland)

LA Sp	Landesarchiv Speyer (Rheinland-Pfalz, Germany)
LHA Ko	Landeshauptarchiv Koblenz (Rheinland-Pfalz, Germany)
PfA WND	Pfarrarchiv Sankt Wendel (Saarland, Germany)
SHD	Service historique de la Défense (Vincennes, France)
StA Tr	Stadtarchiv Trier (Rheinland-Pfalz, Germany)
StA WND	Stadtarchiv Sankt Wendel (Saarland, Germany)

INTRODUCTION

1. AN, F/7/7583, d. 51 (R/841), pièce 64, municipal administration of Hochfelden to minister of police, Hochfelden, 25 thermidor an VII (August 12, 1799).
2. AN, F/7/7583, d. 51 (R/841), pièce 64, municipal administration of Hochfelden to minister of police, Hochfelden, 25 thermidor an VII (August 12, 1799).
3. See Asad, *Formations of the Secular*, esp. 32–35, on the momentous implications of Enlightenment and Revolution; and C. Taylor, *A Secular Age*. Joas, *Die Macht des Heiligen*, offers a brilliant critique of the twin sibling of secularization theory, namely Weberian disenchantment theory.
4. Most important on this point, but largely confined to France during the early years of the Revolution, is Julia, *Le voyage aux saints*, 128–45. See, moreover, the dispersed remarks concerning various parts of France in Boudon, *Napoléon et les cultes*, 106–7; Devos, "Pèlerinages et culte"; and Roche, "Création de cultes." On Germany, see the literature cited below, notes 19–21.
5. See, most recently, Andrés-Gallego, "Catholic Pilgrimages." Likewise, the long eighteenth century is woefully underrepresented in Chantre, d'Hollander, and Grévy, *Politiques du pèlerinage*. My use of the metaphor "eclipse" here is indebted to Julia, *Le voyage aux saints*, 111.
6. Hersche, *Muße und Verschwendung*, 794–838. See also Forster, *Catholic Revival*, esp. 104; Kühtreiber and Schindler, "Wallfahrt und Regionalität"; Dünninger, "Zur Geschichte"; and Baumer, *Wallfahrt als Handlungsspiel*, 42–43.
7. Key contributions include Harris, *Lourdes*; Blackbourn, *Marpingen*; and, more recently, Pazos, *Nineteenth-Century European Pilgrimages*, a volume that tellingly gives short shrift to the time before the 1840s and 1850s.
8. See, e.g., Price, *Religious Renewal*, 141–52; Brophy, *Popular Culture*, 259–69; Clark, "The New Catholicism," esp. 13–15; Gibson, *A Social History*,

229–32; and Sperber, *Popular Catholicism*, 10–38. The time before the mid-nineteenth century is not discussed in Heimann, "Catholic Revivalism."
9. That is not to say that we lack overviews and historiographical reflections attending to religious vitality and renewal around 1800. See, among others, Plongeron, *Histoire du christianisme*, vol. 10, esp. 301–617; Rosa, "Conclusion"; Desan, "The French Revolution and Religion"; and Bourdin and Boutry, "L'Église catholique."
10. Printy, *Enlightenment*, esp. 212–20; Michael Müller, *Fürstbischof Heinrich von Bibra*, esp. 430–31.
11. Schettini, "18th-Century Crusaders"; Krenz, *Druckerschwärze statt Schwarzpulver*; Cole, "Nation, Anti-Enlightenment"; Drascek, "Der Papstbesuch." Often, this development is narrated as an origin story of ultramontanism (see, e.g., Lehner, *The Catholic Enlightenment*, 214–16; and Pelletier, *Rome et la Révolution*). For an interesting intermediate case, the city of Lyon, where enlightened *and* Counter-Enlightenment Catholics shaped the 1790s and both groups left a strong postrevolutionary legacy, see Chopelin, *Ville patriote et ville martyre*.
12. Historians of France have led the way on this issue (see Desan, *Reclaiming the Sacred*; Lagrée, "Religion et chocs"; and Chopelin, "Une affaire de femmes?"). On the revolutionary-era Rhineland, see Zalar, *Reading and Rebellion*, 57–70.
13. See, e.g., McMahon, *Enemies of the Enlightenment*; and J.-C. Martin, *Contre-Révolution, Révolution et Nation*.
14. Simon, *Pastorale Erneuerung*, esp. 21–159 (editor's introduction); Klueting, "Katholische Aufklärung nach 1803?"; Handschuh, *Die wahre Aufklärung*.
15. This heterogeneity is revealed and brilliantly analyzed by Watkins, *Berruyer's Bible*. Relative coherence means that the Baroque and ultramontanism each dominated Roman Catholic culture for longer periods of time, not that they were uncontested within that culture even in their respective heydays (one thinks of the more austere Augustinian Catholicisms of the seventeenth and eighteenth centuries and the liberal Catholicisms of the nineteenth).
16. I borrow this concept from H. G. Brown, *Ending the French Revolution*, 358.
17. Among others, and in addition to the works cited in the next four notes, see Beales, *Joseph II*, 2:314–26; Julia, "Les pèlerins de sainte Reine"; B. Schneider, "Wallfahrtskritik," esp. 298–313; Duhamelle, "Les lumières allemandes"; Hartinger, "Kirchliche und staatliche Wallfahrtsverbote"; and Braubach, "Die kirchliche Aufklärung," esp. 33–34, 46, 62, 195, 198–200, and 216–17.

18. Sperber, *Popular Catholicism*, 30. For similar arguments in studies of other regions, see Gabor, "Das Wallfahrtswesen," esp. 993–95; P. Martin, *Pèlerins de Lorraine*, 79–85; Freitag, *Volks- und Elitenfrömmigkeit*, 351–57; Hüttl, *Marianische Wallfahrten*, 154–84; and Moulinas, "Le pèlerinage."
19. A helpful recent summary of this position is given by Holzem, *Christentum in Deutschland*, 988. For more detail, see Bieg, "'Frommer Glaube und unrichtige Begriffe'"; Planert, *Der Mythos vom Befreiungskrieg*, 363–80; Oswalt, "Frömmigkeit im ländlichen Oberschwaben," esp. 309–14; Freytag, "Wunderglauben und Aberglauben"; Stein, "La République française"; Holzem, "Religiöse Orientierung," esp. 338–41; Buchholz, *Französischer Staatskult*, esp. 140–43, 301–7; Wynands, "Rhein-maasländische Wallfahrten"; and Blanning, *The French Revolution in Germany*, 230–39.
20. Seminal for this interpretation is Brückner, *Die Verehrung*, 161–65. More recently, see Speth, *Katholische Aufklärung*, 141. On similar forms of adaptation, see Kimminich, *Religiöse Volksbräuche*, esp. 200.
21. Rebekka Habermas and Christophe Duhamelle have gone beyond this narrative frame by arguing that late eighteenth-century pilgrims developed a new, intensified, and politically subversive sense of autonomy and Catholic identity (Habermas, *Wallfahrt und Aufruhr*, 129–79; Duhamelle, *La frontière au village*, esp. 252–56). However, neither of them attempts to systematically connect these observations to the historiography of revolutionary and postrevolutionary Europe.
22. For critical reflections on intentionality, agency, and resistance (a kind of conceptual trinity in which each term calls forth the other two), see Cresswell, *In Place/Out of Place*, esp. 21–27; Johnson, "On Agency"; and Asad, *Formations of the Secular*, 67–79.
23. Cresswell, *In Place/Out of Place*, 23. To be sure, when justifying their own transgressions or denouncing those of others, people often do talk about intentions in order to qualify the gravity of the transgression: a deliberate, strident transgression is frequently seen as more severe than an unwitting, accidental one (see Kruijtzer, *Justifying Transgression*, 19–21).
24. Febvre, "Frontière," 17–18.
25. Two seminal works in this regard are Anzaldúa, *Borderlands/La frontera*; and Sahlins, *Boundaries*.
26. On revolutionary-era borderlands, in addition to Sahlins's book, see Rowe, *From Reich to State*; Morieux, *The Channel*; Kaci, *Dans le tourbillon*; and Haynes, *Our Friends the Enemies*. For discussions of recent research, see Rau, "Grenzen und Grenzräume"; Dauphant, "L'historiographie"; and

Akbari et al., "AHR Conversation." See also Windler, "Grenzen vor Ort." On borders as dynamic "filters" rather than barriers or obstacles, see Nail, *Theory of the Border*, esp. 4.

27. Historians of central Europe working on periods before and after the revolutionary era have pioneered the focus on borderlands Catholicism (see Duhamelle, *La frontière au village*; Blackbourn, *Marpingen*, esp. 58–66; and Bjork, *Neither German nor Pole*).
28. Konrad and Amilhat Szary, *Border Culture*, xiii. See also Fassin, "Introduction"; and Di Fiore, "The Production of Borders."
29. Of course, in the chapters that follow, I do delve into the more specific, regional histories of the various borderlands on which this book focuses.
30. G. Braun, *Von der politischen zur kulturellen Hegemonie*, 38–64; Cegielski, *Das alte Reich*, 89–148.
31. Ozouf-Marignier, *La formation des départements*.
32. Klueting, "Quidquid est in territorio"; Dickson, "Joseph II's Reshaping," esp. 104; Langlois et al., *Atlas de la Révolution*, 60.
33. Elliott, "A Europe of Composite Monarchies"; Bretschneider and Duhamelle, "Fraktalität."
34. Ozouf-Marignier, "Le territoire," 353.
35. C. S. Maier, *Once Within Borders*, 3. See also Nordman, *Frontières de France*; Mukerji, *Territorial Ambitions*; Elden, *The Birth of Territory*, esp. 309–30; Foucault, *Sécurité, territoire, population*, esp. 93; and Komlosy, *Grenzen*, esp. 98–105.
36. Scholz, *Borders and Freedom of Movement*, esp. 121–25; see also Rutz, *Die Beschreibung des Raums*, esp. 400–402.
37. Torpey, *The Invention of the Passport*, 21–56; Denis, *Une histoire de l'identité*; Bertrand, "Pour une approche comparée"; Rowe, "Borders, War, and Nation-Building." On the history of French customs authorities, see the numerous works by Jean Clinquart, above all his detailed case study of the Hainaut border province (Clinquart, *Les services extérieurs*).
38. This bottom-up aspect is mostly neglected in histories of revolutionary "respatialization," "the geographical revolution," or "Napoleonic territorial revolution"—concepts that I seek to synthesize and expand upon with my idea of a transformation of border culture (see Maruschke and Middell, "Explaining Revolutionary Upheaval"; Dubois, *La révolution géographique*; and Schnabel-Schüle, "Ansteckungsgefahr und Prophylaxe").
39. Lachenicht, *Information und Propaganda*.
40. Rowe, *From Reich to State*, 197–210.
41. Esser and Ellis, introduction to *Frontier and Border Regions*.

42. Dyas, *The Dynamics of Pilgrimage*, 7. For inspiring recent reflections on the field, see also Coleman, *Powers of Pilgrimage*.
43. Turner and Turner, *Image and Pilgrimage*; Dupront, *Du Sacré*. For important reflections on the political valences of pilgrim spaces, see Eade and Sallnow, *Contesting the Sacred*; Dubisch, *In a Different Place*; and Coleman and Eade, "Introduction." On pilgrimage as movement interacting with landscapes, see, above all, Maddrell et al., *Christian Pilgrimage*. Milestones in historians' usage of these concepts include, for sacred space, Froeschlé-Chopard, *Espace et sacré*; P. Martin, *Les chemins du sacré*; and Doney, *The Persistence*. For landscape and place, see Walsham, *The Reformation of the Landscape*; Reinburg, *Storied Places*; Tingle, *Sacred Journeys*; and Dyas, *The Dynamics of Pilgrimage*.
44. Turner and Turner, *Image and Pilgrimage*, esp. 36.
45. The two noteworthy exceptions here are Duhamelle, *La frontière au village*; and Wingens, *Over de grens*. See also Wingens, "Franchir la frontière." But even Wingens hardly analyzes the border itself, which appears in his work mainly because Dutch Catholics had to leave the United Provinces in order to reach any pilgrimage shrine at all. Ultimately, I question the romanticizing idea that pilgrims throughout history have simply "transcended" or even "ignored" borders, an idea expressed most clearly in the title of Kriss-Rettenbeck and Möhler, *Wallfahrt kennt keine Grenzen*.
46. I borrow the image of the shatterzone from Bartov and Weitz, "Introduction."
47. König and Julien, *Verfeindung und Verflechtung*. See also the other available volumes of the series *Deutsch-französische Geschichte* and, among many important studies and essays, Febvre, *Le Rhin*; Duchhardt, "The Cartographic 'Battle of the Rhine'"; Laux, "Deutschlands Westen—Frankreichs Osten"; and Dunlop, *Cartophilia*.
48. Taveneaux, *Le jansénisme*; Chaunu, "Jansénisme et frontière"; Jalabert, "Frontière de catholicité."
49. See, e.g., Muller, *Dieu est catholique et alsacien*; and Heinen, "Aufbruch—Erneuerung—Politik."
50. Luxembourg and the surroundings of Trier, for instance, were economically rather weak, unlike much of Alsace (Voltmer, "'Krieg, uffrohr und teuffelsgespenst'"; Boehler, *Une société rurale*).
51. Czouz-Tornare, "Une frontière intouchable."
52. For regional overviews of pilgrimage places both big and small, see B. Schneider, "Wallfahrten und Wallfahrts-Prozessionen"; Wynands, *Geschichtlicher Atlas der Rheinlande*; Schiffhauer, "Das Wallfahrtswesen";

Oberhauser, *Wallfahrten und Kultstätten*; P. Martin, *Pèlerins de Lorraine*; and Châtellier and Schon, "Essai de cartographie."

1. HOLY PLACE AND SACRED TERRITORY IN THE AGE OF REVOLUTIONS

1. ADHR, L 987, circular letter, Colmar, 11 floréal an IV (April 30, 1796).
2. On the malleability of place, see Massey, "Power-Geometry"; and Kinnard, *Places in Motion*.
3. Delaney, *Territory*, 14.
4. In some ways, that is still the case today—with the major caveat that, between roughly 1820 and 1918, people began viewing Luxembourgish no longer as a German dialect but as a distinct language (see Péporté et al., *Inventing Luxembourg*, 233–65).
5. Jn 4:21–23, quoted after the King James Version.
6. Dyas, *The Dynamics of Pilgrimage*, 15.
7. On the vagaries and plurality of processes of sacralization, see, most recently, Gissibl and Hofmann, "Sacralizations as Cultural Practices."
8. Older scholarship had assumed such timelessness, as reflected most notably in Kötting, *Peregrinatio religiosa*. The decisive critique of essentializing approaches to "popular religion" with regard to early Christianity was formulated by P. Brown, *The Cult of the Saints*, esp. 13–20.
9. In addition to Brown's work, see Markus, "How on Earth."
10. MacCormack, "Loca Sancta," 17–18. For a nuanced critique of Christianity's difficulties with place-making—and their colonialist ramifications—see Deloria, *God Is Red*, esp. 57–69.
11. Constable, "Opposition to Pilgrimage"; Reiter, "Heiligenverehrung und Wallfahrtswesen," 5–56.
12. Reiter, "Heiligenverehrung und Wallfahrtswesen," 75.
13. Augustine, letter 78, paragraph 3, in *Sancti Aurelii Augustini epistulae*, ed. Daur, 85. See also Bitton-Ashkelony, *Encountering the Sacred*, esp. 115–26.
14. Gretser, *De sacris et religiosis peregrinationibus*, 380.
15. For a magisterial summary, see B. Schneider, "Wallfahrtskritik," esp. 304 and 313, on "spirit and truth." See also B. Schneider, "Reform of Piety," esp. 194. On the precedent of early Protestants rejecting pilgrimage with reference to Jn 4:21–24, see Reiter, "Heiligenverehrung und Wallfahrtswesen," 51 (on Paracelsus); and, above all, Walsham, *The Reformation of the Landscape*, 76.
16. On Catholic sermons that criticized such "abuses" while defending the basic idea and value of pilgrimage, see Bock, *Pastorale Strategien*, 251–53.

17. Here, I follow Reinhardt, "Die Kritik der Aufklärung," esp. 330; and Schmalfeldt, "Sub tuum praesidium," esp. 196–98.
18. Probst, *Gottesdienst in Geist und Wahrheit*, 34–35.
19. See chapter 2 of this book on the concrete measures that Clemens Wenceslaus took in the 1780s to restrict pilgrimage in the Archdiocese of Trier.
20. Sailer, *Vorlesungen aus der Pastoraltheologie*, 3:121–29.
21. Sailer, *Vorlesungen aus der Pastoraltheologie*, 3:127 and 3:129.
22. For a meticulous reconstruction of the debate that pitted Kronenberger against Stammel and Müller, see Kallabis, *Katholizismus im Umbruch*, 419–527. On Kronenberger, see also Groß, "Der Trierer Prediger."
23. Johann Kaspar Müller, *Auch das Volk*, 3 (see also 77 and 120 for Müller's rejection of pilgrimage).
24. Kronenberger, *Polemische Kanzelreden*, 240, 445, 466.
25. Kronenberger, *Polemische Kanzelreden*, 241.
26. Kronenberger, *Polemische Kanzelreden*, 494. On the widespread early modern usage of the word *Gnadenort* to assert God's propensity for dispensing extraordinary favors in some places and not in others, see Brugger, *Gedruckte Gnade*, esp. 57–61; and Sidler, *Heiligkeit aushandeln*, esp. 29–32.
27. For a thorough discussion from a Catholic perspective, see Thettayil, *In Spirit and Truth*, quote on 133, where Thettayil summarizes the position he does not share. For mutually contradictory interpretations by key twentieth-century Protestant exegetes, compare Bauer, *Griechisch-deutsches Wörterbuch*, 1356; and Bultmann, *Das Evangelium des Johannes*, 140–41.
28. Casey, *The Fate of Place*, 134. See also Malpas, "Topologies of History," esp. 11 and 20; and Reddy, "The Eurasian Origins."
29. In addition to Casey's work, see Löw, *Raumsoziologie*, esp. 25–28.
30. Casey, *The Fate of Place*, 334.
31. Lehner, *The Catholic Enlightenment*, 127–30.
32. It may be worth noting that Catholic theology did (and does) not treat the Eucharist as a place-bound sacrament. The eucharistic liturgy can be performed wherever an altar has either been permanently or (in the case of portable altars) temporarily erected, and the consecrated host itself is portable as well (see Bauerschmidt, "The Eucharist," esp. 277 ["liturgies ranging from domestic celebrations in Roman homes to battlefield celebrations on the hood of Jeeps"]).
33. Besides Ulrich Lehner's work, see, above all, Sorkin, *The Religious Enlightenment*; Fillafer, *Aufklärung habsburgisch*, 67–123; Overhoff, "Die Katholische Aufklärung"; and chapter 2 for more on "enlightened Reform

Catholicism." On the critique of miracles in eighteenth-century France, see, most recently, the introductory overview by A. C. Haas, "Enlightenment and the Supernatural"; and Sandrier, *Les Lumières du miracle*.

34. By contrast, the secular Enlightenment and the French Revolution were establishing their own pilgrimages, relics, and shrines, from Rousseau's tomb at Ermenonville and Voltaire's estate at Ferney to the revolutionary Pantheon in Paris (see Ridehalgh, "Preromantic Attitudes"; Flamein, *Voltaire à Ferney*, esp. 104, 251–53, 280–82; and Ozouf, "The Pantheon"). It seems plausible to view these secular pilgrimages as "preromantic" responses to the crisis of place that the widespread ontological prioritization of empty space had triggered. These responses were able to develop precisely because they were unburdened by the issue of divine omnipresence that had (ever since Antiquity, as I have argued above) rendered any Christian theology of place problematic.

35. Bitterling, *L'invention du pré carré*, 31–39; Behrisch, "Vermessen, Zählen, Berechnen."

36. Mazel, *L'évêque et le territoire*.

37. Elden, *The Birth of Territory*, 213–41.

38. A good summary of the issue is given by Whaley, *Germany*, 1:477–79. See also Hardy, "Were There 'Territories,'" esp. 40.

39. Mukerji, *Territorial Ambitions*; Nordman, *Frontières de France*; Bitterling, *L'invention du pré carré*.

40. Sandl, *Ökonomie des Raumes*, esp. 187–201; Garner, *État, économie, territoire*, esp. 64–92.

41. Sahlins, "Natural Frontiers Revisited." See also Schmidt, "Naturgrenzen"; Nordman, *Frontières de France*; and Hayworth, *Revolutionary France's War*.

42. Schwanitz, *Von der Natur gerahmt*. On the Swiss case, see Würgler, "Die Konstruktion."

43. Result obtained by searching gallica.fr and Google Books, as well as using the Google Books Ngram Viewer.

44. Result of a full-text search in the digitized *Archives parlementaires* at https://sul-philologic.stanford.edu/philologic/archparl/.

45. AP 29:426. On the flight to Varennes, see Tackett, *When the King Took Flight*.

46. See Wahnich, *L'impossible citoyen*, esp. 34; and Sewell, "The French Revolution."

47. Tricoire, *Mit Gott rechnen*; Maes, *Le roi, la Vierge*; Ramón Solans, *La Virgen del Pilar*, 51–78; Pípalová, "Bohuslav Balbín," esp. 1011–12; Guth, "Geschichtlicher Abriss," esp. 387–89; Delfosse, *La "protectrice."* For a recent,

more general take on the phenomenon, see Balzamo, "La Vierge en ses royaumes."
48. Christin, "Les topographies sacrées," 192.
49. In addition to Tricoire's work, see Soergel, *Wondrous in His Saints*, 111–30 and 159–62; Czerny, *Die Wittelsbacher*; Lederer, *Madness, Religion and the State*, 101–14; Woeckel, *Pietas Bavarica*, 336–433; and Hüttl, *Marianische Wallfahrten*, 95–124.
50. Coreth, *Pietas Austriaca*; Ducreux, "Emperors, Kingdoms, Territories," esp. 293–96; P. Maier, "Mariazell"; Farbaky and Serfőző, *Ungarn in Mariazell*, esp. the chapters by Gábor Tüskés and Éva Knapp (84–92), Jan Royt (194–202), and Gábor Barna (228–39).
51. Heidegger, "Bauen Wohnen Denken." For a compelling critique, see Günzel, *Raum*, esp. 50–83.
52. I am indebted here to Appadurai, *Modernity at Large*, especially his chapter on the "production of locality" (178–99).
53. I borrow conceptually from Debarbieux, "Le lieu," esp. 103 (on sacred place as "pôle territorial").
54. For a concise introduction, see M. Pauly, *Geschichte Luxemburgs*.
55. Bernard-Lesceux, "Notre-Dame de Luxembourg"; Andriani, "Notre-Dame de Luxembourg"; Maertz, "Entstehung und Entwicklung."
56. Birsens, *Manuels de catéchisme*, 180.
57. Birsens, "Die Bruderschaft."
58. The most detailed analysis of this second consecration is found in M. Schmitt, "Die Erwählung Marias."
59. Parker, *Global Crisis*. More specifically on the crisis in Luxembourg, see Trausch, "Comment rester distincts," esp. 174–85; and M. Pauly, "Pestepidemien."
60. Delfosse, *La "protectrice,"* 64–68.
61. Watelet, *Luxembourg, ville obsidionale*, 46–50.
62. Heinz, "Die Verehrung der 'Luxemburger Muttergottes,'" esp. 453.
63. Heinz, "Die Verehrung der 'Trösterin der Betrübten.'"
64. BA Tr, Abt. 35, Nr. 617, ff. 10–11 and 15, Baroness von Veyder's petition to Luxembourg provincial council, early May 1772, f. 11v; almost identical wording ibid., f. 20, petition by Malberg's *Bürgermeister* and *Gemeindevorsteher* on behalf of the entire community to Bitburg dean, Malberg, August 17, 1772.
65. These places included Auw an der Kyll, Schankweiler, Weidingen, and Igel; see Heinz, "Die Verehrung der 'Trösterin,'" esp. 244 and 251–54. More broadly on offshoot shrines, see P. Martin, "Sanctuaires-mères."

66. Van Kley, *Reform Catholicism*.
67. For previous scholarly glimpses into these changes, see Sprunck, "L'église des Jésuites"; and Faltz, *Heimstätte*, 19.
68. AN Lux, A-XXXVIII-03-0303, extract of minutes from a session of the committee established for the affairs of the ex-Jesuits, March 24, 1774. On continuity and change in the Oktav between 1773 and 1781, see Zago, "Text, Knowledge and Truth," 315–37.
69. AN Lux, A-XXXVIII-03-0303, Gerden to the government in Brussels, Luxembourg City, April 7, 1774.
70. For proof that the chaplain, Jean-Frédéric Hildt, remained in charge of both the chapel and the Oktav at least through 1775 and possibly until 1777, see the chapel's account registers of 1773–78: AN Lux, A-XXXVIII-03-0446, esp. f. 7.
71. AGR, T 460, no. 844/A, Leonardy to Conseil privé, Luxembourg City, May 8, 1777.
72. See Hellinghausen, "Patronne de la Cité," esp. 41.
73. More precisely, the decree stipulated that, instead of Leonardy, there should be three new administrators (*proviseurs*) of the chapel estate: one member of the provincial council, a town magistrate, and the parish priest (*curé*) of Saint Nicholas. In addition, however, the *curé* and his successors "à perpetuité" were appointed chief rectors of the chapel (see ADioc Lux, Pfarrarchiv Luxemburg Notre-Dame, Nr. 21a: Kopiar Paul Feller, vol. II, part q', unpaginated: copy of decree of October 27, 1777, attached to letter from the government to the provincial council, Brussels, November 19, 1777).
74. AN Lux, A-XXXVIII-03-0303, Gerden's letter of April 7, 1774.
75. ADioc Lux, Pfarrarchiv Luxemburg Notre-Dame, Nr. 21a, decree of October 27, 1777.
76. ADioc Lux, Pfarrarchiv Luxemburg Notre-Dame, Nr. 21a, decree of October 27, 1777.
77. BA Tr, Abt. 22, Nr. 18, pp. 44–47, copy of letter in the empress's name to the president of the Luxembourgian provincial council, Brussels, April 29, 1778.
78. For the iconography of the 1781 festivities, see *Description du jubilé*; M. Schmitt, "Die Oktavwallfahrt"; and Faltz, *Heimstätte*, 61–62.
79. "Édit de l'Empereur."
80. Trausch, "L'Octave de Notre-Dame," esp. 352–56.
81. On the organization, activities, and great vitality of the duchy's estates in the eighteenth century, see Thewes, *Stände, Staat und Militär*, esp. 277–83.

82. Putallaz, "Nicolas Dufour," esp. pt. 2, 5–67.
83. AGR, I 071, no. 2611, Commission of ecclesiastical affairs, minutes of the session of March 10, 1787.
84. AGR, T 460, no. 704/A, draft of Dufour's opinion, words crossed out at the end.
85. Dufour ruminated on "l'adoration en esprit et en vérité" in a memorandum "sur l'état dans lequel il a trouvé les affaires ecclésiastiques lorsqu'il a été envoyé aux Pays Bas" (AGR, I 071, no. 2682, pp. 48–49).
86. AGR, T 460, no. 704/A, estates' petition to the government in Brussels, December 8, 1786.
87. AGR, T 460, no. 704/A, estates' petition to the government in Brussels, December 8, 1786.
88. Trausch, "L'Octave de Notre-Dame," 356–58.
89. See ADioc Lux, Pfarrarchiv Luxemburg Notre-Dame, Nr. 137, "Einkünfte und Ausgabenregister der Glaciskapelle" (preserved for the years 1778–85, 1788, 1790, and 1793–95); and other registers of the chapel's accounts for 1778–87 in AN Lux, A-XXXVIII-03-0447. From these sources, 1787 and 1788 emerge as surprisingly ordinary years in terms of expenses incurred for the Oktav, pious offerings received, and number of communion wafers bought and — presumably, at least in their overwhelming majority — distributed to pilgrims (in 1788: 9,900 large ones and 6,000 small ones at the chapel throughout the year, and 850 large ones and 12,900 small ones during the Oktav).
90. See, e.g., a French map of 1737, BnF, GED-4754, https://gallica.bnf.fr/ark:/12148/btv1b84437861/f1.item.
91. AN Lux, B-0847, deliberations of Forêts central administration, pp. 149–51 (session of 23 ventôse an IV). On the first years of French rule in Luxembourg, the most helpful work is still Lefort, *Histoire du département des Forêts*, esp. 257–62, on the fate of the chapel.
92. AN Lux, B-0837, Forêts departmental administration to Lagadine, *chef de brigade* of the engineering corps, 26 prairial an IV (June 14, 1796).
93. See the documents edited by Sprunck, "Les pèlerinages."
94. On the history of the hopping procession and the church of Saint Willibrord, see, for example, Ferrari, Schröder, and Trauffler, *Die Abtei Echternach*; and Langini, *La procession dansante*.
95. For various cases from within (pre-1792) France, see Baciocchi and Julia, "Reliques et Révolution"; and Boutry, "Le procès super non cultu."
96. In addition to Lefort, *Histoire du département des Forêts*, see especially Trausch, "Comment faire," 201–5; and Margue, "Apôtres ou prévaricateurs?"

97. The relevant historiography is vast, but see, above all, J.-C. Martin, *La Vendée et la France*. Also, on the importance of the religious factor in the Vendée, see Rolland-Boulestreau, "Dieu et le roi"; and Woell, *Small-Town Martyrs and Murderers*.
98. See the classic work by Trausch, *La répression des soulèvements*; and, on the wider Belgian context, Dupont-Bouchat, "Les résistances."
99. On this oath and its extraordinary divisiveness in the recently annexed areas, see Minke, *Hommes de Dieu*, 143–97.
100. AM Lux, LU 11 II, no. 381, report by police commissioner Seyler and his assistant Glavet, 16 floréal an VI (May 5, 1798); AM Lux, LU 02.1, no. 5, ff. 194v–197r, minutes of Luxembourg municipality, 17 to 22 floréal an VI (May 6 to 11, 1798); Trausch, "L'octave en 1798," 47–52. For an excellent recent overview of the French police in the revolutionary era, see the chapters by Vincent Denis in Milliot et al., *Histoire des polices*, 201–335.
101. M. Schmitt, "Le Concordat."
102. AN Lux, B-0620, dossier 5272, petition of 14 floréal an X (May 4, 1802). On the petition's success, see ibid., letter from prefect Lacoste to the mayor, 18 floréal an X (May 8, 1802).
103. AN Lux, B-0620, dossier 5272, undated petition from churchwardens Baclesse and Röser to Lacoste. On Baclesse and Röser as members of the urban elite, see N. Franz, *Die Stadtgemeinde Luxemburg*, 249 and 311.
104. AN Lux, B-0062, dossier 663, report to Lacoste by subprefect Wilmar and secretary-general Christiani, undated (probably December 1802).
105. AN, F/19/702/C, dossier Forêts, undated *Projet de Circonscription des Cures & Succursales de l'arrondissement de Luxembourg* (probably late 1802 or early 1803).
106. ADM, 29 J 847, petition of September 28, 1802.
107. ADM, 29 J 847, declaration signed by counselors Baclesse, Dutreux, and Vandernoot, 1er germinal an XI (March 22, 1803).
108. In addition to materials already cited, see many exasperated letters between Bienaymé and Lacoste in AN Lux, B-0062, dossier 663 and B-0620, dossier 5260, as well as in ADM, 29 J 828; and letters from Bienaymé to Portalis (minister of *cultes*), the last one dated Metz, 7 germinal an XII (March 28, 1804): AN, F/19/324.
109. More broadly on the constriction of Luxembourg's urban space by its fortifications, see Thewes, "Luxembourg, ville forteresse."
110. A rich and dispersed documentation reflects the multitude of authorities that intervened to support the project. See, first and foremost, Blum, "Aktenstücke." This edition of copied correspondence preserved in ADioc

Lux, Pfarrarchiv Luxemburg Notre-Dame, Nr. 413, includes letters sent to Paris by the bishop of Metz, Jauffret, and the prefect of the Forêts, Jourdan. Although Blum dates the first two pieces of that dossier to 1803, both must have been first written in the fall of 1804, since they refer to a decision that the minister of war made—as emerges unequivocally from the dossier as a whole—in September 1804. See also AN Lux, B-0880, deliberations of the conseil d'arrondissement of Luxembourg, summaries for the first ten days of germinal an XII (end of March 1804) and for the year 1806; AN Lux, B-0878, deliberations of the conseil général of the Forêts, sessions of 26 germinal an XII (April 16, 1804) and June 15, 1806, the latter also mentioning a previous petition from the municipal council of Luxembourg City to Napoleon; BnF, NAF 28917, vol. 7, letter from Jauffret to the mayor of Luxembourg City, Étalle, July 4, 1807. Finally, in 1810, Jauffret considered petitioning Napoleon directly once more but seems to have decided against sending the letter: see ADM, 29 J 847, Jauffret to Napoleon, letter written in Jauffret's own hand and with his signature crossed out, Compiègne, April 20, 1810.

111. Dondelinger, "Le glacis," esp. 22–32.
112. Blum, "Aktenstücke," 334. For the law in question, see AP 27:727–41, esp. 730.
113. AN, F/19/346, Jauffret to minister Bigot de Préameneu, Metz, July 29, 1810.
114. Blum, "Aktenstücke," 335.
115. ADM, 29 J 824, Neunheuser to vicar-general Oster, February 2, [1805].
116. Hirschhausen et al., *Phantomgrenzen*, 18.
117. Kumor, "Austriackie władze"; on the nineteenth-century continuation of the story, see, e.g., Jabłoński, "Jasna Góra." For more religious, cultural, and political context, see Niedźwiedź, *Obraz i postać;* and Butterwick, *The Polish-Lithuanian Commonwealth.*
118. Very illustrative material on this dilemma in SHD, 1 I 14 (esp. the entry of May 19, 1810 in the correspondence register) and 2 C 416 (*journal de défense* of the fortress, January–May 1814, esp. the preface).
119. Smaller parts of the duchy had fallen to the departments of Sambre-et-Meuse and Ourthe in 1795 (see Dubois, *La révolution géographique*, esp. 134 on Luxembourgian "provincial sentiment" in 1795 and thereafter).
120. AN Lux, B-0878, council session of June 15, 1806: "la reconstruction de la Chapelle de Notre Dame patrone de la [word "ville" struck through] cidevant Province."
121. BnF, NAF 22312, Jauffret's "Mémoires sur ma première visite pastorale

dans le département des Forêts. 1807," f. 156v. This account is corroborated by that of Jauffret's secretary (BnF, NAF 6169, p. 59).
122. AN, F/19/5687, Jauffret to Portalis, Luxembourg City, May 7, 1807.
123. See AN Lux, B-0056, dossier 599, prefect Lacoste to the mayor of Luxembourg City, May 12, 1806; Blum, "Aktenstücke," 394 (Lacoste's successor Jourdan looking back on previous years in 1809); AN, F/7/8069, dossier "Sarre—Préfet—La vraie Robe de Jesus Christ à Trèves," prefect of Moselle department to police ministry, Metz, September 24, 1810 (giving an estimate of fifteen to twenty thousand pilgrims going to Luxembourg City each year around the time of the Oktav).
124. Jacops, "Images et témoignages."
125. E.g., AN, F/19/5541, Jauffret to Bigot de Préameneu, Metz, February 5, 1808; on Luxembourg City as a center, see above all ADM, 19 J 748, memorandum by Jauffret to his successor at the bishopric of Metz.
126. BnF, NAF 22312, f. 157r.
127. ADM, 29 J 132, pp. 2–4 and 13–14, letters from Jauffret to Portalis, February 19 and March 3, 1807.
128. AN, F/19/5687, Jauffret to Portalis, Thionville, May 29, 1807. On the seminaries founded by Jauffret, see R. Schneider, "La réorganisation," 90–126.
129. Other than Faltz, Heimstätte, see Hellinghausen, "Bischof Laurent"; and Hellinghausen, Kleine Diözesangeschichte, esp. 38, on the supposed "Dekadenzphase" of the Oktav from 1795 through the 1830s.
130. Ramón Solans, La Virgen del Pilar, 59 ("vinculación territorial").

2. SHIFTING THE CONFESSIONAL FRONTIER

1. BA Tr, Abt. 40, Nr. 71, pp. 135–42, petition by the Tholey échevins synodaux ("à eux joints le curé, et les elûs": 135) to Weihbischof Hontheim, Tholey, May 19, 1772, quotes from p. 141.
2. BA Tr, Abt. 40, Nr. 71, pp. 135–42, petition by Tholey notables to Hontheim, Tholey, May 19, 1772, 140–41.
3. See the overview in Herrmann, "Die Saarregion," esp. 32–34.
4. See van Kley, Reform Catholicism, esp. 24–30, on Febronius; and Groß, Trierer Geistesleben, esp. 16, 65, 162. Specifically on Hontheim's activities as Weihbischof, see Persch, "Die Bistumsverwaltung," esp. 112–16.
5. On the Catholic Enlightenment as "anti-Baroque," see the powerful synthesis by Hersche, Muße und Verschwendung, 952–1028. Even Benjamin Kaplan's brilliant microhistory tends to reify the binary opposition by con-

struing a "popular backlash against the new ideas" of the Enlightenment (Kaplan, *Cunegonde's Kidnapping*, 236). That said, he has also done much to undermine the tenacious cliché that equates the Age of Enlightenment with the dawn of deconfessionalization and tolerance (Kaplan, *Divided by Faith*, esp. 333–58).

6. BA Tr, Abt. 40, Nr. 71, pp. 135–42, petition by Tholey notables to Hontheim, Tholey, May 19, 1772, 141.
7. Resistance undeniably plays a role in the story that this chapter tells, but resistance is hardly ever the clear-cut other of the power it opposes (see Foucault, *Histoire de la sexualité*, esp. 125–27).
8. In identifying *Wallfahrt* with processional pilgrimage, I pragmatically follow a suggestion first made by Dünninger, "Processio peregrinationis," esp. 30–32. Other scholars have understood *Wallfahrt* as an umbrella term for all kinds of pilgrimage and have, consequently, used the more precise (and more cumbersome) concept of "Prozessionswallfahrt" to designate processional pilgrimage (see, e.g., Berbée, "Zur Klärung," esp. 79).
9. For a concise panorama, see Reader, *Pilgrimage*. For an overview focusing on seventeenth- to nineteenth-century Europe, see Harrer, "Pilgrimage."
10. For this overview paragraph, I draw primarily on Hersche, *Muße und Verschwendung*, 794–838; and Duhamelle, "Le pèlerinage dans le Saint-Empire"; see also Christian, *Local Religion*, esp. 23–69.
11. On the beginnings and breakthrough of *Wallfahrt*, see Guth, "Geschichtlicher Abriss," esp. 360–62; and Duhamelle, "Le pèlerinage dans le Saint-Empire," 73. On the rather different world of pilgrimage in medieval Latin Christianity, see van Herwaarden, "Medieval Pilgrimages"; Webb, *Pilgrims and Pilgrimage*; Vauchez, "Saints and Pilgrimages"; and Sumption, *The Age of Pilgrimage*.
12. This last point is emphasized by Hersche, *Muße und Verschwendung*.
13. On "the cultural cusp of the divide" between the confessions and its increasing sharpness after 1648, see Harrington and Smith, "Confessionalization," esp. 91. Solid empirical grounding of this insight can be found in Katzer, *Konflikt—Konsens—Koexistenz*; Nebgen, *Konfessionelle Differenzerfahrungen*; Duhamelle, *La frontière au village*; Jalabert, *Catholiques et protestants*; Forster, *The Counter-Reformation*, esp. 214–43; François, *Die unsichtbare Grenze*; and Châtellier, *Tradition chrétienne*. A sophisticated early argument for eighteenth-century "reconfessionalization" in the Holy Roman Empire was made by Haug-Moritz, *Württembergischer Ständekonflikt*, 138–63. Haug-Moritz, however, was primarily interested in high politics.
14. Reinhard, "Die lateinische Variante," 250 ("Unterscheidungsriten"). See

also Luebke, *Hometown Religion*, 18–19; and Brückner, "Die Neuorganisation," esp. 163–64.
15. An overview of impressive numbers is given by Duhamelle, "Le pèlerinage dans le Saint-Empire," 69–71.
16. I borrow the concept of "pèlerinage de frontière" from Duhamelle, *La frontière au village*, 167. See also, for the notion of "frontier shrines," Tilatti, *Santuari di confine*.
17. Freitag, *Volks- und Elitenfrömmigkeit*; Zwyssig, *Täler voller Wunder*, esp. 242, on the expression "di frontiera all'eresia" found in a primary source. Further examples of frontier pilgrimages are presented in R. Becker, "Wallfahrt und Geographie," esp. 323–26.
18. For close analysis of this phenomenon, see Duhamelle, *La frontière au village*, 154–71.
19. Corpis, *Crossing the Boundaries*, 37–38, 200–201, 264.
20. Duhamelle, *La frontière au village*, 192–95.
21. See Jalabert, *Catholiques et protestants*, 420–26; Schlenker, *Fördern, Feiern, Verbote*, 87–88; Hegel, "Prozessionen und Wallfahrten," esp. 316; Döring, "Wallfahrtsleben," esp. 45; and Drascek, "Räumliche Horizonte," esp. 297.
22. Kleinehagenbrock, "Der Reicholzheimer Wallfahrtsstreit," esp. 239–40; Goy, *Aufklärung und Volksfrömmigkeit*, 158.
23. Walldürn regularly drew more than one hundred thousand pilgrims annually in the eighteenth century. This shrine was the focus of the classic study by Brückner, *Die Verehrung*.
24. See the remarks in Hersche, *Muße und Verschwendung*, 801.
25. Krämer, "Vom gewerblichen Leben," esp. 175 and 177; Brommer, *Kurtrier*, 2:1048. In 1798, the town had 1,313 inhabitants, according to Hansen, *Quellen zur Geschichte*, 4:771.
26. Selzer, *St. Wendelin*, 91–100.
27. On the Magdalen Chapel, also called Wendelskapelle in the eighteenth century, as a place attracting many pilgrims, see PfA WND, B 28, pp. 628–48, Sankt Wendel parish leaders to the archbishop, February 23, 1794, esp. 646. On St. Anne's Chapel and the Wendelsbrunnenkapelle: G. Schmitt, "Die Annenkapelle und die Wendelskapelle"; and G. Schmitt, *Die St. Sebastianus-Bruderschaft*, 76–108.
28. Selzer, *St. Wendelin*, 172–87, 411.
29. SHD, A 3693, pp. 81–82, *mémoire* signed by the *bailli*(?) Tailleur, Tholey, October 1, 1775, p. 81.
30. For an example of such an extraordinary procession organized in 1788, see Heinz, *Heilige im Saarland*, 74.

31. Hebler and Herrmann, "Tholey," esp. 852–58.
32. F. Pauly, "Die Tholeyer Prozessionsliste"; Kyll, *Pflichtprozessionen und Bannfahrten*, esp. 151–52, on very limited erosion of this custom from the sixteenth century to the 1780s.
33. Naumann, *Die Blasiuskapelle*, esp. 19–23, 61–73.
34. See Seibrich, "Das Erzbistum Trier," esp. 186–93. On the deaconries, see B. Schneider, "Strukturen der Seelsorge." On the complex territorial situation, see also F. Pauly, *Siedlung und Pfarrorganisation*, 113–56.
35. See the expression "low degree of boundary coincidence" in Scholz, *Borders and Freedom of Movement*, 230; see also Bretschneider and Duhamelle, "Fraktalität," esp. 727–32.
36. The same was true for the region's other majority-Protestant territories, including Pfalz-Zweibrücken and Nassau-Saarbrücken. That the treaty of Ryswick and princely conversions crucially accelerated the confessional dynamics in this part of the Empire is shown in great detail by Jalabert, *Catholiques et protestants*.
37. *Kurze Lebensbeschreibung*, 23.
38. LA Sp, Best. B 2, Nr. 169/7, Zweibrücken government to Amt Nohfelden, October 19, 1752.
39. LA Sp, Best. B 2, Nr. 1056/4, ff. 28–29, Pfarrer Löhr to Regierungsrat von Günter, Kübelberg, May 10, 1764, 28r.
40. BA Tr, Abt. 40, Nr. 71, pp. 191–92, report of churchwardens (with confirming signature by the parish priest) of Bleiderdingen, August 20, 1772.
41. These incidents are documented in detail in LA Sp, Best. B 2, Nr. 181/6; see esp. ff. 1r–2r, Oberamt Lichtenberg to the Zweibrücken government, Kusel, May 24, 1769, on the *Kirchenzensor*'s leadership.
42. BA Tr, Abt. 40, Nr. 71, pp. 119–20, Johann Augustin Lauxen to Hontheim, Theley, May 28, 1771, p. 119.
43. Stitz and Naumann, *Pfarrvisitationen*, 250.
44. BA Tr, Abt. 40, Nr. 71, pp. 47–49, excerpt from the minutes of the Trier diocesan officialate, March 18, 1761.
45. I agree with Stitz and Naumann, *Pfarrvisitationen*, 10, on this point.
46. Heinz, "Liturgie und Frömmigkeitsleben," esp. 33–36; Trausch, "L'Octave de Notre-Dame," esp. 339–48.
47. BA Tr, Abt. 40, Nr. 71, p. 9, from the questionnaire of the 1770 visit.
48. BA Tr, Abt. 40, Nr. 71, pp. 15 and 36 ("synodales divisi" in Exweiler and Kastel), p. 17 on lack of answers in Tholey.
49. Stitz and Naumann, *Pfarrvisitationen*, 250.
50. BA Tr, Abt. 40, Nr. 71, p. 19, on Marpingen.

51. BA Tr, Abt. 40, Nr. 71, pp. 53–61, Hontheim's *ordinata*, Kärlich Castle, August 23, 1770, esp. p. 54.
52. Hersche, *Muße und Verschwendung*, 969: "jener katholische Inferioritätskomplex"; Raab, *Clemens Wenzeslaus*, 20: "Ausbildung eines Inferioritätsbewußtseins unter den Katholiken."
53. Historians disagree over whether Febronius took up the ideal of church reunion in earnest or whether foregrounding this cause was primarily a way of packaging Hontheim's more immediate agenda of limiting papal jurisdiction in German dioceses (see Lehner, "Johann Nikolaus von Hontheim's *Febronius*"; Spehr, *Aufklärung und Ökumene*, 34–48; Klueting, "Wiedervereinigung"; and Pitzer, *Justinus Febronius*).
54. For a recent summary and deconstruction of this theme, see Schiersner and Röckelein, "Eine neue Sicht."
55. On this point, see, first and foremost, Duhamelle, *La frontière au village*, 141–46 (and 190–91 on Protestant mockery).
56. BA Tr, Abt. 40, Nr. 71, pp. 53–61, Hontheim's *ordinata*, Kärlich Castle, August 23, 1770, p. 54.
57. BA Tr, Abt. 40, Nr. 71, pp. 151–54, prior of Tholey to Hontheim, Tholey, June 11, 1772, esp. 153, on "Zusammenkunft beyder hiesiger Landspatronen." For a similar, detailed description of the second meeting between the two saints on the Friday after Pentecost, see PfA WND, B 31, pp. 159–61, parish priest and churchwardens of St. Wendel to the General Vicariate, St. Wendel, February 16, 1785.
58. BA Tr, Abt. 40, Nr. 71, p. 101, Lauxen to Hontheim, Theley, April 28, 1771.
59. BA Tr, Abt. 40, Nr. 71, pp. 107–10, correspondence between Hontheim and de Marcol, May 4 and 14, 1771.
60. BA Tr, Abt. 40, Nr. 71, pp. 119–20, Lauxen to Hontheim, Theley, May 28, 1771, p. 119.
61. Lauxen had recently resigned his post at Theley, probably due to old age and bad health. See BA Tr, Abt. 40, Nr. 71, pp. 157–60, Demerath (parish priest at Exweiler) to Hontheim, undated (probably late August 1772), here 158 on Lauxen, "olim pastor in Theley." Lauxen died on November 14, 1772, according to Stitz and Naumann, *Pfarrvisitationen*, 265.
62. BA Tr, Abt. 40, Nr. 71, pp. 185–86, declaration of churchwardens of Bliesen, August 18, 1772, quotes on 185. See also ibid., pp. 177–78, declaration of churchwardens and priest of Freisen, August 19, 1772, esp. 177.
63. BA Tr, Abt. 40, Nr. 71, pp. 157–60, Demerath to Hontheim, p. 159.
64. BA Tr, Abt. 40, Nr. 71, pp. 191–92, report of churchwardens and parish priest of Bleiderdingen, August 20, 1772.

65. BA Tr, Abt. 40, Nr. 71, pp. 185–86, declaration of churchwardens of Bliesen, August 18, 1772, p. 185.
66. BA Tr, Abt. 40, Nr. 71, pp. 177–78, declarations of churchwardens and priest of Freisen, August 19, 1772.
67. BA Tr, Abt. 40, Nr. 71, p. 105, ordinance of the General Vicariate, Trier, April 30, 1771. Lauxen had directly brought the issue to the attention of the General Vicariate (see BA Tr, Abt. 20, Nr. 16, p. 724, protocol entry of April 30, 1771).
68. BA Tr, Abt. 40, Nr. 71, pp. 135–42, petition by Tholey notables to Hontheim, Tholey, May 19, 1772, 140.
69. BA Tr, Abt. 40, Nr. 71, pp. 157–60, Demerath to Hontheim, here 159.
70. BA Tr, Abt. 40, Nr. 71, pp. 143–48, Dean Lochen (parish priest at Hermeskeil) to Hontheim, Hermeskeil, May 25, 1772, pp. 145–46.
71. On this point, see, e.g., van Kley, "Conclusion," esp. 310.
72. Hersche, "'Lutherisch werden'"; further pertinent evidence is found in Duhamelle, *La frontière au village*, 148; Schreiner, "'Abwuerdigung der Feyertage,'" esp. 292; Braubach, "Die kirchliche Aufklärung," esp. 30.
73. Trausch, "L'Octave de Notre-Dame," 347–48.
74. BA Tr, Abt. 40, Nr. 71, p. 195, episcopal ordinance, Trier, September 12, 1772.
75. See specifically for the cities of Trier and Zweibrücken and thus for the region on which this chapter focuses, Drut-Hours, "Promouvoir le 'vrai christianisme.'"
76. PfA WND, B 31, pp. 117–20, protocol of *Kirchenstrafen* (church fines), June 18, 1778.
77. Lees, "Clemens Wenzeslaus," 138.
78. "Ordinatio processiones concernens, in specie quod processiones omnes ultra horam interdictae sint. 29. Novembris 1784," in Blattau, *Statuta synodalia, ordinationes et mandata*, 5:396–97, quote on 396.
79. Heinz, "Prozessionen und Wallfahrten."
80. Cf. PfA WND, B 31, pp. 159, parish and churchwardens of St. Wendel to the General Vicariate, St. Wendel, February 16, 1785; StA WND, A 217, pp. 257ff., gravamina of St. Wendel town delegates, esp. pp. 270–72, on processions and pilgrimages, July 7, 1788; BA Tr, Abt. 20, Nr. 162, General Vicariate protocol entry of May 25, 1789, p. 219v; StA WND, A 116, pp. 265–300, Clemens Wenzeslaus's response to the gravamina of St. Wendel, Koblenz, November 26, 1789, esp. p. 291, for a dilatory remark on the issue of pilgrimage; StA WND, A 232, p. 86, update on the municipal gravamina in the protocols of the St. Wendel Hochgericht, February 17, 1790; PfA

WND, B 28, pp. 245-47, Hofrat and Amtmann Gattermann to Clemens Wenzeslaus, St. Wendel, April 7, 1790.
81. F. Pauly, "Die Pfarrgemeinde Senheim." On Eberhardsklausen more generally, see Dohms and Dohms, *Klausen*.
82. StA WND, A 217, pp. 257ff., gravamina of St. Wendel town delegates, July 7, 1788, quote on p. 271.
83. PfA WND, B 80, *Protocollum synodale* of St. Wendel parish, p. 91, February 13, 1785.
84. BA Tr, Abt. 20, Nr. 25, pp. 313-14, General Vicariate protocol entry of April 19, 1790.
85. See Hebler and Herrmann, "Tholey," 859; and Oberhauser, *Wallfahrten und Kultstätten*, 36-37. For the first statements about this decline, made during and shortly after the Napoleonic period, see ADM, 29 J 360, records of a pastoral visit of 1803/4, report from the parish of Tholey; BA Tr, Abt. 52, Nr. 733, petition of Tholey's notables to the General Vicariate, June 24, 1818.
86. G. Schmitt, "Die Annenkapelle und die Wendelskapelle," 134-36.
87. On the gradual legal integration of the so-called Rhenish departments into France between 1798 and 1802, see, most recently, Lignereux, *L'Empire de la paix*, 34.
88. See Le Roy Ladurie, *Histoire humaine*, 209-33; and Cobb, *The Police and the People*, 246-324.
89. Vallat, *Les bœufs malades*, 76-79, 175-78.
90. Schreiber, "Strukturwandel der Wallfahrt," 69 (on southwestern Germany); Goy, *Aufklärung und Volksfrömmigkeit*, 141 (on Franconia); on St. Wendel itself: StA WND, B 113, *Justizprotokoll* of the District of St. Wendel, p. 65b, August 17, 1796, and PfA WND, B 21, pp. 1-8, vow made by the parish community of St. Wendel, January 18, 1797, esp. p. 1, on the consequences of the epizootic. On the local and regional context, see also J. Schmitt, "Die Saarregion," esp. 83-89; and Max Müller, *Die Geschichte*, esp. 115-16.
91. Selzer, *St. Wendelin*, esp. 353; Goy, *Aufklärung und Volksfrömmigkeit*, 156; Herberich-Marx and Raphaël, "L'imagerie religieuse," esp. 342-43; Schwaller, "Lothringische Tierheilige," esp. 120-21.
92. ADM, 29 J 365-72, diocesan *enquête* of 1807: evidence of particularly strong devotion to Saint Wendelin in Volmerange(-les-Mines) near Cattenom (29 J 366), Hestroff near Bouzonville (ibid.), Hülzweiler near Saarlouis (ibid.), Reinange near Metzervisse (ibid.), and Diebling near Forbach (29 J 368). On this *enquête*, see R. Schneider, "Dévotions et vie spiritu-

elle." For similar evidence from the parish of Momerstroff and Halling-lès-Boulay, see ADM, 29 J 136, no. 181, General Vicariate of Metz to the *curé* of Boulay, May 30, 1809.

93. "Loi sur l'exercice et la police extérieure des cultes" (7 vendémiaire an IV), title IV, section III, in *Bulletin des lois*, no. 186, 1–12.

94. These contentious processions were described in some detail by Gain, "Les processions," esp. 172–84. Gain, however, somewhat underestimated the seriousness of the conflict because he did not consult the numerous relevant police files in the central state archives: AN, F/7/7165, d. B/2/7165 and B/2/7167; F/7/7169, d. B/2/7705 (the phrase "une espece d'insurrection religieuse" in an *arrêté* of the Directory, 12 vendémiaire an V [October 3, 1796]); F/7/7172, d. B/2/8034; F/7/7174, d. B/2/8355; F/7/7175, d. B/2/8405 and B/2/8508; F/7/7179, d. B/2/9013 (united in a single file with numerous other dossiers from the Moselle); F/7/7180, d. B/2/9113. See also, on judicial fallout, two dossiers in BB/18/555. Finally, on the repressive role played by the armed forces in this crisis: SHD, 1 I 7, pp. 60–70, orders of the Third Military Division (Metz) during messidor and thermidor an IV (summer 1796); SHD, 1 I 10, pp. 230–32, relevant correspondence of the same division.

95. For more on Catholic antirevolutionary sentiments and activities in the occupied Rhineland, see Blanning, *The French Revolution in Germany*, 218–39.

96. Paquet, *Bibliographie analytique*, 1160: *directeur des postes* Metzinger to Ministers of Interior and Police, Saarbrücken, 15 thermidor an IV (August 2, 1796).

97. PfA WND, B 28, pp. 850–51, excerpt from the municipal protocol of St. Wendel, August 3, 1796, p. 850.

98. There is evidence, moreover, that an extraordinary number of offerings were made (presumably mostly by pilgrims) to the church of St. Wendel in a short time in 1796: BA Tr, Abt. 20, Nr. 27, pp. 658–59, General Vicariate protocol entry of January 9, 1797, p. 658: "seit Kurzem ad 1000 Gulden Opfer bezogen." See also the high sums recorded for 1796 in the accounting notebook (*"Opferbüchlein"*) of the Wendelsbrunnenkapelle in PfA WND, B 28, pp. 1080–95.

99. AN, F/7/7174, d. B/2/8355, *procès-verbal* of interrogation of seven arrested men by Le Lièvre ("inspecteur de l'administration des pays conquis entre Rhin et Moselle faisant les fonctions de Directeur général"), Saarbrücken, 14 thermidor an IV (August 1, 1796).

100. Another source mentioning the interrupted pilgrimage (Paquet, *Bibliogra-*

phie analytique, 1160: directeur des postes Metzinger to Ministers of Interior and Police, Saarbrücken, 15 thermidor an IV [August 2, 1796]) indicates that the procession had started near Oermingen ("Virmingen, près Sarre-Union"), a village in the Duchy of Saarwerden that had belonged to Nassau-Saarbrücken until the Revolution (see the *notice communale* on Oermingen at http://cassini.ehess.fr/cassini/fr/html/fiche.php?select_resultat=25452, and the map Appendix III c [unpaginated] in Wilhelm, *Nassau-Weilburg*).

101. For a regional overview with lucid remarks on the "porosité opportuniste des enclaves," see Husson and Jalabert, "Les enclaves en Lorraine," quote on 66. See also Duhamelle, "Dedans, dehors."
102. Paquet, *Bibliographie analytique*, 1160, Metzinger to Ministers of Interior and Police, Saarbrücken, 15 thermidor an IV (August 2, 1796).
103. See an anonymous journal article titled "Moselle, Sarreguemines," *Annales de la religion* 1, no. 23 (1795): 543–46, esp. 545.
104. Paquet, *Bibliographie analytique*, 1141 (Cantonal Commissioner Kremer to Ministry of Police, Sarralbe, 25 messidor an IV [July 13, 1796]) and 1143–44 (Cantonal Commissioner Serva to regional *tribunal correctionnel*, Sarreguemines, 27 messidor an IV [July 15, 1796]).
105. On this broader context, see Smith, *The Continuities*, 95–97.
106. BA Tr, Abt. 20, Nr. 17, minutes of the General Vicariate, pp. 54–55.
107. On this mandate, dating to 1699, see Romberg, "Wallfahrten im Bistum," 162.
108. Hersche, "'Lutherisch werden,'" 159.
109. BA Tr, Abt. 20, Nr. 164, minutes of the General Vicariate, pp. 107–10, July 1, 1797, p. 107. On the return of the printing trade to Saarbrücken around 1740, see Jung, "Saarbrücken und St. Johann," 387–89; and Herrmann, "Die Saarregion," 55.
110. That said, the hagiographical part was followed up differently—by a handful of prayers to Saint Wendelin in the 1704 version and by an expanded assortment of litanies, prayers, a novena, and songs in the 1783 one (Keller, *Beschreibung* [1704], 32–47; Keller, *Beschreibung* [1783], 30–79). Why a Protestant printing house would have reprinted such a legend remains inexplicable to me.
111. Keller, *Beschreibung* (1704), 26–27; cf. Keller, *Beschreibung* (1783), 25.
112. *Kurze Lebensbeschreibung*, 24 ("1540 zur Reformationszeit Luthers").
113. On Castello, see Lichter, "Johann Wilhelm Josef Castello."
114. *Kurze Lebensbeschreibung*, xlv–xlvi.
115. *Kurze Lebensbeschreibung*, xl.

116. *Kurze Lebensbeschreibung*, 31–85.
117. *Kurze Lebensbeschreibung*, 24.
118. *Kurze Lebensbeschreibung*, 24.
119. Keller, *Beschreibung (1783)*, 25; cf. Keller, *Beschreibung (1704)*, 27 (almost identical, but the last word is "worden" instead of "geblieben").
120. G. Franz, "Morgenglanz der Toleranz," esp. 120.
121. PfA WND, B 28, pp. 628–48, report by Sankt Wendel parish council to Clemens Wenceslaus, February 23, 1794, esp. 629–30, on the smashed bells.
122. *Kurze Lebensbeschreibung*, 29.
123. My thinking about the dialectics of humiliation and power is indebted to Orsi, *The Madonna*, 214–17.
124. Over the last few decades, historians have thoroughly debunked the myth-making of their interwar predecessors, who had projected the tradition of Franco-German national enmity (*Erbfeindschaft*) back into the revolutionary and Napoleonic era (see, among others, Molitor, *Vom Untertan zum Administré*; Planert, *Der Mythos vom Befreiungskrieg*; Englund, "Monstre sacré," esp. 219–27; G. B. Clemens, "Einleitung"; Owzar, "Liberty," esp. 76–77; and Horn, *Le défi de l'enracinement*, esp. 35–49).
125. This insight may be generalizable beyond the regional frame of the Saar region and the thematic one of pilgrimage. See Hermon-Belot, *Aux sources de l'idée laïque*, esp. 121, on how the Revolution collided and interacted with the outcomes of centuries-long "confessionalization"; and, on southern France, Sottocasa, *Mémoires affrontées*.
126. Rowe, *From Reich to State*, 157. On confessional struggles in the Duchy of Saarwerden around 1792/3, see Wilhelm, *Nassau-Weilburg*, 218–21. For examples of Catholic violence against Protestants in the Northern Rhineland at a slightly later stage of the French occupation (in 1798), see Smets, *Les pays rhénans*, 247–48.
127. On nineteenth-century *Religionspolicey*, see, e.g., Dipper, "Volksreligiosität und Obrigkeit"; and Speth, *Katholische Aufklärung*.
128. Bieg, "'Frommer Glaube und unrichtige Begriffe.'"
129. On the unintended outcomes of state projects to achieve "legibility" and "simplification," see Scott, *Seeing Like a State*, quotes on 2.
130. AN, F/7/7174, d. B/2/8355, *procès-verbal* of interrogation of seven arrested men by Le Lièvre, Saarbrücken, 14 thermidor an IV (August 1, 1796).
131. On confessional strife in modern Europe, see, e.g., Blaschke, "Das 19. Jahrhundert"; and Steinhoff, "Ein zweites konfessionelles Zeitalter?"

3. INVENTING TRANSNATIONAL PILGRIMAGE

1. On these entanglements, see, e.g., Lazer, *State Formation;* and Muller, "Politische Grenze und religiöse Grenze."
2. This point is well summarized by Vogler, "1789–1815."
3. The literature on emigration is awe-inspiring. Still a good starting point for grasping the scale of the phenomenon is Greer, *The Incidence of the Emigration*. The two classic and indispensable works on Alsace are Reuss, *La grande fuite;* and Schaedelin, *L'émigration*. On émigrés in the Franco-German (and Belgian) borderlands, see Blazejewski, "Grenzräume als Zufluchtsräume"; and Winkler, *Revolution und Exil*, esp. 80–98.
4. *Moniteur universel*, September 18, 1793, p. 1107. On how revolutionaries constructed emigration as a betrayal of the French nation, see Ashburn Miller, "The Impossible Émigré"; Heuer, *The Family and the Nation*, 23–43; and Henke, *Coblentz*, 354–67.
5. General Dumouriez, quoted by Pestel, "Französische Revolutionsmigration," n. 77.
6. Saunier, "Transnational," 1048. Therefore, I build on the work of scholars who have rewritten national histories in a transnational key: Penny, *German History Unbound;* Stovall, *Transnational France;* Tyrrell, *Transnational Nation;* Holenstein, *Mitten in Europa*. I also agree with the definition of transnational history developed by Conrad, *What Is Global History?*, 44–48.
7. For the concept of "national awareness," see Ford, *Creating the Nation*, 9. On Catholicism and nationhood in modern Europe more generally, see Altermatt, *Konfession, Nation und Rom*.
8. This point was recently underscored by Ory, *Qu'est-ce qu'une nation?*, esp. 406.
9. Bell, *The Cult of the Nation*.
10. Nora, "Nation," esp. 809. Even where scholarship does attend to counter-revolutionary national awareness, it tends to privilege the later nineteenth century rather than the revolutionary era (see, e.g., Byrnes, *Catholic and French*, esp. 95–119; and Daughton, *An Empire Divided*, esp. 79–82). A partial exception to this focus on the time after 1850 is Jonas, *France and the Cult of the Sacred Heart*. Jonas, however, does not try to write French history in a transnational key.
11. For an isolated complaint about pilgrims clandestinely crossing the Rhine, see ADHR, L 115, dossier "Correspondance générale [1793–96]," undated

letter by someone named Binder to the cantonal administration of Neuf-Brisach.
12. Stannek, "Les pèlerins allemands," esp. 340, 347, 352.
13. For a historical overview, see Schenker, "Beinwil-Mariastein." For a focus on the history of the pilgrimage rather than the monastic community, see Baumann, "Die Wallfahrt von Mariastein." On strong presence of Alsatian pilgrims, see Lüber, "Das Kloster Beinwil-Mariastein," esp. 194 (later eighteenth century), also 190 for estimated number of pilgrims per year; Spycher-Gautschi, "Sundgauer Wallfahrten" (focus on nineteenth and twentieth centuries); Herberich-Marx and Rapp, "Pèlerinages," esp. 5912; and Châtellier and Schon, "Essai de cartographie," esp. 200 (both focused on the present).
14. Ringholz, *Elsass-Lothringen und Einsiedeln*, 27–28.
15. Useful overviews in Schweizer Nationalmuseum, *Kloster Einsiedeln*; Sieber, "Adelskloster, Wallfahrtsort, Gerichtshof" (focus on the later Middle Ages); Böck and Holzherr, *Einsiedeln*; Salzgeber, "Einsiedeln"; and Ringholz, *Kurze chronologische Uebersicht*.
16. The statue present today in the Marian chapel of the abbatial church dates from the early or mid-fifteenth century, according to Birchler, "Das Einsidler [sic] Gnadenbild," 187–88.
17. For an early foray, see Ringholz, *Wallfahrtsgeschichte*, 167–77. See also Lustenberger, "Bild und Abbild" (for a catalogue and overview covering the fifteenth through twentieth centuries); Blanchot, "Le culte de Notre-Dame des Ermites," esp. 159–73 (on Franche-Comté); Scheer, "From Majesty to Mystery," 1425–27 (on the oldest replica of the chapel, in Teising, Bavaria).
18. The most recent hypothesis on the origins of pilgrimage to Einsiedeln points to the Holy Year 1300 as an early catalyst (see Jäggi, "Die Geschichte," 46). On the Baroque apogee, see ibid., 50–51, and Sidler, *Heiligkeit aushandeln*, 76–83. An older, somewhat rosy but still empirically reliable picture in Ringholz, *Wallfahrtsgeschichte*, esp. 81, for numbers of annual pilgrims. These numbers are confirmed by Julia, "Pour une géographie," 47–49.
19. For an intriguing case study on pilgrims from Baden, see Luebke, "Naïve Monarchism"; on Vorarlberg, see Tiefenthaler, "Historische und heutige Pilgerwanderwege"; moreover, at a pilgrim hospital as far away from Switzerland as Nuremberg (Franconia), a considerable 2.95 percent of all guests identified Einsiedeln as the goal of their travels (Duhamelle, "Les pèlerins de passage," 45).
20. Ringholz, *Elsass-Lothringen und Einsiedeln*, 22–25.

21. Châtellier, *Tradition chrétienne*, 192–95; Boehler, *Une société rurale*, 1928.
22. Subirade, "Espace, identité religieuse," esp. 362–64; Blanchot, "Le culte de Notre-Dame des Ermites," esp. 139–46.
23. Jacops, "Les Lorrains," esp. 210–11; P. Martin, *Pèlerins de Lorraine*, 93 and 146.
24. Belmas, "L'interdiction."
25. La Coste-Messelière, "Édits et autres actes royaux," esp. 127.
26. Julia, "Curiosité, dévotion," esp. 308–10.
27. SHD, A 2532, f. 78, summary of a letter from Bouffier (commander at the French border town of Hendaye) to the War Ministry, August 25, 1717.
28. SHD, A 2532, f. 76, summary of Le Gendre's *avis*, fall of 1717.
29. Already in the decades before the Revolution, all three issues were linked in the power struggle between the fiscal-military state and local mobile populations (see Lasconjarias, *Un air de majesté*, esp. 191). On desertion, see Forrest, *Conscripts and Deserters*, esp. 6–11, on Old Regime background. For some links between desertion (or draft-dodging) and pilgrimage in the (later) years of the Revolution, see chapter 4 of this book. On smuggling in the Old Regime, see, above all, Kwass, *Contraband*, esp. 60–63, on Alsace as a hub of European contraband. For scattered evidence of the intersection between pilgrimage and smuggling, see P. Martin, *Les chemins du sacré*, 328; and "Arrest de la Chambre." I thank Laurent Jalabert for drawing my attention to this source.
30. This paragraph summarizes findings that I have presented elsewhere in greater detail (see Harrer, "Wallfahrt als Grenzerfahrung?").
31. This conflict is documented in AAEB, A 109a/12, pastoral visit reports from 1744, p. 15; AAEB, A 25, no. 11, pp. 87–89 (petition by Réchésy community to the *official* of the Elsgau rural chapter), pp. 91–92 and 97 (letter from Réchésy parish priest to Basel bishopric, May 9, 1749).
32. This linguistic issue is very present in the diaries of Abbot Beat Küttel (1780–98), often because his primarily German-speaking monastic community struggled to give pastoral care to the large numbers of Francophone pilgrims (KAE, A 11, A.HB, no. 75/5, p. 5; no. 75/6, p. 33; no. 75/9, p. 27; no. 75/10, p. 19).
33. See the *Chronique d'Einsidlen*, esp. 227–28. On Labre, "popular religion," and the Counter-Enlightenment, see Caffiero, *La fabrique d'un saint*.
34. My tally is based on KAE, A 12, A.11/39 and /40 and B.11/28 and /29. It does not include two additional, undated sermons (in B.11/28) that may have been given either in the 1780s or the 1790s and that also contain Counter-Enlightenment polemics. The quotes are from A.11/40,

"Historische Lob- und Sittenrede auf das jährliche Engelweyh-Fest, der Einsiedlischen Kapelle, dem frommen Pilgrimme gewiedmet," P. Adelricus Rothweiler, 1787; and B.11/28, "Engelweihepredigt v. P. Anselm (Huonder?) v. Dissentis. 1783."

35. On this tortuous intellectual development, see Fässler, *Aufbruch und Widerstand*.
36. Fässler, *Aufbruch und Widerstand*, 165–66. On early modern shrine books, see Brugger, *Gedruckte Gnade*; Maes, *Les livrets de pèlerinage*; and Balzamo, "L'infrastructure."
37. *Chronique d'Einsidlen*, dédicace (unpaginated).
38. This summary of the reform and its implications is based on Tackett, *Religion, Revolution*, 11–26, and (for the argument on polarization) 299–300; van Kley, *The Religious Origins*, 361–67; Fitschen, "Die Zivilkonstitution"; and Maire, *L'Église dans l'État*, 455–75, quote on 473: "la dernière guerre de Religion française."
39. Tackett, *Religion, Revolution*, 41 and 53–54 (statistics and maps showing percentages of jurors in early 1791), 217–24 and 293–94 (for explanation of low oath-taking rates in northeastern France; quote on 294). On a renewal of interconfessional tensions in prerevolutionary Alsace, see Muller, "Pouvoir, société et religion," esp. 306.
40. Tackett, *Religion, Revolution*, 351–52; Varry and Muller, *Hommes de Dieu*, 63–86.
41. See, on Strasbourg, Châtellier, *Tradition chrétienne*, esp. 482–83; and on Basel, P. Braun, *Josef Wilhelm Rinck von Baldenstein*.
42. On the personality and career of Gobel with a focus on Alsace, see Muller, "Mgr Simon Nicolas de Montjoie"; and Muller, "La croix et la cocarde," esp. 107–10. Gobel was elected constitutional bishop of the Haut-Rhin but also of the Department of Paris in early 1791, and he chose the Parisian see. In year II (1793/4), he abdicated and was eventually guillotined.
43. This kind of intracommunal factionalism developed in perhaps as many as half of all southern Alsatian parishes, as suggested by Kammerer, "Documents concernant le clergé," esp. 119–25. For rich local detail, see Fues, *Die Pfarrgemeinden*, 400–461. See also AN, F/1cIII/haut-rhin/6, report from central commissioner of Haut-Rhin, Colmar, 11 ventôse an IV (March 1, 1796); ADHR, L 115 (dossier "District d'Altkirch," late summer 1795), L 116 (dossier "Canton de Hirsingue," early fall 1795), L 740 (pièce 161, Hochstatt and surrounding villages, late spring 1795), L 764 (pièces 15 and 34, Masevaux in 1791/2), L 803 (Masevaux, July 1791).
44. Ragon, *La législation*, 18–22.

45. ADHR, L 743 (for the District of Altkirch) and L 926 (for the District of Colmar), letter from departmental administration, September 12, 1791. The departmental directory had probably made an earlier similar statement in late August or early September, as suggested by KAE, A 11, A.LT, no. 25: copy of a letter of the Altkirch district administration to municipalities, Altkirch, September 7, 1791. On links to Switzerland facilitating resistance to the Constitutional Church in eastern France, see also Chapman-Adisho, *Patriot and Priest*, esp. 10.
46. ADHR, L 642, pièce 361, episcopal *mandement*, Colmar, September 13, 1791; AN, D/XIX/86, pièce 38, Martin to the Ecclesiastical Committee, Colmar, August 3, 1791.
47. See, most explicitly, ADHR, L 642, pièce 360, Martin's vicar-general (Hubert Albert) to central administration, Colmar, September 13, 1791.
48. KAE, A 12, B.16/166.9, Fassbind, *Schwyzer Religionsgeschichte*, pt. 4, vol. 5, f. 95v. See the abbot's diary, KAE, A 11, A.HB, no. 75/11, p. 11, spring 1791. See also KAE, A 11, A.LT, no. 23, p. 32 of Abbot Cölestin Müller's history of the abbey from 1789 to 1818, written in 1820. On Fassbind's life and on dating his *Religionsgeschichte*, see the editor's comments in Dettling, *Schwyzer Geschichte*, vol. 2, esp. 1099.
49. On the burgeoning Germanophone political press in revolutionary Alsace and its detailed treatment of religious issues, see Lachenicht, *Information und Propaganda*, esp. 359–92; Kintz, "Alsace"; Bell, *The Cult of the Nation*, 183; and Krenz, *Druckerschwärze statt Schwarzpulver*, 202–23.
50. ADHR, L 642, pièce 380, *procureur syndic* Rey to central administration, Altkirch, 8 floréal an III (April 27, 1795). Other letters denouncing large groups of pilgrims who went to or returned from Switzerland: L 642, pièce 359, M. Misfeld(?) to central administration, Levoncourt, July 11, 1791; ibid., pièce 301, central commissioner to *accusateur public* of Haut-Rhin, Colmar, 15 prairial an V (June 3, 1797); more than three thousand Alsatian pilgrims went to Mariastein on August 14 and 15, 1796, to celebrate the feast of the Assumption of Mary, and the gendarmerie managed to arrest only fifteen of them, according to AN, F/7/7174, d. B/2/8286, cantonal commissioner of Ferrette to departmental commissioner Resch, 2 fructidor an IV (August 19, 1796).
51. See Schaedelin, *L'émigration*, 2:50 (no. 367).
52. Many Alsatian Catholics equated the Constitutional Church with Lutheranism: for another example, see ADHR, L 671, p. 370, *compte décadaire* from the *agent national* of Bisel, 29 floréal an II (May 18, 1794). See also Marx, *Recherches sur la vie politique*, 123–26.

53. ADHR, L 687, information by Ferrette justice of the peace François-Joseph Faninger against Joseph Bürr, May 26, 1793, quote from B. Rey's testimony. Of course, the City and Canton of Basel were also Protestant; yet, Bürr and his interlocutors would have known that the *episcopal principality* of Basel was a largely Catholic territory.
54. ADHR, 1 Q 1227, interrogation of Christine Beller, Altkirch, May 13, 1793.
55. ADHR, 1 Q 1227, interrogation of Christine Beller, Altkirch, May 13, 1793.
56. On the material culture of Einsiedeln pilgrimage souvenirs and representations of Our Lady of Einsiedeln, see Ringholz, "Die Einsiedler Wallfahrts-Andenken"; Weiller, "Médailles et breloques," esp. 73 (two eighteenth-century medals of Our Lady of Einsiedeln found as far away as present-day Luxembourg); Lerch, "Images et dévotion à Colmar," esp. 265, 276, 279; and Blanchot, "Objets de dévotion."
57. Blanchot, "Le culte de Notre-Dame des Ermites," 137–39. More broadly on proxy pilgrims, see P. Martin, *Pèlerins*, 75–78; P. Martin, *Les chemins du sacré*, 251, on proxy pilgrims as "intermédiaires"; and Carlen, *Wallfahrt und Recht*, 61.
58. Véron-Réville, *Histoire de la Révolution*, 189. Véron-Réville was able to use relevant archival materials that did not survive the German annexation of Alsace in 1871.
59. On the third guillotined pilgrim (Père Zéphirin, a Capuchin from Besançon), see Blanchot, "Le culte de Notre-Dame des Ermites," 154.
60. On the border-policing role of the Bourglibre Bureau de surveillance sur les passeports, see Suratteau, *Le Département du Mont-Terrible*, 473–76. More specifically on its creation and importance in the spring of year II, see ADHR, L 126, esp. *arrêté* of Jean-Baptiste Lacoste, *représentant du peuple près les armées du Rhin et de la Moselle*, Metz, 15 germinal an II (April 4, 1794).
61. ADV, L 897, dossier 133, *séance du tribunal criminel*, Mirecourt, 29 floréal an II (May 18, 1794). The *Ange conducteur* was an immensely popular book in eighteenth-century Catholic France (see P. Martin, *Une religion des livres*, esp. 566).
62. ADV, L 897, dossier 133, *interrogatoire* of 14 floréal an II (May 3, 1794).
63. ADV, L 897, dossier 133, attestation of execution of judgment by *huissier* Joseph Rémy, Mirecourt, 29 floréal an II (May 18, 1794).
64. ADV, L 934, *minutes de jugement* of Vosges revolutionary tribunal, ff. 51v–53r, quotes on ff. 51v and 52r.
65. See Fässler, *Aufbruch und Widerstand*, 273–325 (esp. 276 for the total tally of two thousand émigrés).

66. Several men from her home village, Docelles, confirmed that she had left over a year prior to her return (ADV, L 934, f. 52r).
67. See references to this historiography in Jacops, "Les Lorrains," 212n23 (for Dausson); and Winterer, *La persécution religieuse*, 258: Bernard Meyer among the "martyrs *laïques* du Haut-Rhin" (emphasis in the original).
68. ADHR, L 686, Customs Inspector Godinot to procureur syndic Rey, Bourglibre (Saint-Louis), 20 pluviôse an III (February 8, 1795).
69. ADHR, L 686, Customs Inspector Godinot to procureur syndic Rey, Bourglibre (Saint-Louis), 20 pluviôse an III (February 8, 1795).
70. KAE, A 11, A.SE-06, no. 29.
71. KAE, A 11, A.SE-06, no. 29.
72. On the last years of the *Fürstbistum* of Basel, its annexation by France, and its fate as a revolutionary borderland, see Suratteau, *Le Département du Mont-Terrible*; and Jorio, "Der Untergang des Fürstbistums."
73. See Suratteau, *Le Département du Mont-Terrible*, 471–505, and esp. 509–10, on passports issued in Mariastein.
74. On this broader tendency of the later revolutionary years, see, above all, Desan, *Reclaiming the Sacred*, esp. 197–216.
75. Hunt, *Politics, Culture, and Class*, 85, hearkening back to Agulhon, *1848 ou L'apprentissage*.
76. The literature on this topic is so rich that only a few classic titles can be cited here. Many of them focus on the decades around 1900 (see Weber, *Peasants into Frenchmen*; Applegate, *A Nation of Provincials*; and Confino, *The Nation*). On the revolutionary years, see, among others, Ozouf, *La fête révolutionnaire*; Hunt, *Politics, Culture, and Class*; and Edelstein, *The French Revolution*.
77. Similar points have been made by Muller, "Religion et Révolution," esp. 82; and, more recently, by Brassart and Kaci, "From Rural Homelands" (on France's northern borderlands); and Kaci, "Recompositions frontalières" (on Burgundy and Franche-Comté).
78. In 1795, the National Convention did ban outdoors processions, including the specific kind of pilgrimage I have discussed as *Wallfahrt* (see chapter 2 of this book).
79. *AP* 47:225–26. For more on passports, see chapter 4 of this book.
80. ADHR, L 642, pièce 364.
81. See the previous section on both women. For proof that Beller, too, was added to the list of émigrés, see L. Martin, "Les émigrés du Bas-Rhin," 14.
82. See a more lenient order of the Thermidorian *représentant en mission* Richou: AN, D/§1/30, 2e registre des arrêtés, arrêté no. 269, Strasbourg,

16 prairial an III (June 4, 1795); and AN, F/7/7174, d. B/2/8286, Resch to police ministry, Colmar, 12 fructidor an IV (August 29, 1796).
83. AN, F/7/7174, d. B/2/8286, internal report of the police ministry, 8 vendémiaire an VI (September 29, 1797).
84. ADHR, L 112, draft of an internal note of the departmental administration, undated (probably ca. 1791). For similar insistence on special "surveillance" in "departemens frontieres," see ADHR, L 114, dossier "Lettres et circulaires," Haut-Rhin surveillance committee to departmental administrations of Ain, Jura, Haute-Saône, Bas-Rhin, and Moselle (draft), Colmar, August 4, 1792.
85. Certeau, Julia, and Revel, *Une politique de la langue,* 323 and 326. See also Bell, "Nation-Building," esp. 486–87.
86. Reuss, *La grande fuite.*
87. Dozens of pilgrims only barely escaped arrest. In August 1793, near Bettlach, customs officers stopped and searched a group of twenty-six pilgrims returning from Mariastein but could not actually arrest them because another group of roughly twenty-five men showed up "disposés à se jetté [= jeter] sur nous à coup de trique" (ADHR, L 686, procès-verbal des préposés à la police du commerce extérieur, Hagenthal-le-Bas, August 25, 1793). Another example: when a group of soldiers tried to arrest a group of some thirty apparent Mariastein pilgrims near Altkirch in the spring of 1794, all but three were able to escape (see ADHR, L 687, *arrêté* of Altkirch District Directory, no. 3287bis, 29 floréal an II [May 18, 1794]).
88. The tables are based on the following sources: ADHR, L 642, L 651, L 686, L 687, L 743, 1 Q 1155, 1 Q 1160, 1 Q 1163, 1 Q 1175, 1 Q 1176, 1 Q 1178, 1 Q 1182, 1 Q 1183, 1 Q 1193, 1 Q 1200, 1 Q 1214, 1 Q 1215, 1 Q 1221, 1 Q 1222, 1 Q 1224, 1 Q 1227, 1 Q 1228, 1 Q 1230, EDEPOT/40/5; AN, AF/II/136, F/7/5564, F/7/5567, F/7/5568, F/7/5570, F/7/5573/1; Schaedelin, *L'émigration.*
89. My group profile in many ways confirms the one presented by Varry and Muller, *Hommes de Dieu,* 211. However, Varry and Muller identified a much smaller number of affected pilgrims (only 100), so my research findings underscore more strongly the scope of state repression. Varry and Muller also do not touch on the issue of the pilgrim as émigré.
90. Lobenwein, *Wallfahrt;* Vincent, "Conclusions"; Julia, "Pour une géographie," 94–97 (on familial *Wallfahrt*).
91. Lüber, "Das Kloster Beinwil-Mariastein," 200–209; Suratteau, *Le Département du Mont-Terrible,* 239–40.
92. Cf. ADHR, 1 Q 1214, dossier Schultz, certificates of 29 ventôse an III

(March 19, 1795); ADHR, L 743, *arrêté* of District Directory, March 23, 1793, and L 51/4, pp. 474–75, departmental *arrêté* no. 14462, 12 frimaire an II (December 2, 1793).

93. On the conflict-riddled presence of constitutional priests in Brunstatt during the years 1792–98, see Kammerer, "Le clergé constitutionnel," 7, 14; and Würtz, *Aus dem kirchlichen Leben*, 54–55.
94. ADHR, 1 Q 1178, dossier Gross, undated petition [late March 1793] by Antoine Stirni, Catherine Müller, Antoine Gross, and André Wilhelm, to the Altkirch District Directory.
95. See ADHR, 1 Q 1214, dossier Schultz.
96. ADHR, 1 Q 1230, dossier Schultz, letter from the state prosecutor at the revolutionary tribunal of Haut-Rhin to the national agent of Altkirch District, Colmar, 17 pluviôse an II (February 5, 1794). For a similar case involving a dozen deported pilgrims from the village of Bergholtzzell, see ADHR, 1 Q 1224, dossier Wetterwald.
97. Here I synthesize information from ADHR, L 642, pièces 371 and 372; AN, F/7/3351, émigré-related extract from a *compte décadaire* of the Haut-Rhin, 2ᵉ décade de prairial an II (early June 1794); ADHR, 1 Q 1214, central administration of Haut-Rhin to the Convention's Commission des administrations civiles, police et tribunaux, Colmar, 2 brumaire an III (October 23, 1794).
98. ADHR, L 687, petition by Jean-George Pfleger, Catherine Hibschwirlin, Gothard Mohn, Anne Marie Hanser, Reine Pfleger, Jean Hoff, and Gertrude Herzog [mid-June 1794]. The only relief that administrators granted these petitioners was their transfer from the district jail of Altkirch to the less overcrowded *maison d'arrêt* of Landser (ADHR, L 687, Altkirch District *arrêté* of 5 messidor an II [June 23, 1794]).
99. ADHR, 1 Q 1176, dossier Galliath, undated petition deliberated upon on 6 ventôse an II (February 24, 1794).
100. ADHR, 1 Q 1163, dossier Boll, undated draft of an *arrêté* citing Boll's petition.
101. ADipl, 125CP/426, f. 398, General Pfyffer to Ambassador Barthélemy, Lucerne, April 24, 1792; 125CP/464, ff. 54–57, Ambassador Bacher to the minister, Basel, 30 vendémiaire an VI (October 21, 1797); see also the quoted excerpts of correspondence in Kaulek, *Papiers de Barthélemy*, esp. 1:135, 1:160, 3:243. See also AN, AF/III/51/A, dossier 187, pièce 107, "Extrait d'une lettre sur les moyens dont les Emigrés se servent pour rentrer furtivement en France," 5 prairial an V (May 24, 1797). The embassy also put pressure on the Canton of Solothurn because of alleged counterrevo-

lutionary activity at Mariastein (Lüber, "Das Kloster Beinwil-Mariastein," 207–9).

102. See ADHR, L 55/1, pp. 350–51, *arrêté* of the Conseil Général of Haut-Rhin, July 17, 1793, esp. art. 1; on correspondence about passports between the embassy and Bourglibre (in the early fall of 1794), see Kaulek, *Papiers de Barthélemy*, 4:337 and 4:358.

103. On pilgrims passing through Basel—often because traveling on the Rhine sped up the journey—see Ringholz, *Elsass-Lothringen und Einsiedeln*, 28–30.

104. AN, BB/18/268, dossier no. D 8512, Ferniot to Minister of Justice, Besançon, 4 fructidor an IV (August 21, 1796).

105. AN, BB/18/268, dossier no. D 8512, Ferniot to Minister of Justice, Besançon, 4 fructidor an IV (August 21, 1796) ("un voillage de dévossion"). For more analysis of passport issues, see chapter 4 of this book.

106. See the timeline sketched in her letter, as well as another piece of the same dossier: Lormoy, substitute central commissioner of the Doubs, to the minister, Besançon, 5 vendémiaire an V (September 26, 1796).

107. For recent overviews of the events and related shifts in political culture, see Holenstein, "Beschleunigung und Stillstand," 352–57; Lerner, *A Laboratory of Liberty*, 109–33; G. B. Clemens, "The Swiss Case"; and Dufour, "D'une médiation à l'autre."

108. Fässler, *Aufbruch und Widerstand*, 517–32; Lustenberger, "Das Schicksal des Einsiedler Gnadenbildes"; H. Haas, *Wallfahrtsgeschichte*, 83–84.

109. AN, AF/III/10, dossier 31, p. 112, report from the Minister of War to the Directory, 25 floréal an VI (May 14, 1798).

110. Lustenberger, "Das Schicksal des Einsiedler Gnadenbildes," 204 (solemn procession on September 29, 1803); Lüber, "Das Kloster Beinwil-Mariastein," 268 (August 15, 1804). For Einsiedeln, the timeline is actually more complicated than that: the inhabitants of the village, economically dependent on revenues from pilgrimage, tried to revitalize the Engelweihe festival as early as 1800 (see Glaus, "Helvetische Kloster- und Kirchenpolitik," 185–86).

111. ADBR, 1 VP 571, Desportes to Bishop Saurine, Colmar, 13 messidor an XI (July 2, 1803).

112. ADHR, V 225, *commissaire de police de Colmar* to Desportes, 16 prairial an XI (June 5, 1803), referring to the edicts of 1686 and 1738.

113. ADHR, V 225, Desportes to Minister of Justice, Colmar, 19 prairial an XI (June 8, 1803); Desportes to prefect of the Vosges, Colmar, 13 messidor an

XI (July 2, 1803); prefect of the Vosges to Desportes, Épinal, 24 messidor an XI (July 13, 1803). At that time, the Diocese of Nancy included the Vosges Department.
114. Muller, "'La réunion des esprits.'" For more on the Concordat, see chapter 5 of this book.
115. ADBR, 1 VP 30, Saurine to *ministre des cultes* Portalis, Strasbourg, 11 messidor an XI (June 30, 1803).
116. Muller, *Dieu est catholique*, 918–25.
117. ADHR, V 225, Saurine to Desportes, Strasbourg, 18 messidor an XI (July 7, 1803).
118. KAE, A 12, A.11/39, anonymous Engelweihe sermon of 1808.
119. KAE, A 11, A.CC, no. 16, chapter meeting minutes of March 10, 1809.
120. KAE, A 11, A.WE, no. 3, Talleyrand to the Swiss Landammann, Bern, March 9, 1810. Pilgrims to Einsiedeln also came from German-speaking communities (including Rémering, Vahl-Laning, and Hilsprich) in the even-more-distant Moselle Department (see ADM, 29 J 365–72, pastoral *enquête* of the Bishopric of Metz in 1807). For Mariastein, the evidence from a Strasbourg diocesan *enquête* of the year XII (1803/4) suggests that certain parishes near the border (Hagenthal-le-Bas, Leymen, Liebenswiller) continued to hold annual pilgrimage processions to Mariastein (see Archives de l'Archevêché de Strasbourg, Enquête de l'an XII, vol. 2, pp. 297–99).
121. KAE, A 11, A.WE, no. 7, Abbot Konrad to cantonal government of Schwyz, Einsiedeln, late March 1810.
122. For another supporting piece of evidence, see KAE, A 11, A.CC, no. 17, chapter meeting minutes of April 11, 1810: a deliberation on "quomodo respondendum esset adventantibus huc ex Gallia Peregrinis, ac de negotio nostri aevi Religionem aliquo modo concernentibus [sic] sine dubio interrogaturis." The monks decided to adopt a highly cautious position that would exclude any condemnation of Napoleon's actions.
123. KAE, A 12, B.11/28, Engelweihe sermon of September 22, 1817, given by a Capuchin named P. Anaclet, part II.
124. KAE, A 11, A.RE, no. 29, Johannes Engler to P. Johann Baptist, Strasbourg, August 6, 1828.
125. On the persistence of Alsatian pilgrimage to Einsiedeln and Mariastein in the nineteenth century, see Muller, *Dieu est catholique*, 908.
126. Pinto, "Religious Pilgrimage."
127. Harris, *Lourdes*; Kotulla, *'Nach Lourdes!'*, esp. 514–28.

4. MARY'S OVERFLOWING PRESENCE

1. AN, F/7/7583, d. 51 (R/841), pièce 13, lieutenant Fétré to Buquet, *chef de la 18ᵉ division de la Gendarmerie nationale,* Sarreguemines, 15 prairial an VII (June 3, 1799). On pilgrims from Mannheim and Cologne, see *Journal des départemens de la Moselle, de la Meurthe, etc.,* no. 60, 25 prairial an VII (June 13, 1799), p. 5.
2. AN, F/7/7583, d. 51 (R/841), pièce 10, central administration of Moselle to Ministry of Police, Metz, 20 prairial an VII (June 8, 1799).
3. Harris, *Lourdes;* Blackbourn, *Marpingen.* See also the overview by B. Schneider, "Marienerscheinungen im 19. Jahrhundert."
4. Langlois, "Mariophanies et mariologies"; Zimdars-Swartz, *Encountering Mary;* Marrus, "Cultures on the Move," 217; more recently, see Bouflet, "Institution et charisme"; and Krebs and Laycock, "The American Academy of Religion Exploratory Session," 212. For the concept of a "Tridentine model" of apparitions that dominated from the sixteenth through the first third of the nineteenth century, cutting off the decades around 1800 from the history of later apparitions, see Boutry, "Dévotion et apparition"; and Maes, "Les apparitions mariales."
5. My use of the term "overflow" here is an attempt to spatialize the theoretical insight of Robert Orsi, who argues that the meaning of modern Marian apparitions resides above all in the "abundance" and "excess" of presence that Mary embodies (Orsi, *History and Presence,* 48–71). The Latin etymology of "abundance" (from *unda,* meaning "wave") also dovetails with my reflections on the role of water in this chapter.
6. Dupront, *Du Sacré,* 381.
7. Bouvy, "La fontaine de Host." Bouvy seems to have drawn heavily on MS 759 of the Metz municipal library, a manuscript destroyed in 1944 (I thank Dominique Ribeyre for providing this information). The Moselle departmental archives' entire series L (covering the revolutionary decade) was also lost in 1944, although fortunately, a large number of documents from that series—including dozens on the apparitions of 1799—were edited before the war by Paquet, *Bibliographie analytique.* Overall, little wonder that there is almost no recent scholarship on the apparitions. Ulbrich, "Die Jungfrau," 140–42, and P. Martin, *Pèlerins de Lorraine,* 97–99, aptly connect the phenomena of Hoste to the larger religious resurgence of the Directorial period. Much like Bouvy, however, Ulbrich and Martin treat the apparitions as a merely subregional affair and seem to have left untapped the relevant Parisian sources.

8. KAE, A.11, A.CC, no. 11b, p. 59 (unfortunately, pages 57 and 58, where this entry began, are missing).
9. KAE, A.11, A.HB, no. 74/11, p. 44.
10. See, e.g., Aston, *Religion and Revolution*, 284; and Blanning, *The French Revolution in Germany*, 83–134 and 218–24.
11. Desan, *Reclaiming the Sacred*. For the northern Paris Basin, see Bernet, "Les limites de la déchristianisation"; and Bernet, "Cultes." On Limousin, see Pérouas and d'Hollander, *La Révolution*, 254–59. For a pioneering, still-valuable overview, see Hufton, "The Reconstruction of a Church," esp. 50–51, for remarks on pilgrimage. On de-Christianization in 1793/4, see, above all, Vovelle, *La Révolution contre l'Église*.
12. This was pointed out for Lyon by Chopelin, *Ville patriote et ville martyre*, 323–48. More generally on the fluctuating but overall restrictive religious policies of the Directory, see Suratteau, "Le Directoire"; and Hermant, "Monsieur dimanche."
13. Godechot, *La Grande Nation*, 395–421 (quotes on 419). On the problematic legacy of Godechot's rosy picture, see Desan, "Internationalizing the French Revolution," esp. 149.
14. For short summarizing remarks on this resurgence of pilgrimage, see Aston, *Christianity and Revolutionary Europe*, 230–31.
15. Cattaneo, *Gli occhi di Maria*, esp. 1 (number of statues), 26–29 (Ancona in June 1796), 67 ("flusso migratorio di pellegrini"), 72 ("epicentri").
16. Bazzani, "Miracoli e ierofanie."
17. Cattaneo, *Gli occhi di Maria*, 51, 74.
18. ADM, 19 J 127, p. 87 (and see pp. 87–101 for several similar reports on the Marian miracles happening across the Papal States).
19. ADM, 19 J 127.
20. For a detailed recent account, see Fässler, *Aufbruch und Widerstand*, 480–98.
21. Godel, *Die Zentralschweiz*, esp. 183, 190–91, 198; Fässler, *Aufbruch und Widerstand*, 367–86.
22. For a very instructive overview of this complicated political and administrative history, see Stein, *Die Akten*, 1–46. For a synopsis of Rhenish history between 1792 and 1815, see Gantet and Struck, *Deutsch-Französische Geschichte*, 91–98. See also Dufraisse, "L'installation"; on 1798 as a turning point, see Jürgen Müller, "1798."
23. LHA Ko, Best. 241,016, Nr. 743, pp. 81–88, Dorsch to Special Commissioner Marquis, Aix-la-Chapelle, 11 thermidor an VII (July 29, 1799), quote on p. 83.

24. LHA Ko, Best. 241,015, Nr. 689, pp. 7–13, report by Caselli to the other members of the central administration of the Roër, 13 germinal an VI (April 2, 1798), quote on p. 9.
25. For an *arrêté* of 13 germinal an VI (April 2, 1798), prohibiting all processions (whether to pilgrimage shrines or elsewhere), see LHA Ko, Best. 241,015, Nr. 689, pp. 15–17. This decision was precocious in the sense that the underlying legislation on *police du culte* had not yet been introduced in this region. Thus, on 30 germinal an VI (April 19, 1798), Rudler scrapped the *arrêté*: LHA Ko, Best. 241,015, Nr. 689, pp. 23–24. See also Bormann and Daniels, *Handbuch*, 3:193, on the somewhat later publication, on 8 prairial an VI (May 27, 1798), of parts of the French law of 7 vendémiaire an IV (September 29, 1795) (see chapter 2 of this book for more detail on this law) that banned processions and other outdoors ceremonies of worship.
26. LHA Ko, Best. 241,015, Nr. 689, pp. 33–36, Dorsch to Rudler, Aix-la-Chapelle, 13 prairial an VI (June 1, 1798), quote on p. 34.
27. LHA Ko, Best. 241,016, Nr. 743, pp. 59–60, Dorsch to Marquis, Aix-la-Chapelle, 1er thermidor an VII (July 19, 1799). On these and other miraculous incidents, see also Blanning, *French Revolution in Germany*, 235–39.
28. LHA Ko, Best. 241,019, Nr. 959, pp. 1–4: Nicolas-Sébastien Simon (prefect of the Roër) to Special Commissioner Shée, Aix-la-Chapelle, 23 fructidor an VIII (September 10, 1800), quote on p. 3. The gendarmerie had been established in the occupied Rhineland in 1799 (Lignereux, *Servir Napoléon*, 27). On the politics of pilgrimage in the Rhineland during the late 1790s, see also Carl, "Revolution und Rechristianisierung," esp. 94–95.
29. Paquet, *Bibliographie analytique*, 1071, Thiebault and Helfflinger to central administration of the Moselle, Puttelange, 21 prairial an VII (June 9, 1799). For the name Paul Spaeth, see Bouvy, "La fontaine de Host," 126. On the strong and manifold ties between schoolteachers and communal religious life in eighteenth-century rural France, see Simien, *Le maître d'école*, esp. 79–92; and Bisaro, *Chanter toujours*, esp. chap. 5.
30. AN, F/7/7612, d. 38 (R/1180), pièce 3.
31. AN, F/7/7612, d. 38 (R/1180), pièce 3.
32. AN, F/7/7583, d. 51 (R/841), pièce 13, Fétré to Buquet, Sarreguemines, 15 prairial an VII (June 3, 1799).
33. First piece of the dossier published by Paquet: Thirion, jury director at the tribunal de police correctionnelle of Faulquemont, to central administration of the Moselle, Faulquemont, 15 floréal an VII (May 4, 1799). Paquet, *Bibliographie analytique*, 1060.

34. AN, F/7/7583, d. 51 (R/841), pièce 13, Fétré to Buquet, Sarreguemines, 15 prairial an VII (June 3, 1799).
35. AN, F/7/7583, d. 51 (R/841), pièce 18, lieutenant Rapin to Marchis, capitaine de gendarmerie à Nancy, Pont-à-Mousson, 25 prairial an VII (June 13, 1799).
36. AN, F/7/7583, d. 51 (R/841), pièce 68, cantonal commissioner Umhœfer to the Minister of Police, Bascharage, 25 thermidor an VII (August 12, 1799).
37. Bouflet and Boutry, *Un signe dans le ciel*, 98.
38. AN, F/7/7583, d. 51 (R/841), pièce 35, Saulnier to the Ministry of Police, Nancy, 4 messidor an VII (June 22, 1799).
39. On Chambrey, see AN, F/7/7583, d. 51 (R/841), pièce 38, *état de la situation* written by Saulnier, central commissioner of the Meurthe. On Plaine-de-Walsch and Bertrambois, see Clémendot, *Le Département de la Meurthe*, esp. 489–90, on links established by pilgrims between Rehtal and the Good Well. On pilgrimage to Plaine-de-Walsch, see also AN, F/7/7583, d. 51 (R/841), pièce 39, central administration of Meurthe to Ministry of Police, Nancy, 15 messidor an VII (July 3, 1799).
40. AN, F/7/7583, d. 51 (R/841), pièce 59, central commissioner of the Bas-Rhin to the Ministry of Police, Strasbourg, 16 thermidor an VII (August 3, 1799); ADBR, 1 L 602, pp. 63–66, arrêté no. 29379bis, 3 thermidor an VII (July 21, 1799). See also Burg, *Marienthal*, esp. 196–97, on religious effervescence at Marienthal in the summer of 1799. Burg, who made meticulous use of local archives, offers no evidence that this activity centered around a well.
41. Paquet, *Bibliographie analytique*, 1080–81, cantonal administration of Mars-la-Tour to central administration of Moselle, Mars-la-Tour, 18 fructidor an VII (September 4, 1799); AN, F/7/7583, d. 51 (R/841), pièce 68, Umhœfer to Ministry of Police, Bascharage, 25 thermidor an VII (August 12, 1799) and AN Lux, B-0864, no. 4917, Delattre (central commissioner of the Forêts) to Umhœfer, Luxembourg, 14 thermidor an VII (August 1, 1799); AN, F/7/7615, d. 36 (R/1206), Delattre to Ministry of Police, Luxembourg, 7 fructidor an VII (August 24, 1799).
42. Oberhauser, *Wallfahrten und Kultstätten*, 26.
43. For the repeated mention of bottles used by numerous pilgrims to obtain some water for themselves at the Good Well, see AN, F/7/7583, d. 51 (R/841), pièces 13, 18, 29, 35, 38; and Paquet, *Bibliographie analytique*, 1075 (report of commissioner Legoux, 4 messidor an VII [June 22, 1799]) and 1077 (municipal administration of Puttelange to central administration

of Moselle, Puttelange, 28 messidor an VII [July 16, 1799], on the sale of water at the Good Well).

44. Clémendot, *Le Département de la Meurthe*, 371–75.
45. See Clémendot, *Le Département de la Meurthe*, 54, on glassworks in Plaine-de-Walsch, and 374 on wood (alongside sand) as major local resource used in glassworks.
46. AN, F/7/7583, d. 51 (R/841), pièce 18, Lieutenant Rapin to Captain Marchis.
47. In the late eighteenth century, these bottles with figurines in them began to be sold by the thousands at the famous Marian shrine of Liesse in northern France, not too far from Lorraine (see Maes, *Le roi, la Vierge*, 452–53 [Maes also indicates that other shrines incorporated these bottles into their material culture around the same time]; and McManners, *Church and Society*, 145). See also my remarks in chapter 3 of this book about Christine Beller, who transported such bottles (among many other devotional objects) from Einsiedeln to Alsace in the 1790s.
48. Such aquatic appearances share some features with moving Marian images rather than with more "typical" life-sized apparitions. But the boundaries between image and apparition are often blurry anyway, as demonstrated masterfully by Albert-Llorca, *Les Vierges miraculeuses*, 34–62.
49. AN, F/7/7583, d. 51 (R/841), pièce 38, Saulnier's *état de la situation*.
50. Paquet, *Bibliographie analytique*, 1081, cantonal administration of Mars-la-Tour to central administration of Moselle, 18 fructidor an VII (September 4, 1799).
51. AN, F/7/3676/3, report of central administration of Forêts, Luxembourg, 2 fructidor an VII (August 19, 1799).
52. My reflections here are indebted to Claverie, *Les guerres de la Vierge*.
53. J.-C. Martin, *Contre-Révolution, Révolution et Nation*, esp. 9–13, 291–96.
54. Gainot, *1799, un nouveau jacobinisme?*
55. For two examples, see AN, F/7/3682/22, d. 1, pièce 89, central administration of the Moselle to the Minister of Police, Metz, 3 brumaire an VII (October 24, 1798); and F/7/7215, d. B/3/4368, a schoolteacher named Solms to the Corps législatif, Sarralbe, 22 frimaire an V (December 12, 1796). On fanaticism as a discursive label of radical otherness and inferiority, see Clarke, "'The Rage of the Fanatics'"; and Dupuy, "Ignorance, fanatisme et Contre-Révolution."
56. Laufer, "Seelsorge über Grenzen," esp. 342. For more evidence of this border-crossing movement, see Stein, "La République française," 183.

57. See the numbers broken down by districts in Lesprand, *Le clergé de la Moselle*, 4:461; and the map in Henryot, Jalabert, and Martin, *Atlas de la vie religieuse*, 59.
58. For an anonymous contemporary report on this border-crossing mobility in both directions, see the article "Moselle, Sarreguemines" in the *Annales de la religion* of 1795.
59. AN, F/7/4279, dossier Chavant, esp. his interrogation before the tribunal criminel of the Moselle, Metz, 5 thermidor an IV (July 23, 1796); for further investigations against Chavant in 1797, see AN, F/7/7263, d. B/3/9520; "le Pape du Pays" and authorship of the *Te Deum in Gallos*: AN, F/7/7372, d. B/5/1184, anonymous letter to Reubell, 13 nivôse an VI (January 2, 1798); and on Chavant's connection to Dagstuhl in the French-occupied Rhineland: SHD, 2 B 277, letter from General Laprun to Sauveton (commander at Saarlouis), Metz, 9 vendémiaire an V (September 30, 1796). Chavant also appears as a regional leader of antirevolutionary Catholicism in Ulbrich, "Die Bedeutung der Grenzen," esp. 162. For details on Chavant's career until 1793, see Lesprand, *Le clergé de la Moselle*, 4:95–103.
60. LHA Ko, Best. 241,009, Nr. 319, p. 117, *Direction des pays conquis* to the commissioners of the Moselle Department and the Sarreguemines municipality, Saarbrücken, 17 messidor an IV (July 5, 1796). On three other priests suspected of similar activities, see StA Tr, Fz 681, Hagre (president of the cantonal administration of Sarreguemines) to the *Agence des domaines du pays conquis*, Sarreguemines, 1er nivôse an IV (December 22, 1795).
61. AN, F/7/7583, d. 51 (R/841), pièce 18, Rapin to Marchis, 25 prairial an VII (June 13, 1799). On Spaeth, see also Paquet, *Bibliographie analytique*, 1071, Helfflinger and Thiebaut, letter to the central administration of the Moselle, Puttelange, 21 prairial an VII (June 9, 1799).
62. AN, F/7/7583, d. 51 (R/841), pièce 16, Saulnier to the Ministry of Police, Nancy, 24 prairial an VII (June 12, 1799).
63. AN, F/7/7583, d. 51 (R/841), pièce 63, Marie Anne Mangin "au Citoyen Directeur de la Republic française en secrait," Dieuze, 22 thermidor an VII (August 9, 1799).
64. AN, F/7/7612, d. 38 (R/1180), pièce 3. For mentions of the pamphlet, see ADBR, 1 L 601, pp. 226–30, departmental arrêté no. 28849; Paquet, *Bibliographie analytique*, 1064, municipal administration of Sarrelibre (Saarlouis) to central administration of the Moselle, Sarrelibre, 12 prairial an VII (May 31, 1799); Paquet, *Bibliographie analytique*, 1064, cantonal com-

missioner at Sarreguemines to central administration of the Moselle, Sarreguemines, 13 prairial an VII (June 1, 1799): "se distribue par milliers."
65. AN, F/7/7583, d. 51 (R/841), pièce 6, Thiebault (president of the municipality of Puttelange) and Helfflinger (cantonal commissioner at Puttelange) to central administration of the Moselle, Puttelange, 17 prairial an VII (June 5, 1799).
66. AN, F/7/7612, d. 38 (R/1180), pièce 3.
67. AN, F/7/7612, d. 38 (R/1180), pièce 3.
68. AEA 025, no. 62, quoting here from the interrogation of Charles Thiry, 7 fructidor an VII (August 24, 1799).
69. AEA 025, no. 62, decision of the jury director François-Damien Simonin, 7 fructidor an VII (August 24, 1799).
70. For some remarks on this underresearched revolt, see Lefort, *Histoire du département des Forêts*, 319–20. On the importance of the woods of Virton as a rallying point for rebels during that revolt, see AEA 013, no. 125/43, esp. Gillet (as *directeur du jury d'arrestation*) to special departmental commissioner Légier, Habay-la-Neuve, 27 germinal an IV (April 16, 1796).
71. On the demolition of the Bonlieu hermitage, see AEA 013, no. 415/13, Gillet (as cantonal commissioner of Virton) to special departmental commissioner Duportail, Virton, 20 floréal an IV (May 9, 1796). On the medieval and early modern history of Marian pilgrimage to Bonlieu, see Petit, "L'ermitage Notre-Dame," esp. 67–68 and 98.
72. See chapter 1 of this book.
73. LHA Ko, Best. 276, Nr. 594, p. 19, central administration of Sarre to municipal administration of Trier, Trier, 5 thermidor an VII (July 23, 1799).
74. For more on Kirn's group, including bibliographical and archival references, see chapter 5 of this book.
75. For their identification as "assermentés," see AN, F/7/7583, d. 51 (R/841), pièce 38, Saulnier's report of 1er messidor an VII (June 19, 1799).
76. For an overview of the accomplishments made under Grégoire's leadership, see Dean, *L'abbé Grégoire*.
77. Bouvy, "La fontaine de Host," 145.
78. AN, BB/18/933, printed open letter adressed to the Minister of the Interior, Luxembourg, 3 fructidor an VII (August 20, 1799).
79. AN, F/7/7583, d. 51 (R/841), pièce 50, arrêté of the central administration of the Moselle, 4 messidor an VII (June 22, 1799).
80. This territorial peculiarity resulted from the explicit decision, made by the Constituent Assembly in 1790, against turning Sarreguemines into the *chef-lieu* of a department that would have corresponded to the German-

speaking part of Lorraine (see Bourdon, "La formation des départements," esp. 215–16).

81. On these attempts and their limited success, see Horn, "La monarchie française"; and, most recently, Schmidt, "Die Saar."
82. See Masson, *Histoire administrative*, 348–53.
83. Instead, and relatively late, the departmental administration of the Bas-Rhin finally contacted that of the Moselle about the events of Hoste (see ADBR, 1 L 601, pp. 567–71, arrêté no. 29007, letter of 13 messidor an VII [July 1, 1799]). There is only a shred of evidence of belated horizontal cooperation in this affair between *cantonal* administrations across departmental borders (see ADBR, 1 L 1562, liasse "Instructions," letter from the cantonal administration of Sarralbe [Moselle] to that of Sarre-Union [Bas-Rhin], Sarralbe, 21 messidor an VII [July 9, 1799]).
84. See AN, F/7/7583, d. 51 (R/841), pièce 70, draft of a letter from the Ministry of Police to the departmental commissioner of the Moselle, Paris, 10 fructidor an VII (August 27, 1799).
85. AN, F/7/7583, d. 51 (R/841), pièce 43, internal bulletin of the Ministry of Police, 26 messidor an VII (July 14, 1799); ADBR, 1 L 601, pp. 847–50, Bas-Rhin departmental arrêté no. 29142, 19 messidor an VII (July 7, 1799).
86. Varry and Muller, *Hommes de Dieu*, esp. 63–86.
87. SHD, 2 B 297, p. 19r, Sauveton to the *général de brigade* Belleville, Saarlouis, 4 messidor an VII (June 22, 1799). The registers of the central administration of the Bas-Rhin confirm that draft-dodging and desertion were especially rampant in the Alsace bossue (see ADBR, 1 L 601, pp. 1017–18, arrêté no. 29212, 23 messidor an VII [July 11, 1799]). Finally, from a different part of the Bas-Rhin (the Canton of Villé, southwest of Strasbourg), there is a concrete example of a draft-dodger who on July 19, 1799 had obtained a (procedurally invalid) passport "pour aller à Host et Puttelange" (ADBR, 1 L 605, pp. 27–30, arrêté no. 30977, 2 brumaire an VIII [October 24, 1799]).
88. AN, F/7/7583, d. 51 (R/841), pièce 6, Thiebault and Helfflinger to central administration of the Moselle, Puttelange, 17 prairial an VII (June 5, 1799).
89. AN, F/7/7583, d. 51 (R/841), pièce 18, gendarmerie lieutenant Rapin to his captain Marchis, Pont-à-Mousson, 25 prairial an VII (June 13, 1799). On the language border, see Toussaint, *La frontière linguistique*.
90. Dupront, *Du Sacré*, 381.
91. AN, F/7/7612, d. 38 (R/1180), pièce 3. On the perceived innocence of child-seers as a sacred quality in Spain circa 1500, see Christian, *Apparitions*, 216–20. On the critical role of (often female) child-seers in almost all

of the great modern apparitions (La Salette, Lourdes, Pontmain, Marpingen, Fátima, Medjugorje, . . .), see, e.g., Bouflet and Boutry, *Un signe dans le ciel.*

92. For late medieval and early modern examples of apparitions in which water appears front and center, see Christian, *Apparitions*, 108, 119–21, and 126–32; Chiron, *Enquête sur les apparitions*, 154–56; Reinburg, *Storied Places*, 80; and Vauchez, "L'eau et les sanctuaires," 333.

93. Lotz-Heumann, "Repräsentationen von Heilwassern," esp. 305, 311. Spaeth's miracle report, AN, F/7/7612, d. 38 (R/1180), pièce 3, taps into a Christian tradition of reading the female part in the Song of Songs as pointing to Mary and therefore applying to Mary Solomon's praise of his lover as, among other things, "a spring shut up, a fountain sealed" (4:12, King James Version). On that tradition, see Rubin, *Mother of God*, 15–16 and 158–61.

94. Christian, *Apparitions*, 187 (quote). See also Boutry, "Dévotion et apparition," esp. 120–21.

95. On earlier apparitions as phenomena primarily tied to local religious contexts, see Guyon, "Les apparitions mariales"; and Christian, *Apparitions*, 10–26. On "Personal Experiences and Public Demands" at La Salette, Lourdes, and Fátima, see Zimdars-Swartz, *Encountering Mary*, 25–91.

96. Harris, *Lourdes*; Blackbourn, *Marpingen*; Dabrowski, "Multiple Visions."

97. On the pitfalls of construing "modernity" as a stable package, see Cooper, *Colonialism in Question*, 113–49.

98. Hynes, *Knock*.

99. Reinburg, *Storied Places*, 215–16.

100. Bouflet and Boutry, *Un signe dans le ciel*, 59. On a parallel eighteenth-century crisis of holy wells as pilgrimage goals in France, see Caulier, *L'eau et le sacré*, 135–36; and P. Martin, *Les chemins du sacré*, 245.

101. W. B. Taylor, *Theater*, esp. 46–47; Niedźwiedź, *Obraz i postać*, 142–52. For other case studies, see Cozzo, "Apparizioni"; and Desmette and Martin, *Le miracle de guerre.*

102. Lotz-Heumann, "Repräsentationen von Heilwassern," 297–305; Walsham, *The Reformation of the Landscape*, chap. 6.

103. An earlier apparitional episode, which occurred in 1791 at Saint-Laurent-de-la-Plaine in western France, already displayed similar dynamics of politicization but does not seem to have led to any far-flung offshoot apparitions (see J.-C. Martin, *La Vendée et la France*, 77; and Port, *La Vendée angevine*, 1:262–73, 331, 397–98).

104. See Paquet, *Bibliographie analytique*, 1060–61.
105. AN, F/7/7583, d. 51 (R/841), pièce 2. Administrators of the Directorial period had a general proclivity for enlisting the army's help to impose public order, not least in matters of *police du culte* (see H. G. Brown, *Ending the French Revolution*, 128–41).
106. SHD, 2 B 297, place de Sarrelibre, registre des ordres du jour de la 3e division, f. 13.
107. AN, F/7/7583, d. 51 (R/841), pièce 18, Rapin to Marchis, Pont-à-Mousson, 25 prairial an VII (June 13, 1799).
108. Paquet, *Bibliographie analytique*, 1071–76, for Legoux's reports to central administration of the Moselle; and ibid., 1076, Helfflinger and Thiebaut to central administration of the Moselle, Puttelange, 8 messidor an VII (June 26, 1799). Later in the summer, the influx of pilgrims did grow again, even prompting the municipal administration of Puttelange to request a new military detachment in late July (100 dragoons from Sarreguemines: see AN, F/7/7583, d. 51 [R/841], pièce 66, lieutenant Fétré to captain Dardennes, Sarreguemines, 18 thermidor an VII [August 5, 1799]).
109. AN, F/7/7583, d. 51 (R/841), pièce 13, Fétré to Buquet, Sarreguemines, 15 prairial an VII (June 3, 1799). See also Paquet, *Bibliographie analytique*, 1075, report of commissioner Legoux, 4 messidor an VII (June 22, 1799).
110. AN, F/7/7583, d. 51 (R/841), pièce 38, Saulnier's *état de la situation*.
111. AN, F/7/7583, d. 51 (R/841), pièce 39, central administration of Meurthe to Ministry of Police, Nancy, 15 messidor an VII (July 3, 1799).
112. Denis, *Une histoire de l'identité*, esp. 242–66; Torpey, *The Invention of the Passport*, 21–56.
113. AN, F/7/7583, d. 51 (R/841), pièce 8, copy of a letter from Albert, central commissioner of the Moselle, to the cantonal commissioners of St-Avold, Puttelange, Sarreguemines, Hellimer, Morhange, Forbach, Limberg, Bredembach, and Rohrbach, undated (but probably around 19 prairial an VII [June 7, 1799], judging from surrounding pieces in the dossier).
114. AN, F/7/7468, rapports de gendarmerie, état des arrestations faites dans la Moselle, prairial an VII (May/June 1799). The arrested men came from a handful of villages just southwest of Morhange. Women could face arrest as well (see Paquet, *Bibliographie analytique*, 1067, Boustiquet [chef de brigade commandant la place de Sarreguemines] to General Morlot, Sarreguemines, 15 prairial an VII [June 3, 1799], mentioning fifteen women arrested near the Good Well). For another example of similar gendarmerie

actions, see AN, F/7/7583, d. 51 (R/841), pièce 29, Boucqueau (central commissioner of the Sarre) to the Ministry of Justice, Trier, 29 prairial an VII (June 17, 1799).

115. AN, F/7/7583, d. 51 (R/841), pièce 13, Fétré to Buquet, Sarreguemines, 15 prairial an VII (June 3, 1799).

116. Paquet, *Bibliographie analytique*, 1064, Fétré to Dardenne, Sarreguemines, 15 prairial an VII (June 3, 1799).

117. On passports as territorial technology, see Delaney, *Territory*, 27–28.

118. P. Martin, *Pèlerins*, 92.

119. Julia, *Le voyage aux saints*, 303–13.

120. On source problems, see an especially instructive article by Seifert, "Aus der Franzosenzeit."

121. AN, F/7/7583, d. 51 (R/841), pièce 66, Fétré to Dardenne, Sarreguemines, 18 thermidor an VII (August 5, 1799).

122. See *Recueil des règlemens*, cahier 9, pp. 128–32: on 1er thermidor an VI (July 19, 1798), commissioner Rudler published title III (concerning internal passports) of the law of 10 vendémiaire an IV (October 2, 1795) in the occupied Rhineland. For this reason, the story of passport controls in the borderlands between Lorraine and the Rhineland was a different one in 1799 than in 1796 (compare chapter 2 of this book).

123. AN, F/7/7583, d. 51 (R/841), pièce 29, Boucqueau to the Ministry of Justice, Trier, 29 prairial an VII (June 17, 1799); ibid., pièce 68, Umhœfer, cantonal commissioner of Bascharage (Forêts), to the Ministry of Police, Bascharage, 25 thermidor an VII (August 12, 1799). For a specific mention of a group of "etrangers, munis de passeports du Pays de Treves" (part of the occupied Rhineland) and confronted by French troops at the fountain of Hoste, see AN, F/7/7628, d. 58 (R/1280), pièce 6, cantonal commissioner of Puttelange to central administration of Moselle, 6 fructidor an VII (August 23, 1799).

124. See AN, F/7/7583, d. 51 (R/841), pièce 75, draft of a letter from the Ministry of Police to Thirion (central commissioner of the Moselle), Paris, 24 fructidor an VII (September 10, 1799). According to the central administrators of the Moselle, many local officials continued to facilitate pilgrimage to Hoste by issuing passports for travel to Puttelange or other, nearby cantons (see Paquet, *Bibliographie analytique*, 1079, circular letter by Moselle administrators, Metz, 4 fructidor an VII [August 21, 1799]). For one example of an indulgent cantonal administrator, at Saverne (Bas-Rhin), issuing a passport to a woman who wanted to visit the Good Well, see

Reuss, *La grande fuite*, 257–58. We only know about this case because the official was denounced to the central administration.
125. AN, F/7/7583, d. 51 (R/841), pièce 24, central administration of Moselle to Ministry of Police, Metz, 27 prairial an VII (June 15, 1799).
126. AN, F/7/7583, d. 51 (R/841), pièce 42, Saulnier to the Ministry of Police, Nancy, 22 messidor an VII (July 10, 1799).
127. On the quantitative peak in apparitions in the 1870s, see B. Schneider, "Marienerscheinungen im 19. Jahrhundert," 92–93.
128. Muller, *Dieu est catholique*, 932–34; Bouflet, "Institution et charisme," 71–78; Chiron, *Enquête sur les apparitions*, 307; Hiegel, "Les apparitions," esp. 71–73.
129. Blackbourn, *Marpingen*.
130. Christian, *Visionaries*, esp. 163–213.
131. Blackbourn, *Marpingen*, 334–43.
132. One more example is worth noting: outward from La Salette, secondary apparitions proliferated in southeastern France during the late 1840s, thus coinciding and interacting with the Revolution of 1848 (see Langlois, "Mariophanies et mariologies," 20).
133. In 1799, there was no national newspaper of the nonjuring clergy: the *Annales catholiques* had fallen victim to the Coup d'État of Fructidor an V (September 1797) (see Colot, "Former l'opinion"). The *Annales de la religion*, the (ex-)constitutional equivalent and rival of the *Annales catholiques*, did mention the miracles of Hoste and Plaine-de-Walsch twice, but only briefly and only to denounce them as outgrowths of superstitious fantasies ("Mozelle"; "Église de France," 169–70).
134. Bouvy, "La fontaine de Host," 148–49.
135. "Actuellement, un pèlerinage attire quelques dizaines de fidèles" according to Sbalchiero, "Hoste." In the mid-1990s, however, Yves Chiron noted that "des pèlerins viennent toujours à Host et une procession annuelle est organisée par la paroisse" (Chiron, *Enquête sur les apparitions*, 167).
136. "Populations légales 2020: Commune de Hoste (57337)." Institut national de la statistique et des études économiques, https://www.insee.fr/fr/statistiques/6676182?geo=COM-57337.

5. THE MAKING OF AN IMPERIAL MASS PILGRIMAGE

Parts of this chapter were first published as Kilian Harrer, "Mass Pilgrimage and the Usable Empire in a Napoleonic Borderland," *Historical Journal* 66, no. 4 (2023): 773–94. © The Author, 2023. Published by Cambridge University Press. Open Access article, distributed under the terms of the Creative Commons Attribution license (http://creativecommons.org/licenses/by/4.0). Reprinted with permission.

1. StA Tr, Fz 66, chap. 10 ("police spéciale"), undated letter from Kirn to the municipality.
2. Steinruck, "Charles Mannay."
3. Horn, *Le défi de l'enracinement*, 88.
4. For further historiographical reflections on "usable empire," see Harrer, "Mass Pilgrimage," 775–76.
5. Broers, *The Politics of Religion*; Ramón Solans, *La Virgen del Pilar*, 79–128.
6. Broers, "Napoleon, Charlemagne, and Lotharingia." Broers's distinction among inner, intermediate, and outer imperial zones has proved seminal (see, e.g., Englund, "Monstre sacré," 218; Lignereux, *Les Impériaux*, 219–21).
7. Rowe, *From Reich to State* pioneered the approach of analyzing Napoleonic history, and more particularly the Napoleonic Rhineland, with the tools of border(land) studies.
8. Rowe, "Borders, War, and Nation-Building," 161.
9. I have borrowed this expression from Brambilla, "Exploring the Critical Potential," 20.
10. Julia and Boutry, "Rome, capitale du pèlerinage," esp. 21; see also Ikari, *Wallfahrtswesen in Köln*.
11. According to Acts 1:23–26, Matthias filled the vacancy created by Judas's treason and suicide. On pilgrimage to St. Matthias, see Bernard, *Die Wallfahrten*, esp. 103–35. On the history of the abbey itself, see P. Becker, *Die Benediktinerabtei*.
12. Groß, "Trier als Pilgerziel," esp. 119: 10,438 people in 1759; 11,868 in 1764; 12,189 in 1778. These figures were published at the time by a local newspaper, the *Trierische Wochenblättgen*, probably based on counts that guards conducted at the city gates (see ibid., 120).
13. Groß, "Prozessionen und Wallfahrten," esp. 84. An estimate of forty thousand pilgrims per year for St. Matthias alone in the eighteenth century is given by G. Franz, "Geistes- und Kulturgeschichte," 329.
14. Schmid, "Sancta Treveris"; Reichert, "'Heiliges Trier.'"
15. Just two examples of pilgrimage books that conveyed this tradition throughout the eighteenth century and (in the form of reeditions) into the revolutionary era are Hillar, *Mathianischer Ehren- und Andachts-Tempel*, esp. 44–52; and *Andachts-Uebungen*, esp. 7–30. On how the inhabitants of

Trier in the central medieval period began to narrate a special relationship between their city and Saint Helen, see L. Clemens, "Zum Umgang mit der Antike," 195–96.

16. For a short but insightful overview, see Clemens and Clemens, *Geschichte der Stadt Trier*. For population figures, see Kohl, *Familie und soziale Schichtung*, 212–13.
17. Wolf, "Absolutistische Repräsentation," esp. 334–39 and 361–63; Rapp, *Stadtverfassung und Territorialverfassung*, esp. 367.
18. Ronig, "Die Ausstattung," 285–96. The reliquary was made in 1729–32.
19. Fachbach and Simmer, "Eine höfische Wallfahrt"; Seibrich, "Die Heilig-Rock-Ausstellungen," 213–15.
20. In 1783, moreover, Koblenz's ecclesiastical authorities persuaded the local St. Matthias confraternity to give up its yearly pilgrimage to Trier (BA Tr, Abt. 20, Nr. 21a, pp. 25–26, *Temporale ecclesiasticum* entry of May 23, 1783; see also LHA Ko, Best. 1C, Nr. 11248, p. 23).
21. BA Tr, Abt. 63, Nr. 16, anonymous document dated August 9, 1789: based on a recent episcopal visitation of St. Matthias' Abbey, the author reported among other things that the abbey remained a remarkably well-frequented pilgrimage place all year long (pp. 3–4). But see also BA Tr, Abt. 20, Nr. 24, pp. 72–73, General Vicariate protocol entry of January 11, 1788: one priest in the countryside talked in rather laconic terms about "the processions that were once customarily led to Trier" ("processionibus olim in Treviros duci solitis").
22. Birtsch, "Soziale Unruhen," 153, emphasizes the scale of this sum. See also Schumacher, "Mouvements insurrectionnels."
23. LHA Ko, Best. 1D, Nr. 4102, petition by Trier *Bürgerschaft*, August 29, 1789. See BA Tr, Abt. 20, Nr. 22, pp. 548–49, General Vicariate protocol entry of September 6, 1785.
24. BA Tr, Abt. 71,165, Nr. 25, circular letter from the General Vicariate to all parish priests of the Upper Electorate, January 18, 1790.
25. See my remarks in chapters 2 and 4 of this book on the broader impact of conquest and occupation on civilian populations in the left-bank Rhineland that included Trier and its hinterland.
26. B. Schneider, *Bruderschaften im Trierer Land*, 218–19.
27. Kronenberger, *Fastenreden*, esp. 2:10 and 2:20, and see, for similar exclamations, 2:41 and 2:89; 2:28 on masonic lodges; and 2:34 on recent warfare.
28. Stammel, *Trierische Kronik*, esp. 26–27, 71–72, 87, 117; Kronenberger, *Was ist die stamml'sche Trierische Kronik*, esp. 43–46; Johann Kaspar Müller,

Auch das Volk, esp. 41–46, 76–77, 82–84, 120; Kronenberger, *Polemische Kanzelreden*, esp. 483–507. See also chapter 1 of this book.

29. LHA Ko, Best. 241,015, Nr. 565, report from departmental administration of the Sarre to central government commissioner Rudler for the third *décade* of germinal an VI (mid-April 1798), p. 34. On the laymen's religious protests from 1798 to 1800, see Kallabis, *Katholizismus im Umbruch*, 327–31 and 361–62; B. Schneider, *Bruderschaften im Trierer Land*, 179–81; and Blanning, *The French Revolution in Germany*, 233–34.

30. LHA Ko, Best. 276, Nr. 594, pp. 15–16, petition of sodality members including Karl Kaspar Kirn, Johann Jakob Vacano, and Peter Bartholomae, addressed to the central departmental administration, undated (early April 1798). Although the signatories of those petitions formed a small group, they clearly fed off earlier attempts by larger parts of Trier's *Bürgerschaft* to obtain permission for processions through the city streets. See, on late 1797: StA Tr, Fz 679, military commander of Trier to the civil magistrate, 29 brumaire an VI (November 19, 1797; order to ban processions), and Fz 680, petition by fifteen burghers to the military commander.

31. StA Tr, Fz 68, chap. 20 ("passeports et surveillance"), directorial *arrêté*, 8 fructidor an VII (August 25, 1799). This surveillance was complicated and often unsuccessful, producing a 132-page police dossier (LHA Ko, Best. 276, Nr. 595). For regional context on the policing of pilgrimage during those years, see Stein, "Polizeiüberwachung und politische Opposition," esp. 228–33.

32. BA Tr, Abt. 20, Nr. 27, p. 904, General Vicariate protocol entry no. 637, July 24, 1797. On the relatively accepting attitude of Trier's ecclesiastical leadership toward the French in those years, see Stein, "Die Trierer Reunionsadresse," 215.

33. BA Tr, Abt. 20, Nr. 25, p. 798, General Vicariate protocol entry no. 1260, September 6, 1790.

34. LHA Ko, Best. 241,019, Nr. 960, pp. 51–52, departmental administration to Trier municipality, 15 frimaire an VIII (December 6, 1799), on Kirn's weekly appearances at Beurig (on Fridays). Beurig as a Marian shrine is not well researched; the most helpful work is Schlager, *Marienlob*. On Klausen, see Dohms, "Die Wallfahrt," esp. 18–19, 49.

35. On the procession and prayer session led by Kirn on the Sunday of Pentecost (June 1, 1800/12 prairial an VIII), see LHA Ko, Best. 241,019, Nr. 960, pp. 5–7, General Laroche to central commissioner Shée, Koblenz, 13 prairial an VIII (June 2, 1800); ibid., pp. 21–23, departmental administration to Shée, Trier, 13 prairial an VIII (June 2, 1800); ibid., pp. 27–30,

accusateur public près le tribunal criminel de la Sarre to Shée, Trier, 13 prairial an VIII (June 2, 1800), claiming that the pilgrimage to Klausen had been made by "une centaine d'extravagants"; and StA Tr, Fz 66, chap. 10, Shée's response to the *accusateur public*, Mainz, 25 prairial an VIII (June 14, 1800); LHA Ko, Best. 276, Nr. 595, esp. pp. 65-67, Régnier (military commander of Saar Department) to Shée, Trier, 13 prairial an VIII (June 2, 1800), and pp. 125-26, gendarmerie report of 12 messidor an VIII (July 1, 1800; on the number and gender of arrested pilgrims); LHA Ko, Best. 241,019, Nr. 958, pp. 1-3, General Laroche to Shée, Koblenz, 15 prairial an VIII (June 4, 1800); LHA Ko, Best. 700,062, Nr. 28, diary of Trier citizen Ludwig Müller, year 1800, ff. 21v-22r (prayers to the Sacred Heart; Müller also gives a much lower estimate of the number of people who had accompanied Kirn to Klausen—only "about 28 or 29"). On the Sacred Heart and the Counter-Revolution, see Jonas, *France and the Cult of the Sacred Heart*, 83-90. See further StA Tr, Fz 86, report by municipal commissioner Neveux, Trier, 11 prairial an VIII (May 31, 1800), on a previous "rassemblement de fanatiques" in the early morning of the Saturday before Pentecost. The year 1800 was not the first in which the French administration and gendarmerie intervened against the masses of pilgrims who continued to visit Trier: on actions proposed and taken in 1798, see StA Tr, Fz 678, departmental commissioner Boucqueau to municipal commissioner Lequereux, Trier, 6 prairial an VI (May 25, 1798); LHA Ko, Best. 241,015, Nr. 565, pp. 39-42, *arrêté* of Saar departmental administration, 23 germinal an VI (April 12, 1798); and LHA Ko, Best. 700,062, Nr. 28, Müller's diary, year 1798, f. 26r.

36. BA Tr, Abt. 91, Nr. 265, p. 18, Mannay to French embassy in Munich, undated draft. I date this draft to early 1810 based on directly related correspondence in ADipl, 16CP/186, f. 102, Bogne (secretary at the embassy in Munich) to the French Minister of Foreign Affairs, Munich, March 9, 1810.
37. Kuhn, "Zur Geschichte," 161 and 175-76.
38. On Nassau-Weilburg and its Old Regime left-bank territories for which the princes of Nassau received compensation in 1803, see Wilhelm, *Nassau-Weilburg*. See also Schüler, *Das Herzogtum Nassau*, 8-45 (map on 22). On the right-bank diocesan administration after 1802, see Thomas, "Die Verwaltung," 915-16.
39. Kuhn, "Zur Geschichte," 164, 170, 180-82.
40. On this competition, see Wagner, "Die Rückführung," 220-24.
41. DAL, protocols of the General Vicariate, vol. 20, entry no. 5822, meeting of December 10, 1803; Weber, "Der Heilige Rock," 210-11.
42. DAL, protocols of the General Vicariate, vol. 26, entry no. 8827, meeting of

September 20, 1809. On Napoleonic-era projects for a new episcopal see in Limburg, see Schatz, *Geschichte des Bistums Limburg*, 24–30.
43. LHA Ko, Best. 332, Nr. 907, p. 69, resolution by Prince Friedrich Wilhelm of Nassau-Weilburg, November 10, 1809.
44. LHA Ko, Best. 332, Nr. 907, pp. 71–72, counselor Coll to Ehrenbreitstein regency, July 7, 1810.
45. ADipl, 16CP/186, f. 198, Ambassador Narbonne to minister for foreign affairs, May 28, 1810.
46. LHA Ko, Best. 332, Nr. 907, pp. 143–44, resolution by Friedrich Wilhelm, September 7, 1810.
47. BA Tr, Abt. 52, Nr. 357, ff. 155v–156r, Mannay to Champagny, August 10, 1808.
48. BA Tr, Abt. 91, Nr. 210, f. 71, excerpt from a letter by Count Klemens von Kesselstadt to his brother Philipp, Paris, December 18, 1809; Gagern, *Mein Antheil*, 198–200.
49. Boudon, *Napoléon et les cultes*, 8.
50. More broadly on benefits that Trier derived from Napoleonic rule, see Zenz, *Geschichte der Stadt*, 1:10–58.
51. AN, F/7/8069, folder entitled, "Sarre—Préfet—La vraie Robe de Jesus Christ à Trèves," marginalia on a letter from Vincent-Marie de Vaublanc, prefect of Moselle, to Pierre-François Réal, September 28, 1810.
52. See, e.g., H. G. Brown, *Ending the French Revolution*, 345–48.
53. See esp. the introduction and chapter 1 of this book.
54. Speth, *Katholische Aufklärung*, 124–41.
55. Caiani, *To Kidnap a Pope*.
56. Boudon and Hême de Lacotte, *La crise concordataire*; see also Maréchaux, *Pie VII*, esp. 234–36.
57. Lichter, "Die Rückkehr des Hl. Rockes," 8:248–55 and 9:160–65.
58. AN, F/7/8069, folder entitled, "Sarre—Préfet—La vraie Robe de Jesus Christ à Trèves," brochure: *Exhortation aux fidèles au sujet de l'exposition de la Robe de Notre Seigneur*, p. 6.
59. BA Tr, Abt. 91, Nr. 210, f. 97, "Règlement à l'occasion de l'exposition de la Sainte Robe," sent by Mannay to local civil and military authorities on August 28, 1810. For the cantonal timetable, see BA Tr, Abt. 91, Nr. 211, f. 13.
60. StA Tr, Tb 18/292, printed mayoral resolution of August 27, 1810, reprinted in the local newspaper, the *Journal du Département de la Sarre*, no. 49, September 5, 1810: Stadtbibliothek Trier, T 8. On urban policing under Napoleon, see Renglet, *Policing Cities*.
61. Seibrich, "Die Heilig-Rock-Ausstellungen," 199.

62. Freitag, *Volks- und Elitenfrömmigkeit*, 151–63. On a similar pilgrimage event that brought tens of thousands of pilgrims to Fulda Cathedral in 1755, see Michael Müller, *Fürstbischof Heinrich von Bibra*, 381–82.
63. See ADM, 29 J 824, entry no. 1878, Neunheuser (*provicaire* for Luxembourg) to Oster (vicar-general at the Bishopric of Metz), 2 germinal an XII (March 23, 1804).
64. BnF, NAF 6169, pp. 253–54, description of the Oktav ceremonies of 1810 in Bishop Jauffret's registers. On Mannay's previous trips to Luxembourg, see BA Tr, Abt. 52, Nr. 243, provicaire Neunheuser to Mannay's vicar-general, Garnier, Luxembourg, June 7, 1809; see also, for previous friendly exchanges between Mannay and Jauffret: BnF, NAF 28917, vol. 6, registers of Jauffret's outgoing correspondence, esp. pp. 18 (September 27, 1806), 33 (December 22, 1806), and 56 (January 16, 1808).
65. LHA Ko, Best. 276, Nr. 594, pp. 125–26, prefect Ormechville to General Vicariate, Trier, 16 prairial an X (June 5, 1802), and p. 35, acquiescent reply from the General Vicariate, Trier, 18 prairial an X (June 7, 1802). On March 26, 1804, Mannay also reiterated Clemens Wenceslaus's 1784 decree on processions: "Observatio ordinationis processiones concernentis 29. Novembris 1784, inculcatur. 26. Martii 1804," in Blattau, *Statuta synodalia, ordinationes et mandata*, 7:215–16. On Napoleonic-era pilgrimage policies in this region, see also Wagner, "Revolution, Religiosität," 282–84.
66. AN, F/19/1073/A, folder on Diocese of Trier, Mannay to Bigot de Préameneu, Trier, August 27, 1810; BA Tr, Abt. 91, Nr. 210, f. 94r, margin note at the bottom of a letter from Mannay to the prefect of the Saar, August 2, 1810.
67. BA Tr, Abt. 91, Nr. 210, f. 94r, Mannay to the prefect of the Saar, August 14, 1810.
68. See Uhrmacher, "Neue Staaten—neue Grenzen," 160–61.
69. Delamorre, *Annuaire*, 3.
70. AN, F/7/8069, folder entitled, "Sarre—Préfet—La vraie Robe de Jesus Christ à Trèves," Saar prefecture to Savary, Trier, August 6, 1810.
71. See a draft of that letter in BA Tr, Abt. 91, Nr. 210, f. 94v, with the margin note: "Il n'y a pas eu de réponse à cette lettre."
72. AN, F/7/8069, folder entitled, "Sarre—Préfet—La vraie Robe de Jesus Christ à Trèves," Saar prefecture to police minister Savary, Trier, August 6, 1810.
73. AN, F/7/8069, folder entitled, "Sarre—Préfet—La vraie Robe de Jesus Christ à Trèves," *note pour le Conseil de Police*, August 22, 1810.
74. AN, F/7/8069, folder entitled, "Sarre—Préfet—La vraie Robe de Jesus

Christ à Trèves," *note pour le Conseil de Police*, August 22, 1810, margin note: "Note succincte et substantielle au Bulletin—B(ulle)tin 24 août."
75. AN, F/7/3721, minutes of police bulletins, June thru August 1810; Gotteri, *La police secrète*.
76. See Boudon, *L'Empire des polices*, who ascribes to the Napoleonic police system "une efficacité réelle, sinon complète, sur le contrôle des populations" (p. 8). On Napoleon's police as "generally efficient," see also Sibalis, "The Napoleonic Police State," 93.
77. BA Tr, Abt. 91, Nr. 265, f. 29, draft of letter from Mannay to Gattermann(?), July 19, 1810. For biographical information on Gattermann, see G. B. Clemens, "Die Notabeln," 129–30.
78. Lichter, "Die Rückkehr des Hl. Rockes," 9:169.
79. BA Tr, Abt. 52, Nr. 357, f. 189v, Mannay to *provicaire* Neunheuser, Trier, August 31, 1810.
80. ADM, 29 J 169, entry no. 746, Vicar-General Tournefort to Neunheuser, September 5, 1810.
81. BA Tr, Abt. 91, Nr. 210, f. 99, Neunheuser to Mannay, Luxembourg, September 7, 1810. Neunheuser claimed in this letter that the prefect had been alerted to the dangers of the pilgrimage event by the "Conseiller d'état qui a le département de la Saar." More precisely, information about the upcoming showing of the relic had apparently come from the prefecture of the Saar (see AN, F/1cIII/forets/5, prefectoral report for the third trimester of 1810).
82. BA Tr, Abt. 91, Nr. 210, f. 100, Mannay to Neunheuser, September 14, 1810.
83. LHA Ko, Best. 256, Nr. 7793, pp. 32–34, Adrien de Lezay-Marnésia (prefect of Rhin-et-Moselle) to Marc-Antoine Berdolet (bishop of Aachen), July 9, 1808. On Lezay-Marnésia's attempts to repress pilgrimage, see numerous other pieces in that same dossier, as well as LHA Ko, Best. 261, Nr. 138, circular letters of May 31 and December 4, 1809, from the prefecture of Rhin-de-Moselle to the subprefects and *maires* of that department; and AN, F/7/8068, dossier Rhin-et-Moselle, several letters sent in May and June 1810 by Beving (*conseiller de préfecture* of Rhin-et-Moselle) to the Ministry of Police.
84. AN, F/7/8068, dossier Rhin-et-Moselle, Beving to Ministry of Police, Koblenz, June 25, 1810. See also a tense exchange between the prefects of Rhin-et-Moselle and Saar in 1809, on the topic of transdepartmental pilgrimage: LHA Ko, Best. 276, Nr. 594, pp. 163–73. A strong general case for the importance of urban rivalries in that period is made by Margadant, *Urban Rivalries*.

85. LHA Ko, Best. 655,117, Nr. 466, prefecture of Rhin-et-Moselle to *mairie* of Lutzerath, September 12, 1810.
86. AN, F/7/8068, dossier Rhin-et-Moselle, Beving to Ministry of Police, Koblenz, October 2, 1810, and Fermath (another *conseiller de préfecture*) to Ministry of Police, Koblenz, October 23, 1810.
87. AN, F/7/8069, folder entitled, "Sarre—Préfet—La vraie Robe de Jesus Christ à Trèves," letters from Vaublanc to Ministry of Police, Metz, September 24, 25, 27, and 28 and October 1, 1810. On Vaublanc as a loyal servant of Napoleon and a strict enforcer of state surveillance of religious practice, see Lentz and Imhoff, *La Moselle et Napoléon*, 37–39 and 185; AN, F/7/8066, dossier Moselle, Vaublanc to Ministry of Police, February 3, 1808 (on Catholics' refusal to stop celebrating officially abolished feast days).
88. ADM, 1 V 26, prefectoral *arrêté* of September 24, 1810.
89. AN, AF/IV/1317, pièce 234, report of January 29, 1806, p. 120.
90. AN, F/20/253, report from prefect Keppler to the government, exact date unknown.
91. Dufraisse, "Une rébellion en pays annexé," 5. For additional context and on Mannay's intervention: Gerteis, "Trier—Trèves."
92. AN, F/7/8391, police reports from Trier, May 29, 1810 (for the first trimester of the year) and August 1, 1810 (second trimester).
93. AN, F/7/8069, folder entitled, "Sarre—Préfet—La vraie Robe de Jesus Christ à Trèves," Ministry of Police to Sainte-Suzanne (draft), October 10, 1810, and Sainte-Suzanne to Réal, Trier, October 17, 1810; BA Tr, Abt. 91, Nr. 210, f. 104, Bigot de Préameneu to Mannay, Paris, October 12, 1810, and f. 105, Mannay to Bigot de Préameneu, Trier, October 19, 1810.
94. The key sources in this regard are the registers in BA Tr, Abt. 91, Nr. 211, ff. 81–86, "Registre sur les billets d'entrée à la Cathedrale," and ff. 111–21 (register of information about cantonal processions). For a detailed, critical discussion of the numbers, see Harrer, "Erlaubte und unerlaubte Wallfahrt."
95. Kallabis, *Katholizismus im Umbruch*, 398–404; Schieder, "Der 'Heilige Rock' in Trier," esp. 98; Dipper, "Volksreligiosität und Obrigkeit," esp. 93–94. More nuanced is Wagner, "Die Rückführung," 227–35.
96. Lichter, "Die Rückkehr des Hl. Rockes," 9:168–69.
97. Seibrich, "Das Erzbistum Trier," 163–77. On pilgrimage from Lorraine to Trier Cathedral: LHA Ko, Abt. 276, Nr. 594, p. 35, secretary and assessor Weber to prefect Ormechville, Trier, 18 prairial an X (June 7, 1802).
98. Bernard, *Die Wallfahrten*, esp. the maps on 275–76.

99. Hirschhausen et al., *Phantomgrenzen*.
100. Bernard, *Die Wallfahrten*, esp. 177.
101. BA Tr, Abt. 52, Nr. 169 (St. Matthias parish), esp. the following letters: Trier's mayor Recking to prefect Keppler, Trier, 11 floréal an XII (May 1, 1804); Keppler to Mannay, Trier, 17 floréal an XII (May 7, 1804); Recking to Mannay, Trier, 22 floréal an XII (May 12, 1804). See also LHA Ko, Abt. 276, Nr. 530, statistics on *fabrique* revenues, separate sheet for St. Matthias. On pilgrim booklets, see Dewora, *Andachtsbuch*; Dewora, *Das Wichtigste*; and Dewora, *Bruderschaftsbüchelchen*. On the *Säkularisation* of 1802 in the Rhineland, see Oepen, "Die Säkularisation von 1802"; and Resmini, "Aufklärung und Säkularisation."
102. StA Tr, Ta 43/3, list completed in 1814 or slightly later, mentioning some two dozen candles.
103. Letter by Dewora to the auxiliary bishop of Würzburg, Gregor Zirkel, cited in Ludwig, *Weihbischof Zirkel*, 1:77. For more on Dewora and his moderate pro-Enlightenment views, see Michael Embach's introduction to Dewora, *Ehrendenkmal*, esp. xxix–xxxix.
104. In addition to the materials cited above, see Bernard, *Die Wallfahrten*, 112–18.
105. *Andachts-Uebungen*, 195. Two other examples are *Coblentzer Wallfahrt*, 268; and *Erneuerte Einrichtung*, 360–64.
106. Three examples are found in Hagen, *Die Wallfahrtsmedaillen*, 224–26.
107. See *Kurzer Begriff*, 5 (beginning of third verse).
108. The origins and history of the procession are discussed in some detail in Groß, "Abtei und Kirche," esp. 113–19.
109. Ronig, "Die Ausstattung," 303–4, and plan no. VIII in the annex. For the parallel case of a miraculous Marian statue standing in a chapel of Cologne Cathedral and much visited by pilgrims since the early seventeenth century, see Schmid, *Graphische Medien*, 96–97.
110. This is according to Franz Tobias Müller's manuscript on "The fate of the churches in and near Trier since the hostile arrival of the French in 1794" (BA Tr, Abt. 95, Nr. 342, p. 4).
111. LHA Ko, Best. 256, Nr. 7793, pp. 73–75, mayor of Lutzerath to prefecture, Lutzerath, May 27, 1810.
112. Hagen, *Die Wallfahrtsmedaillen*, 223–24.
113. BA Tr, Abt. 91, Nr. 211, f. 87, healing protocol written on September 20, 1810, quote on f. 87r.
114. BA Tr, Abt. 91, Nr. 211, f. 87v.

115. BA Tr, Abt. 91, Nr. 211, f. 87v.
116. BA Tr, Abt. 91, Nr. 211, ff. 108–9, "Réglement pour l'exposition de la sainte Robe," article 13.
117. BA Tr, Abt. 91, Nr. 211, ff. 111–21; Simmer, "Ein neu entdeckter Bericht," esp. 273.
118. Lichter, "Die Rückkehr des Hl. Rockes," 9:169–70.
119. Simmer, "Ein neu entdeckter Bericht," 273.
120. AN, F/7/8068, prefectoral circular letter, Koblenz, June 1, 1810.
121. Bernard, *Die Wallfahrten*, 112; Dohms, "Die Geschichte der Wallfahrt," 249–50; Poggi, *Cultures of Identification*, 123.
122. This ban was pronounced on February 14, 1810: AN, F/*/19/146, p. 30, Bigot de Préameneu to vicars-general of Aachen, August 14, 1810.
123. ADM, 1 V 26, letters from Metz mayor to Moselle prefect, Metz, September 24 and 25, 1810; ADM, 1 V 26, Metz mayor to prefectoral secretary, Metz, September 25, 1810.
124. AN, F/7/8069, Vaublanc to Ministry of Police, September 28, 1810.
125. AN, F/7/8069, Vaublanc to Ministry of Police, October 1, 1810.
126. They are also mentioned in the correspondence between Koblenz and Paris: AN, F/7/8068, Fermath to Ministry of Police, October 23, 1810.
127. Broers, *The Politics of Religion*, 52–85.
128. Albareda and Massot i Muntaner, *Historia de Montserrat*, 95–102, 124–27. On the Peninsular War, see the numerous works by Charles Esdaile. For his demystification of the *somatenes*, see Esdaile, *Fighting Napoleon*, 44–47, 81–83.
129. Boudon, *Napoléon et les cultes*, 106.
130. Wynands, *Geschichte der Wallfahrten*, 58, 83.
131. On Luxembourg City, see chapter 1 of this book; on Echternach, see Michael Franz Joseph Müller, *Abhandlung*.
132. The idea that the "reactionary Catholicism" of the mid- to late nineteenth century constituted a "populist" current was most clearly expressed by Mergel, *Zwischen Klasse und Konfession*, 5.
133. On southwestern Germany, see Handschuh, *Die wahre Aufklärung*; on the Rhineland, see Speth, *Katholische Aufklärung*; and on Westphalia, see Freitag, *Volks- und Elitenfrömmigkeit*, 317–57.
134. For a new account of the Holy Coat pilgrimages that emphasizes devotional continuities against much of the previous historiography, see Doney, *The Persistence*.
135. B. Schneider, "Die Hl.-Rock-Wallfahrten."

CONCLUSION

1. Jaucourt, "Pélerinage," https://artflsrv04.uchicago.edu/philologic4.7/encyclopedie0922/navigate/12/1048/.
2. See, e.g., Reader, *Pilgrimage*, 117–20; Nolan and Nolan, *Christian Pilgrimage*.
3. Rowe, "Imagining the Rhineland," 85.
4. On confessional tensions in nineteenth-century Alsace, see Muller, *Dieu est catholique et alsacien*, 612–758; on the flourishing of border-crossing mass pilgrimages to Einsiedeln in the later nineteenth century, see Kälin, *Schauplatz katholischer Frömmigkeit*.
5. B. Schneider, "Wallfahrt, Ultramontanismus und Politik," esp. 274–75.
6. Borutta, *Antikatholizismus*, 77–88.
7. Doney, *The Persistence*.
8. Amer Meziane, *Des empires sous la terre*, 23–62.
9. Huber, *Channelling Mobilities*, 204–37 (quote on 204).
10. On the global religious echoes of the French Revolution, see also Banks and Johnson, *Freedom and Faith*.
11. C. Taylor, *A Secular Age*, 445.
12. I draw on Mosse, *The Culture of Western Europe* for ideas about the modern juggling of control and transformation, or order and dynamics. On the ambivalence of place, see Cresswell, *Place*, esp. 39–46 and 165–93.
13. It is worth noting that theorists such as Danièle Hervieu-Léger, James Clifford, and Zygmunt Bauman have had recourse to "pilgrimage" as a master trope for modern religiosity or even modern social life in general (see Hervieu-Léger, *La religion en mouvement*; Coleman, *Powers of Pilgrimage*, 37–42). Likewise, a theorist of science recently included a chapter on pilgrim routes to Santiago de Compostela in a broad reckoning with the notions of place and truth (Gieryn, *Truth-Spots*, 74–99).
14. For a somewhat analogous argument about pilgrimage and modernity that focuses, however, on commoditization and consumption rather than place and space, see Kaufman, *Consuming Visions*.
15. Kmec, "'Marienland Luxemburg.'"
16. See, e.g., Gregory, *Salvation at Stake*.
17. Claverie, *Les guerres de la Vierge*.
18. Kmec, "Notre-Dame de Luxembourg."
19. Gálvez, *Guadalupe in New York*, esp. chap. 6; León, *La Llorona's Children*, 80–126.

BIBLIOGRAPHY

PRINTED PRIMARY SOURCES

Andachts-Uebungen bei einer achttägigen Pilgerfahrt, welche zur Verehrung des Hl. Apostels Mathias und dessen zu Trier aufbehaltenen hl. Reliquien aus der Pfarrkirche der Gemeinde Anrath alle Jahr auf den ersten Freitag nach Christi Himmelfahrt ausgeführt wird. 3rd expanded ed. Krefeld: P. Schüllers Witwe, 1808.

"Arrest de la Chambre des Comptes de Lorraine, qui autorise les employés des Fermes à visiter toutes personnes attroupées, dans le cas de pélerinage ou processions, lorsqu'elles viendront de terreins étrangers [. . .]; & permet aux Employés d'arrêter & emprisonner tous ceux qui feront resistance ou rebellion, de même que ceux qui se trouveront chargés de sels, tabacs, & autres choses prohibées, pour être poursuivis en la maniere ordinaire: Du 24 janvier 1767." In *Recueil des ordonnances et réglemens de Lorraine, du regne de Sa Majesté Louis XV,* vol. 11, 142–45. Nancy: J. & F. Babin, 1772.

Blattau, Johann Jacob, ed. *Statuta synodalia, ordinationes et mandata Archidioecesis Trevirensis.* 8 vols. Trier: Lintz, 1844–49.

Blum, Martin. "Aktenstücke zur Geschichte des Gnadenbildes der Trösterin der Betrübten: XXVII. Dossier relatif au projet de reconstruire l'ancienne chapelle de Notre-Dame sur les glacis de Luxembourg." *Ons Hémecht* 14 (1908): 282–83/334–36/389–95/425.

Bormann, K. Th. F., and A. von Daniels, eds. *Handbuch der für die Königlich Preußischen Rheinprovinzen verkündigten Gesetze, Verordnungen und Regierungsbeschlüsse aus der Zeit der Fremdherrschaft.* 8 vols. Cologne: Hauser, 1833–43.

Brommer, Peter. *Kurtrier am Ende des Alten Reichs: Edition und Kommentierung der kurtrierischen Amtsbeschreibungen von (1772) 1783 bis ca. 1790.* 2 vols. Mainz: Gesellschaft für Mittelrheinische Kirchengeschichte, 2008.

Bulletin des lois de la République française, no. 186. Paris, 1795.

Chronique d'Einsidlen; ou Histoire de l'Abbaye princiere, de la Sainte Chapelle, et du pélerinage de Notre-Dame des Hermites: Avec un récit des principaux Miracles que Dieu y a faits, & des Graces singulieres qu'il y a accordées par l'intercession de la Sainte Vierge. Einsiedeln: Benziger, 1787.

Coblentzer Wallfahrt: Worin alle Stationes daraus nacher der Stadt Trier ordentlich bis zu S. Mathias angezeigt werden [. . .]. Koblenz: Krabben, 1765.

Delamorre, C.-H. *Annuaire topographique et politique du département de la Sarre pour l'an 1810.* Trier: Hæner, 1809.

Description du jubilé, célébré à l'honneur de Marie, Consolatrice des Affligés: Choisie depuis plus de cent ans pour Patronne & Protectrice de la Ville & du Duché de Luxembourg, avec le récit des décorations qui y ont paru. Luxembourg: André Chevalier, 1781.

Dettling, Angela, ed. *Joseph Thomas Fassbind (1755–1824): Schwyzer Geschichte.* 2 vols. Zurich: Chronos, 2005.

Dewora, Viktor Joseph. *Andachtsbuch für die Verehrer des heiligen Mathias.* Trier: Schröll, n.d.

———. *Bruderschaftsbüchelchen für die Verehrer des H. Mathias.* Trier: Schröll, n.d.

———. *'Ehrendenkmal': Quellen zur Geschichte der Koalitionskriege 1792–1801.* Trier: Paulinus-Verlag, 1994.

———. *Das Wichtigste für katholische Christen, welche zum Grabe des heiligen Mathias wallfahrten.* Trier: Schröll, n.d.

"Édit de l'Empereur concernant les processions et les jubilés: Bruxelles, 10 mai 1786." In *Recueil des ordonnances des Pays-Bas autrichiens. Troisième série, 1700–1794,* vol. 12, edited by Paul Verhaegen, 491–92. Brussels: J. Goemaere, 1910.

"Église de France." *Annales de la religion* 10 (1799/1800): 155–78.

Erneuerte Einrichtung der Bruderschaft des H. Apostels Matthias so in der Chur-Cöllnischen Stadt Kempen [. . .] andächtig gehalten wird, samt Ordnung der Pilgerfahrt auf Trier [. . .]. Kempen, 1777.

Gagern, Hans Christoph von. *Mein Antheil an der Politik.* Vol. 1: *Unter Napoleons Herrschaft.* Stuttgart and Tübingen: J. G. Cotta, 1823.

Gotteri, Nicole, ed. *La police secrète du Premier Empire: Bulletins quotidiens adressés par Savary à l'Empereur de juin à décembre 1810.* Paris: H. Champion, 1997.

Gretser, Jacob. *De sacris et religiosis peregrinationibus libri quatuor.* Ingolstadt: Adamus Sartorius, 1606.

Hansen, Joseph, ed. *Quellen zur Geschichte des Rheinlandes im Zeitalter der französischen Revolution, 1780–1801.* 4 vols. Bonn: P. Hanstein, 1931–38.

Hillar, Maurus. *Mathianischer Ehren- und Andachts-Tempel: Darinn vorgestellet die Historie des Gotteshauses S. Mathiæ, die genaue Lebensbeschreibung dieses H. Apostels; Die Geschichten von seinen heiligen Reliquien; vielen und großen Wunderwerken bis auf das laufende Jahrhundert; Die Verzeichnung deren aus alten Schriften bekennten, allhier befindlichen, höchst ehr- und wunderwürdigen Reliquien; Wie auch das Jahr hindurch zu verdienenden Abläßen, mit dero gründlicher Auslegung, samt einem Gebettbüchlein mit schönen Sittenlehren.* 3rd ed. Trier: Steinbüchel, 1793.

Jaucourt, Louis. "Péleringage." In *Encyclopédie, ou dictionnaire raisonné des sciences, des arts et des métiers, etc.*, edited by Denis Diderot and Jean Le Rond d'Alembert [1751–72], vol. 12, 282–83. Chicago: ARTFL Encyclopédie Project, 2017.

Kaulek, Jean, ed. *Papiers de Barthélemy, ambassadeur de France en Suisse, 1792–1797.* 6 vols. Paris: F. Alcan, 1886–1910.

Keller, Nikolaus. *Beschreibung des tugendreichen Lebens des Heiligen Wendelini, Abts und Einsidlers, gebohrnen Königs-Sohn in Schottland.* Colmar, 1704.

———. *Beschreibung des tugendreichen Lebens vom heiligen Einsidler und Abts Wendelini, gebohrnen Königs-Sohn in Schottland.* Saarbrücken: Christian Philipp Hofer, 1783.

Kronenberger, Ernest. *Fastenreden: Ein Betrachtungsbuch für alle Stände.* 1797/98. 2nd ed. 2 vols. Deutz: Haas und Sohn, 1800.

———. *Polemische Kanzelreden über die Verirrungen der Vernunft und schreckliche Lage unserer Zeiten in alphabetischer Ordnung: Ein Handbuch für Diktionairgelehrte.* Cologne: Haas, 1798.

———. *Was ist die stamml'sche Trierische Kronik und Wer sind ihre Vertheidiger?* Luxembourg: Perl & Cercelet, 1797.

Kurze Lebensbeschreibung des heiligen Wendelinus mit angehängten Tagzeiten und andern Gebethen samt einem beigefügten kurzen Gebethbuch für Katholiken. St. Wendel: Johann Steininger, 1797.

Kurzer Begriff der Historie, sammt einem Lobgesang von dem H. ungenähten Rock Jesu Christi: Im Thon: Ist das der Leib Herr Jesu Christ. N.p., [1810].

Lichter, Eduard. "Die Rückkehr des Hl. Rockes aus Augsburg im Jahre 1810." *Kurtrierisches Jahrbuch* 8/9 (1968/1969): 241–55/160–76.

"Moselle, Sarreguemines." *Annales de la religion* 1, no. 23 (1795): 543–46.

"Mozelle." *Annales de la religion* 8 (1799): 361–62.

Müller, Johann Kaspar. *Auch das Volk soll und darf die Wahrheit wissen.* Luxembourg: Perl & Cercelet, 1797.

Müller, Michael Franz Joseph. *Abhandlung über die jährlich am Pfingstdinstage in dem Städtchen Echternach, Herzogthum Luxemburg, gewöhnliche Prozession der sogenannten Springenden Heiligen.* Trier: Leistenschneider, 1816.

Paquet, René. *Bibliographie analytique de l'histoire de Metz, pendant la Révolution (1789–1800): Imprimés et manuscrits.* Paris: Picard, 1926.

Poirson, Jean-Baptiste. *Carte de l'Empire français divisé en 110 départements.* Paris, 1808.

Recueil des règlemens et arrêtés émanés du commissaire du gouvernement dans les quatre nouveaux départemens de la rive gauche du Rhin: V^e tome—9e et 10e cahiers. Strasbourg: Levrault, An VII (1799).

Sailer, Johann Michael. *Vorlesungen aus der Pastoraltheologie: Auf Befehl Sr. Churf. Durchlaucht zu Trier, als Fürstbischofs zu Augsburg, etc. etc. herausgegeben.* 2nd ed. 3 vols. Munich: Joseph Lentner, 1793/94.

Sancti Aurelii Augustini epistulae: LVI–C. Edited by Klaus D. Daur. Corpus Christianorum Series Latina 31A. Turnhout: Brepols, 2005.

Simon, Frederik, ed. *Pastorale Erneuerung in Umbruchszeiten: Bischof Josef von Hommers Visitationen im Bistum Trier zwischen 1827 und 1833.* Münster: Aschendorff, 2023.

Sprunck, Alphonse. "L'église des Jésuites et l'Octave de Luxembourg après 1773." *Academia. Bulletin de l'association catholique des étudiants luxembourgeois* (July 1939): 21–30.

Stammel, Johann Jakob. *Trierische Kronik für den Bürger und Landmann.* Trier: Schröll, 1797.

Stitz, Margarete, and Johannes Naumann. *Pfarrvisitationen im Schaumberger Land: Akten der Pfarreien Tholey, Thalexweiler, Marpingen, Bliesen, Theley und Hasborn von 1569 bis 1781 (Transkription, Übersetzung und Kommentar).* Tholey: Förderverein der Benediktinerabtei St. Mauritius Tholey, 2014.

SECONDARY SOURCES

Agulhon, Maurice. *1848 ou L'apprentissage de la République: 1848–1852.* 1973. Rev. and expanded ed. Paris: Seuil, 1992.

Akbari, Suzanne Conklin, Tamar Herzog, Daniel Jütte, Carl Nightingale, William Rankin, and Keren Weitzberg. "AHR Conversation: Walls, Borders, and Boundaries in World History." *American Historical Review* 122, no. 5 (2017): 1501–53.

Albareda, Anselm M., and Josep Massot i Muntaner. *Historia de Montserrat.* Rev. and expanded ed. Montserrat: Publicacions de l'Abadia de Montserrat, 1974.

Albert-Llorca, Marlène. *Les Vierges miraculeuses: Légendes et rituels.* Paris: Gallimard, 2002.

Altermatt, Urs. *Konfession, Nation und Rom: Metamorphosen im schweizerischen und europäischen Katholizismus des 19. und 20. Jahrhunderts*. Frauenfeld: Huber, 2009.

Amer Meziane, Mohamad. *Des empires sous la terre: Histoire écologique et raciale de la sécularisation*. Paris: La Découverte, 2021.

Andrés-Gallego, José. "Catholic Pilgrimages between c. 1500 and c. 2000." In *Religious Pilgrimages in the Mediterranean World*, edited by Antón M. Pazos, 11–37. London: Routledge, 2023.

Andriani, Giovanni. "Notre-Dame de Luxembourg: Le rayonnement d'un sanctuaire." *Annales de l'Est* 58 (2008): 145–60.

Anzaldúa, Gloria. *Borderlands/La frontera: The New Mestiza*. 1987. 4th ed. San Francisco: Aunt Lute Books, 2012.

Appadurai, Arjun. *Modernity at Large: Cultural Dimensions of Globalization*. Minneapolis: University of Minnesota Press, 1996.

Applegate, Celia. *A Nation of Provincials: The German Idea of Heimat*. Berkeley: University of California Press, 1990.

Asad, Talal. *Formations of the Secular: Christianity, Islam, Modernity*. Stanford, CA: Stanford University Press, 2003.

Ashburn Miller, Mary. "The Impossible Émigré: Moving People and Moving Borders in the Annexed Territories of Revolutionary France." In *French Emigrants in Revolutionised Europe: Connected Histories and Memories*, edited by Laure Philip and Juliette Reboul, 29–44. Cham, Switzerland: Palgrave Macmillan, 2019.

Aston, Nigel. *Christianity and Revolutionary Europe, 1750–1830*. Cambridge: Cambridge University Press, 2002.

———. *Religion and Revolution in France, 1780–1804*. Houndmills, London: Macmillan, 2000.

Baciocchi, Stéphane, and Dominique Julia. "Reliques et Révolution française (1789–1804)." In *Reliques modernes: Cultes et usages chrétiens des corps saints des réformes aux révolutions*, edited by Philippe Boutry, Pierre-Antoine Fabre, and Julia, 2 vols., vol. 2, 483–585. Paris: Éditions de l'EHESS, 2009.

Balzamo, Nicolas. "L'infrastructure de l'*Atlas Marianus*: Les livrets de pèlerinage à l'époque moderne (XVIᵉ–XVIIᵉ siècles)." In *Marie mondialisée: L'Atlas Marianus de Wilhelm Gumppenberg et les topographies sacrées de l'époque moderne*, edited by Olivier Christin, Fabrice Flückiger, and Naïma Ghermani, 121–30. Neuchâtel: Alphil Editions, 2014.

———. "La Vierge en ses royaumes: Images, légendes et patronage marial dans l'Europe moderne (XVIᵉ–XVIIᵉ siècles)." In *Saintetés politiques du IXᵉ au XVIIIᵉ siècle: Autour de la Lotharingie-Dorsale catholique*, edited by Sylvène Édouard, 97–116. Paris: Classiques Garnier, 2020.

Banks, Bryan A., and Erica Johnson, eds. *Freedom and Faith: The French Revolution and Religion in Global Perspective.* Basingstoke: Palgrave Macmillan, 2017.

Bartov, Omer, and Eric D. Weitz. "Introduction: Coexistence and Violence in the German, Habsburg, Russian, and Ottoman Borderlands." In *Shatterzone of Empires: Coexistence and Violence in the German, Habsburg, Russian, and Ottoman Borderlands,* edited by Bartov and Weitz, 1–20. Bloomington: Indiana University Press, 2013.

Bauer, Walter. *Griechisch-deutsches Wörterbuch zu den Schriften des Neuen Testaments und der frühchristlichen Literatur.* 6th rev. ed. Edited by Barbara Aland and Kurt Aland. Berlin: De Gruyter, 1988.

Bauerschmidt, Frederick Christian. "The Eucharist." In *The Oxford Handbook of Catholic Theology,* edited by Lewis Ayres and Medi A. Volpe, 277–93. Oxford: Oxford University Press, 2019.

Baumann, Ernst. "Die Wallfahrt von Mariastein: Ein Beitrag zur religiösen Volkskunde." *Basler Jahrbuch,* 1942, 110–39.

Baumer, Iso. *Wallfahrt als Handlungsspiel: Ein Beitrag zum Verständnis religiösen Handelns.* Bern: Peter Lang, 1977.

Bazzani, Carlo. "Miracoli e ierofanie in epoca rivoluzionaria: Rivoluzionari e controrivoluzionari a confronto attraverso il caso veneto e cisalpino." *Studi e materiali di storia delle religioni* 85, no. 2 (2019): 626–37.

Beales, Derek. *Joseph II.* 2 vols. Cambridge: Cambridge University Press, 1987/2009.

Becker, Petrus. *Die Benediktinerabtei St. Eucharius–St. Matthias vor Trier.* Berlin: De Gruyter, 1996.

Becker, Rainald. "Wallfahrt und Geographie: Zur Raumgeschichte des posttridentinischen Pilgerwesens." In *Andacht oder Abenteuer: Von der Wilsnackfahrt im Spätmittelalter zu Reiselust und Reisefrust in der Frühen Neuzeit,* edited by Hartmut Kühne and Gunhild Roth, 317–49. Tübingen: Narr Francke Attempto, 2020.

Behrisch, Lars. "Vermessen, Zählen, Berechnen des Raums im 18. Jahrhundert." In *Vermessen, zählen, berechnen: Die politische Ordnung des Raums im 18. Jahrhundert,* edited by Behrisch, 7–25. Frankfurt: Campus Verlag, 2006.

Bell, David A. *The Cult of the Nation in France: Inventing Nationalism, 1680–1800.* Cambridge, MA: Harvard University Press, 2001.

———. "Nation-Building and Cultural Particularism in Eighteenth-Century France: The Case of Alsace." *Eighteenth-Century Studies* 21, no. 4 (1988): 472–90.

Belmas, Élisabeth. "L'interdiction des pèlerinages à l'étranger (XVIIe–XVIIIe siècles)." In *Mélanges à la mémoire de Michel Péronnet*, edited by Joël Fouilleron and Henri Michel, 3 vols., vol. 3, 485–98. Montpellier: Centre d'histoire moderne et contemporaine de l'Europe méditerranéenne et de ses périphéries, 2003–6.

Berbée, Paul. "Zur Klärung von Sprache und Sache in der Wallfahrtsforschung: Begriffsgeschichtlicher Beitrag und Diskussion." *Bayerische Blätter für Volkskunde* 14 (1987): 65–82.

Bernard, Birgit. *Die Wallfahrten der St.-Matthias-Bruderschaften zur Abtei St. Matthias in Trier vom 17. Jahrhundert bis zum Ende des Zweiten Weltkrieges.* Heidelberg: Heidelberger Orientverlag, 1995.

Bernard-Lesceux, Isabelle. "Notre-Dame de Luxembourg, naissance et diffusion: XVIIe et XVIIIe siècles." In *Une piété lotharingienne: Foi publique, foi intériorisée (XIIe–XVIIIe siècles)*, edited by Catherine Guyon, Yves Krumenacker, and Bruno Maës, 231–51. Paris: Classiques Garnier, 2022.

Bernet, Jacques. "Cultes chrétiens et civiques en Picardie à l'époque de la première séparation de l'Église et de l'État (1795–1801)." In *Du Directoire au Consulat*, edited by Bernet, Jean-Pierre Jessenne, Christine Le Bozec, and Hervé Leuwers, 4 vols., vol. 2, 165–76. Lille: Centre de recherches sur l'histoire de l'Europe du Nord-Ouest, 1999–2001.

———. "Les limites de la déchristianisation de l'an II éclairées par le retour au culte de l'an III: L'exemple du district de Compiègne." *Annales historiques de la Révolution française* 312 (1998): 285–99.

Bertrand, Gilles. "Pour une approche comparée des modes de contrôle exercés aux frontières des anciens États italiens: Les exemples du Dauphiné et de la Toscane dans la seconde moitié du XVIIIe siècle." In *La mobilité des personnes en Méditerranée de l'Antiquité à l'époque moderne: Procédures de contrôle et documents d'identification*, edited by Claude Moatti, 253–303. Rome: École française de Rome, 2004.

Bieg, Amelie. "'Frommer Glaube und unrichtige Begriffe': Der Umgang der Gläubigen in den Oberämtern Ellwangen und Gmünd mit den Reformen der katholischen Aufklärung." *Rottenburger Jahrbuch für Kirchengeschichte* 39 (2020): 371–82.

Birchler, Linus. "Das Einsidler [sic] Gnadenbild: Seine äussere und innere Geschichte." *Studien und Mitteilungen zur Geschichte des Benediktinerordens und seiner Zweige* 111 (2000): 167–89.

Birsens, Josy. "Die Bruderschaft der Trösterin der Betrübten in Luxemburg: Entstehung und Entwicklung (1652–1795)." *Hémecht* 69, no. 1 (2017): 5–27.

———. *Manuels de catéchisme, missions de campagne et mentalités populaires dans* le duché de Luxembourg aux XVIIe–XVIIIe siècles. Luxembourg: Section Historique de l'Institut Grand-Ducal de Luxembourg, 1990.

Birtsch, Günter. "Soziale Unruhen, ständische Gesellschaft und politische Repräsentation: Trier in der Zeit der Französischen Revolution, 1781–1794." In Mentalitäten und Lebensverhältnisse: Beispiele aus der Sozialgeschichte der Neuzeit. Rudolf Vierhaus zum 60. Geburtstag, 143–59. Göttingen: Vandenhoeck & Ruprecht, 1982.

Bisaro, Xavier. Chanter toujours: Plain-chant et religion villageoise dans la France moderne (XVIe–XIXe siècle). Rennes: Presses universitaires de Rennes, 2010.

Bitterling, David. L'invention du pré carré: Construction de l'espace français sous l'Ancien régime. Paris: Albin Michel, 2009.

Bitton-Ashkelony, Brouria. Encountering the Sacred: The Debate on Christian Pilgrimage in Late Antiquity. Berkeley: University of California Press, 2005.

Bjork, James E. Neither German nor Pole: Catholicism and National Indifference in a Central European Borderland. Ann Arbor: University of Michigan Press, 2008.

Blackbourn, David. Marpingen: Apparitions of the Virgin Mary in Nineteenth-Century Germany. New York: Knopf, 1994.

Blanchot, Jean-Michel. "Le culte de Notre-Dame des Ermites dans le diocèse de Besançon (XVIIIe–XIXe siècle): Militantisme tridentin et culte identitaire." Mémoires de la société d'émulation du Doubs 49 (2007): 133–92.

———. "Objets de dévotion et souvenirs du pèlerinage à Einsiedeln: L'exemple de la Franche-Comté et de ses régions limitrophes au sein de la dorsale catholique." Mémoires de la société d'émulation du Doubs 57 (2015): 279–338.

Blanning, T. C. W. The French Revolution in Germany: Occupation and Resistance in the Rhineland, 1792–1802. Oxford: Clarendon, 1983.

Blaschke, Olaf. "Das 19. Jahrhundert: Ein Zweites Konfessionelles Zeitalter?" Geschichte und Gesellschaft 26, no. 1 (2000): 38–75.

Blazejewski, Jort. "Grenzräume als Zufluchtsräume: Emigranten der Französischen Revolution in Luxemburg und Trier (1789–1795)." In Grenzraum und Repräsentation: Perspektiven auf Raumvorstellungen und Grenzkonzepte in der Vormoderne, edited by Stephan Laux and Maike Schmidt, 145–55. Trier: Kliomedia, 2019.

Bock, Florian. Pastorale Strategien zwischen Konfessionalisierung und Aufklärung: Katholische Predigten und ihre implizite Hörer-/Leserschaft (circa 1670 bis 1800). Münster: Aschendorff, 2023.

Böck, Hanna, and Georg Holzherr. Einsiedeln: Das Kloster und seine Geschichte. Zurich: Artemis, 1989.

Boehler, Jean-Michel. Une société rurale en milieu rhénan: La paysannerie de la *plaine d'Alsace (1648–1789)*. 1994. 2nd rev. ed. 3 vols. Strasbourg: Presses universitaires de Strasbourg, 1995.

Borutta, Manuel. *Antikatholizismus: Deutschland und Italien im Zeitalter der europäischen Kulturkämpfe*. 2010. 2nd rev. ed. Göttingen: Vandenhoeck & Ruprecht, 2011.

Boudon, Jacques-Olivier. *L'Empire des polices: Comment Napoléon faisait régner l'ordre*. Paris: La Librairie Vuibert, 2017.

———. *Napoléon et les cultes: Les religions en Europe à l'aube du XIXe siècle, 1800–1815*. Paris: Fayard, 2002.

Boudon, Jacques-Olivier, and Rémy Hême de Lacotte, eds. *La crise concordataire: Catholiques français et italiens entre Pie VII et Napoléon 1808–1814*. Paris: Éditions SPM, 2016.

Bouflet, Joachim. "Institution et charisme dans l'Église de 1846 à nos jours: La question du jugement épiscopal sur les apparitions mariales modernes et contemporaines." PhD diss., Université Michel de Montaigne-Bordeaux 3, 2014.

Bouflet, Joachim, and Philippe Boutry. *Un signe dans le ciel: Les apparitions de la Vierge*. Paris: Grasset, 1997.

Bourdin, Philippe, and Philippe Boutry. "Introduction. L'Église catholique en Révolution: L'historiographie récente." *Annales historiques de la Révolution française*, no. 355 (2009): 3–23.

Bourdon, Jean. "La formation des départements de l'Est en 1790." *Annales de l'Est*, no. 3 (1951): 187–217.

Boutry, Philippe. "Dévotion et apparition: Le 'modèle tridentin' dans les mariophanies en France à l'époque moderne." *Siècles. Cahiers du Centre d'histoire "Espaces et Cultures,"* no. 12 (2000): 115–31.

———. "Le procès *super non cultu* source de l'histoire des pèlerinages: Germaine Cousin et le sanctuaire de Pibrac au lendemain de la Révolution française." *Bibliothèque de l'École des chartes* 154, no. 2 (1996): 565–90.

Bouvy, A. "La fontaine de Host en l'an VII d'après les documents officiels." In *Études d'histoire ecclésiastique messine offertes à Monseigneur Willibrord Benzler O.S.B. à l'occasion de son jubilé sacerdotal*, edited by N. Hamant, Paul Lesprand, and Bouvy, 121–49. Guénange: Apprentis-Orphelins, 1902.

Brambilla, Chiara. "Exploring the Critical Potential of the Borderscapes Concept." *Geopolitics* 20, no. 1 (2015): 14–34.

Brassart, Laurent, and Maxime Kaci. "From Rural Homelands to National Bordered Lands, 1789–1815?" In *Making Politics in the European Countryside, 1780s–1930s*, edited by Brassart, Corinne Marache, Juan Pan-Montojo, and Leen van Molle, 59–73. Turnhout: Brepols, 2022.

Braubach, Max. "Die kirchliche Aufklärung im katholischen Deutschland im Spiegel des 'Journal von und für Deutschland' (1784–92)." *Historisches Jahrbuch* 54 (1934): 1–63, 178–220.

Braun, Guido. *Von der politischen zur kulturellen Hegemonie Frankreichs 1648–1789.* Darmstadt: Wissenschaftliche Buchgesellschaft, 2008.

Braun, Patrick. *Josef Wilhelm Rinck von Baldenstein (1704–1782): Das Wirken eines Basler Fürstbischofs in der Zeit der Aufklärung.* Fribourg: Universitätsverlag, 1981.

Bretschneider, Falk, and Christophe Duhamelle. "Fraktalität: Raumgeschichte und soziales Handeln im Alten Reich." *Zeitschrift für Historische Forschung* 43, no. 4 (2016): 703–46.

Broers, Michael. "Napoleon, Charlemagne, and Lotharingia: Acculturation and the Boundaries of Napoleonic Europe." *Historical Journal* 44, no. 1 (2001): 135–54.

———. *The Politics of Religion in Napoleonic Italy: The War against God, 1801–1814.* London: Routledge, 2002.

Brophy, James M. *Popular Culture and the Public Sphere in the Rhineland, 1800–1850.* Cambridge: Cambridge University Press, 2007.

Brown, Howard G. *Ending the French Revolution: Violence, Justice, and Repression from the Terror to Napoleon.* Charlottesville: University of Virginia Press, 2006.

Brown, Peter. *The Cult of the Saints: Its Rise and Function in Latin Christianity.* Chicago: University of Chicago Press, 1981.

Brückner, Wolfgang. "Die Neuorganisation von Frömmigkeit des Kirchenvolkes im nachtridentinischen Konfessionsstaat." In *Das Konzil von Trient und die Moderne,* edited by Paolo Prodi and Wolfgang Reinhard, 147–73. Berlin: Duncker & Humblot, 2001.

———. *Die Verehrung des Heiligen Blutes in Walldürn: Volkskundlich-soziologische Untersuchungen zum Strukturwandel barocken Wallfahrtens.* Aschaffenburg: P. Pattloch, 1958.

Brugger, Eva. *Gedruckte Gnade: Die Dynamisierung der Wallfahrt in Bayern (1650–1800).* Affalterbach: Didymos-Verlag, 2017.

Buchholz, Christopher. *Französischer Staatskult 1792–1813 im linksrheinischen Deutschland: Mit Vergleichen zu den Nachbardepartements der habsburgischen Niederlande.* Frankfurt: Lang, 1997.

Bultmann, Rudolf. *Das Evangelium des Johannes.* 1941. Göttingen: Vandenhoeck & Ruprecht, 1968.

Burg, André Marcel. *Marienthal: Histoire du couvent et du pèlerinage sous les*

Guillelmites, les Jésuites et le Clergé séculier. Phalsbourg: Imprimerie franciscaine, 1959.

Butterwick, Richard. *The Polish-Lithuanian Commonwealth, 1733–1795: Light and Flame*. New Haven, CT: Yale University Press, 2020.

Byrnes, Joseph F. *Catholic and French Forever: Religious and National Identity in Modern France*. University Park: Pennsylvania State University Press, 2005.

Caffiero, Marina. *La fabrique d'un saint à l'époque des Lumières*. 1996. Paris: Éditions de l'EHESS, 2006.

Caiani, Ambrogio. *To Kidnap a Pope: Napoleon and Pius VII*. New Haven, CT: Yale University Press, 2021.

Carl, Horst. "Revolution und Rechristianisierung: Soziale und religiöse Umbruchserfahrung im Rheinland bis zum Konkordat von 1801." In *Zerfall und Wiederbeginn: Vom Erzbistum zum Bistum Mainz (1792/97–1830). Ein Vergleich*, edited by Walter G. Rödel and Regina E. Schwerdtfeger, 87–102. Würzburg: Echter, 2002.

Carlen, Louis. *Wallfahrt und Recht im Abendland*. Fribourg: Universitätsverlag, 1987.

Casey, Edward S. *The Fate of Place: A Philosophical History*. Berkeley: University of California Press, 1997.

Cattaneo, Massimo. *Gli occhi di Maria sulla Rivoluzione: "Miracoli" a Roma e nello Stato della Chiesa (1796–1797)*. Rome: Istituto nazionale di studi romani, 1995.

Caulier, Brigitte. *L'eau et le sacré: Les cultes thérapeutiques autour des fontaines en France, du Moyen Âge à nos jours*. Paris: Beauchesne, 1990.

Cegielski, Tadeusz. *Das alte Reich und die erste Teilung Polens 1768–1774*. Stuttgart: Steiner, 1988.

Certeau, Michel de, Dominique Julia, and Jacques Revel. *Une politique de la langue: La Révolution française et les patois. L'enquête de Grégoire*. 1975. Paris: Gallimard, 2002.

Chantre, Luc, Paul d'Hollander, and Jérôme Grévy, eds. *Politiques du pèlerinage du XVIIe siècle à nos jours*. Rennes: Presses universitaires de Rennes, 2014.

Chapman-Adisho, Annette. *Patriot and Priest: Jean-Baptiste Volfius and the Constitutional Church in the Côte-d'Or*. Montreal: McGill-Queen's University Press, 2019.

Châtellier, Louis. *Tradition chrétienne et renouveau catholique: Dans le cadre de l'ancien diocèse de Strasbourg (1650–1770)*. Paris: Ophrys, 1981.

Châtellier, Louis, and Annik Schon. "Essai de cartographie des pèlerinages alsaciens: Réflexions en marge d'une enquête en cours." *Annales de Bretagne et des Pays de l'Ouest* 90, no. 2 (1983): 197–202.

Chaunu, Pierre. "Jansénisme et frontière de catholicité (XVIIᵉ et XVIIIᵉ siècles): À propos du Jansénisme lorrain." *Revue Historique* 227, no. 1 (1962): 115–38.
Chiron, Yves. *Enquête sur les apparitions de la Vierge.* Paris: Perrin/Mame, 1995.
Chopelin, Paul. "Une affaire de femmes? Les résistances laïques à la politique religieuse d'État sous la Révolution française." In *Genre et christianisme: Plaidoyers pour une histoire croiseé,* edited by Matthieu Brejon de Lavergnée and Magali Della Sudda, 155–79. Paris: Beauchesne, 2015.

———. *Ville patriote et ville martyre: Lyon, l'Église et la Révolution, 1788–1805.* Paris: Letouzey et Ané, 2010.

Christian, William A. *Apparitions in Late Medieval and Renaissance Spain.* Princeton, NJ: Princeton University Press, 1981.

———. *Local Religion in Sixteenth-Century Spain.* Princeton, NJ: Princeton University Press, 1981.

———. *Visionaries: The Spanish Republic and the Reign of Christ.* Berkeley: University of California Press, 1996.

Christin, Olivier. "Les topographies sacrées de la période moderne et l'espace de la catholicité." In *Dorsale catholique, jansénisme, dévotions (XVIᵉ–XVIIIᵉ siècles): Mythe, réalité, actualité historiographique,* edited by Gilles Deregnaucourt, Yves Krumenacker, Philippe Martin, and Frédéric Meyer, 189–206. Paris: Riveneuve, 2014.

Clark, Christopher. "The New Catholicism and the European Culture Wars." In *Culture Wars: Secular–Catholic Conflict in Nineteenth-Century Europe,* edited by Clark and Wolfram Kaiser, 11–46. Cambridge: Cambridge University Press, 2003.

Clarke, Joseph. "'The Rage of the Fanatics': Religious Fanaticism and the Making of Revolutionary Violence." *French History* 33, no. 2 (2019): 236–58.

Claverie, Élisabeth. *Les guerres de la Vierge: Une anthropologie des apparitions.* Paris: Gallimard, 2003.

Clémendot, Pierre. *Le Département de la Meurthe à l'époque du Directoire.* Raon-l'Étape: Fetzer, 1966.

Clemens, Gabriele B. "Einleitung: Franzosen und Deutsche im napoleonischen Empire. Konsens, Kollaboration oder Konfrontation?" In *Erbfeinde im Empire? Franzosen und Deutsche im Zeitalter Napoleons,* edited by Jacques-Olivier Boudon, Clemens, and Pierre Horn, 7–15. Ostfildern: Thorbecke, 2016.

———. "Die Notabeln der Franzosenzeit." In *Unter der Trikolore: Trier in Frankreich—Napoleon in Trier (1794–1814),* edited by Elisabeth Dühr, 2 vols., vol. 1, 105–80. Trier: Städtisches Museum Simeonstift, 2004.

———. "The Swiss Case in the Napoleonic Empire." In *The Napoleonic Empire and the New European Political Culture,* edited by Michael Broers, Peter Hicks, and Agustín Guimerá Ravina, 132–42. Basingstoke: Palgrave Macmillan, 2012.

Clemens, Gabriele B., and Lukas Clemens. *Geschichte der Stadt Trier.* Munich: Beck, 2007.

Clemens, Lukas. "Zum Umgang mit der Antike im hochmittelalterlichen Trier." In *2000 Jahre Trier,* edited by Universität Trier, 3 vols., vol. 2, 167–202. Trier: Spee-Verlag, 1985–96.

Clinquart, Jean. *Les services extérieurs de la Ferme générale à la fin de l'Ancien Régime: L'exemple de la direction des fermes du Hainaut.* Paris: Comité pour l'Histoire Économique et Financière de la France, 1995.

Cobb, Richard. *The Police and the People: French Popular Protest 1789–1820.* Oxford: Clarendon, 1970.

Cole, Laurence. "Nation, Anti-Enlightenment, and Religious Revival in Austria: Tyrol in the 1790s." *Historical Journal* 43, no. 2 (2000): 475–97.

Coleman, Simon. *Powers of Pilgrimage: Religion in a World of Movement.* New York: NYU Press, 2022.

Coleman, Simon, and John Eade. "Introduction: Reframing Pilgrimage." In *Reframing Pilgrimage: Cultures in Motion,* edited by Coleman and Eade, 1–25. London: Routledge, 2004.

Colot, Guillaume. "Former l'opinion des Catholiques sous le Directoire: *Les Annales de la religion* et *Les Annales catholiques.*" In *La Révolution française au miroir des recherches actuelles: Actes du colloque tenu à Ivry-sur-Seine, 15–16 juin 2010,* edited by Cyril Triolaire, 207–19. Paris: Société des études robespierristes, 2011.

Confino, Alon. *The Nation as a Local Metaphor: Württemberg, Imperial Germany, and National Memory, 1871–1918.* Chapel Hill: University of North Carolina Press, 1997.

Conrad, Sebastian. *What Is Global History?* Princeton, NJ: Princeton University Press, 2016.

Constable, Giles. "Opposition to Pilgrimage in the Middle Ages." *Studia Gratiana* 19 (1976): 125–46.

Cooper, Frederick. *Colonialism in Question: Theory, Knowledge, History.* Berkeley: University of California Press, 2005.

Coreth, Anna. *Pietas Austriaca: Österreichische Frömmigkeit im Barock.* 1959. Munich: Oldenbourg, 1982.

Corpis, Duane J. *Crossing the Boundaries of Belief: Geographies of Religious Conversion in Southern Germany, 1648–1800.* Charlottesville: University of Virginia Press, 2014.

Cozzo, Paolo. "Apparizioni fra 'dubbiezze, dissenzioni e guerre': L'uso pubblico delle ierofanie nel Piemonte meridionale tra fine Cinquecento e metà Seicento." *Studi e materiali di storia delle religioni* 85, no. 2 (2019): 573–86.
Cresswell, Tim. *In Place/Out of Place: Geography, Ideology, and Transgression.* Minneapolis: University of Minnesota Press, 1996.
———. *Place: An Introduction.* 2nd ed. Malden, MA: Wiley-Blackwell, 2015.
Czerny, Helga. *Die Wittelsbacher und der Wallfahrtsort Altötting: Tradition und Traditionsbildung im bayerischen Herrscherhaus.* Regensburg: Pustet, 2018.
Czouz-Tornare, Alain-Jacques. "Une frontière intouchable: Les limites entre la France et les Cantons suisses sous la Révolution et l'Empire." In *Frontières et espaces frontaliers du Léman à la Meuse: Recompositions et échanges de 1789 à 1814 (actes du colloque de Nancy, 25–27 novembre 2004),* edited by Claude Mazauric and Jean-Paul Rothiot, 155–84. Nancy: Presses universitaires de Nancy, 2007.
Dabrowski, Patrice M. "Multiple Visions, Multiple Viewpoints: Apparitions in a German–Polish Borderland, 1877–1880." *Polish Review* 58, no. 3 (2013): 35–64.
Daughton, J. P. *An Empire Divided: Religion, Republicanism, and the Making of French Colonialism, 1880–1914.* New York: Oxford University Press, 2006.
Dauphant, Léonard. "L'historiographie des frontières et des espaces frontaliers en France depuis trente ans." *Francia. Forschungen zur westeuropäischen Geschichte* 47 (2020): 295–306.
Dean, Rodney J. *L'abbé Grégoire et l'Église constitutionnelle après la terreur, 1794–1797.* Paris: Picard, 2008.
Debarbieux, Bernard. "Le lieu, le territoire et trois figures de rhétorique." *Espace géographique* 24, no. 2 (1995): 97–112.
Delaney, David. *Territory: A Short Introduction.* Malden, MA: Wiley-Blackwell, 2005.
Delfosse, Annick. *La "protectrice du Païs-Bas": Stratégies politiques et figures de la Vierge dans les Pays-Bas espagnols.* Turnhout: Brepols, 2009.
Deloria, Vine, Jr. *God Is Red: A Native View of Religion.* 30th anniversary ed. Golden, CO: Fulcrum, 2003.
Denis, Vincent. *Une histoire de l'identité: France, 1715–1815.* Seyssel: Champ Vallon, 2008.
Desan, Suzanne. "The French Revolution and Religion, 1795–1815." In *Enlightenment, Reawakening and Revolution 1660–1815,* edited by Stewart J. Brown and Timothy Tackett, vol. 7 of *The Cambridge History of Christianity,* 556–74. Cambridge: Cambridge University Press, 2006.

———. "Internationalizing the French Revolution." *French Politics, Culture & Society* 29, no. 2 (2011): 137–60.

———. *Reclaiming the Sacred: Lay Religion and Popular Politics in Revolutionary France*. Ithaca, NY: Cornell University Press, 1990.

Desmette, Philippe, and Philippe Martin, eds. *Le miracle de guerre dans la chrétienté occidentale*. Paris: Hémisphères Éditions, 2018.

Devos, Roger. "Pèlerinages et culte des saints à l'épreuve de la Révolution: L'exemple du diocèse de Genève." In "Confréries et dévotions à l'épreuve de la Révolution," edited by Marie-Hélène Froeschlé-Chopard, special issue, *Provence historique* 39, no. 156 (1989): 317–26.

Di Fiore, Laura. "The Production of Borders in Nineteenth-Century Europe: Between Institutional Boundaries and Transnational Practices of Space." *European Review of History* 24, no. 1 (2017): 36–57.

Dickson, P. G. M. "Joseph II's Reshaping of the Austrian Church." *Historical Journal* 36, no. 1 (1993): 89–114.

Dipper, Christof. "Volksreligiosität und Obrigkeit im 18. Jahrhundert." In *Volksreligiosität in der modernen Sozialgeschichte*, edited by Wolfgang Schieder, 73–96. Göttingen: Vandenhoeck & Ruprecht, 1986.

Dohms, Peter. "Die Geschichte der Wallfahrt nach Kevelaer." In *Consolatrix afflictorum: Das Marienbild zu Kevelaer. Botschaft, Geschichte, Gegenwart*, edited by Josef Heckens and Richard Schulte Staade, 227–74. Kevelaer: Butzon & Bercker, 1992.

———. "Die Wallfahrt nach Klausen in Geschichte und Gegenwart." In *500 Jahre Wallfahrtskirche Klausen*, edited by Martin Persch, Michael Embach, and Dohms, 9–68. Mainz: Gesellschaft für Mittelrheinische Kirchengeschichte, 2003.

Dohms, Peter, and Wiltrud Dohms. *Klausen: Geschichte der Wallfahrt und Nachweis der Prozessionen*. Siegburg: Schmitt, 2005.

Dondelinger, Patrick. "Le glacis de la forteresse de Luxembourg, lieu(e) de mémoire nationale." *Hémecht* 60, no. 1 (2008): 5–78.

Doney, Skye. *The Persistence of the Sacred: German Catholic Pilgrimage, 1832–1937*. Toronto: University of Toronto Press, 2022.

Döring, Alois. "Wallfahrtsleben im 18. Jahrhundert." In *Hirt und Herde: Religiosität und Frömmigkeit im Rheinland des 18. Jahrhunderts*, edited by Frank G. Zehnder, 37–58. Cologne: DuMont, 2000.

Drascek, Daniel. "Der Papstbesuch in Wien und Augsburg 1782: Zum Wandel spätbarocker Alltags- und Frömmigkeitskultur unter dem Einfluß süddeutscher Gegenaufklärer." In *Volkskundliche Fallstudien: Profile empirischer*

Kulturforschung heute, edited by Burkhart Lauterbach and Christoph Köck, 25–44. Münster: Waxmann, 1998.

———. "Räumliche Horizonte: Zur Konstruktion von Räumlichkeit durch frühneuzeitliche Mobilität zu süddeutschen Kultstätten." *Jahrbuch des italienisch-deutschen historischen Instituts in Trient* 29 (2003): 287–306.

Drut-Hours, Marie. "Promouvoir le 'vrai christianisme': La question religieuse et l'*Aufklärung* dans les communautés catholique de Trèves et protestante des Deux-Ponts." *Dix-huitième siècle* 34 (2002): 41–52.

Dubisch, Jill. *In a Different Place: Pilgrimage, Gender, and Politics at a Greek Island Shrine*. Princeton, NJ: Princeton University Press, 1995.

Dubois, Sébastien. *La révolution géographique en Belgique: Départementalisation, administration et représentations du territoire de la fin du XVIIIe au début du XIXe siècle*. Brussels: Académie royale de Belgique, 2008.

Duchhardt, Heinz. "The Cartographic 'Battle of the Rhine' in the Eighteenth Century." In *Bordering Early Modern Europe*, edited by Maria Baramova, Grigor Boykov, and Ivan Parvev, 3–13. Wiesbaden: Harrassowitz, 2015.

Ducreux, Marie-Élizabeth. "Emperors, Kingdoms, Territories: Multiple Versions of the *Pietas Austriaca*?" *Catholic Historical Review* 97, no. 2 (2011): 276–304.

Dufour, Alfred. "D'une médiation à l'autre." In *Bonaparte, la Suisse et l'Europe: Actes du colloque européen d'histoire constitutionnelle pour le bicentenaire de l'Acte de Médiation (1803–2003)*, edited by Dufour, Till Hanisch, and Victor Monnier, 7–37. Brussels, Berlin, and Geneva: Bruylant/Berliner Wissenschafts-Verlag/Schulthess, 2003.

Dufraisse, Roger. "L'installation de l'institution départementale sur la rive gauche du Rhin (4 novembre 1797–23 septembre 1802)." In *L'Allemagne à l'époque napoléonienne: Questions d'histoire politique, économique et sociale*, 77–103. Bonn: Bouvier, 1992.

———. "Une rébellion en pays annexé: Le 'soulevement' des gardes nationales de la Sarre en 1809." *Bulletin de la Société d'histoire moderne* 68, no. 10 (1969): 2–6.

Duhamelle, Christophe. "Dedans, dehors: Espace et identité de l'exclave dans le Saint-Empire après la paix de Westphalie." In *Espaces de pouvoir, espaces d'autonomie en Allemagne*, edited by Hélène Miard-Delacroix and Maurice Blanc, 93–115. Villeneuve-d'Ascq: Presses universitaires du Septentrion, 2010.

———. *La frontière au village: Une identité catholique allemande au temps des Lumières*. Paris: Éditions de l'EHESS, 2010.

———. "Les lumières allemandes, les pèlerins et les moines (1778–1784)." In

Contre les moines: L'antimonachisme, des Réformes à la Révolution, edited by Fabienne Henryot and Philippe Martin, 329–40. Paris: Cerf, 2023.

———. "Le pèlerinage dans le Saint-Empire au XVIIIe siècle: Pratiques dévotionnelles et identités collectives." *Francia. Forschungen zur westeuropäischen Geschichte* 33, no. 2 (2006): 69–96.

———. "Les pèlerins de passage à l'hospice zum Heiligen Kreuz de Nuremberg au XVIIIe siècle." In *Rendre ses vœux: Les identités pèlerines dans l'Europe moderne (XVIe–XVIIIe siècle)*, edited by Philippe Boutry, Pierre-Antoine Fabre, and Dominique Julia, 39–56. Paris: Éditions de l'EHESS, 2000.

Dunlop, Catherine Tatiana. *Cartophilia: Maps and the Search for Identity in the French–German Borderland*. Chicago: University of Chicago Press, 2015.

Dünninger, Hans. "Processio peregrinationis: Volkskundliche Untersuchungen zu einer Geschichte des Wallfahrtswesens im Gebiet der heutigen Diözese Würzburg [1961/62]." In *Wallfahrt und Bilderkult: Gesammelte Schriften*, edited by Wolfgang Brückner, Jürgen Lenssen, and Klaus Wittstadt, 10–268. Würzburg: Echter, 1995.

———. "Zur Geschichte der barocken Wallfahrt im deutschen Südwesten [1981]." In *Wallfahrt und Bilderkult: Gesammelte Schriften*, edited by Wolfgang Brückner, Jürgen Lenssen, and Klaus Wittstadt, 305–20. Würzburg: Echter, 1995.

Dupont-Bouchat, Marie-Sylvie. "Les résistances à la Révolution: 'La Vendée belge' (1798–1799), nationalisme ou religion?" In *La Belgique criminelle: Droit, justice, société (XIVe–XXe siècles)*, 183–233. Louvain-la-Neuve: Bruylant-Academia/Université catholique de Louvain, 2006.

Dupront, Alphonse. *Du Sacré: Croisades et pèlerinages, images et langages*. Paris: Gallimard, 1987.

Dupuy, Roger. "Ignorance, fanatisme et Contre-Révolution." In *Les résistances à la Révolution: Actes du colloque de Rennes (17–21 sept. 1985)*, edited by François Lebrun and Dupuy, 37–42. Paris: Imago, 1988.

Dyas, Dee. *The Dynamics of Pilgrimage: Christianity, Holy Places, and Sensory Experience*. New York: Routledge, 2021.

Eade, John, and Michael J. Sallnow, eds. *Contesting the Sacred: The Anthropology of Christian Pilgrimage*. 1991. Urbana: University of Illinois Press, 2000.

Edelstein, Melvin. *The French Revolution and the Birth of Electoral Democracy*. Farnham, UK: Ashgate, 2014.

Eismann, Adam. *Umschreibung der Diözese Trier und ihrer Pfarreien (1802–1821)*. Saarbrücken: Verlag für religiöses Schrifttum Krueckemeyer, 1941.

Elden, Stuart. *The Birth of Territory*. Chicago: University of Chicago Press, 2013.

Elliott, John H. "A Europe of Composite Monarchies." *Past & Present* 137, no. 1 (1992): 48–71.

Englund, Steven. "Monstre sacré: The Question of Cultural Imperialism and the Napoleonic Empire." *Historical Journal* 51, no. 1 (2008): 215–50.

Esdaile, Charles J. *Fighting Napoleon: Guerrillas, Bandits and Adventurers in Spain, 1808–1814.* New Haven, CT: Yale University Press, 2004.

Esser, Raingard, and Steven G. Ellis. Introduction to *Frontier and Border Regions in Early Modern Europe,* edited by Esser and Ellis, 7–18. Hannover: Wehrhahn, 2013.

Fabricius, Wilhelm. *Erläuterungen zum Geschichtlichen Atlas der Rheinprovinz.* Vol. 2: Die *Karte von 1789. Einteilung und Entwickelung der Territorien von 1600 bis 1794.* Bonn: Hermann Behrendt, 1898.

Fachbach, Jens, and Mario Simmer. "Eine höfische Wallfahrt: Die Ausstellung des Heiligen Rockes auf dem Ehrenbreitstein 1765." *Archiv für mittelrheinische Kirchengeschichte* 65 (2013): 235–80.

Faltz, Michael. *Heimstätte U. L. Frau von Luxemburg.* 1920. 3rd expanded ed. Luxembourg: Sankt-Paulus-Druckerei, 1948.

Farbaky, Péter, and Szabolcs Serfőző, eds. *Ungarn in Mariazell—Mariazell in Ungarn: Geschichte und Erinnerung.* Budapest: Historisches Museum der Stadt Budapest, 2004.

Fassin, Didier. "Introduction: Connecting Borders and Boundaries." In *Deepening Divides: How Territorial Borders and Social Boundaries Delineate Our World,* edited by Fassin, 1–18. London: Pluto, 2019.

Fässler, Thomas. *Aufbruch und Widerstand: Das Kloster Einsiedeln im Spannungsfeld von Barock, Aufklärung und Revolution.* Egg bei Einsiedeln: Thesis Verlag, 2019.

Febvre, Lucien. "Frontière: Le mot et la notion." In *Pour une histoire à part entière,* 11–24. Paris: S.E.V.P.E.N., 1962.

———. *Le Rhin: Histoire, mythes et réalités.* New ed. Paris: Perrin, 1997.

Ferrari, Michele Camillo, Jean Schröder, and Henri Trauffler, eds. *Die Abtei Echternach: 698–1998.* Luxembourg: CLUDEM, 1999.

Fillafer, Franz Leander. *Aufklärung habsburgisch: Staatsbildung, Wissenskultur und Geschichtspolitik in Zentraleuropa 1750–1850.* Göttingen: Wallstein, 2020.

Fitschen, Klaus. "Die Zivilkonstitution des Klerus von 1790 als revolutionäres Kirchenreformprogramm im Zeichen der Ecclesia primitiva." *Historisches Jahrbuch* 117 (1997): 378–405.

Flamein, Richard. *Voltaire à Ferney: Adresse à la postérité moderne (1758–2015).* Paris: Classiques Garnier, 2019.

Ford, Caroline C. *Creating the Nation in Provincial France: Religion and Political Identity in Brittany*. Princeton, NJ: Princeton University Press, 1993.

Forrest, Alan. *Conscripts and Deserters: The Army and French Society during the Revolution and Empire*. Oxford: Oxford University Press, 1989.

Forster, Marc R. *Catholic Revival in the Age of the Baroque: Religious Identity in Southwest Germany, 1550–1750*. New York: Cambridge University Press, 2001.

———. *The Counter-Reformation in the Villages: Religion and Reform in the Bishopric of Speyer, 1560–1720*. Ithaca, NY: Cornell University Press, 1992.

Foucault, Michel. *Histoire de la sexualité*. Vol. 1: *La volonté de savoir*. Paris: Gallimard, 1976.

———. *Sécurité, territoire, population: Cours au Collège de France, 1977–1978*. Paris: Seuil/Gallimard, 2004.

François, Étienne. *Die unsichtbare Grenze: Protestanten und Katholiken in Augsburg 1648–1806*. Sigmaringen: Thorbecke, 1991.

Franz, Gunther. "Geistes- und Kulturgeschichte 1560–1794." In *2000 Jahre Trier*, edited by Universität Trier, 3 vols., vol. 3, 203–373. Trier: Spee-Verlag, 1985–96.

———. "Morgenglanz der Toleranz: Clemens Wenzeslaus und die Toleranz im Herzogtum Luxemburg und im Trierer Kurstaat." In *Der Trierer Erzbischof und Kurfürst Clemens Wenzeslaus (1739–1812), eine historische Bilanz nach 200 Jahren: Vorträge einer Tagung in der Stadtbibliothek Trier im November 2012*, edited by Michael Embach, 97–136. Mainz: Gesellschaft für Mittelrheinische Kirchengeschichte, 2014.

Franz, Norbert. *Die Stadtgemeinde Luxemburg im Spannungsfeld politischer und wirtschaftlicher Umwälzungen (1760–1890): Von der Festungs- und Garnisonsstadt zur offenen multifunktionalen Stadt*. Trier: Kliomedia, 2001.

Freitag, Werner. *Volks- und Elitenfrömmigkeit in der frühen Neuzeit: Marienwallfahrten im Fürstbistum Münster*. Paderborn: Schöningh, 1991.

Freytag, Nils. "Wunderglauben und Aberglauben: Wallfahrten und Prozessionen im Bistum Trier im 18. und 19. Jahrhundert." In *500 Jahre Wallfahrtskirche Klausen*, edited by Martin Persch, Michael Embach, and Peter Dohms, 261–82. Mainz: Gesellschaft für Mittelrheinische Kirchengeschichte, 2003.

Froeschlé-Chopard, Marie-Hélène. *Espace et sacré en Provence (XVIe–XXe siècle): Cultes, images, confréries*. Paris: Cerf, 1994.

Fues, Franz Joseph. *Die Pfarrgemeinden des Kantons Hirsingen, ihre Alterthümer und Gotteshäuser, ihre Weltpriester und Ordensleute, ihre adeligen Familien und namhaften Privatpersonen: Ein Beitrag zur Geschichte des Elsasses*. Rixheim: Sutter, 1876.

Gabor, Ingo. "Das Wallfahrtswesen vor und nach der Säkularisation." In *Alte Klöster, neue Herren: Die Säkularisation im deutschen Südwesten 1803*, edited by Volker Himmelein and Hans U. Rudolf, 979–98. Ostfildern: Thorbecke, 2003.

Gain, André. "Les processions religieuses en Moselle pendant la Révolution et l'Empire." *Annuaire de la Fédération historique lorraine (Annales de l'Est)* 3 (1930): 167–202.

Gainot, Bernard. *1799, un nouveau jacobinisme? La démocratie représentative, une alternative à brumaire*. Paris: CTHS, 2001.

Gálvez, Alyshia. *Guadalupe in New York: Devotion and the Struggle for Citizenship Rights among Mexican Immigrants*. New York: NYU Press, 2010.

Gantet, Claire, and Bernhard Struck. *Deutsch-Französische Geschichte 1789 bis 1815: Revolution, Krieg und Verflechtung*. Darmstadt: Wissenschaftliche Buchgesellschaft, 2008.

Garner, Guillaume. *État, économie, territoire en Allemagne: L'espace dans le caméralisme et l'économie politique, 1740–1820*. Paris: Éditions de l'EHESS, 2005.

Gerteis, Klaus. "Trier—Trèves: Die 'Franzosenzeit' in Trier 1794–1814. Ein Überblick." In *Unter der Trikolore: Trier in Frankreich—Napoleon in Trier (1794–1814)*, edited by Elisabeth Dühr, 2 vols., vol. 1, 59–83. Trier: Städtisches Museum Simeonstift, 2004.

Gibson, Ralph. *A Social History of French Catholicism 1789–1914*. London: Routledge, 1989.

Gieryn, Thomas F. *Truth-Spots: How Places Make People Believe*. Chicago: University of Chicago Press, 2018.

Gissibl, Bernhard, and Andrea Hofmann. "Sacralizations as Cultural Practices: An Introduction." In *Multiple Sacralities: Rethinking Sacralizations in European History*, edited by Gissibl and Hofmann, 9–38. Göttingen: Vandenhoeck & Ruprecht, 2023.

Glaus, Beat. "Helvetische Kloster- und Kirchenpolitik in Einsiedeln 1798–1803." *Mitteilungen des Historischen Vereins des Kantons Schwyz* 109 (2017): 179–91.

Godechot, Jacques. *La Grande Nation: L'expansion révolutionnaire de la France dans le monde de 1789 à 1799*. 2nd rev. ed. Paris: Aubier, 1983.

Godel, Eric. *Die Zentralschweiz in der Helvetik (1798–1803): Kriegserfahrungen und Religion im Spannungsfeld von Nation und Region*. Münster: Aschendorff, 2009.

Goy, Barbara. *Aufklärung und Volksfrömmigkeit in den Bistümern Würzburg und Bamberg*. Würzburg: Schöningh, 1969.

Greer, Donald. *The Incidence of the Emigration during the French Revolution.* Cambridge, MA: Harvard University Press, 1951.

Gregory, Brad S. *Salvation at Stake: Christian Martyrdom in Early Modern Europe.* Cambridge, MA: Harvard University Press, 1999.

Groß, Guido. "Abtei und Kirche St. Matthias und die Trierer Familie Neurohr im 18. und 19. Jahrhundert." *Neues trierisches Jahrbuch* 41 (2001): 113–37.

———. "Prozessionen und Wallfahrten nach Trier im Widerstreit geistiger Strömungen und ökonomischer Interessen." In *Zwischen Andacht und Andenken: Kleinodien religiöser Kunst und Wallfahrtsandenken aus Trierer Sammlungen— ein Katalog zur Gemeinschaftsausstellung des Bischöflichen Dom- und Diözesanmuseums Trier und des Städtischen Museums Simeonstift Trier vom 16. Oktober 1992 bis 17. Januar 1993*, edited by Elisabeth Dühr, Markus Groß-Morgen, and Burkhard Kaufmann, 79–88. Trier: Selbstverlag des Bischöflichen Dom- und Diözesanmuseums Trier und des Städtischen Museums Simeonstift Trier, 1992.

———. "Trier als Pilgerziel in der 2. Hälfte des 18. Jahrhunderts: Ein Beitrag zur Wallfahrtsgeschichte des Trierer Raumes." In *Corona amicorum: Alois Thomas zur Vollendung des 90. Lebensjahres*, edited by Andreas Heinz and Martin Persch, 112–23. Trier: Selbstverlag, 1986.

———. *Trierer Geistesleben unter dem Einfluß von Aufklärung und Romantik (1750–1850).* Trier: Lintz, 1956.

———. "Der Trierer Prediger P. Ernst Kronenberger OESA: Ein Beitrag zum Kirchenkampf im Zeitalter der Französischen Revolution." *Archiv für mittelrheinische Kirchengeschichte* 11 (1959): 207–25.

Günzel, Stephan. *Raum: Eine kulturwissenschaftliche Einführung.* 2017. 3rd ed. Bielefeld: transcript, 2020.

Guth, Klaus. "Geschichtlicher Abriss der marianischen Wallfahrtsbewegungen im deutschsprachigen Raum." In *Handbuch der Marienkunde*, edited by Wolfgang Beinert and Heinrich Petri, 2nd rev. ed., 2 vols., vol. 2, 321–448. Regensburg: F. Pustet, 1997.

Guyon, Catherine. "Les apparitions mariales dans l'espace français et ses marges et les mutations de la fin du XVe et du début du XVIe siècle." *Studi e materiali di storia delle religioni* 85, no. 2 (2019): 509–22.

Haas, Angela C. "Enlightenment and the Supernatural: Popular Religious Practice in the Eighteenth Century." In *The Routledge Handbook of French History*, edited by David Andress, 293–303. New York: Routledge, 2024.

Haas, Hieronymus. *Wallfahrtsgeschichte von Mariastein.* Mariastein: Editio de Consolatione, 1973.

Habermas, Rebekka. *Wallfahrt und Aufruhr: Zur Geschichte des Wunderglaubens in der frühen Neuzeit*. Frankfurt: Campus Verlag, 1991.

Hagen, Ursula. *Die Wallfahrtsmedaillen des Rheinlandes in Geschichte und Volksleben*. Cologne: Rheinland-Verlag, 1973.

Handschuh, Christian. *Die wahre Aufklärung durch Jesum Christum: Religiöse Welt- und Gegenwartskonstruktion in der Katholischen Spätaufklärung*. Stuttgart: Franz Steiner Verlag, 2014.

Hardy, Duncan. "Were There 'Territories' in the German Lands of the Holy Roman Empire in the Fourteenth to Sixteenth Centuries?" In *Constructing and Representing Territory in Late Medieval and Early Modern Europe*, edited by Mario Damen and Kim Overlaet, 29–52. Amsterdam: Amsterdam University Press, 2022.

Harrer, Kilian. "Erlaubte und unerlaubte Wallfahrt: Neue Erkenntnisse zum Andrang bei der Trierer Heilig-Rock-Zeigung von 1810." *Archiv für mittelrheinische Kirchengeschichte* 75 (2023): 199–219.

———. "Mass Pilgrimage and the Usable Empire in a Napoleonic Borderland." *Historical Journal* 66, no. 4 (2023): 773–94.

———. "Pilgrimage." In *Europäische Geschichte Online (EGO)*, edited by Leibniz-Institut für Europäische Geschichte (IEG). Mainz, 2025. https://www.ieg-ego.eu/harrerk-2025-en.

———. "Wallfahrt als Grenzerfahrung? Zur Sakralmobilität zwischen Ostfrankreich und dem schweizerischen Raum im XVIII. Jahrhundert." In *Le Corps helvétique et la France, 1660–1792 = Das Corps helvétique und Frankreich, 1660–1792: Transferts, asymétries et interdépendances entre des partenaires inégaux = Transfers, Asymmetrien und Interdependenzen zwischen ungleichen Partnern*, edited by Simona Boscani Leoni, Claire Gantet, André Holenstein, Timothée Léchot, and Bérangère Poulain, 145–57. Geneva: Slatkine, 2024.

Harrington, Joel F., and Helmut Walser Smith. "Confessionalization, Community, and State Building in Germany 1555–1870." *Journal of Modern History* 69, no. 1 (1997): 77–101.

Harris, Ruth. *Lourdes: Body and Spirit in the Secular Age*. New York: Viking, 1999.

Hartinger, Walter. "Kirchliche und staatliche Wallfahrtsverbote in Altbayern." In *Staat, Kultur, Politik: Beiträge zur Geschichte Bayerns und des Katholizismus. Festschrift zum 65. Geburtstag von Dieter Albrecht*, edited by Winfried Becker and Werner Chrobak, 119–36. Kallmünz/Opf.: Laßleben, 1992.

Haug-Moritz, Gabriele. *Württembergischer Ständekonflikt und deutscher Dua-

lismus: Ein Beitrag zur Geschichte des Reichsverbands in der Mitte des 18. Jahrhunderts. Stuttgart: Kohlhammer, 1992.
Haynes, Christine. *Our Friends the Enemies: The Occupation of France after Napoleon*. Cambridge, MA: Harvard University Press, 2018.
Hayworth, Jordan R. *Revolutionary France's War of Conquest in the Rhineland: Conquering the Natural Frontier, 1792–1797*. Cambridge: Cambridge University Press, 2019.
Hebler, Makarios, and Hans-Walter Herrmann. "Tholey." In *Die Männer- und Frauenklöster der Benediktiner in Rheinland-Pfalz und Saarland*, edited by Friedhelm Jürgensmeier and Regina E. Schwerdtfeger, 849–94. St. Ottilien: EOS-Verlag, 1999.
Hegel, Eduard. "Prozessionen und Wallfahrten im alten Erzbistum Köln im Zeitalter des Barock und der Aufklärung." *Zeitschrift des Aachener Geschichtsvereins* 84/85 (1977/78): 301–19.
Heidegger, Martin. "Bauen Wohnen Denken (1951)." In *Vorträge und Aufsätze (1936–1953)*, 145–64. Frankfurt: Klostermann, 2000.
Heimann, Mary. "Catholic Revivalism in Worship and Devotion." In *World Christianities c. 1815–c. 1914*, edited by Brian Stanley and Sheridan Gilley, vol 8. of *The Cambridge History of Christianity*, 70–83. Cambridge: Cambridge University Press, 2006.
Heinen, Ernst. "Aufbruch—Erneuerung—Politik: Rheinischer Katholizismus im 19. Jahrhundert." *Rheinische Vierteljahrsblätter* 64 (2000): 266–89.
Heinz, Andreas. *Heilige im Saarland*. 2nd rev. and expanded ed. Saarbrücken: Saarbrücker Druckerei und Verlag, 1991.
———. "Liturgie und Frömmigkeitsleben im Erzbistum Trier unter Erzbischof Clemens Wenzeslaus (1768–1801)." In *Der Trierer Erzbischof und Kurfürst Clemens Wenzeslaus (1739–1812), eine historische Bilanz nach 200 Jahren: Vorträge einer Tagung in der Stadtbibliothek Trier im November 2012*, edited by Michael Embach, 21–44. Mainz: Gesellschaft für Mittelrheinische Kirchengeschichte, 2014.
———. "Prozessionen und Wallfahrten im Gegenwind der Aufklärung." *Kurtrierisches Jahrbuch* 58 (2018): 155–71.
———. "Die Verehrung der 'Luxemburger Muttergottes' in der einst zum Herzogtum Luxemburg gehörenden Südeifel." *Hémecht* 65, no. 4 (2013): 449–63.
———. "Die Verehrung der 'Trösterin der Betrübten' in den alt-luxemburgischen Gebieten der Eifel und an der Obermosel: Ein Beitrag zur Geschichte der Marienfrömmigkeit und des Wallfahrtswesens im trierisch-luxemburgischen Raum." *Hémecht* 30, no. 2 (1978): 233–58.
———. "Die Verehrung der 'Trösterin der Betrübten' in der Schlosskapelle

von Malberg." In *Schloss Malberg: Das Barockjuwel in der Südeifel*, edited by Förderverein Schloss Malberg, 160–71. Bitburg: Förderverein Schloss Malberg, 2021.

Hellinghausen, Georges. "Bischof Laurent und die Wiederbelebung der Oktave." *Nos cahiers. Lëtzeburger Zäitschrëft fir Kultur* 18, no. 2 (1997): 9–39.

———. *Kleine Diözesangeschichte Luxemburgs*. Münster: Aschendorff, 2020.

———. "Patronne de la Cité: Tradition et traditions." In *Notre-Dame de Luxembourg: Dévotion et patrimoine*, edited by Sébastien Pierre, 35–50. Bastogne: Musée en Piconrue, 2016.

Henke, Christian. *Coblentz, Symbol für die Gegenrevolution: Die französische Emigration nach Koblenz und Kurtrier 1789–1792 und die politische Diskussion des revolutionären Frankreichs 1791–1794*. Stuttgart: J. Thorbecke, 2000.

Henryot, Fabienne, Laurent Jalabert, and Philippe Martin, eds. *Atlas de la vie religieuse en Lorraine à l'époque moderne*. Metz: Serpenoise, 2011.

Herberich-Marx, Geneviève, and Freddy Raphaël. "L'imagerie religieuse durant la Révolution en Alsace: L'Œuvre au noir." *Revue d'Alsace* 116 (1989–90): 333–55.

Herberich-Marx, Geneviève, and Francis Rapp. "Pèlerinages." In *Encyclopédie de l'Alsace*, edited by Agnès Acker, 12 vols., vol. 10, 5910–25. Strasbourg: Éditions Publitotal, 1982–86.

Hermant, Maxime. "Monsieur dimanche face au citoyen décadi: Les autorités révolutionnaires et la liberté de culte." In *Le Directoire: Forger la République, 1795–1799*, edited by Loris Chavanette, 179–96. Paris: CNRS Éditions, 2020.

Hermon-Belot, Rita. *Aux sources de l'idée laïque: Révolution et pluralité religieuse*. Paris: Odile Jacob, 2015.

Herrmann, Hans-Christian. "Die Saarregion im Alten Reich." In *Das Saarland: Geschichte einer Region*, edited by Herrmann and Johannes Schmitt, 11–59. St. Ingbert: Röhrig Universitätsverlag, 2012.

Hersche, Peter. "'Lutherisch werden'—Rekonfessionalisierung als paradoxe Folge aufgeklärter Religionspolitik." In *Ambivalenzen der Aufklärung: Festschrift für Ernst Wangermann*, edited by Gerhard Ammerer and Hanns Haas, 155–68. Vienna: Verlag für Geschichte und Politik/R. Oldenbourg, 1997.

———. *Muße und Verschwendung: Europäische Gesellschaft und Kultur im Barockzeitalter*. 2 vols. Freiburg: Herder, 2006.

Hervieu-Léger, Danièle. *La religion en mouvement: Le pèlerin et le converti*. Paris: Flammarion, 1999.

Heuer, Jennifer Ngaire. *The Family and the Nation: Gender and Citizenship in Revolutionary France, 1789–1830*. Ithaca, NY: Cornell University Press, 2007.

Hiegel, Henri. "Les apparitions de la Sainte-Vierge en Lorraine de langue allemande en 1799 et 1873." *Les Cahiers Lorrains*, no. 4 (1957): 68–74.

Hirschhausen, Béatrice von, Hannes Grandits, Claudia Kraft, Dietmar Müller, and Thomas Serrier. *Phantomgrenzen: Räume und Akteure in der Zeit neu denken*. Göttingen: Wallstein, 2015.

Holenstein, André. "Beschleunigung und Stillstand: Spätes Ancien Régime und Helvetik (1712–1802/03)." In *Die Geschichte der Schweiz*, edited by Georg Kreis, 311–61. Basel: Schwabe, 2014.

——. *Mitten in Europa: Verflechtung und Abgrenzung in der Schweizer Geschichte*. Baden: Hier und Jetzt, 2014.

Holzem, Andreas. *Christentum in Deutschland 1550–1850: Konfessionalisierung—Aufklärung—Pluralisierung*. 2 vols. Paderborn: Schöningh, 2015.

——. "Religiöse Orientierung und soziale Ordnung: Skizzen zur Wallfahrt als Handlungsfeld und Konfliktraum zwischen Frühneuzeit und Katholischem Milieu." In *Institutionen und Ereignis: Über historische Praktiken und Vorstellungen gesellschaftlichen Ordnens*, edited by Reinhard Blänkner and Bernhard Jussen, 327–54. Göttingen: Vandenhoeck & Ruprecht, 1998.

Horn, Pierre. *Le défi de l'enracinement napoléonien entre Rhin et Meuse, 1810–1814: L'opinion publique dans les départements de la Roër, de l'Ourthe, des Forêts et de la Moselle*. Berlin: De Gruyter, 2017.

——. "La monarchie française et l'espace frontalier sarro-lorrain: La régularisation de la seconde moitié du XVIIIe siècle." *Annales de l'Est* 60 (2010): 169–88.

Huber, Valeska. *Channelling Mobilities: Migration and Globalisation in the Suez Canal Region and Beyond, 1869–1914*. Cambridge: Cambridge University Press, 2013.

Hufton, Olwen H. "The Reconstruction of a Church, 1796–1801." In *Beyond the Terror: Essays in French Regional and Social History 1794–1815*, edited by Gwynne Lewis and Colin Lucas, 21–52. Cambridge: Cambridge University Press, 1983.

Hunt, Lynn. *Politics, Culture, and Class in the French Revolution*. Berkeley: University of California Press, 1984.

Husson, Jean-Pierre, and Laurent Jalabert. "Les enclaves en Lorraine au XVIIIe siècle: De l'objet spatial complexe et vivant à la marginalisation." In *Frontières et espaces frontaliers du Léman à la Meuse: Recompositions et échanges de 1789 à 1814 (actes du colloque de Nancy, 25–27 novembre 2004)*, edited by Claude Mazauric and Jean-Paul Rothiot, 55–68. Nancy: Presses universitaires de Nancy, 2007.

Hüttl, Ludwig. *Marianische Wallfahrten im süddeutsch-österreichischen Raum:*

Analysen von der Reformations- bis zur Aufklärungsepoche. Cologne: Böhlau, 1985.

Hynes, Eugene. *Knock: The Virgin's Apparition in Nineteenth-Century Ireland.* Cork: Cork University Press, 2008.

Ikari, Yuki. *Wallfahrtswesen in Köln vom Spätmittelalter bis zur Aufklärung.* Cologne: SH-Verlag, 2009.

Irsigler, Franz. *Geschichtlicher Atlas der Rheinlande, 1. Lieferung.* Vol. 5, fasc. 1: *Herrschaftsgebiete im Jahre 1789.* Cologne: Rheinland-Verlag, 1982.

Jabłoński, Zachariasz S. "Jasna Góra w drugiej połowie XIX wieku i na początku XX wieku: Jej udział w dążeniach niepodległościowych." In *Częstochowa: Dzieje miasta i klasztoru jasnogórskiego,* edited by Marceli Antoniewicz and Ryszard Kołodziejczyk, 4 vols., vol. 3, 165–94. Częstochowa: Urząd Miasta Częstochowy, 2002–7.

Jacops, Marie-France. "Images et témoignages de la dévotion des habitants du nord de la Lorraine à Notre-Dame de Luxembourg, consolatrice des affligés." *Le pays gaumais* 54–57 (1993–96): 267–82.

———. "Les Lorrains, pèlerins et dévots de la Vierge noire d'Einsiedeln." *Pays lorrain* 71, no. 3 (1990): 193–213.

Jäggi, Gregor. "Die Geschichte der Einsiedler Wallfahrt." In *Kloster Einsiedeln: Pilgern seit 1000 Jahren,* edited by Schweizerisches Nationalmuseum, 45–53. Berlin: Hatje Cantz, 2017.

Jalabert, Laurent. *Catholiques et protestants sur la rive gauche du Rhin: Droits, confessions et coexistence religieuse de 1648 à 1789.* Brussels: Peter Lang, 2009.

———. "Frontière de catholicité et coexistence confessionnelle sur le Rhin (XVIIe siècle): Aux marges de la dorsale catholique." In *Dorsale catholique, jansénisme, dévotions (XVIe–XVIIIe siècles): Mythe, réalité, actualité historiographique,* edited by Gilles Deregnaucourt, Yves Krumenacker, Philippe Martin, and Frédéric Meyer, 415–25. Paris: Riveneuve, 2014.

Joas, Hans. *Die Macht des Heiligen: Eine Alternative zur Geschichte von der Entzauberung.* Berlin: Suhrkamp, 2017.

Johnson, Walter. "On Agency." *Journal of Social History* 37, no. 1 (2003): 113–24.

Jonas, Raymond Anthony. *France and the Cult of the Sacred Heart: An Epic Tale for Modern Times.* Berkeley: University of California Press, 2000.

Jorio, Marco. "Der Untergang des Fürstbistums Basel (1792–1815): Der Kampf der beiden letzten Fürstbischöfe Joseph Sigismund von Roggenbach und Franz Xaver von Neveu gegen die Säkularisation." *Zeitschrift für Schweizerische Kirchengeschichte* 75/76 (1981/1982): 1–230/115–72.

Julia, Dominique. "Curiosité, dévotion et *politica peregrinesca:* Le pèlerinage de Nicola Albani, melfitain, à Saint-Jacques-de-Compostelle (1743–1745)." In

Rendre ses vœux: Les identités pèlerines dans l'Europe moderne (XVIe–XVIIIe siècle), edited by Philippe Boutry, Pierre-Antoine Fabre, and Julia, 239–314. Paris: Éditions de l'EHESS, 2000.

———. "Les pèlerins de sainte Reine au XVIIIe siècle." In *Reine au Mont Auxois: Le culte et le pèlerinage de sainte Reine des origines à nos jours*, edited by Philippe Boutry and Julia, 243–76. Dijon: Ville de Dijon, 1997.

———. "Pour une géographie européenne du pèlerinage à l'époque moderne et contemporaine." In *Pèlerins et pèlerinages dans l'Europe moderne*, edited by Julia and Philippe Boutry, 3–126. Rome: École française de Rome, 2000.

———. *Le voyage aux saints: Les pèlerinages dans l'Occident moderne, XVe–XVIIIe siècle*. Paris: Éditions de l'EHESS, 2016.

Julia, Dominique, and Philippe Boutry. "Rome, capitale du pèlerinage: Traditions modernes et recompositions postrévolutionnaires." In *Capitales européennes et rayonnement culturel: XVIIIe–XXe siècle*, edited by Christophe Charle, 19–54. Paris: Éditions Rue d'Ulm, 2004.

Jung, Michael. "Saarbrücken und St. Johann während der Fürstenzeit (1741–89)." In *Geschichte der Stadt Saarbrücken*, edited by Rolf Wittenbrock, 2 vols., vol. 1, 353–453. Saarbrücken: Saarbrücker Druckerei und Verlag, 1999.

Kaci, Maxime. *Dans le tourbillon de la Révolution: Mots d'ordre et engagements collectifs aux frontières septentrionales, 1791–1793*. Rennes: Presses universitaires de Rennes, 2016.

———. "Recompositions frontalières en révolution: Quand les affrontements politiques transcendent les appartenances provinciales et nationales (1789–1798)." In *Deux frontières aux destins croisés? Étude interdisciplinaire et comparative des délimitations territoriales entre la France et la Suisse, entre la Bourgogne et la Franche-Comté (XIVe siècle–XXIe siècle)*, edited by Benjamin Castets Fontaine, Kaci, Jérôme Loiseau, and Alexandre Moine, 47–61. Besançon: Presses universitaires de Franche-Comté, 2019.

Kälin, Kari. *Schauplatz katholischer Frömmigkeit: Wallfahrt nach Einsiedeln von 1864 bis 1914*. Fribourg: Academic Press Fribourg, 2005.

Kallabis, Anna. *Katholizismus im Umbruch: Diskurse der Elite im (Erz-)Bistum Trier zwischen Aufklärung und französischer Herrschaft*. Berlin: De Gruyter, 2020.

Kammerer, Louis. "Le clergé constitutionnel en Alsace, 1791–1802." Unpublished manuscript, 1987. ADHR, 19 US 20.

———. "Documents concernant le clergé du Haut-Rhin pendant la Révolution: La correspondance et les cahiers du provicaire général Didner, conservés aux Archives de l'évêché de Bâle, à Soleure." *Archives de l'Église d'Alsace* 41 (1982): 95–136.

Kaplan, Benjamin J. *Cunegonde's Kidnapping: A Story of Religious Conflict in the Age of Enlightenment.* New Haven, CT: Yale University Press, 2014.

———. *Divided by Faith: Religious Conflict and the Practice of Toleration in Early Modern Europe.* Cambridge, MA: Belknap Press of Harvard University Press, 2007.

Katzer, Carolin. *Konflikt—Konsens—Koexistenz: Konfessionskulturen in Worms im 18. Jahrhundert.* Münster: Aschendorff, 2022.

Kaufman, Suzanne K. *Consuming Visions: Mass Culture and the Lourdes Shrine.* Ithaca, NY: Cornell University Press, 2005.

Kimminich, Eva. *Religiöse Volksbräuche im Räderwerk der Obrigkeiten: Ein Beitrag zur Auswirkung aufklärerischer Reformprogramme am Oberrhein und in Vorarlberg.* Frankfurt: Lang, 1989.

Kinnard, Jacob N. *Places in Motion: The Fluid Identities of Temples, Images, and Pilgrims.* New York: Oxford University Press, 2014.

Kintz, Jean-Pierre. "Alsace: Départements du Bas-Rhin et du Haut-Rhin." In *Dictionnaire de la presse française pendant la Révolution: 1789–1799*, edited by Gilles Feyel, 7 vols., vol. 1, 189–278. Ferney-Voltaire: Centre International d'Étude du XVIIIe Siècle, 2005.

Kleinehagenbrock, Frank. "Der Reicholzheimer Wallfahrtsstreit: Eine Dorfgemeinde im Konflikt mit ihrem Pfarrer." In *Forschungen zu Stadt und Grafschaft Wertheim: Festschrift für Erich Langguth zum 95. Geburtstag,* edited by Monika Schaupp, Kleinehagenbrock, and Jörg Paczkowski, 237–59. Wertheim: Verlag des Historischen Vereins Wertheim, 2018.

Klueting, Harm. "Katholische Aufklärung nach 1803? Theologie und Kirche unter dem Eindruck des Umbruchs." *Rottenburger Jahrbuch für Kirchengeschichte* 34 (2015): 23–34.

———. "'Quidquid est in territorio, etiam est de territorio': Josephinisches Staatskirchentum als rationaler Territorialismus." *Der Staat* 37, no. 3 (1998): 417–34.

———. "Wiedervereinigung der getrennten Konfessionen oder episkopalistische Nationalkirche? Nikolaus von Hontheim (1701–1790), der *Febronius* (1763) und die Rückkehr der Protestanten zur katholischen Kirche." In *Irenik und Antikonfessionalismus im 17. und 18. Jahrhundert,* edited by Klueting, 259–77. Hildesheim: Olms, 2003.

Kmec, Sonja. "'Marienland Luxemburg': L'historiographie du culte de Notre-Dame de Luxembourg entre aspirations universalistes et ancrage national." *Hémecht* 66, no. 3/4 (2014): 493–512.

———. "Notre-Dame de Luxembourg et sa fête annuelle: L'Octave comme lieu de mémoire." In *Notre-Dame de Luxembourg: Dévotion et patrimoine*, edited by Sébastien Pierre, 223–28. Bastogne: Musée en Piconrue, 2016.

Kohl, Thomas. *Familie und soziale Schichtung: Zur historischen Demographie Triers, 1730–1860*. Stuttgart: Klett-Cotta, 1985.

Komlosy, Andrea. *Grenzen: Räumliche und soziale Trennlinien im Zeitenlauf*. Vienna: Promedia, 2018.

König, Mareike, and Élise Julien. *Verfeindung und Verflechtung: Deutschland und Frankreich 1870–1918*. Darmstadt: Wissenschaftliche Buchgesellschaft, 2019.

Konrad, Victor, and Anne-Laure Amilhat Szary. *Border Culture: Theory, Imagination, Geopolitics*. London: Routledge, 2023.

Kötting, Bernhard. *Peregrinatio religiosa: Wallfahrten in der Antike und das Pilgerwesen in der alten Kirche*. Münster: Regensberg, 1950.

Kotulla, Andreas J. *'Nach Lourdes!': Der französische Marienwallfahrtsort und die Katholiken im Deutschen Kaiserreich, 1871–1914*. Munich: M. Meidenbauer, 2006.

Krämer, Paul. "Vom gewerblichen Leben einer Kleinstadt: Ein Beitrag zur wirtschaftlichen Entwicklung der Stadt St. Wendel vom 17. bis 20. Jahrhundert." *Zeitschrift für die Geschichte der Saargegend* 17/18 (1969/70): 171–92.

Krebs, Jill M., and Joseph Laycock. "The American Academy of Religion Exploratory Session on Marian Apparitions and Theoretical Problems in Religious Studies (2015)." *Religious Studies Review* 43, no. 3 (2017): 207–18.

Krenz, Jochen. *Druckerschwärze statt Schwarzpulver: Wie die Gegenaufklärung die Katholische Aufklärung nach 1789 mundtot machte. Die Perzeption der kirchenpolitischen Vorgänge der Französischen Revolution in der oberdeutschen theologischen Publizistik des Alten Reichs*. Bremen: Edition Lumière, 2016.

Kriss-Rettenbeck, Lenz, and Gerda Möhler, eds. *Wallfahrt kennt keine Grenzen: Themen zu einer Ausstellung des Bayerischen Nationalmuseums und des Adalbert Stifter Vereins, München*. Munich: Schnell & Steiner, 1984.

Kruijtzer, Gijs. *Justifying Transgression: Muslims, Christians, and the Law—1200 to 1700*. Berlin: De Gruyter, 2024.

Kuhn, Hans Wolfgang. "Zur Geschichte des Trierer und des Limburger Domschatzes: Die Pretiosenüberlieferung aus dem linksrheinischen Erzstift Trier seit 1792." *Archiv für mittelrheinische Kirchengeschichte* 28 (1976): 155–207.

Kühtreiber, Thomas, and Jacqueline Schindler. "Wallfahrt und Regionalität in Mitteleuropa—einleitende Gedanken zu einem Rahmenkonzept." *MEMO Sonderband*, no. 1 (2022): 1–18.

Kumor, Bolesław. "Austriackie władze zaborcze wobec kultu Królowej Polski i pielgrzymek na Jasną Górę (1772–1809)." *Studia Claromontana* 1 (1981): 77–97.

Kwass, Michael. *Contraband: Louis Mandrin and the Making of a Global Underground.* Cambridge, MA: Harvard University Press, 2014.

Kyll, Nikolaus. *Pflichtprozessionen und Bannfahrten im westlichen Teil des alten Erzbistums Trier.* Bonn: Röhrscheid, 1962.

La Coste-Messelière, René de. "Édits et autres actes royaux contre les abus des pèlerinages à l'étranger aux XVIIe et XVIIIe siècles et la pérennité du pèlerinage à Saint-Jacques de Compostelle." In *Les relations franco-hispaniques*, vol. 1 of *Actes du quatre-vingt-quatorzième congrès national des sociétés savantes. Pau, 1969: Section d'histoire moderne et contemporaine*, edited by Comité des travaux historiques et scientifiques, 115–28. Paris: Bibliothèque nationale, 1971.

Lachenicht, Susanne. *Information und Propaganda: Die Presse deutscher Jakobiner im Elsaß (1791–1800).* Munich: Oldenbourg, 2004.

Lagrée, Michel. "Religion et chocs révolutionnaires en Bretagne." In *Chocs et ruptures en histoire religieuse (fin XVIIIe–XIXe siècles)*, edited by Lagrée, 167–81. Rennes: Presses universitaires de Rennes, 1998.

Langini, Alex. *La procession dansante d'Echternach: Son origine et son histoire.* Echternach: Société d'embellissement et de tourisme, 1977.

Langlois, Claude. "Mariophanies et mariologies au XIXe siècle: Méthode et histoire." In *Théologie, histoire et piété mariale: Actes du colloque, Université Catholique de Lyon, 1–3 octobre 1996*, edited by Jean Comby, 19–36. Lyon: Profac, 1997.

Langlois, Claude, Timothy Tackett, Michel Vovelle, Serge Bonin, and Madeleine Bonin, eds. *Atlas de la Révolution française.* Vol. 9: *Religion.* Paris: Éditions de l'EHESS, 1996.

Lasconjarias, Guillaume. *Un air de majesté: Gouverneurs et commandants dans l'Est de la France au XVIIIe siècle.* Paris: CTHS, 2010.

Laufer, Wolfgang. "Seelsorge über Grenzen: Taufen und Heiraten von Lothringern in grenznahen deutschen Pfarreien während der Französischen Revolution." *Archiv für mittelrheinische Kirchengeschichte* 62 (2010): 313–47.

Laux, Stephan. "Deutschlands Westen—Frankreichs Osten: Überlegungen zur Historiographie und zu den Perspektiven der rheinischen Landesgeschichte in der Frühen Neuzeit." *Rheinische Vierteljahrsblätter* 79 (2015): 143–63.

Lazer, Stephen A. *State Formation in Early Modern Alsace, 1648–1789.* Rochester, NY: University of Rochester Press, 2019.

Le Roy Ladurie, Emmanuel. *Histoire humaine et comparée du climat*. Vol. 2: *Disettes et révolutions (1740–1860)*. Paris: Fayard, 2006.

Lederer, David. *Madness, Religion and the State in Early Modern Europe: A Bavarian Beacon*. Cambridge: Cambridge University Press, 2006.

Lees, James. "Clemens Wenzeslaus, Ultramontanismus und die Gegenaufklärung." In *Der Trierer Erzbischof und Kurfürst Clemens Wenzeslaus (1739–1812), eine historische Bilanz nach 200 Jahren: Vorträge einer Tagung in der Stadtbibliothek Trier im November 2012*, edited by Michael Embach, 137–62. Mainz: Gesellschaft für Mittelrheinische Kirchengeschichte, 2014.

Lefort, Alfred. *Histoire du département des Forêts (le duché de Luxembourg de 1795 à 1814) d'après les archives du gouvernement grand-ducal et des documents français inédits*. Luxembourg: Worré-Mertens, 1905.

Lehner, Ulrich. *The Catholic Enlightenment: The Forgotten History of a Global Movement*. New York: Oxford University Press, 2016.

———. "Johann Nikolaus von Hontheim's *Febronius*: A Censored Bishop and His Ecclesiology." *Church History and Religious Culture* 88, no. 2 (2008): 205–33.

Lentz, Thierry, and Denis Imhoff. *La Moselle et Napoléon: Étude d'un département sous le Consulat et l'Empire*. Metz: Serpenoise, 1986.

León, Luis D. *La Llorona's Children: Religion, Life, and Death in the U.S.–Mexican Borderlands*. Berkeley: University of California Press, 2004.

Lerch, Dominique. "Images et dévotion à Colmar au XVIIIe siècle: Les dominicaines d'Unterlinden au miroir du monde catholique." *Revue d'Alsace* 127 (2001): 239–82.

Lerner, Marc H. *A Laboratory of Liberty: The Transformation of Political Culture in Republican Switzerland, 1750–1848*. Leiden: Brill, 2012.

Lesprand, Paul. *Le clergé de la Moselle pendant la Révolution*. 4 vols. Montigny-lès-Metz: Paul Lesprand, 1934–39.

Lichter, Eduard. "Johann Wilhelm Josef Castello und die Aufklärung in Trier." *Archiv für mittelrheinische Kirchengeschichte* 21 (1969): 179–227.

Lignereux, Aurélien. *L'Empire de la paix. De la Révolution à Napoléon: Quand la France réunissait l'Europe*. Paris: Passés composés, 2023.

———. *Les Impériaux: Administrer et habiter l'Europe de Napoléon*. Paris: Fayard, 2019.

———. *Servir Napoléon: Policiers et gendarmes dans les départements annexés, 1796–1814*. Seyssel: Champ Vallon, 2012.

Lobenwein, Elisabeth. *Wallfahrt—Wunder—Wirtschaft: Die Wallfahrt nach Maria Luggau (Kärnten) in der Frühen Neuzeit*. Bochum: Winkler, 2013.

Lotz-Heumann, Ute. "Repräsentationen von Heilwassern und -quellen in der

Frühen Neuzeit: Badeorte, lutherische Wunderquellen und katholische Wallfahrtsorte." In *Säkularisierungen in der Frühen Neuzeit: Methodische Probleme und empirische Fallstudien,* edited by Matthias Pohlig, Lotz-Heumann, Vera Isaiasz, Ruth Schilling, Heike Bock, and Stefan Ehrenpreis, 277–330. Berlin: Duncker & Humblot, 2008.

Löw, Martina. *Raumsoziologie.* Frankfurt: Suhrkamp, 2001.

Lüber, Alban Norbert. "Das Kloster Beinwil-Mariastein von 1765 bis 1815." *Jahrbuch für solothurnische Geschichte* 70 (1997): 105–300.

Ludwig, August Friedrich. *Weihbischof Zirkel von Würzburg in seiner Stellung zur theologischen Aufklärung und zur kirchlichen Restauration: Ein Beitrag zur Geschichte der katholischen Kirche Deutschlands um die Wende des achtzehnten Jahrhunderts.* 2 vols. Paderborn: Schöningh, 1904/1906.

Luebke, David M. *Hometown Religion: Regimes of Coexistence in Early Modern Westphalia.* Charlottesville: University of Virginia Press, 2016.

———. "Naïve Monarchism and Marian Veneration in Early Modern Germany." *Past & Present,* no. 154 (1997): 71–106.

Lustenberger, Othmar. "Bild und Abbild: Einsiedler Pilgerzeichen, Einsiedler (Gnaden-)Kapellen, Einsiedler Gnadenbilder." *Studien und Mitteilungen zur Geschichte des Benediktinerordens und seiner Zweige* 111 (2000): 257–95.

———. "Das Schicksal des Einsiedler Gnadenbildes zur Zeit der Helvetik." *Mitteilungen des Historischen Vereins des Kantons Schwyz* 97 (2005): 175–209.

MacCormack, Sabine. "Loca Sancta: The Organization of Sacred Topography in Late Antiquity." In *The Blessings of Pilgrimage,* edited by Robert G. Ousterhout, 7–40. Urbana: University of Illinois Press, 1990.

Maddrell, Avril, Veronica Della Dora, Alessandro Scafi, and Heather Walton. *Christian Pilgrimage, Landscape and Heritage: Journeying to the Sacred.* New York: Routledge, 2014.

Maertz, Joseph. "Entstehung und Entwicklung der Wallfahrt zur Trösterin der Betrübten in Luxemburg (1624–1666)." *Hémecht* 18, no. 1 (1966): 7–132.

Maes, Bruno. "Les apparitions mariales à l'époque moderne, ou l'émergence du modèle tridentin." *Studi e materiali di storia delle religioni* 85, no. 2 (2019): 587–99.

———. *Les livrets de pèlerinage: Imprimerie et culture dans la France moderne.* Rennes: Presses universitaires de Rennes, 2016.

———. *Le roi, la Vierge et la nation: Pèlerinages et identité nationale entre guerre de Cent Ans et Révolution.* Paris: Publisud, 2003.

Maier, Charles S. *Once Within Borders: Territories of Power, Wealth, and Belonging since 1500.* Cambridge, MA: Harvard University Press, 2016.

Maier, Peter. "Mariazell." In *Die benediktinischen Mönchs- und Nonnenklöster* in *Österreich und Südtirol*, edited by Ulrich Faust and Waltraud Krassnig, 3 vols., vol. 2, 395–448. St. Ottilien: EOS-Verlag, 2000–2002.

Maire, Catherine. *L'Église dans l'État: Politique et religion dans la France des Lumières*. Paris: Gallimard, 2019.

Malpas, Jeff. "Topologies of History." *History and Theory* 58, no. 1 (2019): 3–22.

Maréchaux, Xavier. *Pie VII: Le pape qui défia Napoléon*. Paris: Passés composés, 2024.

Margadant, Ted W. *Urban Rivalries in the French Revolution*. Princeton, NJ: Princeton University Press, 1992.

Margue, Paul. "Apôtres ou prévaricateurs? Remarques sur l'Administration du Département des Forêts à l'époque du Directoire." *Hémecht* 50, no. 3 (1998): 363–71.

Markus, Robert A. "How on Earth Could Places Become Holy? Origins of the Christian Idea of Holy Places." *Journal of Early Christian Studies* 2, no. 3 (1994): 257–71.

Marrus, Michael R. "Cultures on the Move: Pilgrims and Pilgrimage in Nineteenth-Century France." *Stanford French Review* 1, no. 2 (1977): 205–20.

Martin, Jean-Clément. *Contre-Révolution, Révolution et Nation en France, 1789–1799*. Paris: Seuil, 1998.

———. *La Vendée et la France*. Paris: Seuil, 1987.

Martin, Louis. "Les émigrés du Bas-Rhin: Liste alphabétique." Unpublished manuscript, 1969, accessible at the ADBR.

Martin, Philippe. *Les chemins du sacré: Paroisses, processions, pèlerinages en Lorraine, du XVIe au XIXe siècle*. Metz: Serpenoise, 1995.

———. *Pèlerins de Lorraine*. Metz: Serpenoise, 1997.

———. *Pèlerins: XVe–XXIe siècle*. Paris: CNRS Éditions, 2016.

———. *Une religion des livres: 1640–1850*. Paris: Cerf, 2003.

———. "Sanctuaires-mères et pèlerinages-relais." In *Identités pèlerines: Actes du colloque de Rouen, 15–16 mai 2002*, edited by Catherine Vincent, 107–22. Rouen: Publications de l'Université de Rouen, 2004.

Maruschke, Megan, and Matthias Middell. "Explaining Revolutionary Upheaval: From Internal Societal Developments to Global Processes of Respatialization." In *The French Revolution as a Moment of Respatialization*, edited by Maruschke and Middell, 1–19. Berlin: De Gruyter, 2019.

Marx, Roland. *Recherches sur la vie politique de l'Alsace prérévolutionnaire et révolutionnaire*. Strasbourg: Istra, 1966.

Massey, Doreen. "Power-Geometry and a Progressive Sense of Place." In *Mapping the Futures: Local Cultures, Global Change*, edited by Jon Bird, Barry

Curtis, Tim Putnam, George Robertson, and Lisa Tickner, 59–69. London: Routledge, 1993.

Masson, Jean-Louis. *Histoire administrative de la Lorraine: Des provinces aux départements et à la région.* Paris: Éditions Fernand Lanore, 1982.

Mazel, Florian. *L'évêque et le territoire: L'invention médiévale de l'espace.* Paris: Seuil, 2016.

McMahon, Darrin M. *Enemies of the Enlightenment: The French Counter-Enlightenment and the Making of Modernity.* New York: Oxford University Press, 2001.

McManners, John. *Church and Society in Eighteenth-Century France.* Vol. 2: *The Religion of the People and the Politics of Religion.* Oxford: Clarendon, 1998.

Mergel, Thomas. *Zwischen Klasse und Konfession: Katholisches Bürgertum im Rheinland 1794–1914.* Göttingen: Vandenhoeck & Ruprecht, 1994.

Milliot, Vincent, Emmanuel Blanchard, Vincent Denis, and Arnaud-Dominique Houte. *Histoire des polices en France: Des guerres de religion à nos jours.* Paris: Belin, 2020.

Minke, Alfred. *Hommes de Dieu et Révolution: Entre Meuse, Rhin et Moselle.* Turnhout: Brepols, 1992.

Molitor, Hansgeorg. *Vom Untertan zum Administré: Studien zur französischen Herrschaft und zum Verhalten der Bevölkerung im Rhein-Mosel-Raum von den Revolutionskriegen bis zum Ende der napoleonischen Zeit.* Wiesbaden: F. Steiner, 1980.

Morieux, Renaud. *The Channel: England, France and the Construction of a Maritime Border in the Eighteenth Century.* Cambridge: Cambridge University Press, 2016.

Mosse, George L. *The Culture of Western Europe: The Nineteenth and Twentieth Centuries.* 1961. Madison: University of Wisconsin Press, 2022.

Moulinas, René. "Le pèlerinage, victime des Lumières." In *Les chemins de Dieu: Histoire des pèlerinages chrétiens des origines à nos jours,* edited by Jean Chélini and Henry Branthomme, 259–92. Paris: Hachette, 1982.

Mukerji, Chandra. *Territorial Ambitions and the Gardens of Versailles.* Cambridge: Cambridge University Press, 1997.

Muller, Claude. "La croix et la cocarde: Les évêques constitutionnels alsaciens." In *Gouverner une église en révolution: Histoires et mémoires de l'épiscopat constitutionnel,* edited by Paul Chopelin, 99–123. Lyon: Laboratoire de Recherche Historique Rhône-Alpes, 2017.

———. *Dieu est catholique et alsacien: La vitalité du diocèse de Strasbourg au XIXe siècle (1802–1914).* Haguenau: Société d'Histoire de l'Église d'Alsace, 1987.

———. "Mgr Simon Nicolas de Montjoie, les Klinglin et les Gobel (1762–1775):

Contribution à l'histoire du diocèse de Bâle au XVIIIe siècle." *Revue d'Alsace* 128 (2002): 281–313.

———. "Politische Grenze und religiöse Grenze: Das Elsass im 18. Jahrhundert." *Zeitschrift für die Geschichte des Oberrheins* 154 (2006): 241–70.

———. "Pouvoir, société et religion en Alsace au XVIIIe siècle." In *Regards sur l'Alsace du XVIIIe siècle*, edited by Muller and Valentin Kuentzler, 271–313. Strasbourg: Éditions du Signe, 2017.

———. "Religion et Révolution en Alsace." *Annales historiques de la Révolution française*, no. 337 (2004): 63–83.

———. "'La réunion des esprits': Jean Pierre Saurine, évêque constitutionnel et évêque concordataire." *Revue de l'Institut Napoléon*, no. 206 (2013): 7–27.

Müller, Jürgen. "1798: Das Jahr des Umbruchs im Rheinland." *Rheinische Vierteljahrsblätter* 62 (1998): 205–37.

Müller, Max. *Die Geschichte der Stadt St. Wendel: Von ihren Anfängen bis zum Weltkriege*. St. Wendel: Verlag der Stadt St. Wendel, 1927.

Müller, Michael. *Fürstbischof Heinrich von Bibra und die Katholische Aufklärung im Hochstift Fulda (1759–88): Wandel und Kontinuität des kirchlichen Lebens*. Fulda: Parzeller, 2005.

Nail, Thomas. *Theory of the Border*. Oxford: Oxford University Press, 2016.

Naumann, Johannes. *Die Blasiuskapelle bei Bergweiler: Wallfahrtskirche der Benediktinerabtei Tholey*. Bergweiler: Förderverein Blasiuskapelle Bergweiler, 2005.

Nebgen, Christoph. *Konfessionelle Differenzerfahrungen: Reiseberichte vom Rhein (1648–1815)*. Berlin: De Gruyter, 2014.

Niedźwiedź, Anna. *Obraz i postać: Znaczenia wizerunku Matki Boskiej Częstochowskiej*. Kraków: Wydawnictwo Uniwersytetu Jagiellońskiego, 2005.

Nolan, Mary Lee, and Sidney Nolan. *Christian Pilgrimage in Modern Western Europe*. Chapel Hill: University of North Carolina Press, 1989.

Nora, Pierre. "Nation." In *Dictionnaire critique de la Révolution française*, edited by François Furet and Mona Ozouf, 801–12. Paris: Flammarion, 1988.

Nordman, Daniel. *Frontières de France: De l'espace au territoire, XVIe–XIXe siècle*. Paris: Gallimard, 1998.

Oberhauser, Gabriele. *Wallfahrten und Kultstätten im Saarland: Von der Quellenverehrung zur Marienerscheinung*. Saarbrücken: Saarbrücker Druckerei und Verlag, 1992.

Oepen, Joachim. "Die Säkularisation von 1802 in den vier rheinischen Departements." In *200 Jahre Reichsdeputationshauptschluss: Säkularisation, Mediatisierung und Modernisierung zwischen Altem Reich und neuer Staatlichkeit*, edited by Harm Klueting, 87–114. Münster: Aschendorff, 2005.

Orsi, Robert A. *History and Presence.* Cambridge, MA: Belknap Press of Harvard University Press, 2016.

———. *The Madonna of 115th Street: Faith and Community in Italian Harlem, 1880–1950.* 3rd ed. New Haven, CT: Yale University Press, 2010.

Ory, Pascal. *Qu'est-ce qu'une nation? Une histoire mondiale.* Paris: Gallimard, 2020.

Oswalt, Vadim. "Frömmigkeit im ländlichen Oberschwaben—nach der Säkularisation." In *Die Säkularisation im Prozess der Säkularisierung Europas,* edited by Peter Blickle and Rudolf Schlögl, 299–315. Epfendorf: Bibliotheca Academica Verlag, 2005.

Overhoff, Jürgen. "Die Katholische Aufklärung als bleibende Forschungsaufgabe: Grundlagen, neue Fragestellungen, globale Perspektiven." *Das Achtzehnte Jahrhundert* 41, no. 1 (2017): 11–27.

Owzar, Armin. "Liberty in Times of Occupation: The Napoleonic Era in German Central Europe." In *Napoleon's Empire: European Politics in Global Perspective,* edited by Ute Planert, 67–83. New York: Palgrave Macmillan, 2016.

Ozouf, Mona. *La fête révolutionnaire 1789–1799.* Paris: Gallimard, 1976.

———. "The Pantheon: The École Normale of the Dead." In *Realms of Memory: Rethinking the French Past,* edited by Pierre Nora, 3 vols., vol. 3, 325–46. New York: Columbia University Press, 1996–98.

Ozouf-Marignier, Marie-Vic. *La formation des départements: La représentation du territoire français à la fin du 18ᵉ siècle.* Paris: Éditions de l'EHESS, 1988.

———. "Le territoire: Représentations géographiques et pratiques politiques." In *Histoires d'espaces: Territoires et limites, autour de Daniel Nordman,* edited by Hélène Blais, Claire Fredj, Alain Messaoudi, and Isabelle Surun, 341–54. Saint-Denis: Éditions Bouchène, 2018.

Parker, Geoffrey. *Global Crisis: War, Climate Change and Catastrophe in the Seventeenth Century.* New Haven, CT: Yale University Press, 2013.

Pauly, Ferdinand. "Die Pfarrgemeinde Senheim a. d. Mosel und ihre Wallfahrt nach Eberhards-Klausen im ausgehenden 18. Jahrhundert." *Annalen des Historischen Vereins für den Niederrhein* 177 (1975): 92–102.

———. "Die Tholeyer Prozessionsliste von 1454." *Rheinische Vierteljahrsblätter* 29 (1964): 331–36.

———. *Siedlung und Pfarrorganisation im alten Erzbistum Trier: Das Landkapitel Wadrill.* Trier: Bistumsarchiv Trier, 1965.

Pauly, Michel. *Geschichte Luxemburgs.* 2011. 2nd rev. ed. Munich: C. H. Beck, 2013.

———. "Pestepidemien in Mittelalter und Früher Neuzeit: Eine Chronik der

Ausbrüche und Gegenmaßnahmen im Herzogtum Luxemburg." *Hémecht* 73, no. 2 (2021): 133–58.

Pazos, Antón M., ed. *Nineteenth-Century European Pilgrimages: A New Golden Age.* London: Routledge, 2020.

Pelletier, Gérard. *Rome et la Révolution française: La théologie et la politique du Saint-Siège devant la Révolution française (1789–1799).* Rome: École française de Rome, 2004.

Penny, H. Glenn. *German History Unbound: From 1750 to the Present.* Cambridge: Cambridge University Press, 2022.

Péporté, Pit, Sonja Kmec, Benoît Majerus, and Michel Margue. *Inventing Luxembourg: Representations of the Past, Space and Language from the Nineteenth to the Twenty-First Century.* Leiden: Brill, 2010.

Pérouas, Louis, and Paul d'Hollander. *La Révolution française: Une rupture dans le christianisme? Le cas du Limousin (1775–1822).* Treignac: Les Monédières, 1988.

Persch, Martin. "Die Bistumsverwaltung." In *Kirchenreform und Konfessionsstaat (1500–1801),* edited by Bernhard Schneider, vol. 3 of *Geschichte des Bistums Trier,* 102–30. Trier: Paulinus-Verlag, 2010.

Pestel, Friedemann. "Französische Revolutionsmigration nach 1789." In *Europäische Geschichte Online (EGO),* edited by Leibniz-Institut für Europäische Geschichte (IEG). Mainz, 2017. http://www.ieg-ego.eu/pestelf-2017-de.

Petit, André. "L'ermitage Notre-Dame de Bonlieu dans le bois de Virton du XIe au XVIIIe siècle." *Annales de l'Institut archéologique du Luxembourg à Arlon* 106/107 (1975/1976): 67–136.

Pinto, Paulo G. "Religious Pilgrimage." In *The Palgrave Dictionary of Transnational History,* edited by Akira Iriye and Pierre-Yves Saunier, 901–4. Basingstoke: Palgrave Macmillan, 2009.

Pípalová, Anna-Marie. "Bohuslav Balbín and the Patriotic Reconceptualization of Bohemia, c. 1650–1675." *Historical Journal* 65, no. 4 (2022): 992–1014.

Pitzer, Volker. *Justinus Febronius: Das Ringen eines katholischen Irenikers um die Einheit der Kirche im Zeitalter der Aufklärung.* Göttingen: Vandenhoeck & Ruprecht, 1976.

Planert, Ute. *Der Mythos vom Befreiungskrieg: Frankreichs Kriege und der deutsche Süden—Alltag, Wahrnehmung, Deutung (1792–1841).* Paderborn: Schöningh, 2007.

Plongeron, Bernard, ed. *Histoire du christianisme: Des origines à nos jours.* Vol. 10: *Les défis de la modernité (1750–1840).* Paris: Desclée, 1997.

Poggi, Stefano. *Cultures of Identification in Napoleonic Italy, c.1800–1814.* New York: Routledge, 2024.

Port, Célestin. *La Vendée angevine*. 2 vols. Paris: Hachette, 1888.
Price, Roger. *Religious Renewal in France, 1789–1870: The Roman Catholic Church between Catastrophe and Triumph*. New York: Palgrave Macmillan, 2018.
Printy, Michael. *Enlightenment and the Creation of German Catholicism*. Cambridge: Cambridge University Press, 2009.
Probst, Manfred. *Gottesdienst in Geist und Wahrheit: Die liturgischen Anschauungen und Bestrebungen Johann Michael Sailers*. Regensburg: Pustet, 1976.
Putallaz, Pierre-Alain. "Nicolas Dufour (1746–1809), prévôt mitré de la Collégiale Saint-Venceslas de Nikolsbourg: Monographie pouvant servir à l'élaboration d'une biographie détaillée." *Vallesia* 64/72 (2009/2017): 247–360/1–134.
Raab, Heribert. *Clemens Wenzeslaus von Sachsen und seine Zeit (1739–1812): Dynastie, Kirche und Reich im 18. Jahrhundert*. Freiburg: Herder, 1962.
Ragon, Marcel. *La législation sur les émigrés 1789–1825*. Paris: Arthur Rousseau, 1904.
Ramón Solans, Francisco Javier. *La Virgen del Pilar dice . . . : Usos políticos y nacionales de un culto mariano en la España contemporánea*. Zaragoza: Prensas de la Universidad de Zaragoza, 2014.
Rapp, Wolf-Ulrich. *Stadtverfassung und Territorialverfassung: Koblenz und Trier unter Kurfürst Clemens Wenzeslaus (1768–1794)*. Frankfurt: Peter Lang, 1995.
Rau, Susanne. "Grenzen und Grenzräume in der deutschsprachigen Geschichtswissenschaft." *Francia. Forschungen zur westeuropäischen Geschichte* 47 (2020): 307–22.
Reader, Ian. *Pilgrimage: A Very Short Introduction*. Oxford: Oxford University Press, 2015.
Reddy, William M. "The Eurasian Origins of Empty Time and Space: Modernity as Temporality Reconsidered." *History and Theory* 55, no. 3 (2016): 325–56.
Reichert, Sabine. "'Heiliges Trier': Die Sakralisierung des städtischen Raumes im Mittelalter." In *Die Stadt im Raum: Vorstellungen, Entwürfe und Gestaltungen im vormodernen Europa*, edited by Karsten Igel and Thomas Lau, 89–99. Cologne: Böhlau, 2016.
Reinburg, Virginia. *Storied Places: Pilgrim Shrines, Nature, and History in Early Modern France*. New York: Cambridge University Press, 2019.
Reinhard, Wolfgang. "Die lateinische Variante von Religion und ihre Bedeutung für die politische Kultur Europas: Ein Versuch in historischer Anthropologie." *Saeculum* 43, no. 2–3 (1992): 231–55.
Reinhardt, Rudolf. "Die Kritik der Aufklärung am Wallfahrtswesen." In *Bausteine*

zur geschichtlichen Landeskunde von Baden-Württemberg: Herausgegeben von der Kommission für geschichtliche Landeskunde in Baden-Württemberg anläßlich ihres 25jährigen Bestehens, 319–45. Stuttgart: Kohlhammer, 1979.

Reiter, Günther. "Heiligenverehrung und Wallfahrtswesen im Schrifttum von Reformation und katholischer Restauration." PhD diss., Universität Würzburg, 1970.

Renglet, Antoine. *Policing Cities in Napoleonic Europe.* Cham, Switzerland: Palgrave Macmillan, 2023.

Resmini, Bertram. "Aufklärung und Säkularisation im Trierer Erzstift, vornehmlich bei den Klostergemeinschaften in der Eifel und in der Stadt Trier." In *Klosterkultur und Säkularisation im Rheinland,* edited by Georg Mölich, Joachim Oepen, and Wolfgang Rosen, 81–104. Essen: Klartext-Verlag, 2002.

Reuss, Rodolphe. *La grande fuite de décembre 1793 et la situation politique et religieuse du Bas-Rhin de 1794 à 1799.* Strasbourg: Istra, 1924.

Ridehalgh, Anna. "Preromantic Attitudes and the Birth of a Legend: French Pilgrimages to Ermenonville, 1778–1789." *Studies on Voltaire and the Eighteenth Century,* no. 215 (1982): 231–52.

Ringholz, Odilo. "Die Einsiedler Wallfahrts-Andenken einst und jetzt." *Schweizerisches Archiv für Volkskunde* 22 (1919): 176–91, 232–42.

———. *Elsass-Lothringen und Einsiedeln in ihren gegenseitigen Beziehungen.* Einsiedeln: Benziger, 1914.

———. *Kurze chronologische Uebersicht der Geschichte des fürstlichen Benediktinerstiftes Unserer Lieben Frau von Einsiedeln.* Einsiedeln: Stift Einsiedeln, 1900.

———. *Wallfahrtsgeschichte Unserer Lieben Frau von Einsiedeln: Ein Beitrag zur Culturgeschichte.* Freiburg: Herder, 1896.

Roche, Jehanne. "Création de cultes autour de nouveaux 'corps saints' victimes de la Révolution." In *Pratiques religieuses, mentalités et spiritualités dans l'Europe révolutionnaire (1770–1820): Actes du colloque, Chantilly 27–29 novembre 1986,* edited by Bernard Plongeron, Paule Lerou, and Raymond Dartevelle, 618–25. Turnhout: Brepols, 1988.

Rolland-Boulestreau, Anne. "Dieu et le roi en Vendée militaire (1793–1796)." *Annales historiques de la Révolution française,* no. 403 (2021): 97–117.

Romberg, Winfried. "Wallfahrten im Bistum und Hochstift Würzburg im Zeitalter von Konfessionalismus und Aufklärung (ca. 1600–1803): Zur Ambivalenz katholischer Frömmigkeitsgestaltung in der Frühen Neuzeit." *Biuletyn Polskiej Misji Historycznej* 10 (2015): 151–79.

Ronig, Franz J. "Die Ausstattung." In *Der Trierer Dom,* edited by Gustav Bereths and Ronig, 225–362. Neuss: Verlag Gesellschaft für Buchdruckerei, 1980.

Rosa, Mario. "Conclusion." In *Religions en transition dans la seconde moitié du dix-huitième siècle*, edited by Louis Châtellier, 281–93. Oxford: Voltaire Foundation, 2000.

Rowe, Michael. "Borders, War, and Nation-Building in Napoleon's Europe." In *Borderlands in World History, 1700–1914*, edited by Paul Readman, Cynthia Radding, and Chad Bryant, 143–65. Basingstoke: Palgrave Macmillan, 2014.

———. *From Reich to State: The Rhineland in the Revolutionary Age, 1780–1830*. Cambridge: Cambridge University Press, 2003.

———. "Imagining the Rhineland: Region- and Nation-Building in France and Germany, 1790–1840." In *Belonging across Borders: Transnational Practices in the Nineteenth and Twentieth Centuries*, edited by Levke Harders and Falko Schnicke, 61–85. Oxford: Oxford University Press, 2022.

Rubin, Miri. *Mother of God: A History of the Virgin Mary*. New Haven, CT: Yale University Press, 2009.

Rutz, Andreas. *Die Beschreibung des Raums: Territoriale Grenzziehungen im Heiligen Römischen Reich*. Cologne: Böhlau, 2018.

Sahlins, Peter. *Boundaries: The Making of France and Spain in the Pyrenees*. Berkeley: University of California Press, 1989.

———. "Natural Frontiers Revisited: France's Boundaries since the Seventeenth Century." *American Historical Review* 95, no. 5 (1990): 1423–51.

Salzgeber, Joachim. "Einsiedeln." In *Helvetia sacra, Abt. III, Bd. 1, Erster Teil: Frühe Klöster, Die Benediktinerinnen und Benediktiner in der Schweiz*, edited by Rudolf Henggeler, Albert Bruckner, Antonietta Moretti, Franz X. Bischof, and Yvon Beaudoin, 517–94. Bern: Francke, 1986.

Sandl, Marcus. *Ökonomie des Raumes: Der kameralwissenschaftliche Entwurf der Staatswirtschaft im 18. Jahrhundert*. Cologne: Böhlau, 1999.

Sandrier, Alain. *Les Lumières du miracle*. Paris: Classiques Garnier, 2015.

Saunier, Pierre-Yves. "Transnational." In *The Palgrave Dictionary of Transnational History*, edited by Akira Iriye and Saunier, 1047–55. Basingstoke: Palgrave Macmillan, 2009.

Sbalchiero, Patrick. "Hoste." In *Dictionnaire des "apparitions" de la Vierge Marie: Inventaire des origines à nos jours, méthodologie, bilan interdisciplinaire, prospective*, edited by René Laurentin and Sbalchiero, 438. Paris: Fayard, 2007.

Schaedelin, Félix. *L'émigration révolutionnaire du Haut-Rhin*. 3 vols. Colmar: Paul Hartmann, 1937–46.

Schatz, Klaus. *Geschichte des Bistums Limburg*. Mainz: Gesellschaft für Mittelrheinische Kirchengeschichte, 1983.

Scheer, Monique. "From Majesty to Mystery: Change in the Meanings of Black Madonnas from the Sixteenth to Nineteenth Centuries." *American Historical Review* 107, no. 5 (2002): 1412–40.

Schenker, Lukas. "Beinwil-Mariastein." In *Helvetia sacra, Abt. III, Bd. 1, Erster Teil: Frühe Klöster, Die Benediktinerinnen und Benediktiner in der Schweiz*, edited by Rudolf Henggeler, Albert Bruckner, Antonietta Moretti, Franz X. Bischof, and Yvon Beaudoin, 384–421. Bern: Francke, 1986.

Schettini, Glauco. "18th-Century Crusaders: The War against France and the Catholic Counterrevolution, 1789–99." In *Cosmopolitan Conservatisms: Countering Revolution in Transnational Networks, Ideas and Movements (c. 1700–1930)*, edited by Matthijs Lok, Friedemann Pestel, and Juliette Reboul, 152–71. Boston: Brill, 2021.

Schieder, Wolfgang. "Der 'Heilige Rock' in Trier als Erinnerungsort." In *Erinnerungsorte in Rheinland-Pfalz*, edited by Franz J. Felten, 85–101. Stuttgart: Franz Steiner Verlag, 2015.

Schiersner, Dietmar, and Hedwig Röckelein. "Eine neue Sicht auf den Geistlichen Staat der Frühen Neuzeit." In *Weltliche Herrschaft in geistlicher Hand: Die Germania Sacra im 17. und 18. Jahrhundert*, edited by Schiersner and Röckelein, 3–22. Berlin: De Gruyter, 2018.

Schiffhauer, Joachim. "Das Wallfahrtswesen im Bistum Trier unter Bischof Josef von Hommer." In *Festschrift für Alois Thomas: Archäologische, kirchen- und kunsthistorische Beiträge*, 345–58. Trier: Bistumsarchiv Trier, 1967.

Schlager, Patricius. *Marienlob: Wallfahrtsbüchlein enthaltend die Geschichte des Gnadenbildes in Beurig, nebst Gebeten und Liedern für die Wallfahrer.* Trier: Paulinus-Verlag, 1907.

Schlenker, Max. *Fördern, Feiern, Verbote: Studien zum Wallfahrtswesen in der Markgrafschaft Baden-Baden (1535–1771).* Ubstadt-Weiher: Verlag Regionalkultur, 2020.

Schmalfeldt, Christiane. "Sub tuum praesidium confugimus: Unsere Liebe Frau in der Tanne zu Triberg." *Freiburger Diözesan-Archiv* 108 (1988): 5–302.

Schmid, Wolfgang. *Graphische Medien und katholische Reform: Reliquienverehrung, Goldschmiedekunst und Wallfahrt in rheinischen Städten nach dem Dreißigjährigen Krieg.* Trier: Paulinus-Verlag, 2008.

———. "Sancta Treveris: Zur Bedeutung der Formel vom Heiligen Trier in Mittelalter und Früher Neuzeit." *Rheinische Heimatpflege* 37 (2000): 12–18.

Schmidt, Maike. "Naturgrenzen—Stand der Forschung und Problemaufriss aus deutscher Perspektive." *Comparativ: Zeitschrift für Globalgeschichte und vergleichende Gesellschaftsforschung* 34, no. 4–5 (2024): 381–403.

———. "Die Saar als *limite naturelle*: Grenz- und Flussregulierung am Vorabend der Französischen Revolution." *Comparativ: Zeitschrift für Globalgeschichte und vergleichende Gesellschaftsforschung* 34, no. 4–5 (2024): 518–41.

Schmitt, Gerd. "Die Annenkapelle und die Wendelskapelle: Zwei Wallfahrtstätten und ihre Beziehung zu St. Wendel." *Heimatbuch des Landkreises St. Wendel* 25 (1993/94): 131–37.

———. *Die St. Sebastianus-Bruderschaft von St. Wendel: Ihr Wirken und ihre Bedeutung im Leben unserer Stadt.* Merzig: Krüger Druck + Verlag, 2016.

Schmitt, Johannes. "Die Saarregion zur Zeit der Französischen Revolution und im Französischen Kaiserreich (1789–1815)." In *Das Saarland: Geschichte einer Region*, edited by Hans-Christian Herrmann and Schmitt, 61–110. St. Ingbert: Röhrig Universitätsverlag, 2012.

Schmitt, Michel. "Le Concordat de 1801 et son application." In *À l'épreuve de la révolution: L'Église en Luxembourg de 1795 à 1802*, edited by André Neuberg, 197–200. Bastogne: Musée en Piconrue, 1996.

———. "Die Erwählung Marias zur Landespatronin im Jahre 1678." *Hémecht* 30, no. 2 (1978): 161–83.

———. "Die Oktavwallfahrt in künstlerischen Darstellungen." *Nos cahiers. Lëtzeburger Zäitschrëft fir Kultur* 18, no. 2 (1997): 91–101.

Schnabel-Schüle, Helga. "Ansteckungsgefahr und Prophylaxe: Französische Revolution und Napoleonische Territorialrevolution." In *Die großen Revolutionen im deutschen Südwesten*, edited by Hans-Georg Wehling and Angelika Hauser-Hauswirth, 15–33. Stuttgart: Kohlhammer, 1998.

Schneider, Bernhard. *Bruderschaften im Trierer Land: Ihre Geschichte und ihr Gottesdienst zwischen Tridentinum und Säkularisation.* Trier: Paulinus-Verlag, 1989.

———. "Die Hl.-Rock-Wallfahrten von 1810 und 1844." In *Auf dem Weg in die Moderne (1802–1880)*, edited by Martin Persch and Schneider, vol. 4 of *Geschichte des Bistums Trier*, 567–79. Trier: Paulinus-Verlag, 2000.

———. "Marienerscheinungen im 19. Jahrhundert: Ein Phänomen und seine Charakteristika." In *"Wahre" und "falsche" Heiligkeit: Mystik, Macht und Geschlechterrollen im Katholizismus des 19. Jahrhunderts*, edited by Hubert Wolf, 87–110. Munich: Oldenbourg, 2013.

———. "Reform of Piety in German Catholicism, 1780–1920." In *Piety and Modernity*, edited by Anders Jarlert, 193–224. Leuven: Leuven University Press, 2012.

———. "Strukturen der Seelsorge und kirchlichen Verwaltung: Archidiakonat, Landkapitel und Pfarrei." In *Kirchenreform und Konfessionsstaat (1500–*

1801), edited by Schneider, vol. 3 of *Geschichte des Bistums Trier*, 131–46. Trier: Paulinus-Verlag, 2010.

——. "Wallfahrt, Ultramontanismus und Politik: Studien zu Vorgeschichte und Verlauf der Trierer Hl.-Rock-Wallfahrt von 1844." In *Der heilige Rock zu Trier: Studien zur Geschichte und Verehrung der Tunika Christi anlässlich der Heilig-Rock-Wallfahrt 1996*, edited by Erich Aretz, Michael Embach, Martin Persch, and Franz Ronig, 237–80. Trier: Paulinus-Verlag, 1995.

——. "Wallfahrten und Wallfahrts-Prozessionen im frühneuzeitlichen Erzbistum Trier." In *Wege zum Heil: Pilger und heilige Orte an Mosel und Rhein*, edited by Thomas Frank, 19–80. Stuttgart: Franz Steiner Verlag, 2009.

——. "Wallfahrtskritik im Spätmittelalter und in der 'Katholischen Aufklärung': Beobachtungen zu Kontinuität und Wandel." In *Wallfahrt und Kommunikation, Kommunikation über Wallfahrt*, edited by Schneider, 281–316. Mainz: Gesellschaft für Mittelrheinische Kirchengeschichte, 2004.

Schneider, René. "Dévotions et vie spirituelle dans les paroisses de Moselle selon une enquête de 1807." In *Pratiques religieuses, mentalités et spiritualités dans l'Europe révolutionnaire (1770–1820): Actes du colloque, Chantilly 27–29 novembre 1986*, edited by Bernard Plongeron, Paule Lerou, and Raymond Dartevelle, 626–33. Turnhout: Brepols, 1988.

——. "La réorganisation du diocèse de Metz durant l'épiscopat de Monseigneur Gaspard-Jean-André-Joseph Jauffret (1806–1823)." PhD diss., Pontificia studiorum Universitas, 1968.

Scholz, Luca. *Borders and Freedom of Movement in the Holy Roman Empire*. Oxford: Oxford University Press, 2020.

Schreiber, Georg. "Strukturwandel der Wallfahrt." In *Wallfahrt und Volkstum in Geschichte und Leben*, edited by Schreiber, 1–183. Düsseldorf: Schwann, 1934.

Schreiner, Klaus. "'Abwuerdigung der Feyertage'—Neuordnung der Zeit im Widerstreit zwischen religiöser Heilssorge und wirtschaftlichem Fortschritt." In *Die Autorität der Zeit in der Frühen Neuzeit*, edited by Arndt Brendecke, Ralf-Peter Fuchs, and Edith Koller, 257–304. Münster: LIT-Verlag, 2007.

Schüler, Winfried. *Das Herzogtum Nassau (1806–1866): Deutsche Geschichte im Kleinformat*. Wiesbaden: Historische Kommission für Nassau, 2006.

Schumacher, Alois. "Mouvements insurrectionnels à Trèves à l'époque de la Révolution française 1781 à 1792." In *Échanges internationaux idéologiques et culturels dans la mouvance de la Révolution française*, edited by Michel Baridon, 67–89. Paris: Les Belles Lettres, 1987.

Schwaller, Joseph. "Lothringische Tierheilige und Tierwallfahrten." *Neuer Elsässer Kalender* 22 (1933): 119–22.

Schwanitz, Henrik. *Von der Natur gerahmt: Die Idee der "natürlichen Grenzen" als Identitätsressource um 1800*. Leipzig: Leipziger Universitätsverlag, 2021.

Schweizerisches Nationalmuseum, ed. *Kloster Einsiedeln: Pilgern seit 1000 Jahren*. Berlin: Hatje Cantz, 2017.

Scott, James C. *Seeing Like a State: How Certain Schemes to Improve the Human Condition Have Failed*. New Haven, CT: Yale University Press, 1999.

Seibrich, Wolfgang. "Das Erzbistum Trier als Teil der Gesamtkirche." In *Kirchenreform und Konfessionsstaat (1500–1801)*, edited by Bernhard Schneider, vol. 3 of *Geschichte des Bistums Trier*, 147–99. Trier: Paulinus-Verlag, 2010.

———. "Die Heilig-Rock-Ausstellungen und Heilig-Rock-Wallfahrten von 1512 bis 1765." In *Der heilige Rock zu Trier: Studien zur Geschichte und Verehrung der Tunika Christi anlässlich der Heilig-Rock-Wallfahrt 1996*, edited by Erich Aretz, Michael Embach, Martin Persch, and Franz Ronig, 175–217. Trier: Paulinus-Verlag, 1995.

Seifert, Hans-Ulrich. "Aus der Franzosenzeit: die 'Registres des passeports pour l'Intérieur': Eine wenig genutzte Quelle zur Sozial- und Kulturgeschichte des Saardepartements im Stadtarchiv Trier." *Landeskundliche Vierteljahresblätter* 44, no. 4 (1998): 133–52.

Selzer, Alois. *St. Wendelin: Leben und Verehrung eines alemannisch-fränkischen Volksheiligen*. 1935. 2nd rev. ed. Mödling bei Wien: St. Gabriel-Verlag, 1962.

Sewell, William H., Jr. "The French Revolution and the Emergence of the Nation Form." In *Revolutionary Currents: Nation Building in the Transatlantic World*, edited by Michael A. Morrison and Melinda Zook, 91–125. Lanham, MD: Rowman & Littlefield, 2004.

Sibalis, Michael. "The Napoleonic Police State." In *Napoleon and Europe*, edited by Philip G. Dwyer, 79–94. Harlow: Longman, 2001.

Sidler, Daniel. *Heiligkeit aushandeln: Katholische Reform und lokale Glaubenspraxis in der Eidgenossenschaft (1560–1790)*. Frankfurt: Campus Verlag, 2017.

Sieber, Christian. "Adelskloster, Wallfahrtsort, Gerichtshof, Landesheiligtum: Einsiedeln und die Alte Eidgenossenschaft." *Mitteilungen des Historischen Vereins des Kantons Schwyz* 88 (1996): 41–51.

Simien, Côme. *Le maître d'école du village au temps des Lumières et de la Révolution*. Paris: CTHS, 2023.

Simmer, Mario. "Ein neu entdeckter Bericht über die Wallfahrt zum Heiligen Rock im Jahre 1810 von Franz Tobias Müller." *Kurtrierisches Jahrbuch* 53 (2013): 251–74.

Smets, Josef. *Les pays rhénans (1794–1814): Le comportement des Rhénans face à l'occupation française.* Bern: Lang, 1997.

Smith, Helmut Walser. *The Continuities of German History: Nation, Religion, and Race across the Long Nineteenth Century.* New York: Cambridge University Press, 2008.

Soergel, Philip M. *Wondrous in His Saints: Counter-Reformation Propaganda in Bavaria.* Berkeley: University of California Press, 1993.

Sorkin, David. *The Religious Enlightenment: Protestants, Jews, and Catholics from London to Vienna.* Princeton, NJ: Princeton University Press, 2008.

Sottocasa, Valérie. *Mémoires affrontées: Protestants et catholiques face à la Révolution dans les montagnes du Languedoc.* Rennes: Presses universitaires de Rennes, 2004.

Spehr, Christopher. *Aufklärung und Ökumene: Reunionsversuche zwischen Katholiken und Protestanten im deutschsprachigen Raum des späteren 18. Jahrhunderts.* Tübingen: Mohr Siebeck, 2005.

Sperber, Jonathan. *Popular Catholicism in Nineteenth-Century Germany.* Princeton, NJ: Princeton University Press, 1984.

Speth, Volker. *Katholische Aufklärung, Volksfrömmigkeit und 'Religionspolicey': Das rheinische Wallfahrtswesen von 1814 bis 1826 und die Entstehungsgeschichte des Wallfahrtsverbots von 1826. Ein Beitrag zur aufklärerischen Volksfrömmigkeitsreform.* 2008. 2nd rev. ed. Frankfurt: Lang, 2014.

Sprunck, Alphonse. "Les pèlerinages et la basilique d'Echternach sous le Directoire." *Jonghemecht* 14, no. 1/2 (1940): 9–15.

Spycher-Gautschi, Albert. "Sundgauer Wallfahrten nach Mariastein." *Baselbieter Heimatblätter* 76, no. 3 (2011): 49–78.

Stannek, Antje. "Les pèlerins allemands à Rome et à Lorette à la fin du XVIIe et au XVIIIe siècle." In *Pèlerins et pèlerinages dans l'Europe moderne*, edited by Dominique Julia and Philippe Boutry, 327–54. Rome: École française de Rome, 2000.

Stein, Wolfgang Hans. *Die Akten der französischen Besatzungsverwaltungen 1794–1797: Landeshauptarchiv Koblenz, Bestand 241,001–241,014.* Koblenz: Landesarchivverwaltung Rheinland-Pfalz, 2009.

———. "Polizeiüberwachung und politische Opposition im Saar-Departement unter dem Direktorium 1798–1800." *Rheinische Vierteljahrsblätter* 64 (2000): 208–65.

———. "La République française et la Rhénanie annexée: Frontière religieuse et autonomie paroissiale." In *Du Directoire au Consulat*, edited by Jacques Bernet, Jean-Pierre Jessenne, Christine Le Bozec, and Hervé Leuwers, 4 vols., vol. 2, 177–98. Lille: Centre de recherches sur l'histoire de l'Europe du Nord-Ouest, 1999–2001.

———. "Die Trierer Reunionsadresse vom April 1798 und ihre Signatare." *Kurtrierisches Jahrbuch* 61 (2021): 203–66.

Steinhoff, Anthony. "Ein zweites konfessionelles Zeitalter? Nachdenken über die Religion im langen 19. Jahrhundert." *Geschichte und Gesellschaft* 30, no. 4 (2004): 549–70.

Steinruck, Josef. "Charles Mannay (1802–1816)." In *Auf dem Weg in die Moderne (1802–1880)*, edited by Martin Persch and Bernhard Schneider, vol. 4 of *Geschichte des Bistums Trier*, 55–63. Trier: Paulinus-Verlag, 2000.

Stovall, Tyler Edward. *Transnational France: The Modern History of a Universal Nation*. Boulder, CO: Westview, 2015.

Subirade, Patricia. "Espace, identité religieuse, identité provinciale dans la Franche-Comté à l'âge baroque (XVIIe–XVIIIe siècles)." In *Topographien des Sakralen: Religion und Raumordnung in der Vormoderne*, edited by Susanne Rau and Gerd Schwerhoff, 348–69. Munich: Dölling & Galitz, 2008.

Sumption, Jonathan. *The Age of Pilgrimage: The Medieval Journey to God*. 1975. Mahwah, NJ: HiddenSpring, 2003.

Suratteau, Jean-René. *Le Département du Mont-Terrible sous le régime du Directoire (1795–1800): Étude des contacts humains, économiques et sociaux dans un pays annexé et frontalier*. Paris: Les Belles Lettres, 1964.

———. "Le Directoire avait-il une politique religieuse?" *Annales historiques de la Révolution française*, no. 283 (1991): 79–92.

Tackett, Timothy. *Religion, Revolution, and Regional Culture in Eighteenth-Century France: The Ecclesiastical Oath of 1791*. Princeton, NJ: Princeton University Press, 1986.

———. *When the King Took Flight*. Cambridge, MA: Harvard University Press, 2004.

Taveneaux, René. *Le jansénisme en Lorraine, 1640–1789*. Paris: J. Vrin, 1960.

Taylor, Charles. *A Secular Age*. Cambridge, MA: Belknap Press of Harvard University Press, 2007.

Taylor, William B. *Theater of a Thousand Wonders: A History of Miraculous Images and Shrines in New Spain*. New York: Cambridge University Press, 2016.

Thettayil, Benny. *In Spirit and Truth: An Exegetical Study of John 4:19–26 and a Theological Investigation of the Replacement Theme in the Fourth Gospel*. Leuven: Peeters, 2007.

Thewes, Guy. "Luxembourg, ville forteresse: L'impact de la fortification sur l'organisation de l'espace urbain (XVIe–XIXe siècle)." *Revue belge de philologie et d'histoire* 89, no. 2 (2011): 787–801.

———. *Stände, Staat und Militär: Versorgung und Finanzierung der Armee in den Österreichischen Niederlanden 1715–1795*. Vienna: Böhlau, 2012.

Thomas, Alois. "Die Verwaltung des rechtsrheinischen Bistums Trier 1802–1825." In *Römische Kurie. Kirchliche Finanzen. Vatikanisches Archiv: Studien zu Ehren von Hermann Hoberg*, edited by Erwin Gatz, 913–79. Rome: Pontificia Universitas Gregoriana, 1979.

Tiefenthaler, Helmut. "Historische und heutige Pilgerwanderwege von Vorarlberg nach Einsiedeln." *Montfort* 54, no. 2 (2002): 97–123.

Tilatti, Andrea, ed. *Santuari di confine: Una tipologia? Atti del convegno di studi, Gorizia, Nova Gorica, 7–8 ottobre 2004*. Gorizia: Istituto di Storia Sociale e Religiosa, 2008.

Tingle, Elizabeth C. *Sacred Journeys in the Counter-Reformation: Long-Distance Pilgrimage in Northwest Europe*. Boston: De Gruyter, 2020.

Torpey, John C. *The Invention of the Passport: Surveillance, Citizenship and the State*. Cambridge: Cambridge University Press, 2000.

Toussaint, Maurice. *La frontière linguistique en Lorraine: Les fluctuations et la délimitation actuelle des langues française et germanique dans la Moselle*. Paris: A. et J. Picard, 1955.

Trausch, Gilbert. "Comment faire d'un État de convention une nation?" In *Histoire du Luxembourg: Le destin européen d'un petit pays*, edited by Trausch, 201–74. Toulouse: Privat, 2003.

———. "Comment rester distincts dans le filet des Pays-Bas?" In *Histoire du Luxembourg: Le destin européen d'un petit pays*, edited by Trausch, 149–200. Toulouse: Privat, 2003.

———. "L'Octave de Notre-Dame de Luxembourg aux prises avec le joséphisme et les réformes catholiques du 18e siècle." *Hémecht* 18, no. 3 (1966): 333–62.

———. "L'octave en 1798: La ville de Luxembourg à l'heure républicaine." In *Un passé resté vivant: Mélanges d'histoire luxembourgeoise*, 47–52. Luxembourg: Lions Club Luxembourg Doyen, 1995.

———. *La répression des soulèvements paysans de 1798 dans le Département des Forêts*. Luxembourg: Beffort, 1967.

Tricoire, Damien. *Mit Gott rechnen: Katholische Reform und politisches Kalkül in Frankreich, Bayern und Polen-Litauen*. Göttingen: Vandenhoeck & Ruprecht, 2013.

Turner, Victor, and Edith Turner. *Image and Pilgrimage in Christian Culture*. 1978. New York: Columbia University Press, 2011.

Tyrrell, Ian. *Transnational Nation: United States History in Global Perspective since 1789*. 2007. 2nd ed. New York: Palgrave Macmillan, 2015.

Uhrmacher, Martin. "Neue Staaten—neue Grenzen: Die Rhein-Maas-Mosel-

Region zwischen den Grenzbereinigungen des Ancien Régime und der Neuordnung durch den Wiener Kongress (1779–1816)." In *Repression, Reform und Neuordnung im Zeitalter der Revolutionen: Die Folgen des Wiener Kongresses für Westeuropa*, edited by Andreas Fickers, Norbert Franz, and Stephan Laux, 155–83. Berlin: Peter Lang, 2019.

Ulbrich, Claudia. "Die Bedeutung der Grenzen für die Rezeption der französischen Revolution an der Saar." In *Aufklärung, Politisierung und Revolution*, edited by Winfried Schulze, 147–74. Pfaffenweiler: Centaurus-Verlagsgesellschaft, 1991.

———. "Die Jungfrau in der Flasche: Ländlicher Traditionalismus in Deutschlothringen während der Französischen Revolution." *Historische Anthropologie* 3, no. 1 (1995): 125–43.

Vallat, François. *Les bœufs malades de la peste: La peste bovine en France et en Europe, XVIIIe–XIXe siècle*. Rennes: Presses universitaires de Rennes, 2009.

van Herwaarden, Jan. "Medieval Pilgrimages." In *Between Saint James and Erasmus: Studies in Late-Medieval Religious Life: Devotion and Pilgrimage in the Netherlands*, 125–210. Leiden: Brill, 2003.

van Kley, Dale K. "Conclusion: The Varieties of Enlightened Experience." In *God in the Enlightenment*, edited by William J. Bulman and Robert G. Ingram, 278–316. New York: Oxford University Press, 2016.

———. *Reform Catholicism and the International Suppression of the Jesuits in Enlightenment Europe*. New Haven, CT: Yale University Press, 2018.

———. *The Religious Origins of the French Revolution: From Calvin to the Civil Constitution, 1560–1791*. New Haven, CT: Yale University Press, 1996.

Varry, Dominique, and Claude Muller. *Hommes de Dieu et Révolution en Alsace*. Turnhout: Brepols, 1993.

Vauchez, André. "L'eau et les sanctuaires chrétiens dans le monde méditerranéen, du Moyen Âge à nos jours." In *L'eau en Méditerranée de l'Antiquité au Moyen Âge: Actes du 22e colloque de la Villa Kérylos à Beaulieu-sur-Mer, les 7 et 8 octobre 2011*, edited by Jacques Jouanna, Pierre Toubert, and Michel Zink, 325–38. Paris: Académie des inscriptions et belles-lettres, 2012.

———. "Saints and Pilgrimages: New and Old." In *Christianity in Western Europe, c. 1100–1500*, edited by Miri Rubin, vol. 4 of *The Cambridge History of Christianity*, 324–39. Cambridge: Cambridge University Press, 2009.

Véron-Réville, Armand-Antoine. *Histoire de la Révolution française dans le département du Haut-Rhin*. Paris: Durand, 1865.

Vincent, Catherine. "Conclusions." In *Femmes et pèlerinages: Women and pilgrimages*, edited by Juliette Dor and Marie-Élisabeth Henneau, 209–21. Santiago de Compostela: Compostela Group of Universities, 2007.

Vogler, Bernard. "1789–1815, une rupture dans l'histoire régionale." In *Nouvelle histoire de l'Alsace: Une région au cœur de l'Europe*, edited by Vogler, 181–97. Toulouse: Privat, 2003.

Voltmer, Rita. "'Krieg, uffrohr und teuffelsgespenst': Das Erzbistum Trier und seine Bevölkerung während der Frühen Neuzeit." In *Kirchenreform und Konfessionsstaat (1500–1801)*, edited by Bernhard Schneider, vol. 3 of *Geschichte des Bistums Trier*, 20–37. Trier: Paulinus-Verlag, 2010.

Vovelle, Michel. *La Révolution contre l'Église: De la Raison à l'Être suprême*. Brussels: Éditions Complexe, 1988.

Wagner, Elisabeth. "Revolution, Religiosität und Kirchen im Rheinland um 1800." In *Franzosen und Deutsche am Rhein, 1789, 1918, 1945*, edited by Peter Hüttenberger and Hansgeorg Molitor, 267–88. Essen: Klartext, 1989.

———. "Die Rückführung des Heiligen Rockes nach Trier und die Heilig-Rock-Wallfahrt im Jahre 1810." In *Der heilige Rock zu Trier: Studien zur Geschichte und Verehrung der Tunika Christi anlässlich der Heilig-Rock-Wallfahrt 1996*, edited by Erich Aretz, Michael Embach, Martin Persch, and Franz Ronig, 219–36. Trier: Paulinus-Verlag, 1995.

Wahnich, Sophie. *L'impossible citoyen: L'étranger dans le discours de la Révolution française*. Paris: Albin Michel, 1997.

Walsham, Alexandra. *The Reformation of the Landscape: Religion, Identity, and Memory in Early Modern Britain and Ireland*. Oxford: Oxford University Press, 2011.

Watelet, Michel. *Luxembourg, ville obsidionale: Cartographie et ingénierie européennes d'une place forte du XVIe au XIXe siècle*. Luxembourg: Musée d'histoire de la Ville de Luxembourg, 1998.

Watkins, Daniel J. *Berruyer's Bible: Public Opinion and the Politics of Enlightenment Catholicism in France*. Montreal: McGill-Queen's University Press, 2021.

Webb, Diana. *Pilgrims and Pilgrimage in the Medieval West*. London: I. B. Tauris, 1997.

Weber, Eugen. *Peasants into Frenchmen: The Modernization of Rural France, 1870–1914*. Stanford, CA: Stanford University Press, 1976.

Weber, Leo. "Der Heilige Rock und Augsburg." *Jahrbuch des Vereins für Augsburger Bistumsgeschichte* 31 (1997): 197–221.

Weiller, Raymond. "Médailles et breloques de pèlerinages trouvées au Grand-Duché de Luxembourg." In *Sociologie et mentalités religieuses au Luxembourg d'Ancien Régime*, edited by Jean-Claude Muller, 71–79. Luxembourg: Les Amis de l'Histoire, 1990.

Whaley, Joachim. *Germany and the Holy Roman Empire, 1493–1806*. 2 vols. Oxford: Oxford University Press, 2012.

Wilhelm, Andreas. *Nassau-Weilburg 1648–1806: Territorialverfassung und Reichsrechtsordnung.* Wiesbaden: Historische Kommission für Nassau, 2007.

Windler, Christian. "Grenzen vor Ort." *Rechtsgeschichte—Legal History* 1 (2002): 122–45.

Wingens, Marc. "Franchir la frontière: Le pèlerinage des catholiques néerlandais aux XVIIe et XVIIIe siècles." In *Rendre ses vœux: Les identités pèlerines dans l'Europe moderne (XVIe–XVIIIe siècle)*, edited by Philippe Boutry, Pierre-Antoine Fabre, and Dominique Julia, 75–85. Paris: Éditions de l'EHESS, 2000.

———. *Over de grens: De bedevaart van katholieke Nederlanders in de zeventiende en achttiende eeuw.* Nijmegen: SUN, 1994.

Winkler, Matthias. *Revolution und Exil: Französische Emigranten in der Habsburgermonarchie 1789–1815.* Göttingen: Wallstein, 2024.

Winterer, Landolin. *La persécution religieuse en Alsace pendant la Grande Révolution, de 1789 à 1801.* Rixheim: Sutter, 1876.

Wisniewski, Clément, and Jean-Philippe Droux. "Carte administrative de l'Alsace en 1790." In *Atlas historique d'Alsace*, edited by Université de Haute-Alsace. Mulhouse, 2007. http://www.atlas.historique.alsace.uha.fr/fr/par-periodes/86-carte-administrative-de-l-alsace-en-1790.html.

Woeckel, Gerhard P. *Pietas Bavarica: Wallfahrt, Prozession und Ex-voto-Gabe im Hause Wittelsbach in Ettal, Wessobrunn, Altötting und der Landeshauptstadt München von der Gegenreformation bis zur Säkularisation und der "Renovatio Ecclesiae."* Weissenhorn: Konrad, 1992.

Woell, Edward J. *Small-Town Martyrs and Murderers: Religious Revolution and Counterrevolution in Western France, 1774–1914.* Milwaukee, WI: Marquette University Press, 2006.

Wolf, Klaus. "Absolutistische Repräsentation und zweckrationale Reformpolitik: Clemens Wenceslaus von Sachsen als Kurfürst und Erzbischof von Trier in den Jahren 1768 bis 1794." *Historisches Jahrbuch* 135 (2015): 307–63.

Würgler, Andreas. "Die Konstruktion der 'natürlichen' Schweizergrenzen um 1700: Politik, Diplomatie und Kartographie." In *Politische, gelehrte und imaginierte Schweiz = Suisse politique, savante et imaginaire: Kohäsion und Disparität im Corpus helveticum des 18. Jahrhunderts = Cohésion et disparité du Corps helvétique au XVIIIe siècle*, edited by André Holenstein, Claire Jaquier, Timothée Léchot, and Daniel Schläppi, 127–41. Geneva: Slatkine, 2019.

Würtz, Emil. *Aus dem kirchlichen Leben der Pfarrei Brunstatt: Festschrift bei Anlass der Konsekration der Pfarrkirche, Sonntag, den 12. Oktober 1924.* Rixheim: Sutter, 1924.

Wynands, Dieter P. J. *Geschichte der Wallfahrten im Bistum Aachen.* Aachen: Einhard-Verlag, 1986.

———. *Geschichtlicher Atlas der Rheinlande, Beiheft XI/12: Wallfahrten 1000–2000.* Cologne: Rheinland-Verlag, 2002.

———. "Rhein-maasländische Wallfahrten des 19. Jahrhunderts im Spannungsfeld von Politik und Frömmigkeit." *Annalen des Historischen Vereins für den Niederrhein* 191 (1988): 115–31.

Zago, Tom. "Text, Knowledge and Truth in the Duchy of Luxembourg, 1666–1781." PhD diss., University of Cambridge, 2022.

Zalar, Jeffrey T. *Reading and Rebellion in Catholic Germany, 1770–1914.* New York: Cambridge University Press, 2019.

Zenz, Emil. *Geschichte der Stadt Trier im 19. Jahrhundert.* 2 vols. Trier: Spee-Verlag, 1979/80.

Zimdars-Swartz, Sandra. *Encountering Mary: From La Salette to Medjugorje.* Princeton, NJ: Princeton University Press, 1991.

Zimmer, Nikolaus, and Hans-Ernst Noack. *Archiepiscopatus Trevirensis: Das Erzbistum Trier bis um 1800.* Map, 1952, accessible at the BA Tr.

Zwyssig, Philipp. *Täler voller Wunder: Eine katholische Verflechtungsgeschichte der Drei Bünde und des Veltlins (17. und 18. Jahrhundert).* Affalterbach: Didymos-Verlag, 2018.

INDEX

Aachen: bishopric of, 161; city of, 163
Alsace, 1, 12, 16, 81–108, 163; and apparitions, 109, 136; German Jacobins in, 10; "hunchback" region of, 72–73, 126–27; and Saint Wendelin, 71. *See also* Bas-Rhin Department; Haut-Rhin
Altkirch, district of, 90, 92, 93, 99, 101, 102; town of, 96, 204n87
Altötting, 28–29
Alzette River, 35
Amilhat Szary, Anne-Laure, 8
Ancona, 111, 113
Andechs, 54
Anrath, 158
anticlericalism, 16, 24, 168; and French expansion, 113, 115; of French soldiers, 112; of revolutionaries, 2, 39, 47, 100; —, in late 1790s, 115, 121, 122, 125
apparitions, 1, 6, 15, 108–38, 170–71, 210n103; and messages from Mary, 129, 130; and modernity, 110, 129–31; rare in the eighteenth century, 131; scholarship on, 110, 128; waves of, 15–16, 110, 117–19, 129, 135–37, 167
Ardennes Department, 46
armies: of Austria, 100; at border fortresses, 9, 44; of Spain, 87. *See also* French army
Augsburg, Peace of, 26
Augustine (saint and theologian), 22–23

Augustinian friars, 144
Austrian Netherlands, 28, 39, 57, 124, 126
Auw an der Kyll, 182n65

backwardness discourse, 2, 6, 63, 70, 121, 168
Baclesse, Jean-François, 40, 42
Bacourt, 117, 119, 124, 128, 132–33, 135
Baden, 77, 78, 86
Barère, Bertrand, 100
Baroque, 3–4, 13, 50–53, 129; and Enlightenment, 66–68, 75; and mass pilgrimage, 150–51; and notions of holy place, 20, 25; and Pietas Austriaca, 29
Bartenheim, 96
Barthélemy, François, 104
Bascharage, 117, 118, 127
Basel: city of, 13, 90, 93, 95, 168; diocese of, 89, 90; episcopal principality of, 85, 87, 97, 202n53
Bas-Rhin Department, 73, 90, 105, 118, 123, 125–27, 136
Bavaria, 23, 28–29, 86, 147
Belfort, district of, 90
Beller, Christine, 93–94, 96, 98, 99, 212n47
bells, 76
Benedictines, 56, 85
Benoît Labre (saint), 88
Bergholtzzell, 103, 205n96

Bertrambois, 118
Bettlach, 93, 96, 204n87
Beurig, 145
Bieg, Amelie, 78
Bienaymé, Pierre-François, 41, 43
Bigot de Préameneu, Félix Julien Jean, 151–52
Birkenfeld, 159
Blackbourn, David, 110
Blaise (saint), 56
Blasiusberg, 15, 49–51, 56, 61, 64
Bleiderdingen (Hoppstädten-Weiersbach), 57, 59, 65
Bliesen, 64, 65
Boll, Elisabeth, 103
Bonlieu. *See* Virton
border culture: ambiguities of, 73, 141; concept of, 7–8; pilgrims' impact on, 13, 79–80, 107, 138, 166–67, 172; transformation of, 1, 8–11, 12, 17, 121–22. *See also* phantom borders
borderlands: and cultural creativity, 2; exposed to military threats, 100, 121, 125–26, 127–28; local politics of, 8, 10; regional cultures of, 8; as spaces of entanglement, 12–13; specificities of, 79, 99–100, 110, 152, 167. *See also* borders; territory
borders: and cameralism, 27; complexity of, 32, 57–60, 67, 78–79, 126–28, 152; crossed by pilgrims, 1, 6, 11, 15, 134; —, without authorization, 2, 16, 86–87, 156–57; —, going across the Rhine, 83, 154, 161; —, going to Switzerland, 81–108; —, within Holy Roman Empire, 53, 59; and local politics, 8, 10; meanings of, 7, 9–11, 167; as natural frontiers, 27, 79; policed, 9–11, 83, 87, 95–97, 134, 141; scholarship on, 7, 11–12, 44, 220n7; shifting, 8–9, 12, 44, 77, 134–35, 146–49. *See also* phantom borders; security; territory

Boudon, Jacques-Olivier, 163
Bouflet, Joachim, 117
Boutry, Philippe, 117
Brabant Revolution, 37
Broers, Michael, 162, 220n6
Brumaire coup, 39–40, 120
Brunstatt, 102
Burgundy, 113
Bürr, Joseph, 93, 98, 102

Campoformio, Treaty of, 115
canton, as French territorial unit, 126–27, 133, 141, 150, 164
Capuchins, 53, 202n59, 207n123
Caselli, L. P., 115
Casey, Edward, 25
Castello, Johann, 75
Catholic Reformation, 12–13, 28–29, 66–67
Catholic renewal, 4–6, 17, 47, 112–13, 162–64, 167
Cattaneo, Massimo, 113, 114
Chambrey, 118, 119, 124, 128, 132–33, 136
Champagny, Jean-Baptiste Nompère de, 148
chapels, 66, 115; and Marian devotion, 123–24, 137, 159–60, 170; —, in Luxembourg, 30–34, 37–38, 41–45; in Sankt Wendel, 55, 70–71, 72
Chavant, Jean
children, 124, 129, 134, 136
Christin, Olivier, 28
churchwardens, 40, 49–50, 59, 61–62, 64–65, 67
Civil Constitution of the Clergy, 9, 89, 97, 102, 107, 219n133; viewed as heretical, 90, 93. *See also* clergy
Clemens Wenceslaus of Saxony, 23, 69, 143, 146–47
clergy, 6, 46, 67, 150; affected by revolution, 4; in conflict with pilgrims, 23, 61, 87; of Luxembourg City, 33–34, 39–40;

as pilgrims, 101, 161. *See also* Civil Constitution of the Clergy; revolutionary oaths; *names of episcopal sees and bishops*
Cobenzl, Johann Philipp von, 37
Colmar, 95, 105
Cologne, 109, 142, 157, 228n109
Concordat (of 1801), 40, 105, 146, 149
Confederation of the Rhine, 148
confession. *See* Penance, Sacrament of
confessional diversity, 13, 57–60, 78, 155; in revolutionary Alsace, 90, 93; and rivalry, 15, 50, 59–70, 73–79, 166, 168
confessionalization, 26, 60, 66–68, 188n13, 196n125
confraternities, 52; devoted to Mary, 29, 31, 124, 144–45, 163; devoted to Saint Matthias, 142, 157–58, 221n20
Congress of Vienna, 8
conscription. *See* armies
Constitutional Church. *See* Civil Constitution of the Clergy
conversions, 49, 53–54, 74
Cordel, Anton, 150, 153, 157, 160
Counter-Enlightenment, 4, 24, 30, 88–89, 106–7, 144
counter- or antirevolution, 4, 75–77, 82–83, 98, 120–21; denounced by revolutionaries, 1, 19, 91, 96, 99; and royalism, 82–83, 122, 125, 128; and the Sacred Heart, 145; and Swiss shrines, 101, 107, 114–15
Cresswell, Tim, 7
crowds, 23, 36, 43, 52, 130, 149
cultes, French Ministry of, 42–43, 151, 155
customs agents, 9, 96, 141
Częstochowa, 44, 131

Dangolsheim, 93
Dausson, Anne, 95–96, 99, 107
Deggendorf, 74
Delamorre, C.-H., 152

department, as French territorial unit, 9, 89, 115, 126, 156, 163
Derving, Gertrude, 116, 129, 132
deserters, 11, 87, 128, 167
Desportes, Félix, 104–5
Dewora, Viktor, 158
Dieuze, 122
dioceses, 26, 38; boundaries of, 9, 89, 141
diplomacy, 103–4, 106, 147–48, 163
Directory (French government, 1795–99), 112, 115, 120, 122, 144. *See also* Fructidor coup
Dittrichswalde (Gietrzwałd), 136
Docelles, 95
Dorsch, Anton, 115
Doubs Department, 104
Dufour, Nicolas, 35–36
Dufraisse, Roger, 155
Duhamelle, Christophe, 54
Dupront, Alphonse, 11, 110, 128
Dutch Republic, 13
Dyas, Dee, 11

Eberhardsklausen, 70, 145
Echternach, 38, 163
economy, 44, 71, 112, 115; influenced by pilgrimage, 5, 70, 105, 118
Ehrenbreitstein, 143, 146–47, 153
Eichsfeld, 54
Einsiedeln, 13, 15, 38, 83–108, 111–12, 114, 168
émigrés and emigration, 10, 11, 95–96, 114, 128; criminalized by revolutionaries, 82, 91, 166–67; social background of, 100. *See also* pilgrims: as émigrés
enclaves and exclaves, 85, 93, 97, 121, 152; as Catholic outposts, 54, 57, 62; eliminated by the Revolution, 73, 126; eliminated by treaties, 27, 169
Engelweihe. *See* feasts and festivals
engineering corps, 41–43, 44, 47

Enlightenment: Catholic, 3–5, 23–26, 50–51, 75, 144; French, 21, 25, 106, 165; German, 63, 68; Josephist, 5, 9, 29, 35–37, 44, 47; Kantian, 24; under Napoleon, 105, 158, 164; and religious reform, 15, 17, 23–25, 35, 66, 166. *See also* pilgrimage bans and legal restrictions; worship, in spirit and truth
epizootics, 55, 71–72, 73, 76, 121
Erb, Joseph, 97, 98
Eucharist, 25
expropriations of the Church by the state, 4, 8, 32, 39, 41, 78
Exweiler, 62, 64, 65

fairs, 56, 61, 109
"fanaticism": denounced by French revolutionaries, 1, 68, 72, 95–96, 100, 115–17, 121, 125, 127, 128; denounced under Napoleon, 105; revolutionaries accused of, 106
Fassbind, Joseph Thomas, 91
Fátima, 110, 130–31
feasts and festivals, 52, 66, 163, 201n50; at Einsiedeln (Engelweihe), 88, 106, 206n110; of the French Revolution, 93, 98; in Luxembourg (Muttergottesoktav), 32–33, 35–37, 40, 45–47, 151, 171; at Saar region shrines, 56, 61, 70; in Trier, 144, 157
Febronius. *See* Hontheim, Johann Nikolaus von
Febvre, Lucien, 7
Feller, Paul, 34
Ferdinand II (Habsburg emperor), 29
Ferniot, *citoyenne*, 103–4
Final Recess of the Imperial Deputation, 146, 148
Fislis, 93
Forêts Department, 40–41, 45–48, 124, 135, 152, 153–54
Fouché, Joseph, 155

Foussedoire, André, 102
Franche-Comté, 86, 90, 103–4, 106
Franconia, 54, 71, 198n19
freedom of worship, 19, 113
Freisen, 64
French army, 28, 38–39, 87, 100, 103; and 1810 Trier pilgrimage, 151, 160; and conscription, 39; eluded by pilgrims, 118; invasions by, 76, 104, 114, 162; joined by volunteers, 98; as occupation force, 112, 115, 144, 159; pilgrim crowds dispersed by, 72, 109–10, 122, 132; pilgrims arrested by, 95, 123, 133, 204n87; revolts crushed by, 39, 155; shrines sacked by, 70, 114. *See also* deserters; military engineers; war
French Revolution, 81–82; in crisis, 15, 120–21, 127–28; and de-Christianization, 25, 112; radical phase of (Terror), 2, 70, 73, 96, 101–2, 107; religious policies of, 70, 73, 83, 89–92, 112, 120; revolts against, 39, 72, 114, 124; supported by Catholics, 4, 92, 103, 120, 125; and territorial expansion, 8, 13, 15, 112–13, 119; —, to Luxembourg, 37–38, 126; —, to the Rhineland, 27, 70–71, 79–80, 126, 144
Fribourg, Canton of, 88
Friedrich Wilhelm of Nassau-Weilburg, 148
Friesen, 102
frontier of Catholicity, 13, 15, 50, 53, 65, 80
Fructidor coup, 39, 99, 104, 113, 219n133

Gagern, Hans Christoph von, 148
Galliath, Sebastian and Anne-Marie, 103
Gallican Church, 57, 89, 90, 106
Gattermann, Franz Richard, 153
Geilenkirchen, 115, 116
gendarmes, policing pilgrims, 16, 72, 145, 153, 201n50; around Hoste, 116, 118, 122, 132–34, 137–38

gender, 4, 98, 100–101, 134
General Vicariate, 57, 65, 70, 74, 144. *See also* Cordel, Anton
geopolitics, 7–10, 12, 44
Gerden, François-Chrétien, 33
German language, 20, 66, 88, 123; in Napoleonic France, 46; in revolutionary France, 90, 99–100
Gietrzwałd (Dittrichswalde), 136
Girsterklaus, 169–72
Gobel, Jean-Baptiste, 90
Godechot, Jacques, 113
Grégoire, Henri, 125
Gretser, Jacob, 22, 25–26
Grisons, 53
Guadalupe, Mexico, 131, 171–72
Guerber, Jean, 125, 128

Habay-la-Neuve, 16, 123
Habsburg lands, 9, 28, 83–84, 86. *See also* Austrian Netherlands; Luxembourg
Habsheim, 93
hagiography, 55, 74–76, 88, 94, 142
Haguenau, 97, 105
Harris, Ruth, 110
Haut-Rhin, bishopric of, 91; department of, 19, 90, 91, 100–104, 106
healings, 22, 24, 31, 109, 159–60; at apparition sites, 116, 118, 122, 124, 129, 137
Heede, 136
Heidegger, Martin, 30
Heinsberg, 115
Heinz, Andreas, 61
Helvetic Revolution, 104, 114
hermits, 55, 56, 72, 85
Hersche, Peter, 66
Hesse, 54, 77
Hindlingen, 102–3
Hochfelden, 1
Hofer (Saarbrücken court printer), 75
Hollerich, 33

Holy Coat of Jesus, 139, 142, 144; 1810 showing of, 15–16, 139–41; 1844 showing of, 164, 168; pre-1810 showings of, 142, 150–51, 153, 158; returned to Trier, 146–49, 150, 163
Holy Land, 142
Holy Nail (relic), 142, 144
holy place, changing notions of, 6, 19–25, 42–44, 47, 88. *See also* place; sacred space; shrines
Holy Roman Empire, 8–10, 26, 53–55, 81, 83–84, 126; Estates of, 27, 57–59; *Mediatisierung* in, 8, 78
holy wells, 1, 118, 129, 131
Homatt, Johann Georg, 96, 98
honor, 35, 54, 60, 65
Hontheim, Johann Nikolaus von, 50, 60–68, 70, 79
Hoste, 1, 15, 109–38, 166
Huber, Valeska, 168
Hülfensberg, 54, 55

Igel, 145, 182n65
Île-de-France, 113
Illingen, 62, 67, 118
images. *See* sacred images and statues
inferiority complex, 51, 62–63, 79, 166, 168
Interior, French Ministry of the, 42
Italy, 88, 111–14, 119, 140, 162

Jacobins, 10, 121, 149
Jaucourt, Louis de, 165
Jauffret, Gaspard-Jean-André-Joseph, 42–43, 45–46, 186n110
Jerusalem, 21, 144
Jesuits, 20, 22, 30–31, 54; suppressed (in 1773), 20, 32–34, 47, 144
Jews, 49, 73–74, 77. *See also* conversions; violence
Jura Department, 106
Justice, French Ministry of, 103

Kastel, 62
Käuffer, Jean-Baptiste, 40
Keller, Nikolaus, 55, 75
Kevelaer, 115
Kirn, Karl Kaspar, 124, 139, 141, 144–45, 163
Klausen. *See* Eberhardsklausen
Klein, Elisabetha, 159–60
Kleppelkrich, 39
Knock, 130
Koblenz, 143, 154, 157
Konrad, Victor, 7–8
Kronenberger, Ernst, 24–25, 30, 144
Kübelberg, 57, 59
Kulturkampf, 129, 130, 136, 138
Kusel, 57
Küttel, Beat, 91, 111–12
Kyllburg, 32

Lacoste, Jean-Baptiste, 42, 43
language. *See* German language
La Salette, 110, 130–31, 137, 219n132
Lauxen, Johann Augustin, 61–64
laypeople, 16, 41–42, 66, 91, 121; defending pilgrimage, 50–51, 64–65, 87, 143–45, 166; as pilgrimage leaders, 5, 59, 116, 157. *See also* churchwardens
Leibniz, Gottfried Wilhelm, 25
Le Laus, 130
Leonardy, Jean-Baptiste, 34
Leyen, Imperial Counts von der, 57
Leyen, Karl Kaspar von der, 150, 158
liberalism, 3, 168
Libis, Anna, 93
Liesse, 212n47
Limburg, 147
Limousin, 113
liturgy, 52, 61, 66, 74, 180n32
livestock diseases. *See* epizootics
Lombardy, 113
Loreto, 83, 165
Lorraine, 46, 163; as a borderland, 12, 16, 57, 126; German-speaking parts of, 15, 71–72, 90, 109–38; as home region of pilgrims, 30, 86, 106, 157. *See also* Meurthe Department; Moselle Department; Vosges Department
Louis XIV, 8, 26, 32, 58, 81, 86, 143
Louis XV, 27, 86
Louis XVI, 27, 28, 89, 91, 94, 99
Louise de France (aunt of Louis XVI), 89
Lourdes, 108, 110, 129–31, 137, 165, 170–71
Lunéville, Treaty of, 146
Lutzerath, 159
Luxembourg City, 15, 24, 30–48, 151, 163; fortifications of, 31–32, 42–44; plans to reconstruct Marian chapel in, 42–45
Luxembourg, (Grand) Duchy of, 30–48, 71, 117, 169–71; as a borderland, 12, 16, 20; French conquest of, 21, 37–38, 47; as home region of pilgrims, 109, 157, 168; part of Trier Archdiocese, 23; provincial estates of, 35–37; towns of, 35

Mainz, Archbishopric-Electorate of, 54
Malberg, 32
Mangin, Marie Anne, 122–23, 125
Mannay, Charles, 140, 146–56, 163
Mannheim, 109
Marcol, Pascal-Joseph de, 64
Mariastein, 13, 15, 19, 83–108, 168
Maria Theresa (Habsburg empress), 32, 34–35
Mariazell, 29
Marienthal, 105, 118, 136, 163
markets. *See* fairs
Marpingen, 62, 64, 67, 110, 136
Mars-la-Tour, 118, 119, 128
Martin, Arbogaste, 91, 92
martyrs, 22, 96, 170
Mary: devotion to, 3, 53, 145, 158–60, 170; as Our Lady of Einsiedeln, 85–86, 94, 97; as Our Lady of Luxem-

bourg, 20, 30–48, 145, 167, 171; as patroness, 20–21, 28–30, 31–32, 123; as Queen of Poland, 44
Mass, 24, 56, 61, 113, 151
material culture of pilgrimage, 94, 95, 96–97, 119, 143, 158–60. *See also* sacred images and statues
Matthias' Abbey (Trier), 142, 144, 157–58, 160, 221n20
Maurice (saint), 56, 63
Mecca, 27, 168
Mediation Act, 104
Medjugorje, 130, 170–71
Meinrad (saint), 85
Merlin de Douai, Philippe-Antoine, 82
Metz: city of, 161; diocese of, 41, 43, 45–48, 114, 151, 153
Meurthe Department, 106, 116–18, 122, 125–26, 135–36
Meyer, Bernard, 95, 100
military. *See* armies; French army
military engineers, 41–43, 44, 47
ministries. See *cultes*, French Ministry of; Interior, French Ministry of the; Justice, French Ministry of; police: French Ministry of; war: French Ministry of
miracles, 1, 32, 75, 111–20; belief in, 20, 22, 25, 144; reports of, 109, 114, 116, 123, 129; at Swiss shrines, 85, 89, 97, 104. *See also* healings
Mirecourt, 95
mobility, 11, 17, 82, 154; seasonal, 7, 96
mockery, 49, 51, 60, 65–68, 76, 79
Montbéliard, 90
Montmorency-Laval, Cardinal Joseph-Louis de, 114
Montserrat, 87, 162–63
Mont-Terrible Department, 97
Morhange, 127, 133
Morlot (French general), 132
Moselle Department, 1, 114, 117, 121, 126, 207n120; administration of, 72, 126, 135, 154–55

Moselle River, 12, 35, 70, 86
Muespach, 95
Mulhouse, 93, 103
Muller, Claude, 90, 204n89
Müller, Franz Tobias, 228n110
Müller, Johann Kaspar, 24
Müller, Ludwig, 223n35
Münchweiler, 57, 59
Münster, Prince-Bishopric of, 53, 114, 151
Muttergottesoktav. *See* feasts and festivals

Nancy: bishopric of, 105; French sovereign court in, 64
Naples, 113
Napoleon (Bonaparte), 152, 162, 163; and Charles Mannay, 140, 155; in Italy, 112–13; and Pius VII, 140, 150. *See also* Brumaire coup
Napoleonic Empire, 8, 11, 15–16, 44, 46, 105–6; Church-state collaboration in, 148, 150, 163; core areas of, 140, 150, 155, 162–64; and territorial expansion, 140, 146–49, 150; and vassal states of France, 9
Narbonne-Lara, Louis-Marie de, 147
Nassau, Duchy of, 146–48, 153
Nassau-Saarbrücken, County of, 50, 57, 73, 90
National Assembly (French), 27–28, 89, 91, 102, 214n80
national guards, 134, 155
nation-building, 11, 15, 82, 98–100, 166; awareness of, 6, 82, 93, 102–3; and betrayal, 10, 82, 103, 107, 166; and territorial ideas, 81–82, 107, 166
Neuchâtel, 90
Neunheuser, Henry, 43
newspapers, 10, 91–92, 219n133, 220n12, 224n60
Nohfelden, 59
Nora, Pierre, 83
Nunkirchen, 159
nuns, 89, 101, 122

Ohmbach, 59
omnipresence of God, 19, 23, 26, 181n34
order: ideals of, 5, 10, 51, 60, 79, 151; under Napoleon, 141, 152, 153–54, 161–62, 166
Ottobeuren, 54
Ozouf-Marignier, Marie-Vic, 9

Palatinate, 13, 57–59
papacy, 85, 89, 90, 105–6
Papal States, 105, 111, 113–14, 150
Paris, 28; apparitions in, 137
parish, 32, 36–37, 40, 47; and pilgrimage organization, 52, 149, 151; of Saint Nicholas (later Saints Nicholas and Theresa, Saint Pierre) in Luxembourg City, 33–35, 40–41, 45
parish churches, 38, 55, 70, 132–33, 158
passports, 95, 97, 103–4, 152, 154; laws and rules on, 10, 99, 126, 133, 141, 161; for travel abroad, 9, 73, 99, 135, 161; used by pilgrims, 1, 87, 134–35, 161, 169
pastoral visits and inquiries, 16, 49, 61–63, 71, 207n120, 221n21
Peace of Westphalia, 8, 53, 59, 77
Penance, Sacrament of, 88, 91, 93, 95, 106, 122
Perugia, 113
petitions, 16–17; by local notables, 40–42, 49, 64–65, 69–70, 143, 147; by pilgrims and their relatives, 102–3, 124; by provincial elites, 35–36, 42
Pfalz-Zweibrücken, Duchy of, 50, 57, 70
phantom borders, 44–45, 73, 157
Philipp Wilhelm of Pfalz-Neuburg, 58
pilgrimage bans and legal restrictions, 4–5; before the Revolution, 35, 60–68, 69–70, 86, 143; during the Revolution, 71–72, 91, 99, 115; after the Revolution, 78, 151, 161, 163, 168–69. See also passports; pilgrims: as émigrés; pilgrims: policed; police

pilgrims: adapting to change, 5–6, 48; arrested, 72, 87, 92–103; —, by gendarmes or soldiers, 16, 95, 123, 133–34, 145, 201n50, 204n87; bottling water at holy wells, 117–19, 124, 132; denounced (see "fanaticism"; "superstition"); as émigrés, 82, 93–95, 98–104, 107; guillotined, 2, 94–95, 100–101; mass participation of, 136, 140, 156–57, 160, 164, 168; numbers of, 5; —, after the Revolution, 46, 156, 168, 171; —, before the Revolution, 37, 53, 55–56, 85–87, 142, 151, 189n23; —, during the Revolution, 72, 76, 92–93, 115, 116–17, 136, 201n50; offerings by, 34, 52, 56, 137, 158, 184n89, 194n98; persistence of, 5–6, 47–48, 76, 207n125; policed, 11, 87, 129–37, 154, 168–69; prayers said by, 52, 74, 116, 123, 145, 159–60; scholarship on, 4–6, 11–12; sensory experiences of, 23–24; sexual excesses of, 23, 52, 61; socioeconomic backgrounds of, 101, 161; songs chanted by, 52, 59, 93, 116, 158. See also borders: crossed by pilgrims; Wallfahrten
Pius VII (pope), 105, 140, 149–50, 162
place: concepts of, 11, 24–26; fluidity of, 44, 47–48, 110, 129–30, 135–38; sense of, 6, 30, 31, 63, 145, 169. See also holy place, changing notions of
Plaine-de-Walsch, 118, 136
Poland-Lithuania, 28, 131; partitions of, 8, 44
police, 40, 87, 99, 105; French Ministry of, 99, 127, 135, 149, 152, 154–55; reports written by, 16, 111, 116, 118–19, 132; of worship (Religionspolizei, police du culte), 69, 71–72, 77–78, 115, 131–38, 149, 168–69. See also gendarmes, policing pilgrims; pilgrimage bans and legal restrictions
Pont-à-Mousson, 116, 118, 128

popes. *See* papacy
Portalis, Jean-Marie-Étienne, 155
pride, 2, 6, 76
processions, 38, 74, 115–16, 132, 151, 158; through Luxembourg City, 35–37, 40, 45; obligatory character of, 52, 56, 69; through Trier, 124, 139, 143–45, 150, 158, 159–60. *See also* Wallfahrten
Prost, Jean, 121
Protestantism, 2, 3, 22, 53, 88. *See also* confessional diversity; conversions; frontier of Catholicity; violence
provinces of France, 9, 27
Puttelange, 125, 127, 132, 133, 135

Ravensberg, Duchy of, 53
Réal, Pierre-François, 149
Réchésy, 87
Reichsdeputationshauptschluss. *See* Final Recess of the Imperial Deputation
Reichskammergericht, 54
relics, 15, 23, 56, 63, 142, 181n34. *See also* Holy Coat of Jesus; Holy Nail
religious orders, 89. *See also* Augustinian friars; Benedictines; Capuchins; Jesuits
Rencurel, Benoîte, 130
resistance, 5–7, 80, 123–24, 166, 188n7; to Napoleonic Empire, 140, 160–61, 162–64. *See also* counter- or antirevolution
revival. *See* Catholic renewal
revolutionary oaths: and refractory clergy, 89–91, 95–96, 99–100, 121–23, 127; sworn by clergy, 40, 89–91, 124–25. *See also* Civil Constitution of the Clergy
Rhineland, 5, 12, 77–78, 86; under French occupation, 112, 115–16, 135; under Napoleon, 10, 140, 149, 163; as part of Prussia, 164, 168; pilgrims from, 142, 158
Rhin-et-Moselle Department, 154–55, 160–61

Roër Department, 115–16, 161
Rohan, Cardinal Louis-René de, 127
Rome, 83, 88, 111, 113, 142
Röser, François, 40
Rowe, Michael, 77
Rudler, François Joseph, 115, 210n25, 218n122
Ryswick, Peace of, 32, 59

Saarbrücken, town of, 72–73, 74, 75, 127
Saar Department, 127, 135, 151, 152, 155, 156–57, 169
Saarlouis, 132
Saar region, 12, 13, 15, 16, 49–80, 136
Saarwerden, County of, 73, 126
Sacred Heart, devotion to the, 145
sacred images and statues, 23, 31, 85, 145, 158–59, 170; and apparitions, 119, 212n48; in Luxembourg City, 33, 35–36, 40; moving miraculously, 111, 113; replicas of, 32, 85–86, 104, 145, 170–71; surviving pillage, 104, 162–63. *See also* material culture of pilgrimage
sacred space, 2, 3, 11–12, 15, 21–30; rhizomatic, 110, 117–19, 135–37. *See also* holy place, changing notions of; shrines
Sailer, Johann Michael, 23, 25–26
Saint-Avold, 72, 135
Saint-Louis (Bourglibre), 95, 103
saints: cult of, 3, 23, 43, 170; as patrons, 63, 71–72
Saint-Ursanne, 87
Säkularisation. *See* expropriations of the Church by the state
Sankt Wendel, 15, 49–51, 55–56, 57–78, 121, 159
Santiago de Compostela, 83, 87, 165
Sarralbe, 73
Sarreguemines, 73, 77, 116, 126, 132, 134, 214n80
Sarre-Union, 127
Sauer River, 35, 171

Saulnier, 122, 125
Saurine, Jean Pierre, 105, 163
Savary, Anne Jean Marie René, 155
Savoy, 86
Schambourg, Bailliage de, 55, 57, 64, 70
Schankweiler, 182n65
Schauenburg (French general), 104, 114
Scholz, Luca, 10
Schultz, Jean, 102
Schwyz, Canton of, 85, 91
secularization theories, 2, 17
security, at the border, 2, 9–10, 87, 107, 166–67, 172
seers (of apparitions), 111, 128–31
seminaries, 46
sermons, 23, 45, 66, 105, 106; against Enlightenment and Revolution, 24, 30, 88, 114, 144
shrines, 22, 53, 55, 162, 181n34; at/near borders, 17, 32, 53–54, 171, 189n16; demolished or damaged, 37–38, 47–48, 70–71, 76, 104, 124; interconnected, 33, 37, 55, 63, 158–60; as offshoots of bigger shrines, 6, 32; as waystations to other shrines, 52, 85, 97. *See also* holy place, changing notions of; holy wells; sacred space
sister republics, 9, 104
smuggling, 7, 10, 11, 87, 97, 167; by pilgrims, 154, 199n29
Solothurn, Canton of, 19, 85, 205n101
space, as a container, 25–26, 32. *See also* sacred space; territory
Spaeth, Paul, 116, 118, 122, 123, 128, 131
Spain, 28, 87, 136, 140, 162
Sperber, Jonathan, 5
"spirit and truth." *See* worship, in spirit and truth
Sponheim, Lower County of, 57
Sprinkange, 118
Stammel, Johann Jakob, 24
statues. *See* sacred images and statues
Steininger, Johann, 74–76

Strasbourg, 10, 97, 106; diocese of, 90, 99, 105, 127, 207n120
Sundgau, 85
"superstition," 2, 3, 5, 22, 79, 168; denounced by enlighteners, 36, 63, 66, 165; denounced by French revolutionaries, 19, 68, 100, 113, 115, 219n133; denounced under Napoleon, 105, 149, 154, 158
Surveillance. *See* police; security, at the border
Swabia, 54, 71
Switzerland, 9, 13, 53, 81–108, 111–12, 114–15

Tackett, Timothy, 89–90
Talleyrand, Auguste de, 106
Talleyrand-Périgord, Charles-Maurice de, 148
Tanner, Konrad, 106
Taylor, Charles, 169
Telgte, 53, 151
territory, 3, 12, 15; annexed by France, 12, 31–32, 37–39, 81, 115, 124, 126; and confessional belonging, 26; and jurisdictional power, 26, 33–34, 41; in the Middle Ages, 26; occupied by France, 39, 71–73, 112, 121, 144, 163; as *pré carré*, 27, 32; sacralized, 1, 21, 26–30; and state-building, 17, 19, 30, 81–82; subdivisions of, 9, 27, 126–28, 141, 149. *See also* borders; canton, as French territorial unit; department, as French territorial unit; French Revolution; Holy Roman Empire: Estates of; Napoleonic Empire; provinces of France
Theley, 61
theology of pilgrimage, 21–26
Thirty Years' War, 76
Tholey, 15, 38, 49–51, 55–56, 57–71
tolerance and toleration, 50, 76, 113, 188n5

transgression, concept of, 6–7
transnational history, 82, 92
Trausch, Gilbert, 61
Treaty of the Pyrenees, 32
tribunals, prosecuting pilgrims, 16, 95, 102, 123, 133–34. *See also* Reichskammergericht
Trier: Archbishopric-Electorate of, 23–24, 30, 32, 57, 65, 68–69, 71, 76, 142–43, 146, 157, 169; burghers of, 69, 144, 222n30; cathedral chapter of, 143, 146–47; cathedral of, 143, 144, 150, 158–59; Church of Our Lady in, 124, 159, 160; city of, 16, 109, 124, 143; —, as a holy city (Sancta Treveris), 141, 142–45, 157, 160; municipality of, 139, 143, 144, 150; Napoleonic diocese of, 146–48, 150, 155, 156–57; old archdiocese of, 49–50, 57, 142, 147, 157
Trois-Épis, 85
Turner, Victor and Edith, 11

ubiquity. *See* omnipresence of God
ultramontanism, 3–4, 80, 90, 106, 164
universality, Catholic standard of, 66
usable empire, 140, 156, 161–62, 164

vagabondage, 5, 11, 87, 134, 152, 167
Varry, Dominique, 90, 204n89
Vauban, 32
Vaublanc, Vincent-Marie Viénot de, 154, 161–62
Vendée, 39, 123, 126
Verona, 113

Vicenza, 113
Vinnenberg, 53
violence, 2, 40, 61, 79; against Jews, 73–74, 77; between pilgrims and Protestants, 54, 59–60, 62, 64–65, 196n126
Virton, 118, 119, 123–24, 125, 128
Vosges Department, 95, 105, 106, 125
vows, 31–33, 52–53, 78, 103, 123

Wadrill, Deaconry of, 57, 61, 66, 69
Walderdorff, Johann Philipp von, 143
Walldürn, 54, 78
Wallfahrten, 52–80, 100, 145, 150–54, 157–58; distances covered in, 52, 69. *See also* processions; pilgrims
war: affecting borderlands, 7, 8; and devotion to Mary, 131; French Ministry of, 42–43, 87, 104, 186n110; under Louis XIV, 32, 87, 158; during the Revolution, 39, 70–71, 76, 99–100, 120–21, 127–28
Weidingen, 182n65
Wendelin (saint), 55, 63, 71, 75–76
Wertheim, 54
Westphalia, 53, 151. *See also* Peace of Westphalia
Wittenheim, 103
worship, in spirit and truth, 21–25, 30, 36, 75, 88. *See also* freedom of worship; place: of worship
Württemberg, 77, 78
Würzburg, Prince-Bishopric of, 54, 74

Zurich, 168

STUDIES IN EARLY MODERN GERMAN HISTORY

The Great Elector's Table: The Politics of Food in Seventeenth-Century Brandenburg-Prussia
Molly Taylor-Poleskey

Bedazzled Saints: Catacomb Relics in Early Modern Bavaria
Noria K. Litaker

Music and Urban Life in Baroque Germany
Tanya Kevorkian

Strange Brethren: Refugees, Religious Bonds, and Reformation in Frankfurt, 1554–1608
Maximilian Miguel Scholz

A German Barber-Surgeon in the Atlantic Slave Trade: The Seventeenth-Century Journal of Johann Peter Oettinger
Edited and translated by Craig M. Koslofsky and Roberto Zaugg

Furnace and Fugue: A Digital Edition of Michael Maier's "Atalanta fugiens" (1618) with Scholarly Commentary
Edited by Donna Bilak and Tara Nummedal

The Devil's Art: Divination and Discipline in Early Modern Germany
Jason Philip Coy

Four Fools in the Age of Reason: Laughter, Cruelty, and Power in Early Modern Germany
Dorinda Outram

The Executioner's Journal: Meister Frantz Schmidt of the Imperial City of Nuremberg
Translated by Joel F. Harrington

Hometown Religion: Regimes of Coexistence in Early Modern Westphalia
David M. Luebke

www.ingramcontent.com/pod-product-compliance
Lightning Source LLC
Chambersburg PA
CBHW021651230426
43668CB00008B/590